Left: Faneuil Hall (p85)

Above: Massachusetts Institute of Technology (p147)

Right: Wally's Café (p104)

Cambridge
p144

Charlestown
p44

West End &
North End
p52

Beacon Hill &
Boston Common
p66

Downtown &
Waterfront
p78

Back Bay
p110

Seaport District
South Boston
p134

Kenmore
Square &
Fenway
p123

South End &
Chinatown
p96

Streetcar
Suburbs
p162

Welcome to Boston

Boston's history recalls revolution and renewal, and it's still among the country's most progressive and barrier-breaking cities.

Art & Architecture

The arts have thrived in Boston ever since the 19th century, when this cultural capital was dubbed the Athens of America. Certainly, the intellectual elite enjoyed their fine paintings and their classical music, but they were also dedicated to spreading the cultural wealth, establishing museums, libraries and symphony orchestras that could be appreciated by the masses. Today the lucky residents of (and visitors to) Boston benefit from such largesse. These venerable institutions play an integral role on Boston's cultural stage, which has significantly expanded to include dynamic contemporary art and music scenes.

Sports

'Fanatic' is no idle word here. Boston fans are passionate about sports, and it's easy to understand why. The three-time world-champion Patriots; the long-overdue World Series–winning Red Sox; the winningest basketball team in history, the Celtics; and 2011 Stanley Cup victors the Bruins: there's a lot to be passionate about. Boston's college teams also inspire fierce loyalties and staunch rivalries. No less spirited are the country's oldest and most celebrated running event, the Boston Marathon, and the world's largest two-day rowing event, the Head of the Charles Regatta.

Food

A word of advice: when in Boston, eat as much seafood as possible. Local specialties include the 'sacred cod,' fresh steamed lobster, oysters on the half-shell and thick, creamy chowder. You can eat seafood around the city, but especially in the fish-centered Seaport District, where it's accompanied by spectacular harbor views. The creatures of the sea are your top priority, but don't miss the chance to devour delicious plates of pasta in the North End and to sample exotic Asian dishes in Chinatown. Trendy fusion restaurants draw on all of these eclectic influences to present contemporary cuisine that is uniquely Boston.

History

For all intents and purposes, Boston is the oldest city in America. And you can hardly walk a step over its cobblestone streets without running into some historic site. The Freedom Trail winds its way around the city, connecting 16 sites of varying historical significance; and that's just the beginning of the history lesson. These are the very places where history unfolded. In effect, Boston is one enormous outdoor history museum, where visitors can remember and relive the events of centuries past.

Why I Love Boston
By Mara Vorhees, Author

Boston is wicked *smaaht*. I love that Boston is motivated not by money or politics, but by learning. The academic institutions are a source of innovative art, architecture and ideas that we all benefit from. The students provide a renewable source of energy and vibrancy that permeates the city. Yet for all the fancy buildings and big ideas, Boston is still a city of neighborhoods and local people. The students may or may not be here in four years, but my neighbors are here for the long haul. They are the cogs that keep the city running, moving, growing, remembering the past and creating the future.

For more about our authors, see p272.

For more about our authors, see p272.

Financial District, viewed from the Northern Avenue Bridge

Boston's
Top 10

Fenway Park (p133)

1 There might as well be signs on I-90 reading 'Now entering Red Sox Nation.' The intensity of baseball fans has only grown since the Boston Red Sox broke their agonizing 86-year losing streak and won the 2004 World Series. The hometown team repeated its feat in 2007 and has come awfully close in years since, which means it continues to sell out every game. Catch the boys at Fenway Park, the iconic old-style ball park that has hosted the Sox for over a century.

🏃 *Kenmore Square & Fenway*

Freedom Trail (p215)

2 For a sampler of Boston's revolutionary sights, follow the red brick road. It leads 2.4 miles through the center of Boston, from Boston Common to the Bunker Hill Monument, and traces the events leading up to and following the War for Independence. The Freedom Trail is well marked and easy to follow on your own – an ideal strategy if you actually wish to enter some of the historic buildings and museums. Otherwise, there are plenty of tours that follow this trail, including the National Park Service's free option. (OLD SOUTH MEETING HOUSE, P217)

🏃 *Freedom Trail*

RICHARD CUMMINS / LONELY PLANET IMAGES ©

Boston Harbor Islands *(p80)*

3 If you're dreaming of an island vacation, you've come to the right place. The Boston Harbor Islands consist of 34 islands, many of which are open for trail-walking, bird-watching, camping, kayaking and swimming. Explore a 19th-century fort at Georges Island; walk the trails and lounge on the beach at Spectacle Island; or climb to the top of Boston's iconic oldest lighthouse at Little Brewster. Mostly operated by the National Park Service, the Harbor Islands offer a unique opportunity for outdoor adventure – and they're just a quick boat ride from downtown Boston.

🏃 *Downtown &
Waterfront*

Harvard Square *(p148)*

4 Harvard Sq overflows with bookstores and boutiques, coffee shops and record shops, street performers and street dwellers. Although many Cantabridgians rightly complain that the square has lost its edge – as once independently owned shops are continually gobbled up by national chains – Harvard Sq is still a vibrant, exciting place to hang out. The university is the centerpiece of the square, with ivy-covered architecture and excellent museums. Harvard Sq is also a hotbed of colonial and revolutionary history, from Mt Auburn Cemetery to the Cambridge Common.

◉ *Cambridge*

Copley Square *(p112, 114, 116)*

5 Boston's most exquisite architecture is clustered around this stately Back Bay plaza. The square's centerpiece is the celebrated Romanesque masterpiece by Henry Hobson Richardson: Trinity Church. It's lovely in person and even lovelier when reflected in the mirrored facade of the modernist John Hancock Tower. This assemblage faces off against the elegant neo-Renaissance Boston Public Library. The plaza itself is peppered with whimsical and serious pieces commemorating the city's biggest sporting event, the Boston Marathon, for which Copley Sq is the finish line.

◉ *Back Bay*

Art Museums *(p207)*

6 Boston's museums are famed for their collections of Asian, American and European art from days gone by. But this is the 21st century, and Boston artists and curators still have something to say about it – as indicated by the city's flourishing contemporary scene. All of Boston's major art institutions have undergone massive upgrades in recent years, demonstrating that this city is on the forefront of artistic endeavors. The only disappointment is that there is never enough time to see them all. (ISABELLA STEWART GARDNER MUSEUM, P127)

◉ *Arts & Architecture*

Charles River Esplanade *(p115)*

7 When we talk about the 'waterfront,' we're usually talking about the Boston Harbor. But there's a second, equally appealing waterfront along Charles River. The Esplanade is a long and narrow riverside park that offers endless opportunities for outdoor recreation, from playgrounds to picnic areas, and bike trails to ball parks. There's no swimming in the river, but there is sunbathing, sailing, kayaking and canoeing. The Hatch Memorial Shell is a venue for (free) outdoor entertainment, including the annual July 4 concert by the Boston Pops.

🏃 *Back Bay*

North End (p58)

8 What's so special about eating in the North End? For starters, it actually feels like you're in Italy. One of Boston's oldest neighborhoods, its narrow streets and brick buildings exude an Old World ambience that is only enhanced by its Italian-American population. It sounds like Italy too, with local residents carrying on lively conversations in the mother tongue. Most importantly, it tastes like Italy. Packed with romantic restaurants, cozy cafes and aromatic bakeries, the North End will delight the senses and the stomach. (GIACOMO'S RISTORANTE, P59)

🍴 *West End & North End*

Beacon Hill (p75)

9 With an intriguing history, distinctive architecture and unparalleled neighborhood charm, Beacon Hill is Boston's most prestigious address. It's hard to beat the utter loveliness of the place: the narrow cobblestone streets lit with gas lanterns; the distinguished brick town houses decked with purple windowpanes and blooming flower boxes; and streets such as stately Louisburg Sq that capture the neighborhood's grandeur. Charles St, the commercial street that traverses the flat of the hill, is Boston's most enchanting spot for browsing boutiques and haggling over antiques.

Beacon Hill & Boston Common

Walden Pond (p174)

10 In 1854, Henry David Thoreau left the comforts of Concord and built himself a rustic cabin on the shores of Walden Pond, where he lived for two years. From this retreat, he wrote his famous treatise on nature, *Walden; or, Life in the Woods*. Surrounded by acres of forest, the glacial pond remains a respite for children and swimmers who frolic in its cool waters, bird-watchers and walkers who stroll along the pleasant footpath, and nature lovers of all sorts.

Day Trips from Boston

What's New

Rose Kennedy Greenway

After two decades of construction and $15 billion in cost, the infamous Central Artery/Tunnel Project is complete (see p87). Above ground, the project reclaimed about 27 acres of industrial wasteland for parks and plazas. Ever evolving, the Greenway now hosts a weekly open market for Saturday shoppers and a slew of food trucks for weekday lunchers. Coming soon: a custom-designed Boston-themed carousel for kiddies and a daily local farmers market for foodies.

Boston Tea Party Ships & Museum

A decade after being destroyed by fire, the Tea Party ships are once again docked at Griffin's Wharf, alongside an interactive history museum. (p137)

Museum of Fine Arts

It's the same beloved MFA, but now with impressive new wings showcasing its expanded collections of American and contemporary art. (p125)

Isabella Stewart Gardner Museum

Mrs Jack's Italian palazzo now boasts a stunning glass addition, designed by Renzo Piano and housing new facilities for performance and ongoing creation. (p127)

Harvard Art Museum

Keeping up with its counterparts across the river, Harvard's expansion and renovation (2013) will allow all three of the university's collections to co-exist under one exquisite roof. (p148)

Seaport District

The Seaport District is now officially a destination, with three state-of-the-art museums and a slew of trendy new restaurants, some of which offer amazing harbor views. (p134)

New Balance Hubway

Boston has a brand-new bike-share program, with stations all around the city and hundreds of bikes that are available to cycling mavens and casual riders alike. (p222)

Kayaking & Canoeing

Kayak or canoe in the heart of Boston, launching your boat from the new Kendall Sq location of Charles River Canoe & Kayak Center, and even paddling out to the harbor if you dare. (p158)

NPS Visitors Centre in Faneuil

Faneuil Hall and Quincy Market have long been tourist central in Boston. Now the National Park Service is in the thick of it, with its revamped digs situated in the old marketplace. (p228)

Boston Harbor Islands Pavillion

Sitting pretty on the Greenway, this information center is the new gateway to the glorious Boston Harbor Islands. (p228)

For more recommendations and reviews, see **lonelyplanet.com/boston**

Need to Know

Currency
US dollar ($)

Language
English

Visas
Citizens of many countries are eligible for the Visa Waiver Program, which requires prior approval via Electronic System for Travel Authorization (ESTA).

Money
ATMs widely available. Credit cards accepted at most hotels, restaurants and shops.

Cell Phones
Most US cell-phone systems are incompatible with the GSM 900/1800 standard used throughout Europe and Asia.

Time
Eastern Standard Time (GMT/UTC minus 5)

Tourist Information
Boston Common Information Kiosk (GBCVB Visitors Center; www.bostonusa.com; Boston Common; ⊘8:30am-5pm; ⓜPark St) is the starting point for many walking tours.

Your Daily Budget
The following are average costs per day.

Budget less than $80
➡ Dorm bed $30–$50

➡ Cheap fast food, ethnic food and self-catering

➡ Take advantage of free museum nights and walking tours

Midrange $150–$300
➡ Double room in a midrange hotel $125–$250

➡ At least one proper sit-down meal per day $20–$30

➡ Includes admission to museums, tours and other activities

Top End more than $300
➡ Double room in a top-end hotel from $250

➡ Eat at the city's finest restaurants

➡ Enjoy concerts, events and other activities

Advance Planning

One month before Reserve a place to stay, especially if you are coming during late spring or fall. Budget travelers, this means you!

Two weeks before Buy your tickets for the Boston Symphony Orchestra, the Boston Red Sox or your favorite Boston band.

One week before Catch up on the latest news and find out about special events.

One day before Check the weather forecast so you know what to pack.

Useful Websites

Lonely Planet (www.lonely planet.com/boston) Destination information, hotel bookings, traveler forum and more.

Boston.com (www.boston. com) The online presence of the Boston Globe, with event listings, restaurant reviews, local news, weather and more.

Universal Hub (www.universal hub.com) Bostonians talk to each other about whatever is on their mind (sometimes nothing).

Sons of Sam Horn (www. sonsofsamhorn.com) Dedicated to discussion of all things Red Sox. Curt Schilling used to occasionally post.

WHEN TO GO

Peak travel times are fall and spring, with lovely weather and many events. Summer is humid but also busy.

Boston

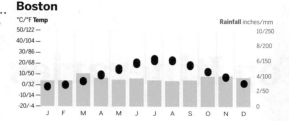

Arriving in Boston

Boston Logan International Airport Subway (blue line) and bus (silver line) to central Boston 5:30am to 12:30am $1.70–$2; taxi $15–$25.

South Station Located in central Boston on the red line.

Manchester Airport Shuttle bus to Logan $39; should be booked in advance.

TF Green Airport Commuter rail to South Station $8.25.

For much more on **arrival** see p220

Getting Around

➡ **T (Subway)** The quickest and easiest way to get to most destinations. Runs from 5:30am or 6am until 12:30am or 1am.

➡ **Hubway** Boston's new bike-share program, with hundreds of bikes available for travelers to borrow.

➡ **MBTA bus** Supplements the subway system.

For much more on **getting around** see p221

Sleeping

Boston is a relatively expensive place to stay, due to its busy conference and academic calendars and popular tourist appeal. Book in advance online for the best prices. Budget travelers, especially, will find there is a shortage of hostels and other affordable options, so book your beds as early as possible. Plenty of welcoming guesthouses and smaller hotels welcome midrange travelers, while many hotels of all sizes cater to high-enders. Prices increase dramatically during peak travel times, especially in autumn.

Useful Websites

➡ **Boston Green Tourism** (www.bostongreentourism. org) Includes up-to-date listings of green hotels.

➡ **Boston Luxury Hotels** (www.bostonluxuryhotels. com) Individualized service for upscale travelers.

➡ **University Hotels** (www. universityhotels.net) Perfect for finding accommodations near a particular university.

For much more on **sleeping** see p182

IT'S NOT EASY BEING GREEN

Sure it is! Here are some simple steps you can take to enjoy and protect Boston's natural beauty.

➡ Get around town by walking, biking or taking the T.

➡ Patronize hotels and restaurants that are making efforts to reduce their environmental impact. Look for the 🌿 icon in the listings.

➡ Check out the environmental education exhibits at the Harvard Museum of Natural History, the Museum of Science and the New England Aquarium.

Top Itineraries

Day One

Downtown & Waterfront

 Spend your first day in Boston following the **Freedom Trail**, which starts on the Boston Common and continues through Downtown. There's not time to go inside every museum, but you can admire the architecture and learn the history. Highlights are the **Old South Meeting House**, the **Old State House** and **Faneuil Hall**.

> **Lunch** Grab lunch from one of the many outlets in Quincy Market (p88).

West End & North End

 In the afternoon, the Freedom Trail continues into the North End, where you can visit the historic **Paul Revere House**, **Old North Church** and **Copp's Hill Burying Ground**.

> **Dinner** You are perfectly poised for an Italian feast along Hanover St (p58).

West End & North End

For the evening, perhaps you have tickets to an event at the **TD Garden**. If not, head to the exquisite **Liberty Hotel**, the former Charles St Jail. After admiring the impressive architectural transformation in the lobby, head downstairs for after-dinner drinks in the former 'drunk tank,' which now houses the ultracool club **Alibi**.

Day Two

Back Bay

 Spend the morning admiring Boston's most architecturally significant collection of buildings, clustered around **Copley Sq**. Admire the art and books at the **Boston Public Library**, ogle the magnificent stained-glass windows at **Trinity Church**, and gaze at the clean lines on the **John Hancock Tower**.

> **Lunch** Treat yourself to some smart fine dining at the Courtyard (p116).

Kenmore Square & Fenway

Your afternoon is reserved for one of Boston's magnificent art museums. Unfortunately, you'll have to choose between the excellent, encyclopaedic collection at the **Museum of Fine Arts** and the smaller but no less extraordinary exhibits at the **Isabella Stewart Gardner Museum**. Either way, you won't be disappointed.

> **Dinner** Eat raw oysters and drink craft beer at Citizen Public House (p130).

Kenmore Square & Fenway

There is music in the air this evening. It might be emanating from the acoustically perfect **Symphony Hall**, where you can hear the world-renowned Boston Symphony Orchestra (procure tickets in advance). Alternatively, rock out at the **House of Blues** or check out the local scene at **Church**.

Or, since you're in the neighborhood, you could always go to a baseball game instead.

Day Three

Cambridge

 Rent a bicycle – or borrow one from Hubway – and spend the morning cycling along the **Charles River**. You don't have to stay in Cambridge the whole time; the Charles River route has cycling paths on both sides of the river. Feel free to stop for scenic views of scullers and sailboats on the Charles, with the Boston city skyline as the backdrop.

> **Lunch** Grab a bite at Clover Food Lab's food truck or storefront (p150).

Cambridge

While away an afternoon in Harvard Sq, browsing the bookstores and cruising the cafes. Catch a free campus tour (try the unofficial **Harvard Tour** for a laugh) and rub John Harvard's shoe for good luck. If you're in the mood for a museum, the university offers several excellent options.

> **Dinner** Casual Cambridge, 1 or classy Russell House Tavern (p150).

Cambridge

 Don't miss the chance to see whatever brilliant or bizarre production is playing at the **American Repertory Theater** or at the company's second venue, **Club Oberon**. If that doesn't take your fancy, catch a band at the **Lizard Lounge**.

Day Four

Downtown & Waterfront

 Spend the morning on the water. In the best-case scenario, the weather is fine and you book yourself on a **whale-watching tour** to Stellwagen Bank. Alternatively, get a closer view of the marine life inside the **New England Aquarium**. Afterwards, stroll along the HarborWalk and across the Old North Bridge, admiring the harbor views along the way.

> **Lunch** Have lunch with a view at Sam's or Legal Harborside (p139).

Seaport District & South Boston

Follow along the HarborWalk to the **ICA** for an afternoon of provocative contemporary art. Don't miss the amazing view from the Founders' Gallery.

> **Dinner** Choose either colorful Chinatown (p100) or hip South End (p98).

South End & Chinatown

 A night on the town in this neighborhood offers virtually unlimited possibilities. Don your finest duds and go out to one of the Theater District's glittering venues for music, dance or drama. If you prefer to participate instead of watch, opt for one of the district's many flashy nightclubs. Or join the sophisticates sipping cocktails and listening to jazz at the **Beehive** in the South End.

If You Like...

Revolutionary History

Freedom Trail The 2.4-mile walking trail includes Boston's most important revolutionary sites, from the Boston Common to the Bunker Hill Monument. (p215, p68, p48)

Lexington & Concord An easy day trip from Boston, these towns are the sites of the first battles in the War for Independence. (p172)

Boston Tea Party Ships & Museum This excellent new museum includes replicas of the merchant ships that hosted the historic tea party. (p137)

Contemporary Art

Institute of Contemporary Art Boston's pre-eminent venue for contemporary art boasts a dramatic waterside setting. (p136)

Museum of Fine Arts The new and improved Linde Family Wing for Contemporary Art has tripled the exhibition space for its growing collection. (p125)

Isabella Stewart Gardner Museum A dynamic artist-in-residency program ensures a rich rotation of innovative exhibits and performances. (p127)

SoWa Artists Guild Visit on the first Friday of the month, when artists open their studios to the public. (p98)

JFK

John F Kennedy National Historic Site See where the

LOU JONES / LONELY PLANET IMAGES ©

Union Oyster House (p88)

35th US president was born and raised. (p164)

John F Kennedy Library & Museum Learn about Kennedy's political legacy at the official presidential library. (p138)

Harvard Yard Wander the hallowed halls of JFK's alma mater; afterwards, sun yourself in nearby JFK park. (p146)

Union Oyster House Request the JFK booth and order the lobster bisque. (p88)

Rose Kennedy Greenway Pay your respects to the matriarch of the Kennedy clan. (p87)

Literature

Concord Visit the homes and gravesites of Concord's literary masters; take a detour to Walden Pond to experience *Life in the Woods*. (p174)

Longfellow National Historic Site See where the Fireside Poet composed *Paul Revere's Ride*. (p149)

Public Garden Don't miss *Make Way for Ducklings*, a whimsical statue based on Robert McCloskey's children's book. (p70)

Boston Athenaeum Since 1807 this esteemed institution has counted many noteworthy writers and thinkers among its members. (p72)

Architecture

Copley Square Some of Boston's most stunning signature buildings are clustered around this plaza, including Trinity Church, the Boston Public Library and the John Hancock Tower. (p114, p112, p116)

Harvard Yard Features the best of all eras, including buildings by Henry Hobson Richardson, Walter Gropius and Le Corbusier. (p146)

Massachusetts Institute of Technology The campus contains the masterful examples of 20th-century modernism and architecture that have brought the institution into the 21st century. (p147)

Animals

New England Aquarium Explore the most exotic of natural environments... under the sea. (p83)

New England Aquarium Whale Watch Sightings of whales, dolphins and other marine life are practically guaranteed. (p92)

Franklin Park Zoo Visit the Serengeti plain, the Australian outback and the Amazonian rain forest all in one afternoon. (p165)

Harvard Museum of Natural History Hundreds of (stuffed) animals peer out of glass showcases, representing all classes and continents. (p149)

Gardens

Public Garden The Victorian-era Public Garden is an island of loveliness, always awash in blooms and breezes. (p70)

Arnold Arboretum Flowering trees galore, with special collections of bonsai, lilacs, conifers, rosaceous and fruit-laden *malus*. (p164)

Back Bay Fens At the end of June, the Kelleher Rose Garden

For more top Boston spots, see the following:
➡ Eating (p27)
➡ Drinking & Nightlife (p30)
➡ Entertainment (p33)
➡ Shopping (p35)
➡ Sports & Activities (p38)

PLAN YOUR TRIP IF YOU LIKE...

explodes in fireworks of colors and scents. (p129)

Old North Church Boston's oldest church is surrounded by delightfully secluded gardens, including an 18th-century garden that features annuals and perennials from the days of yore. (p55)

Free Stuff

Freedom Trail The National Park Service offers a free walking tour; several sites along the route – including the Massachusetts State House and the USS *Constitution* – do not charge admission. (p92, p71, p46)

Free Museum Nights The Museum of Fine Arts is free on Wednesdays after 4pm, while the Institute of Contemporary Art is free on Thursdays after 5pm; admission to the Children's Museum is $1 on Fridays from 5pm to 9pm. (p125, p136, p137)

Universities Both MIT and Harvard offer free campus tours. (p147, p146)

New HI Boston Plenty of free and discounted activities for guests. (p188)

Month by Month

January

The month of January represents the deepest, darkest part of winter. Expect snow and cold temperatures – great weather for sledding and skating.

🎆 Chinese New Year

In late January or early February, Chinatown lights up with a colorful parade, firecrackers, fireworks and lots of food.

February

The weather is still cold, but the days are getting longer. Tourists are few and far between, so prices are cheap.

🏃 Beanpot

Local college hockey teams face off against each other in the hotly contested Beanpot Tournament (www.beanpothockey.com). The men's teams play the first two Mondays of February, while the women play the first two Tuesdays.

March

By March, Boston is officially sick of winter. On March 17 the city celebrates Evacuation Day, when the British pulled out of Boston Harbor in 1776.

🎆 St Patrick's Day

The large and vocal South Boston Irish community hosts a parade (www.southbostonparade.org) on West Broadway, which has come under fire for its exclusion of gay and lesbian groups.

🍴 Restaurant Week

Two weeks, really. At the end of March, scores of venues participating in Restaurant Week (www.restaurantweekboston.com) offer prix-fixe menus: $20 for lunch, $30 for dinner. The menus are usually excellent value. This event repeats in August (so that actually makes it four weeks).

April

Emerging crocuses and blooming forsythias signal the arrival of spring in April, when baseball fans await opening day at Fenway Park. Temperatures range from 40°F to 55°F, although the occasional snowstorm can also occur.

🎆 Patriots' Day

On the third Monday in April, history buffs commemorate the start of the American Revolution (www.battleroad.org), with a reenactment of the battle on Lexington Green (11 miles west of Boston) and a commemoration ceremony at the North Bridge in Concord (17 miles west of Boston).

🏃 Boston Marathon

This is the world's oldest marathon (www.bostonmarathon.org), and it attracts tens of thousands of ambitious runners who pound the pavement for 26.2 miles. Held on Patriots' Day (the third Monday in April).

☆ Independent Film Festival of Boston

During the last week in April, venues around the city host screenings of independent films (www.iffboston.org), including shorts, documentaries and drama produced locally and nationally.

May

In May – one of Boston's most beautiful months – the sun comes out on a semi-permanent basis and the magnolia trees bloom all along Newbury St and Commonwealth Ave. Memorial Day, on the last Monday in May, officially kicks off the summer season.

🏠 Mayfair

When the sun comes out, so do the good folks in Harvard Sq, for Mayfair (www.harvardsquare.com). On the first or second Sunday in May, artists, merchants and restaurants set up booths on the streets, while children's events and live entertainment take place on stages around the square.

⚜ Lilac Sunday

On the third Sunday in May, the Arnold Arboretum celebrates the arrival of spring on Lilac Sunday (www.arboretum.harvard.edu), when more than 400 varieties of fragrant lilac are in bloom. It is the only day of the year that visitors can picnic on the grass.

June

June brings temperatures ranging from 55°F to 70°F, and lots of rain. Student calendars are packed with end-of-academic-year events and graduation ceremonies. Then the students depart the city, causing a noticeable decline in traffic and noise.

⚜ Boston Pride Festival

The week-long GLBT festival (www.bostonpride.org) kicks off with the raising of a rainbow flag on City Hall Plaza. On the second Saturday the Pride Parade attracts tens of thousands of participants, decked out in outrageous costumes and showing off their gay pride, culminating in a huge party on the Boston Common.

⚜ Bunker Hill Day

Charlestown historians remember the crucial Battle of Bunker Hill. The city celebrates with a road race, followed by a parade.

July

By July the city has emptied out, as the students vacate for the summer and Bostonians head to their summerhouses. It's also Boston's hottest month, with temperatures ranging from 70°F to 85°F, and there's always a week or two when the mercury shoots to the high 90s.

⚜ Harborfest

The week-long Independence Day festival (www.bostonharborfest.com) starts on the last weekend in June. It includes events like Children's Day, with face painting and children's entertainment, as well as Chowderfest, where you can sample dozens of chowders prepared by Boston's top chefs.

⚜ Independence Day

On July 4 Boston hosts a line-up of free performances (www.july4th.org), concluding with the Boston Pops playing Tchaikovsky's *1812 Overture*, complete with brass cannon and synchronized fireworks. Half a million people descend on the Esplanade to watch it live.

August

Summer in the city continues in August; only at the end of the month will you begin to feel fall coming.

⚜ Boston Carnival

Boston's Caribbean community re-creates Carnival (www.bostoncarnival.org), a celebration of Caribbean culture complete with spectacular costumes, sultry music and spicy cooking. Includes a Kiddies Carnival Celebration and an all-out, over-the-top 'Trini-style' Carnival parade in Franklin Park.

⚜ Italian Festivals

Throughout July and August, the North End's religious societies sponsor feasts and processions honoring their patron saints. Major celebrations include the Fisherman's Feast (www.fishermansfeast.com) on the third weekend in August, and St Anthony's Feast (www.stanthonys feast.com) on the last weekend in August.

Top: July 4 fireworks over the Charles River and the Massachusetts State House.
Bottom: Head of the Charles Regatta.

September

By September the humidity disappears, leaving slightly cooler temperatures and a crispness in the air. The students return and the streets are filled with U-Haul trailers during the first week. The first Monday in September is Labor Day, the official end of the summer season.

☆ Boston Comedy Festival

The second week in September is dedicated to the funny guys and gals, who cut up at venues all around town as a part of the Boston Comedy Festival (www. bostoncomedyfest.com).

☆ Boston Film Festival

For 10 days in mid-September, all Bostonians become film critics at the Boston Film Festival (www.boston filmfestival.org), where they are invited to attend screenings of some 50 different films at theaters around the city.

☆ Beantown Jazz Festival

The Berklee College of Music sponsors this free two-day festival (www. beantownjazz.org) in the South End. Three stages show performances by jazz greats as well as local artists and Berklee students. Panel discussions, food vendors, kids activities and all that jazz.

☆ Life is Good Festival

This local (and optimistic!) company sponsors the Life is Good Festival (www.

lifeisgood.com), a day of music and fun in Canton, 16 miles south of Boston. Families are invited to groove to the music and play backyard games, ranging from home run hero to seed-spitting.

Hub on Wheels

On the third Sunday in September, the citywide bicycle ride, Hub on Wheels (www.bostoncyclingcelebration.com), starts at City Hall Plaza and offers three different scenic routes (10, 30 or 50 miles).

October

October is Boston's best month. The academic year is rolling; the weather is crisp and cool; and the trees take on shades of red, gold and amber.

Oktoberfest

On the first or second Sunday in October, Harvard Sq artisans and entertainers take to the streets. This annual street fair (www.harvardsquare.com) is great for kids, with puppet shows, face painting, fair rides and dance troupes.

Head of the Charles Regatta

Spectators line the banks of the Charles River on a weekend in mid-October to watch the world's largest rowing event, the Head of the Charles (www.hocr.org).

Haunted Happenings

Salem (16 miles north of Boston) goes all out for Halloween (www.hauntedhappenings.org). The city celebrates for much of the month of October, when there are parades, concerts, pumpkin carvings, costume parties and trick-or-treating.

November

In November, you can feel winter in the air. You may even see snow flurries. Thanksgiving Day – the third Thursday in November – kicks off the holiday season.

America's Hometown Thanksgiving Celebration

Plymouth (40 miles south of Boston) is the birthplace of Thanksgiving, so it's appropriate that the town celebrates this heritage with a parade, concerts, crafts and – of course – food.

December

In early December, the huge Christmas trees at the Prudential Center and the Boston Common are lit, lending the city a festive air that remains throughout the month. There is usually at least one good snow storm this month.

☆ Boston Tea Party Reenactment

On the Sunday prior to December 16, costumed actors march from Old South Meeting House to the waterfront and toss crates of tea into the harbor. Nowadays, the event takes place on the newly rebuilt Griffin's Wharf, where the Tea Party ships are docked.

First Night

New Year celebrations (www.firstnight.org) begin early and continue past midnight, culminating in fireworks over the harbor. Purchase a special button (see the website for button vendors) that permits entrance into events citywide.

With Kids

Boston is a giant history museum, the setting for many educational and lively field trips. Cobblestone streets and costume-clad tour guides bring to life the events that kids read about in history books. Hands-on experimentation and interactive exhibits fuse learning and entertainment.

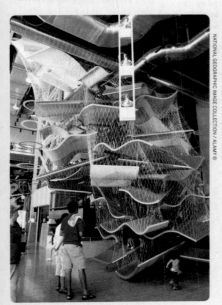

Boston Children's Museum (p137)

Kids' History

USS Constitution & Museum

Aside from exploring the warship, kids can swing in hammocks and experience life as a sailor (see p46).

Massachusetts State House

Check out the Kids' Zone on the State House website. It features word games, trivia quizzes and the priceless Ladybug Story, a story of how a group of kids used the legislative process to make the ladybug the official bug of Massachusetts (see p71).

Old South Meeting House

Scavenger hunts and activity kits direct children's exploration of the historic building (see p87).

Old State House

Most of the exhibits are not particularly kid-friendly, but the 'Hands-on History' exhibition allows kids to build with blocks and peek behind the hidden doors of the State House facade (see p84).

Prudential Center Skywalk Observatory

Assuming your kids are not acrophobes, they will be thrilled to see Boston from above. A special audio tour caters to little ones (see p116).

Kids' Art

Museum of Fine Arts

Offers loads of programs for kids of all ages. For example, Family Place (open Tuesday and Thursday) teaches children over age four to use art, music and poetry to explore the gallery's collections. Every second Monday there's a program for toddlers, and different series of Saturday classes target kids and teens (see p125).

Institute of Contemporary Art (ICA)

The ICA (see p136) offers innovative programs for families including Sunday afternoon art classes and monthly 'play dates,' as well as a supercool program organized by teens for teens (www.icateens.org).

NEED TO KNOW

➡ Boston Central (www.bostoncentral.com) is a fantastic resource for families, with listings for activities, outings, shops and playgrounds that are good for kids.

➡ Look for the ⊞ icon in the listings indicating family-friendly restaurants, shops and hotels.

➡ Kids under 11 ride the T for free, while junior high and high school students pay half-price. Most taxi companies can provide a child seat if you reserve in advance.

➡ Most upscale hotels offer babysitting services or referrals. You can also try Boston's Best Babysitters (☎617-268-7148; www.bbbabysitters.com; 1/2/3 children per day $40/70/105) and Nanny Poppins (☎617-227-5437; www.nannypoppins.com; per hour $12-20, plus $30 placement fee).

Kids' Science

Museum of Science

More opportunities to combine fun and learning than anywhere in the city. Most of the museum is good for older children and teenagers, while the Discovery Center is designed for kids under eight (see 54).

New England Aquarium

Special hands-on exhibits give kids the chance to pet sharks and rays or even pick up a starfish or a sea urchin (see p83). Toddlers will appreciate the toys and activities in the (tiny) Curious George Discovery Corner.

Boston Children's Museum

Hours of fun climbing, constructing and creating. The museum is especially good for kids aged three to eight years, although the PlaySpace is designed specifically for toddlers under the age of three (see p137).

Franklin Park Zoo

The zoo often hosts special events (eg Little Joe the gorilla's birthday party), which children adore. Otherwise, the hands-on exhibits like Franklin Farm and Aussie Aviary let them get up close and interact with the animals (see p165).

Harvard Museum of Natural History

It's almost as good as the zoo. Sure, the stuffed animals don't move, but they let the kids get really close and look them in the eye. Nature story hours target young audiences (see p149).

MIT Museum

It's too complicated for small kids, but teenagers will get a kick out of the robots, holograms and other fascinating science stuff (see p147).

Kids' Outdoor Adventures

Boston Harbor Islands

Spectacle Island has family-friendly facilities (and a beach), while Georges Island has Fort Warren, which is fun for older children to explore. Check the website for lots of kid-oriented activities on weekends (see p80).

Castle Island & Fort Independence

Lots of run-around space and a fort to explore, plus beaches and a playground, make this an excellent adventurous outing for kids (see p137).

New England Aquarium Whale Watch

The boat ride can be a thrill, and whale sightings are practically guaranteed. That said, they are not usually very close, and it can turn into a long trip for smaller children (see p92).

Swan Boats

Boat rides on the Public Garden lagoon are short (15 minutes) and sweet (read: tame). Perfect for little tykes, but perhaps boring for older kids (see p70).

ERIC FOWKE / ALAMY ©

Franklin Park Zoo (p165)

Kids' Tours

Boston by Foot
'Boston by Little Feet' is the only Freedom Trail walking tour designed especially for children age six to 12 (see p224).

Boston Duck Tours
Kids of all ages are invited to drive the duck on the raging waters of the Charles River. Bonus: quacking loudly is encouraged (see p223).

Freedom Trail Foundation
Older kids will appreciate the guides in costume. Download a scavenger hunt or reading list for your child before setting out (see p224).

Urban AdvenTours
This bike tour is great for all ages. Kids' bikes and helmets are available for rent, as are bike trailers for toddlers (see p223).

Kids' Entertainment

Quincy Market
There are always jugglers, puppeteers, break-dancers and acrobats performing on weekends at Quincy Market (see p88).

Boston Symphony Orchestra
The BSO has a rich 'Youth & Family' program, with weekend concerts designed to introduce young people to classical music. Come early for instrument demonstrations and other interactive fun. Recommended for ages five to 12 (see p132).

Improv Boston
Improv Boston presents *The Family Show* on Saturdays at 6pm (www.improvboston.com). Kids aged four and up can watch and engage in improvised song and dance (see Map p268).

Coolidge Corner Theatre
Sunday morning movies especially for little people (see p168).

Mugar Omni & Simons Theaters
Nature and science come alive at these multi-sensory IMAX cinemas (see p62, p91).

Parks & Playgrounds

Charlesbank Playground
Aka the Esplanade playground (see Map p246).

Boston Common Playground
Bonus: summertime spray pool on the Frog Pond (see Map p250).

Stoneman Playground
Two gated areas target different age-groups (see Map p260).

Cambridge Common Playground
Features swings, climbing structures and ramps (see Map p266).

Eating

The Boston area is the home of the first Thanksgiving and of bountiful autumnal harvests. It is America's seafood capital, the origin of dishes such as clam chowder and boiled lobster. This regional cuisine has deep cultural roots and, like all things cultural, it is dynamic and continuously developing.

International Influences

The international influence on Boston cuisine cannot be underestimated. Italian, Irish and Portuguese is already old hat. Now Bostonians are sampling Brazilian, Chinese, Indian, Korean, Thai and Vietnamese. Immigrants open restaurants to cater to their own community, but these exotic eateries are also attracting the attention of well-traveled Bostonians who are curious about global cultures.

Local, Seasonal, Organic

In this era of creative culinary discovery, more and more Bostonians are reclaiming their roots in one crucial way: their appreciation of local, seasonal and organic products. A thriving 'locavore' movement highlights the bounty from the local waters and from rich New England farms.

Vegetarians & Vegans

The **Boston Vegetarian Society** (www.bostonveg.org) is a great resource for vegetarian eaters, with extensive restaurant reviews and lots of links to veggie-friendly organizations. It also organizes a fabulous two-day food festival in October.

Cooking Courses

Patron food saint Julia Child, long-time Cambridge resident and star of many cooking shows, spent four decades teaching people to cook before she died in 2004. If you want to embody Julia's *bon vivant, bon appétit* spirit, take a class at the Cambridge School of Culinary Arts (p161).

Eating by Neighborhood

➡ **Charlestown** (p49) A small selection of welcoming restaurants on Main St and City Sq.

➡ **West End & North End** (p57) Hearkening back to Italy, the North End is Boston's most authentic and abundant Old World eating destination.

➡ **Beacon Hill & Boston Common** (p73) A mix of cute cafes, business lunches and gourmet delicatessens, with no shortage of swanky spots.

➡ **Downtown & Waterfront** (p88) Sandwich shops and lunch spots catering to the workaday world.

➡ **South End & Chinatown** (p98) Boston's best eating, overflowing with ethnic eateries, trendy restaurants and neighborhood cafes.

➡ **Back Bay** (p116) Classy grills and cozy cafes lined up along Newbury St and Boylston St.

➡ **Kenmore Square & Fenway** (p129) Cheap ethnic eats and burger joints, with a few excellent upscale options.

➡ **Seaport District & South Boston** (p138) Seafood, seafood and more seafood, with a few arty cafes and restaurants thrown into the mix.

➡ **Cambridge** (p150) Coffeehouses, sandwich shops, multicultural eateries and upscale restaurants to suit every taste.

➡ **Streetcar Suburbs** (p165) An eclectic assortment of dining options, including kosher delis, Russian restaurants and other ethnic eats.

NEED TO KNOW

Opening Hours

➡ Breakfast 7am to 10am

➡ Lunch 11:30am to 2:30pm or 3pm

➡ Dinner 5pm to 9pm or 10pm

In this book, opening hours are listed only where they differ from this standard.

Price Guide

$ Less than $12

$$ Between $12 and $25

$$$ More than $25

Prices listed are for main courses.

Booking Tables

Reservations are recommended for most top-end restaurants, especially on Friday and Saturday evenings. Make reservations at www.opentable.com.

Tipping

In restaurants with sit-down service, customers should leave a 15% tip for acceptable service and a 20% tip for good service; tipping at a lower level reflects dissatisfaction with the service. Waiters and bartenders are paid significantly below minimum wage and they depend on tips for their earnings.

Lonely Planet's Top Choices

Pomodoro (p58) The quintessential romantic North End hideaway with great Italian food.

Hungry Mother (p151) Sophisticated Southern fare in a cozy cottage.

El Pelon (p130) Cheap and delicious tacos galore.

Neptune Oyster (p58) A casual but classy seafood restaurant with a well-stocked raw bar.

Tres Gatos (p166) Tapas, wine, music, books... good times.

Gourmet Dumpling House (p100) Ridiculously good soup dumplings in a no-nonsense setting.

Best By Budget

$
Clover Food Lab (p150)
India Quality (p130)

$$
Giacomo's Ristorante (p59)
Grotto (p73)
Courtyard (p116)

$$$
Bondir (p151)
Ten Tables (p166)
L'Espalier (p117)
O Ya (p102)

Best by Cuisine

Italian
Marco (p58)
Giacomo's Ristorante (p59)
Trattoria Toscana (p130)
Scampo (p57)

Chinese
Café de Lulu (p101)
Winsor Dim Sum Cafe (p101)
Taiwan Cafe (p101)
Jumbo Seafood (p101)

Best Eat Streets

Hanover St, North End (p58)

Tremont St, South End (p98)

Main St, Cambridge (p151)

Best for Vegetarians

Veggie Galaxy (p152)
Kookoo Café (p166)
My Thai Vegan Café (p101)
Life Alive (p151)
Clover Food Lab (p150)
Veggie Planet (p150)

Best for Kids

Full Moon (p151)
Summer Shack (p118)
Friendly Toast (p152)
Flatbread Co (p160)
Mr Bartley's Burger Cottage (p150)
Quincy Market (p88)

Best Seafood

Yankee Lobster Fish Co (p139)
Atlantic Fish Co (p117)
B&G Oysters (p98)
Daily Catch (p59)
Legal Harborside (p139)

Best Sandwiches

Volle Nolle (p59)
Chacarero (p89)
Darwin's Ltd (p150)
Sam LaGrassa's (p89)

Best Pizza

Emma's Pizza (p151)
Galleria Umberto (p59)

Santarpio's (p60)

Cambridge, 1 (p150)

Best Burgers

Uburger (p130)

Tasty Burger (p130)

The Haven (p168)

Mr Bartley's Burger Cottage (p150)

Best Sushi

O Ya (p102)

Douzo (p117)

Kaze Shabu Shabu (p101)

Fugakyu (p166)

Zen Sushi Bar & Grill (p74)

Best Ice Cream

Christina's (p151)

Toscanini's (p152)

JP Licks (p167)

Best Historic Restaurants

Marliave (p89)

Warren Tavern (p50)

Red House (p150)

Durgin Park (p88)

Union Oyster House (p88)

Best Diners

Mike's City Diner (p100)

Charlie's Kitchen (p153)

Veggie Galaxy (p152)

South Street Diner (p102)

Best Bakeries

Maria's Pastry (p58)

Flour (p139)

South End Buttery (p100)

Best Late-night Grub

Bar Lola (p117)

Franklin Café (p100)

Market in the Square (p151)

South Street Diner (p102)

Best Brunch

Centre Street Café (p168)

Winsor Dim Sum Café (p101)

The Gallows (p103)

Gaslight, Brasserie du Coin (p100)

Union Bar & Grille (p100)

Zaftigs Delicatessen (p165)

Best Neighborhood Restaurants

Navy Yard Bistro & Wine Bar (p49)

75 Chestnut (p73)

Franklin Café (p100)

Audubon Circle (p130)

Green Street Grill (p151)

Regal Beagle (p166)

Best Hidden Haunts

Marco (p58)

Casa Romero (p117)

Courtyard (p116)

Channel Café (p139)

Grotto (p73)

Bar Lola (p117)

PLAN YOUR TRIP EATING

Drinking & Nightlife

Despite the city's Puritan roots, modern-day Bostonians like to get their drink on. While the city has more than its fair share of Irish pubs, it also has a dynamic craft beer movement, with a few homegrown microbreweries; a knowledgeable population of wine drinkers (and pourers); and a red-hot cocktail scene, thanks to some talented local bartenders. So pick your poison...and drink up!

Where to Drink

ALCOHOL

Boston's drinking scene is dominated by four categories: dive bars, Irish bars, sports bars and a new breed of truly hip cocktail bar. Any of these types might cater to discerning beer drinkers, with craft local brews on tap or a wide selection of imported bottles. Some also morph into dance clubs as the night wears on. Boston also boasts a few sophisticated and semi-swanky wine bars, which are delightful for a glass of Pinot (and usually accompanying food).

CAFFEINE

Aside from Dunkin' Donuts on every corner, there are scores of cute cafes and cool coffeehouses, many of which serve dynamite sandwiches and pastries. Many coffee shops offer wireless internet access (sometimes for a fee), which is basically an invitation to stay all day.

Where to Dance

There's really only one neighborhood in Boston where the dancing goes down: the Theater District. Boylston St is the main drag for over-the-top megaclubs, but there are other venues all over this groovy 'hood. There are a few classier clubs in Back Bay, Cambridge and Downtown. Most clubs organize thematic dance parties, often centered on a particular type of music, clientele or DJ. As such, the atmosphere can vary greatly from night to night.

Drinking & Nightlife by Neighborhood

➡ **Charlestown** (p50) An eclectic mix of drinking options, ranging from historic to exotic.

➡ **West End & North End** (p60) Drink beer (West End) or Campari (North End) with your sports on the tube.

➡ **Beacon Hill & Boston Common** (p74) There are only a few local watering holes in the bastion of Brahmin.

➡ **Downtown & Waterfront** (p89) Some perennial favorites are embedded in the streets away from the Freedom Trail.

➡ **South End & Chinatown** (p102) Gay-friendly and ubertrendy places to drink; plus the city's hottest clubbing scene.

➡ **Back Bay** (p118) Divey student haunts at one end, trendy yuppy bars at the other (with plenty in between).

➡ **Kenmore Square & Fenway** (p131) Overflowing with drinking joints for students and sports-lovers.

➡ **Seaport District & South Boston** (p140) Salty treats in Seaport for the diligent drinker, but head deeper into Southie for a Boston Irish experience.

➡ **Cambridge** (p152) Students and scholars congregate at creative cafes and beloved dives.

➡ **Streetcar Suburbs** (p168) Some of Boston's best beer pubs and music clubs are in these outlying areas.

Lonely Planet's Top Choices

Delux Café (p102) A friendly South End dive with delicious food.

Casablanca (p152) A long-standing favorite among Cambridge literati; excellent wine list.

Café Pamplona (p152) A quintessentially Cambridge Euro-style cafe.

Bleacher Bar (p131) Sneak a peek inside Fenway Park at this sweet sports bar.

Drink (p140) Sets the standard for Boston cocktail bars, with the industry's most knowledge-able mixologists.

Beehive (p103) Enjoy a little jazz at this hip place to drink and be seen.

Best for Beer

Boston Beer Works (p131)

Cambridge Brewing Co (p154)

Bukowski Tavern (p118)

Cornwall's (p131)

Lower Depths (p131)

Best for Wine

Troquet (p103)

Sonsie (p118)

Bin 26 Enoteca (p75)

Navy Yard Bistro & Wine Bar (p49)

Shay's Pub (p153)

Best for Cocktails

Flash's Cocktails (p118)

Eastern Standard (p131)

The Gallows (p103)

Brick & Mortar (p154)

28 Degrees (p103)

Woodward (p90)

Best for Coffee

Equal Exchange Cafe (p60)

Pavement Coffeehouse (p131)

Thinking Cup (p90)

Best for Tea

Algiers Coffee House (p153)

Karma Yoga Studio (p107)

Upstairs on the Square (p153)

Best for Hot Chocolate

LA Burdick (p152)

Caffé Vittoria (p61)

Thinking Cup (p90)

Best Irish Pubs

Brendan Behan Pub (p168)

Mr Dooley's Boston Tavern (p90)

Croke Park Whitey's (p140)

Plough & Stars (p153)

Best Sports Bars

Baseball Tavern (p132)

West End Johnnies (p60)

Caffé dello Sport (p61)

Fritz (p103)

Fours (p61)

Best Hidden Haunts

Lucky's Lounge (p140)

Café Pamplona (p152)

Tavern on the Water (p50)

Alley Bar (p90)

Corner Pub (p118)

NEED TO KNOW

Opening Hours

➜ Most drinking venues open from 11:30am until midnight, and until 1am or 2am on Friday and Saturday.

➜ A few upscale venues open only in the evening at 5pm.

➜ Clubs are open 10pm to 2am, but most of the action goes down after midnight.

➜ Remember that the T stops running around 12:20am – a good 1½ hours before last call.

Tipping

➜ Tip your bartender! As when dining, the going rate is 15% to 20% of the tab.

➜ If you are paying as you go, it is standard to leave your change for the folks who made your drinks (eg leave $10 if your total due is $8).

Clubbing

➜ Expect to pay a cover charge of $10 to $20.

➜ Most clubs enforce a dress code at the door.

➜ To avoid being turned away at the door, go online to get on the guest list or make a reservation.

Best Cafe Scene

Voltage Coffee & Art (p153)

Algiers Coffee House (p153)

Zumes Coffee House (p50)

Best Dance Scene

Good Life (p90)

Ryles Jazz Club (p156)

Rise (p119)

Underbar (p103)

Storyville (p119)

6B Lounge (p74)

Best Gay & Lesbian Scene

Midway Café (p168)

Alley Bar (p90)

Club Café (p119)

Machine (p132)

Fritz (p103)

Underbar (p103)

Best Student Scene

Shay's Pub (p153)

Miracle of Science Bar & Grill (p152)

Pavement Coffeehouse (p131)

Pour House (p119)

Best DJs

River Gods (p154)

Middlesex (p154)

Good Life (p90)

Middle East (p156)

Best Views

Barking Crab (p139)

Tavern on the Water (p50)

Top of the Hub (p119)

Best Trivia Nights

Brendan Behan Pub (p168)

21st Amendment (p74)

The Haven (p168)

6B Lounge (p74)

Warren Tavern (p50)

Entertainment

Welcome to the Athens of America, a city rich with artistic and cultural offerings. With the world-class Boston Symphony Orchestra, two opera companies, a ballet company and several nationally ranked music schools, Boston is a true musical mecca. The Theater District is packed with venues showcasing the city's opera, dance and dramatic prowess, while more innovative experimental theaters are in Cambridge and the South End.

Music

CLASSICAL MUSIC

Home to the Boston Symphony Orchestra and the New England Conservatory of Music, Boston boasts some of the country's oldest and most prestigious houses for symphonic experiences.

ROCK, HIP-HOP & INDIE

Boston's modern music scene is centered in the student areas of Cambridge and Allston/Brighton. To figure out who's playing where, take a look at the clubs' websites or listings in the *Phoenix* or *Weekly Dig*. Most shows are for those aged 21 and over.

JAZZ CLUBS

Since jazz is the music of intellectuals, it comes as no surprise that Boston has a thriving scene. It starts with the students and faculty of the excellent music institutes in town, and ends with intimate venues that attract the biggest names in the genre.

Comedy

Boston is a funny place, and we mean funny ha-ha. To cite some famous examples, Conan O'Brian, Jay Leno and Denis Leary are all from Boston. The Wilbur Theater is Boston's largest comedy venue, but there are smaller funny outlets all around town.

Theater

In the Theater District, several big-ticket venues consistently book top shows, produce premieres and serve as testing grounds for many plays that eventually become hits on Broadway. The Theater District is also home to two professional opera companies and the Boston Ballet. For innovative, independent and sometimes wacky theater, leave the gilded halls of the Theater District and check out the smaller venues in Cambridge and the South End.

Entertainment by Neighborhood

➡ **Charlestown** The closest thing to 'cultcha' is trivia night at the Warren Tavern.

➡ **West End & North End** (p61) Aside from big-name concerts at the Garden, there's one lone comedy venue.

➡ **Beacon Hill & Boston Common** (p75) Shakespeare on the Common but nothing on the hill.

➡ **Downtown & Waterfront** (p91) The spillover from the Theater District includes several Downtown venues.

➡ **South End & Chinatown** (p104) The epicenter of Boston's cultural life, with dozens of theaters.

➡ **Back Bay** (p119) Home to a few music venues associated with the Berklee College of Music.

➡ **Kenmore Square & Fenway** (p132) Avenue of the Arts includes Symphony Hall and other esteemed venues.

➡ **Seaport District & South Boston** (p140) One outdoor concert venue, plus whatever goes down at the ICA.

➡ **Cambridge** (p154) A huge selection of innovative, independent music, theater, dance and comedy.

➡ **Streetcar Suburbs** (p168) Pretty quiet for entertainment, but Boston's best indie music scene is up the street in Allston/Brighton.

NEED TO KNOW

Tickets

➡ Tickets for opera, theater and dance are available online or at each theater's box office.

➡ At most rock, indie and jazz clubs, you can buy tickets at the door at performance time. For bigger or popular shows in danger of selling out, many venues allow advance online purchases.

Opening Hours

Classical music, theater and dance performances usually start at 7pm or 8pm, while there may be matinee performances on weekends. Concerts at music clubs often start at 9pm or 10pm, though clubs might offer an early show at 7pm or 8pm.

BosTix

BosTix (www.bostix.org; ⊙10am-6pm Tue-Sat, 11am-4pm Sun) offers discounted tickets to theater productions citywide (up to 25% off for advance purchases online). Discounts up to 50% are available for same-day purchase: check the website to see what's available. Purchases must be made in person, in cash, at outlets on Copley Sq or at Quincy Market.

Internet Resources

➡ **Band in Boston** (www.bandinboston podcast.com)

➡ **World Music** (www.worldmusic.org)

➡ **Comedy Boston** (www.comedyboston. com)

Lonely Planet's Top Choices

Wally's (p104) A low-down blues bar with funky live music seven nights a week.

Café 939 (p119) A Berklee–student–run venue that showcases up-and-coming stars in a super intimate setting.

Lizard Lounge (p154) The Boston area's best small music venue, for diversity of music and coolness of club.

Club Passim (p154) The legendary club that constitutes the folk scene in Boston.

Comedy Studio (p154) Cutting-edge comedy every night of the week, upstairs from the Chinese restaurant-club.

Lily Pad (p156) A super-small space for music, dance and performance art, in bizarre and beautiful forms.

Best for Indie Rock

Great Scott (p169)

Brighton Music Hall (p169)

Paradise Rock Club (p169)

Church (p132)

Best for Jazz

Regatta Bar (p155)

Scullers Jazz Club (p169)

Ryles Jazz Club (p156)

Berklee Performance Center (p119)

Best for Classical Music

Boston Symphony Orchestra (p132)

New England Conservatory (p133)

Longy School of Music (p155)

Best for Opera, Dance & Musical Theater

Opera House (p91)

Citi Performing Arts Center (p105)

Paramount Center (p91)

Cutler Majestic Theater (p104)

Club Oberon (p155)

Best for Drama

American Repertory Theater (p155)

Huntington Theatre Company (p132)

Boston Center for the Arts (p104)

Best for Comedy

Wilbur Theatre (p105)

Dick's Beantown Comedy Vault (p105)

Great Scott (p169)

Improv Asylum (p62)

Best for Film

Coolidge Corner Theatre (p168)

Brattle Theatre (p155)

Modern Theatre (p91)

Harvard Film Archive Cinematheque (p155)

Best for Poetry

Lizard Lounge (p154)

Grolier Poetry Bookshop (p157)

Cantab Lounge (p156)

Best for Gay Cabaret

Jacques Cabaret (p105)

Shopping

Boston is known for its intellect and its arts, so it goes without saying that it's good for bookstores, art galleries and music shops. These days, the streets are also sprinkled with offbeat boutiques – some carrying vintage treasures and local designers. Besides to-die-for duds, indie shops hawk handmade jewelry, exotic household decorations and arty, quirky gifts. Boston's stores are a treat to browse, even if you don't intend to buy.

Fashion

Fashionistas continue to take their cues from New York, but a few local designers are trying to put Boston on the map *à la mode.* Recognizing Boston's conservative tastes in clothes, the styles tend to be relatively down-to-earth and decidedly wearable compared to what you might see in *Vogue* magazine. That Boston's most famous names in the fashion industry are Bert and John Jacobs (Life is Good) proves the point.

Recycled Stuff

Vintage is very hot in Boston. Sure, you can buy 'vintage-inspired' clothing; or you can go for the real deal at one of Boston's many second-hand clothing stores. Other popular recyclables include books, records, jewelry and wicked nice furniture.

Locally Made

Boston's vibrant art scene makes its presence known in local shops, galleries and markets that are dedicated to arts and crafts. High-quality handmade items run the gamut from designer clothes and jewelry to colorful ceramics and housewares. Sometimes quirky and clever, sometimes sophisticated and stylish, these handmade, locally made items are hard to classify but easy to appreciate.

Shopping by Neighborhood

➡ **Charlestown** (p51) Pick up an 'I climbed the Bunker Hill Monument' T-shirt.

➡ **West End & North End** (p61) Get some gourmet treats from the Italian grocers in the North End.

➡ **Beacon Hill & Boston Common** (p75) Cutesy boutiques and scads of antiques.

➡ **Downtown & Waterfront** (p91) One large department store and smaller practical retail outlets cater to workaday Boston.

➡ **South End & Chinatown** (p105) Fast becoming Boston's best shopping destination, with trendy boutiques and excellent galleries.

➡ **Back Bay** (p120) The traditional 'shopping and lunch' destination.

➡ **Kenmore Square & Fenway** (p133) Not much appeal, unless you're in the market for used records.

➡ **Seaport District & South Boston** (p141) One iconic fashion center and one art gallery. Period.

➡ **Cambridge** (p156) Long famous for its used bookstores and second-hand record shops.

➡ **Streetcar Suburbs** (p168) Charming strips lined with eclectic collections of interesting shops.

NEED TO KNOW

Opening Hours

Stores are generally open Monday through Saturday from 10am or 11am until 6pm or 7pm, unless otherwise noted. Most are also open on Sunday from noon to 5pm.

Sales Tax – Not!

There is no sales tax in Massachusetts on clothing up to $175 because – get this – it's a necessity! Now, if we could only convince our frugal partner of the *necessity* of those designer jeans...

Lonely Planet's Top Choices

Ward Maps (p157) Awesome antique and reproduction maps; get one printed on a T-shirt or a tote.

Artifaktori Vintage (p75) Super-stylish vintage-inspired and ethically produced clothing.

Weirdo Records (p158) A tiny shopped packed with music you never knew you loved.

Salmagundi (p169) Hip hats for everyone's heads.

Tayrona (p157) Exquisite, internationally inspired jewelry, hand bags and other irresistible odds and ends.

South End Open Market (p105) A weekly (seasonal) outdoor extravaganza of arts and crafts and other creations.

Best for Women's Fashion

Crush Boutique (p75)

In-Jean-ius (p62)

LIT Boutique (p63)

Turtle (p107)

Louis Boston (p141)

Best for Men's Fashion

Bobby from Boston (p106)

Sault New England (p106)

Uniform (p107)

Louis Boston (p141)

Best for Vintage

Bobby from Boston (p106)

SoWa Vintage Market (p106)

Oona's Experienced Clothing (p158)

Second Time Around (p121)

Closet, Inc (p120)

Best for Local Designers

Wild Indigo (p106)

Cibeline (p76)

Lunarik Fashions (p120)

Best for Locally Made

Greenway Open Market (p91)

Society of Arts & Crafts (p121)

Made In Fort Point (p141)

Cambridge Artists Cooperative (p157)

MassArt Made (p133)

North Bennet Street School (p62)

Best for Shoes & Accessories

Berk's (p157)

Helen's Leather (p76)

Moxie (p77)

Lunarik Fashions (p120)

Best for Sportswear

Ibex (p121)

Eastern Mountain Sports (p120)

Core de Vie (p76)

City Sports Outlet (p91)

Best for Sneakers

New Balance Factory Store (p159)

Marathon Sports (p121)

Converse (p120)

Bill Rodgers Running Center (p92)

Best for Kids

Red Wagon & Pixie Stix (p77)

Coco Baby (p107)

Tadpole (p106)

Boing! (p169)

Eureka Puzzles (p169)

Hatched (p170)

Best Bookstores

Brookline Booksmith (p168)

Trident Booksellers (p121)

Harvard Bookstore (p157)

Brattle Book Shop (p91)

Raven Used Books (p157)

Lorem Ipsum (p159)

Best Specialty Bookstores

Grolier Poetry Bookshop (p157)

Ars Libri (p106)

Schoenhof's Foreign Books (p158)

Calamus Bookstore (p106)

Best for Music & Records

Newbury Comics (p121)

Cheapo Records (p159)

Looney Tunes (p133)

In Your Ear (p158)

Nuggets (p133)

Best for Gifts

Blackstone's of Beacon Hill (p75)

Motley (p106)

On Centre (p169)

Shake the Tree (p62)

Fairy Shop (p120)

Gracie Finn (p106)

Best for Boston Souvenirs

Lucy's League (p92)

Motley (p106)

Blackstone's of Beacon Hill (p75)

Sault New England (p106)

Best for Antiques

Cambridge Antique Market (p159)

SoWa Vintage Market (p106)

Marika's Antique Shop (p76)

Eugene Galleries (p76)

Best for Jewelry

Twentieth Century Ltd (p77)

Ruby Door (p76)

Geoclassics (p92)

Local Charm (p92)

Jewelers Exchange Building (p92)

Bling! of Boston (p63)

Best for Food & Drink

Cardullo's Gourmet Shop (p158)

Salumeria Italiana (p62)

Polcari's Coffee (p62)

Beacon Hill Chocolates (p76)

South End Formaggio (p106)

Best for Housewares

Kitchenwitch (p169)

Dickson Bros (p158)

Lekker Home (p107)

Best for Sex

Good Vibrations (p170)

French Dressing (p76)

Sedurre (p62)

Condom World (p120)

Best for Crafts

Newbury Yarns (p121)

Windsor Button (p92)

Sports & Activities

Considering Boston's large student population and extensive green spaces, it's no surprise to see so many urban outdoorsy people running along the Esplanade and cycling the Emerald Necklace. For seafaring types, the Charles River and the Boston Harbor offer opportunities for kayaking, sailing and even swimming. Meanwhile, the keenest of sports fans are planted in front of their televisions watching the Red Sox (or the Patriots, or the Bruins).

Spectator Sports

BASEBALL

The intensity of baseball fans has only grown since the Boston Red Sox broke their agonizing 86-year losing streak and won the 2004 World Series. The Red Sox play from April to September at Fenway Park (133), the nation's oldest (and most expensive) ball park.

BASKETBALL

The Boston Celtics have won more basketball championships than any other NBA team, most recently in 2008. From October to April, the Celtics play at TD Garden (p61).

The Boston College Eagles basketball team is competitive in the Atlantic Coast Conference (ACC) and is usually still standing for March Madness. The Eagles play at **Conte Forum** (🖉617-552-3000; www.bceagles.com; 140 Commonwealth Ave; ⊙Nov-Mar; Ⓜ Boston College).

FOOTBALL

Super Bowl champions in 2002, 2004 and 2005 (that's a 'three-peat' for football fans), the New England Patriots are considered a football dynasty. They play in the state-of-the-art **Gillette Stadium** (🖉508-543-8200, 800-543-1776; www.patriots.com; ⊙Aug-Dec; ℝFoxborough), 32 miles south of Boston.

Now part of the competitive Atlantic Coast Conference (ACC), the Boston College Eagles football team plays in the new **Alumni Stadium** (🖉617-552-3000; www.bceagles.com; 140 Commonwealth Ave; Ⓜ Boston College) every second Saturday from September to November. Staunch Ivy League rivalries bring out alumni and fans to see the Harvard Crimson play at **Harvard Stadium** (🖉617-495-2211; www.gocrimson.com; N Harvard St & Soldiers Field Rd; Ⓜ Harvard), across the river from Harvard Sq.

HOCKEY

The Boston Bruins play ice hockey at the **TD Garden** (Map p246; 🖉information 617-624-1900, tickets 617-931-2000; www.bostonbruins.com; 150 Causeway St; ⊙Oct-Apr; Ⓜ North Station). College hockey is also huge in Boston, with the various university teams earning the devotion of spirited fans. Local rivalries emerge in full force during the annual **Beanpot Tournament** (p20; www.beanpothockey.com; ⊙Feb).

Sports & Activities by Neighborhood

➡ **Charlestown** (p51) Set sail on the Boston Harbor.

➡ **West End & North End** (p63) Home of TD Garden, the venue for the Bruins and the Celtics.

➡ **Beacon Hill & Boston Common** (p77) Outdoor fun on the Boston Common and the Charles River.

➡ **Downtown & Waterfront** (p92) The waterfront offers many boating excursions, including the Boston Harbor Islands.

➡ **South End & Chinatown** (p107) Take a tour or a class.

➡ **Back Bay** (p122) The Charles River Esplanade is prime for running, cycling, sunning and funning.

➡ **Kenmore Square & Fenway** (p133) Baseball at Fenway Park and loads more opportunities for fun in the Back Bay Fens.

➡ **Seaport District & South Boston** (p141) Boston's best city beaches.

➡ **Cambridge** (p159) Easy access to the city's best cycling and kayaking routes.

➡ **Streetcar Suburbs** (p170) The Emerald Necklace traverses these leafy 'burbs.

Lonely Planet's Top Choices

New England Aquarium Whale Watch (p92) Journey out to Stellwagen Bank, a feeding ground for ample marine life.

Urban AdvenTours (p223) The best way to see the city is on two wheels.

Fenway Park (p133) See the Red Sox battle it out at America's oldest ball park.

Boston Common Frog Pond (p77) Ice skating on the Boston Common is the quintessential Boston winter activity.

Best Sporting Events

Boston Marathon (p20)

Head of the Charles Regatta (p23)

Beanpot Tournament (p20)

Hub on Wheels (p23)

Best for Bicycling

Charles River Bike Path (p160)

Minuteman Bikeway (p159)

Emerald Necklace (p165)

Southwest Corridor (p122)

Best for Swimming

Walden Pond (p174)

Boston Harbor Islands (p80)

Carson Beach (p141)

Best for Sailing & Kayaking

Charles River Canoe & Kayak Center (p160)

Courageous Sailing (p51)

Jamaica Pond (p170)

Best for Winter Sports

Community Ice Skating @ Kendall Square (p160)

Rink at the Charles (p160)

Best for Bowling & Billiards

Sacco's Bowl Haven (p160)

Kings (p122)

Jillian's & Lucky Strike (p133)

Flat Top Johnny's (p160)

Best for Yoga

Karma Yoga Studio (p159)

Core de Vie (p76)

Exhale Spa (p107)

Back Bay Yoga Studio (p122)

Best Boat Rides

Swan Boats (p70)

Codzilla (p93)

Liberty Clipper (p92)

Gondola di Venezia (p77)

Best Walking Tours

Chinatown Market Tour (p107)

Black Heritage Trail (p77)

Old Boston Original Secret Tour (p63)

On Location Tours (p224)

Harvard Tour (p160)

Best Riding Tours

Boston Duck Tours (p223)

Old Town Trolley Tours (p224)

Upper Deck Trolley Tours (p224)

Ghosts & Gravestones (p224)

NEED TO KNOW

Tickets

Tickets for Boston's professional sports teams are hard to come by, although it's sometimes possible to procure them from the teams' websites. Otherwise, online ticket agents always offer tickets for marked-up prices, as do scalpers hanging out around the venues.

Equipment Rental

Bicycles are available for rent through the city's bike-share program or at several bike shops around town (p222). Ice skates can be rented on site at the rinks, while golf clubs are available at the courses.

Internet Resources

➡ **Boston Yoga** www.bostonyoga.com

➡ **Inline Club of Boston** www.sk8net.com

➡ **Mass Bike** www.massbike.org

➡ **Charles River Swimming Club** www.charlesriverswimmingclub.org

Best Courses

Boston Center for Adult Education (p107)

Cambridge Center for Adult Education (p160)

Grub Street (p107)

Cambridge School of Culinary Arts (p161)

PLAN YOUR TRIP SPORTS & ACTIVITIES

Explore Boston

BOSTON'S
TOP SIGHTS

Neighborhoods at a Glance

❶ Charlestown (p44)

The site of the original settlement of the Massachusetts Bay Colony, Charlestown is the terminus for the Freedom Trail. Many tourists tromp across these historic cobblestone sidewalks to admire the USS *Constitution* and climb to the top of the Bunker Hill Monument, which towers above the neighborhood.

❷ West End & North End (p52)

Although the West End and North End are physically adjacent, they are atmospherically worlds apart. The West End is an institutional area without much zest. By contrast, the North End is delightfully spicy, thanks to the many Italian *ristoranti* and *salumeria* that line the streets.

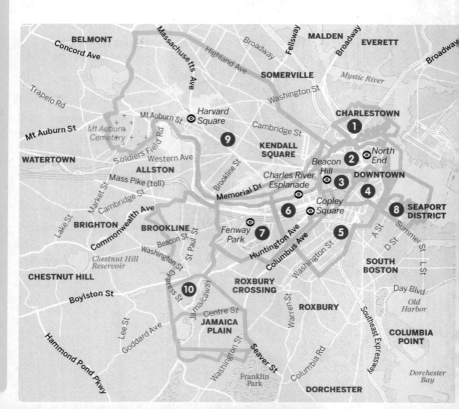

➌ Beacon Hill & Boston Common (p66)

Abutted by the Boston Common (the nation's original public park and the centerpiece of the city) and topped with the gold-domed Massachusetts State House, Beacon Hill is the neighborhood most often featured on Boston postcards. The retail and residential streets on Beacon Hill are delightfully, quintessentially Boston.

➍ Downtown & Waterfront (p78)

Much of Boston's business and tourist activity takes place in this central neighborhood. Downtown is a bustling district crammed with modern complexes and colonial buildings, including Faneuil Hall and Quincy Market. The Waterfront is home to the HarborWalk, the Harbor Island ferries and the New England Aquarium.

➎ South End & Chinatown (p96)

The Chinatown area teems with cheap eats glitzy theaters and the remnants of Boston's leather industry (now clubs and lofts). The once rough South End has been reclaimed by artists and the gay community, who have created a vibrant dining and gallery scene.

➏ Back Bay (p110)

Back Bay includes the city's most fashionable window-shopping, latte-drinking and people-watching area, Newbury St, as well as its most elegant architecture, around Copley Sq.

➐ Kenmore Square & Fenway (p123)

Kenmore Sq and Fenway attract club-goers and baseball fans to the streets surrounding Fenway Park, as well as art lovers and culture vultures to the artistic institutions along the Avenue of the Arts (Huntington Ave).

➑ Seaport District & South Boston (p134)

The Seaport District is a section of South Boston that is fast developing as an attractive waterside destination, thanks to the dynamic contemporary art museum and the explosion of new dining options. Travel deeper into Southie for seaside breezes, a little history and a lot of beer.

➒ Cambridge (p144)

Spanning the north shore of the Charles River, Cambridge boasts two distinguished universities, and historic and cultural attractions galore. The restaurants, bars and clubs around Harvard Sq and Central Sq all rival their counterparts across the river.

➓ Streetcar Suburbs (p162)

A chain of parks known as the Emerald Necklace leads south to the Streetcar Suburbs. Brookline was the birthplace of John F Kennedy; Jamaica Plain is a progressive community with gracious Victorian architecture and a cutting-edge music scene.

Charlestown

Neighborhood Top Five

1 Counting the 294 steps as you climb to the top of the **Bunker Hill Monument** (p48), then catching your breath while you admire the 360-degree view of Boston, Cambridge and beyond.

2 Sipping an ale at the same bar that propped up the founding fathers in the **Warren Tavern** (p50).

3 Learning about the long and storied history of the **USS Constitution** (p46) from US Navy sailors.

4 Watching the sun set behind the city skyline from **Tavern on the Water** (p50).

5 Taking your kids to the **USS Constitution Museum** (p47) to experience the life of a sailor.

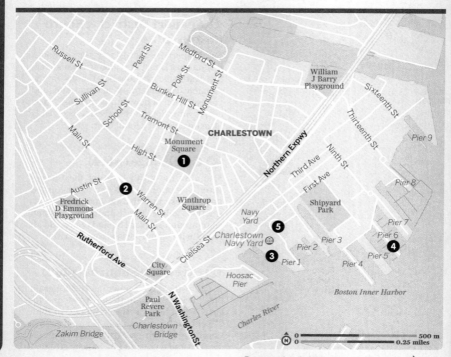

For more detail of this area, see Map p245 ▶

Explore Charlestown

Spend a day following the Freedom Trail and you will end up in Charlestown, as the final two sites are located here. Besides seeing the historic USS *Constitution* and the commemorative Bunker Hill Monument, strolling inland from the Charlestown waterfront provides an opportunity to explore the neighborhood's aged narrow streets, lined with 19th-century Federal and colonial houses. Afterwards, there are a handful of restaurants and cafes surrounding City Sq and lining Main St.

Despite the historic significance, Charlestown retains the distinctive atmosphere of a local neighborhood, with real people (known as 'Townies') inhabiting the restored town houses and working in the granite buildings. Even the eateries – however recommended – are places to patronize if you happen to be in the area, not normally meriting a special trip.

Charlestown was incorporated into Boston in 1873; but this neighborhood remains apart, both geographically and atmospherically. On the north shore of the Charles River, it is connected to the rest of the city by the Old Charlestown Bridge. So even though C-town sees its fair share of tourists trudging along the Freedom Trail, the sights and streets will not be as crowded as those in downtown Boston.

Local Life

→ **Coffee with Kids** Townies of all ages love the coffee and doughnuts at Zumes Coffee House (p50); but it's especially popular among the mommy set, who bring their kids to play with puzzles and eat grilled cheese sandwiches.

→ **Sundowners** Little known outside of Charlestown, the Tavern on the Water (p50) attracts the local after-work crowd with its informal atmosphere and unbeatable city view.

→ **Historic Hang-out** Even though the Warren Tavern (p50) is a historic site of sorts, it's still a favorite place for Townies to drink beers and eat burgers.

Getting There & Away

→ **Metro** The closest T-stations are Community College station (orange line) and North Station (junction of orange and green lines), both a 20-minute walk from the Charlestown sights.

→ **Boat** The MBTA runs the F4 ferry (Map p245; $1.70) every 15 to 30 minutes between Pier 3 in Charlestown and Long Wharf on the Boston waterfront.

Lonely Planet's Top Tip

For a unique perspective on Charlestown and Boston, walk east from the Navy Yard, following the shoreline from pier to pier. Crowded with boats, this working waterfront boasts one of the best views of the Boston Harbor and skyline.

CHARLESTOWN

 **Best Places to Eat**

→ Navy Yard Bistro & Wine Bar (p49)
→ Figs (p49)
→ Max & Dylan's (p49)

For reviews, see p49 →

 **Best Places to Drink**

→ Tavern on the Water (p50)
→ Warren Tavern (p50)
→ Zumes Coffee House (p50)

For reviews, see p50 →

 Best Boats

→ USS Constitution (p46)
→ USS Cassin Young (p47)
→ Green Turtle (p185)
→ MBTA Inner Harbor Ferry (F4; Map p245)

For reviews, see p46

TOP SIGHTS
CHARLESTOWN NAVY YARD

No longer operational, the Charlestown Navy Yard stands as an architectural and historical monument to the US Navy and its vessels. The oldest commissioned US Navy ship, the USS Constitution, has been moored here since 1897. Another formidable warship, the USS Cassin Young, also docks here, inviting visitors to learn about its feats during WWII. There is an excellent museum dedicated to the USS Constitution and more general naval history, while the rest of the shipyard remembers the history of the shipbuilding industry.

DON'T MISS

➡ Guided tour of the USS *Constitution*

➡ Exhibit on the Barbary War and the birth of the US Navy at the USS *Constitution* Museum

➡ Model Shipwright Guild workshop

PRACTICALITIES

➡ Map p245

➡ www.nps.gov/bost

➡ admission free

➡ ⊘9am-5pm

➡ M North Station, ⛴F4 from Long Wharf

USS Constitution

'Her sides are made of iron!' So cried a crewman as he watched a shot bounce off the thick oak hull of the USS *Constitution* during the War of 1812. This earned the legendary ship her nickname, 'Old Ironsides.' Indeed, she won no fewer than three battles during that war, and she never went down in a battle. For her last mission in 1853 she seized an American slave ship off the coast of Africa.

The **USS Constitution** (Map p245; www.oldironsides.com; Charlestown Navy Yard; admission free; ⊘10am-6pm Tue-Sun Apr-Oct, 10am-4pm Thu-Sun Nov-Mar; M North Station, ⛴F4 from Long Wharf) is still the oldest commissioned US Navy ship, dating to 1797, and she is taken out onto Boston Harbor every July 4 in order to maintain her commissioned status.

Make sure you bring a photo ID to go aboard the *Constitution*. Navy personnel give 30-minute guided tours of the top deck, gun deck and cramped quarters (last tour 4:30pm in summer, 3:30pm in winter). You can also wander around the top deck by yourself, but access is limited. Plus, you won't learn all the USS *Constitution* fun facts, like how the captain's son died on her maiden voyage (an inauspicious start).

USS Constitution Museum

For a play-by-play account of the various battles of the USS *Constitution*, as well as her current role as the flagship of the US Navy, head to the **USS Constitution Museum** (Map p245; www.ussconstitutionmuseum.org; First Ave, Charlestown Navy Yard; adult/senior/child $5/3/2; ☺9am-6pm Apr-Oct, 10am-5pm Nov-Mar; ⊞; ⓂNorth Station, ⛴F4 from Long Wharf). Most interesting is the exhibit on the Barbary War, which explains the birth of the US Navy during this relatively unknown conflict – America's first war at sea.

On the ground floor of the museum, the Model Shipwright Guild operates a workshop, where visitors can see volunteer modelers working on fantastically detailed miniatures of the USS *Constitution* and other ships.

Upstairs, kids can experience what it was like to be a sailor on the USS *Constitution* in 1812. The interactive exhibit *All Hands on Deck* showcases the swashbuckling lifestyle, from recruitment to embarkation to life at sea.

USS Cassin Young

This formidable vessel is an example of a Fletcher-class destroyer – this WWII craft was the navy's fastest, most versatile ship at the time. This 376ft destroyer was designed as an all-purpose ship, able to fight off attacks on all fronts (air, surface and below). Able to refuel at sea, the destroyer could travel further and operate more effectively in the vastness of the Pacific.

USS Cassin Young (Map p245; Charlestown Navy Yard; ☺10am-5pm Jul & Aug, noon-3pm Sep-Jun, tours 11am & 2pm; ⓂNorth Station, ⛴F4 from Long Wharf) participated in the 1944 Battle of Leyte Gulf, as well as the 1945 invasion of Okinawa. Here, the ship sustained two kamikaze hits, leaving 23 crew members dead and many more wounded. These days she has been completely refurbished, as you can see during a free, 45-minute tour, or you can explore the main deck on your own.

Charlestown Navy Yard

Besides the historic ships docked here, the Charlestown Navy Yard is a living monument to its own history of shipbuilding and naval command. It was a thriving shipbuilding center throughout the 19th century, finally closing in 1974, ushering in a new era for the neighborhood. (Nowadays, it's tourists, not sailors, who come ashore)

Most of the buildings are closed to the public, but you can wander around the dry docks and see how the ships were repaired while resting on wooden blocks. The oldest building here is the imposing Federal-style Commandant's House, dating to 1805.

CHARLESTOWN CHARLESTOWN NAVY YARD

Old Ironsides never lost a battle during her active service from 1797 to 1855.

USS CONSTITUTION MUSEUM

The USS *Constitution* Museum is a private, nonprofit organization dedicated to preserving the memory of, and promoting education about, the historic ship, so your admission donation goes to a good cause.

The copper fastenings for the interior of the USS Constitution were made in Paul Revere's metalworks shop.

FREE FILM

Don't miss the free 10-minute introductory film about the history of the Charlestown Navy Yard, shown throughout the day at the NPS visitor center.

A former commanding officer of the USS Constitution, Tyron Martin, spent 30 years compiling a database of some 15,000 sailors who served on the ship over the years, including the 1182 individuals who served during the War of 1812.

TOP SIGHTS
BUNKER HILL MONUMENT

'Don't fire until you see the whites of their eyes!' came the order from Colonel Prescott to revolutionary troops on June 17, 1775. Considering the ill-preparedness of the revolutionary soldiers, the bloody battle that followed resulted in a surprising number of British casualties. Ultimately, the Redcoats prevailed, but the victory was bittersweet. They lost more than one-third of their deployed forces, while the colonists suffered relatively few casualties. Equally importantly, the battle demonstrated the gumption of the upstart revolutionaries.

Bunker Hill Monument

Climb the 294 steps of the Bunker Hill Monument to enjoy the panorama of the city. The 220ft granite obelisk monument was built between 1827 and 1843, overseen by a design team that included such local luminaries as orator Daniel Webster and artist Gilbert Stuart. Long on ideas but short on cash, the team had to sell off most of the battleground to fund the monument, retaining only the land at the summit. The monument is constructed of granite from Quincy, Massachusetts.

Bunker Hill Museum

Opposite the monument, the **Bunker Hill Museum** (Map p245; 43 Monument Sq; admission free; ☺9am-5pm Sep-Jun, to 6pm Jul & Aug; Ⓜ Community College, ☻F4 from Long Wharf) contains two floors of exhibits, including historical dioramas, a few artifacts and an impressive 360-degree mural depicting the battle. National Park Service (NPS) rangers give battle talks and musket-firing demonstrations.

DON'T MISS

➡ The view from the top!

➡ Bunker Hill Day reenactment and parade

➡ Diorama of the Battle of Bunker Hill

PRACTICALITIES

➡ Map p245

➡ www.nps.gov/bost

➡ Monument Sq

➡ admission free

➡ ☺9am-5pm Sep-Jun, to 6pm Jul & Aug

➡ Ⓜ Community College, ☻F4 from Long Wharf

 **SIGHTS**

CHARLESTOWN NAVY YARD MUSEUM
See p46.

BUNKER HILL MONUMENT MONUMENT
See p48.

GREAT HOUSE SITE ARCHAEOLOGICAL SITE
Map p245 (City Sq; ◷dawn-dusk; ⓂNorth Station, ⚓F4 from Long Wharf) Besides being an urban plaza, the aptly named City Sq is also an archaeological site. Big Dig construction unearthed the foundation for a structure called the Great House, widely believed to be John Winthrop's house and the seat of government in 1630.

Winthrop soon moved across the Charles to the Shawmut Peninsula, and the Great House became the Three Cranes Tavern, as documented in 1635. Informative dioramas demonstrate the remains of the kitchen, the main hall and the wine cellar.

JOHN HARVARD MALL SQUARE
Map p245 (btwn Main & Harvard Sts; ◷dawn-dusk; ⓂNorth Station, ⚓F4 from Long Wharf) North of City Sq, a shady, brick plaza leads up Town Hill. Back in the days of the earliest settlements, a fort crowned Town Hill, which you can read about on the bronze plaques along the mall.

Before the local minister – one John Harvard – died of consumption, he donated half his £800 estate and all 300 of his books to a young Cambridge college, which saw fit to name its school after him.

 **EATING**

NAVY YARD BISTRO & WINE BAR FRENCH **$$**
Map p245 (www.navyyardbistro.com; cnr Second Ave & Sixth St; mains $15-25; ◷dinner; ⓂNorth Station, ⚓F4 from Long Wharf) Dark and romantic, this hideaway is tucked into an unlikely spot behind the Tedeschi convenience store. It does not sound like an ideal location, but it faces a pedestrian walkway, allowing for comfortable outdoor seating in summer months. Inside, the cozy, carved-wood interior is an ideal date destination – perfect for tuna tartare or brined pork chops.

The menu always features seasonal vegetables and an excellent wine list, from which the owner will be pleased to help you make a selection.

FIGS ITALIAN **$$**
Map p245 (www.toddenglish.com; 67 Main St; mains $15-20; ◷lunch & dinner; ✍❢; ⓂCommunity College) This creative pizzeria – which also has an outlet in Beacon Hill – is the brainchild of celebrity chef Todd English, who tops whisper-thin crusts with interesting, exotic toppings. Case in point: the namesake fig and prosciutto with gorgonzola cheese. The menu also includes sandwiches and fresh pasta. While the food tastes gourmet, the dining room is dark, comfy and casual.

MAX & DYLAN'S MODERN AMERICAN **$$**
Map p245 (www.maxanddylans.com; 1 Chelsea St; mains $10-16; ◷lunch & dinner; ✍❢; ⓂNorth Station, ⚓F4 from Long Wharf) This is a modern family eatery and trendy

CHARLESTOWN SIGHTS

LENNY ZAKIM & BUNKER HILL
....
Driving north from Boston on the Central Artery, your car emerges from the Tip O'Neill Tunnel into the open air, where you are surrounded on all sides by the Boston city skyline and the crisp white cables of the Leonard Zakim Bunker Hill Bridge. Capped with obelisks that mirror its namesake monument, it is the widest cable-stayed bridge in the world. And against the clear blue or dark night, it is stunning.

Lenny Zakim was a local human-rights activist who spent years railing against racism. Bunker Hill was the battle where the patriots first proved their potency in the War for Independence. As Mayor Menino said at the dedication: 'The Leonard P Zakim Bunker Hill Bridge will showcase the diversity and the unity of race, religion and personal background that exist in Boston today, because of the work of community leaders like Lenny Zakim and because patriots fought long ago in Charlestown to make our country independent.' It's a stretch, but he managed to merge these disparate dedicatees.

The name is nonetheless unwieldy, so don't be afraid to take short cuts. Either the Zakim Bridge or the Bunker Hill Bridge will do.

WARREN TAVERN

Eliphelet Newell was an ardent supporter of the revolutionary cause and a supposed participant in the Boston Tea Party. When the War for Independence was over, he opened a tavern and named it after his dear friend General Joseph Warren. Although Warren had died in the Battle of Bunker Hill, he had been an active member of the Sons of Liberty and a respected leader of the revolution. Indeed, the prime minister of Great Britain described him as 'the greatest incendiary in North America.'

So when the Warren Tavern was opened in 1780 it quickly became a popular meeting place, especially among admirers of General Warren. Over the years Paul Revere was a regular and even George Washington stopped by for a visit when he was in town. Nowadays locals still love to gather here to drink a few pints and engage in debates (perhaps not the heady discussions of building a new nation, but important stuff nonetheless).

bar with a classy but casual atmosphere. The unusual menu features a wide array of sliders (from BBQ pork to Kobe beef), five kinds of mac-n-cheese and some exotic flatbread sandwiches. The big windows yield views of the Zakim Bridge, while the big-screen TVs show whatever sport is in season.

TANGIERINO   MOROCCAN $$$

Map p245 (☎617-242-6009; www.tangierino.com; 83 Main St; mains $25-40; ☺dinner; ⓜCommunity College) This unexpected gem transports guests from a colonial town house in historic Charlestown to a sultan's palace in the Moroccan desert. North African specialties include *harira* (a traditional tomato and lentil soup), couscous and tajine, all with a modern flair. But the highlight is the sexy interior, complete with thick Oriental carpets, plush pillows and rich, jewel-toned tapestries. For a romantic date, reserve a secluded cabana table.

Belly dancers may or may not enhance the atmosphere. For more exotic fun, Koullshi lounge is downstairs.

ZUMES COFFEE HOUSE   CAFE

(www.zumescoffeehouse.blogspot.com; 223 Main St; ☺6am-6pm Mon-Fri, 7am-6pm Sat & Sun; ☎⏺; ⓜCommunity College) This is slightly off the beaten path (aka the Freedom Trail), but locals love it for the comfy leather chairs, big cups of coffee and decadent doughnuts; other bakery items get rather mixed reviews. Also on the menu: soup, sandwiches and lunchy items. Paintings and photographs by local artists adorn the walls; books and games keep the kiddies busy.

DRINKING & NIGHTLIFE

WARREN TAVERN   PUB

Map p245 (www.warrentavern.com; 2 Pleasant St; ☺11am-1am; ⓜCommunity College) One of the oldest pubs in Boston, the Warren Tavern has been pouring pints for its customers since George Washington and Paul Revere drank here. It is named for General Joseph Warren, a fallen hero of the Battle of Bunker Hill (shortly after which – in 1780 – this pub was opened).

TAVERN ON THE WATER   BAR

Map p245 (www.tavernonthewater.com; 1 8th St, Pier 6; ☺11:30am-11:30pm, later in summer; ⓜNorth Station, ⛴F4 from Long Wharf) Set at the end of the pier behind the Navy Yard, this understated tavern offers one of the finest views of the Boston Harbor and city skyline. The food is not so memorable, but it's a fine place to go to catch some rays on your face, the breeze off the water, and an ice cold one from behind the bar.

KOULLSHI   LOUNGE

Map p245 (☎617-242-6001; www.tangierino. com; 83 Main St; ☺5pm-1:30am; ⓜCommunity College) First and foremost, it's a hookah lounge, with plush furniture, ornately carved woodwork, nightly belly-dancing shows and sophisticated flavors of tobacco. A little bit exotic, a little bit erotic (a little bit expensive). Since people are smoking anyway, they added a cigar bar with a walk-in humidor. Perhaps exotic, but not so erotic.

Alas, there are also the obligatory flat-screen TVs behind the bar, so you can watch sports while you smoke. Not exotic or erotic.

Booking ahead is recommended if you want a private hookah room.

FIREHOUSE VENDING
MACHINE
VENDING MACHINE

Map p245 (34 Winthrop St; M Community College) The kind firefighters at Engine Company 50 work in a sweet 19th-century firehouse with the Freedom Trail passing close by. On most summer days, they open up one of the bays so that hot walkers have access to a vending machine that sells cold drinks, embedded in some old wooden lockers covered in departmental patches. Sit on the bench out front and admire the charming streetscape.

 **SHOPPING**

OLIVIA BROWNING
GIFTS

Map p245 (www.oliviabrowning.com; 20 City Sq; M North Station) Whether you need a gift for a birthday, baby shower or bridal shower – or simply a unique local souvenir – Olivia Browning will provide. There are survival packs for every major life event, gourmet treats from around New England, and Townie gear you won't find anywhere else. Show your Charlestown pride!

 **SPORTS & ACTIVITIES**

COURAGEOUS SAILING
SAILING

Map p245 (☎617-242-3821; www.courageous sailing.org; 1 First Ave; 12hr course $295; ⊕; ⊒F4 from Long Wharf) Named after a two-time America's Cup winner, Courageous Sailing offers instruction and boat rental for sailors and would-be sailors.

A unique public-private partnership, this outfit was established by the City of Boston with the support of private individuals, with the aim of making sailing accessible to kids and adults of all ages, incomes and abilities.

West End & North End

Neighborhood Top Five

❶ Strolling the cobblestone streets, browsing the boutiques and soaking up the Old World atmosphere in the North End, then squeezing into one of the candlelit tables at **Pomodoro** or **Marco** (p58) for amazing Italian food and service.

❷ Gawking at the architecture and appreciating the irony at the **Liberty Hotel** (p185).

❸ Gazing at the steeple of the **Old North Church** (p55) and imagining the lanterns signalling the Redcoats' approach.

❹ Discovering how fun science can be at the **Museum of Science** (p54).

❺ Exploring the quaint but cramped quarters at the **Paul Revere House** (p56), Boston's oldest home.

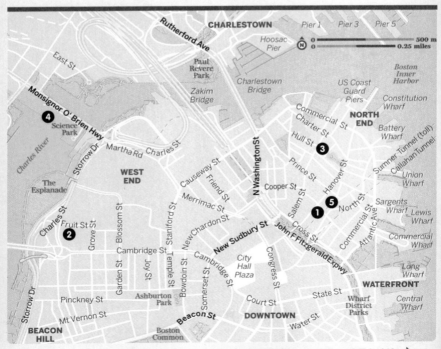

For more detail of this area, see Maps p246 & p248 ➡

Explore West End & North End

These side-by-side neighborhoods could not be more different from each other. The West End – formerly a vibrant multicultural neighborhood – was virtually razed by 'urban renewal' in the 1950s. Now its streets are dominated by concrete monoliths and institutional buildings, including the extensive facilities of Mass General Hospital and many government buildings. Most visitors to Boston bypass this bleak district, unless they are catching a train at North Station or attending an event at the Garden.

That said, the West End borders Beacon Hill and downtown Boston, putting many historic and cultural sites within walking distance. The West End is actually a convenient and comfortable place to stay, and there are a few fine hotels that offer excellent value for the location.

By contrast, the North End feels like an Old World enclave that has hardly changed in the last century. Italian immigrants and their descendants have held court in this warren of narrow streets and alleys since the 1920s. Old-timers still carry on passionate discussions in Italian and play bocce in the park. The neighborhood's main streets are packed with *ristoranti* and *salumerie* (Italian delis), not to mention bakeries, pizzerias, coffee shops, wine shops and cheese mongers. The North End is a required destination for everyone who likes to eat.

The Freedom Trail also winds through the North End, past the Paul Revere House, the Old North Church and Copp's Hill Burying Ground. Indeed, this peninsula was an integral part of Boston long before the Italians arrived: some of these landmarks date back to the 17th century.

So come during the day to see the sights and learn the history, but by all means come back at night for dinner.

Local Life

→ **Drinks** Watch *futbol*, drink Campari and speak Italian (or just listen) at Caffé dello Sport or Caffé Paradiso (p61).

→ **Saints** North Enders get lively in August, when they celebrate their favorite saints during the weekend Italian Festivals (p61). If you can't come in August, visit All Saints Way (p57) to see the locals' fervor.

Getting There & Away

→ **Metro** For the West End, use the red-line Charles/MGH or the blue-line Bowdoin station to access sites along Cambridge St. At the junction of the green and orange lines, North Station is more convenient for the northern part of the neighborhood. For the North End, the closest T-station is Haymarket, which lies on both the green and the orange lines.

Lonely Planet's Top Tip

Bad news: it's impossible to park in the North End. Good news: **Parcel 7**'s parking garage (p88) offers three hours of parking for $3 if you get your ticket validated by a North End establishment.

 Best Places to Eat

→ Marco (p58)

→ Pomodoro (p58)

→ Neptune Oyster (p58)

→ Volle Nolle (p59)

For reviews, see p57 →

 Best Places to Drink

→ Caffé Vittoria (p61)

→ Boston Beer Works (p61)

→ West End Johnnies (p60)

For reviews, see p60 →

 Best Places to Stock your Kitchen

→ Salumeria Italiana (p62)

→ Polcari's Coffee (p62)

→ DePasquale's Homemade Pasta Shoppe (p62) Fresh Cheese Deli (p63)

→ Wine Bottega (p63)

For reviews, see p62 →

WEST END & NORTH END

This educational playground has more than 600 interactive exhibits. Favorites include the world's largest lightning-bolt generator, a full-scale space capsule, a world population meter and a butterfly house. The amazing array of exhibits and presentations explores computers and technology; maps and models; the human body and human evolution; and the birds and the bees (literally and figuratively).

Dinosaurs

One of the museum's main attractions is its excellent collection of dinosaur fossils and life-size models, including the rare 23ft-long Triceratops Cliff. The centerpiece of the exhibit is the enormously impressive Tyrannosaurus rex model, which has evolved significantly from the original T rex model that was built in the 1960s. The exhibit demonstrates how paleontologists use fossils to learn about extinct animals and their evolutionary predecessors.

Cahners Computerplace

This hands-on technological playground will delight technophiles and technophobes alike, with programmable robots, remote-control rovers and models for building your own computers. Various programs allow would-be inventors to design their own computer games, create thier own animations and imagine other electronic inventions. Your hosts are Ada and Grace, two 'virtual' guides.

DON'T MISS
➡ Tyrannosaurus rex
➡ A full-size model of the *Apollo* command module that landed on the moon
➡ Cahners Computerplace

PRACTICALITIES
➡ Map p246
➡ www.mos.org
➡ Science Park, Charles River Dam
➡ adult/child/senior $22/19/20
➡ ⊘9am-5pm Sat-Thu Sep-Jun, to 7pm Jul & Aug, 9am-9pm Fri year-round
➡ P 🚼
➡ Ⓜ Science Park

Alternative Energy

There are excellent exhibits on alternative sources of energy, including a detailed look at how energy is generated from wind turbines and solar power. *Catch the Wind* allows visitors to monitor the electricity being produced by turbines on the museum's roof. *Energized* follows the path of energy as it travels from sunlight to rooftop panels to the 'Theater of Electricity.'

Discovery Center

This hands-on play area and educational center is specifically designed for children under the age of eight. Museum staff oversee science experiments, engineering projects and live-animal presentations. Costumes and oversized climbing structures invite little ones to imagine life inside a beehive or a bird's nest. Other educational fun includes a water table, building blocks and 'Discovery boxes.'

Charles Hayden Planetarium & Mugar Omni Theater

The museum also houses the **Charles Hayden Planetarium** (Map p246; adult/senior/child $10/8/9) and Mugar Omni Theater (p62). The planetarium boasts a state-of-the-art projection system that casts a heavenly star show, programs about black holes and other astronomical mysteries, and evening laser light shows with rock music.

TOP SIGHTS
OLD NORTH CHURCH

'Hang a lantern aloft in the belfry arch / Of the North Church tower as a signal light / One if by land, two if by sea / And I on the opposite shore will be...' Everyone knows the line from Longfellow's poem 'Paul Revere's Ride.' It was here, on the night of April 18, 1775, that the sexton hung two lanterns from the steeple, as a signal that the British would march on Lexington and Concord via the sea route.

Also called Christ Church, this 1723 place of worship is Boston's oldest church. Many of the tall pew boxes bear the brass nameplates of early parishioners who had to purchase their pews. The brass chandeliers used today were first lit on Christmas in 1724. Note the candles – there is no electric lighting in the church. This remains an active church; the grand organ is played at the 11am Sunday service.

The 175ft **steeple** houses the oldest bells (1744) still rung in the US. Restored in 1975, the eight bells are normally rung on Saturday mornings. Today's steeple is a 1954 replica, since severe weather toppled two prior ones, but the 1740 weather vane is original.

All visitors are invited to enjoy a 10-minute presentation about the history of the Old North Church. For more detailed information, a **Behind the Scenes tour** (adult/child/ student & senior $8/5/6; ⊘hourly Jul-Oct) takes visitors up into the belfry and down into the crypt.

Behind the church, several hidden brick courtyards offer quiet respite for a moment of peaceful meditation. Heading down the hill, shady **Paul Revere Mall** perfectly frames the Old North Church. Often called 'the prado' by locals, it is a lively meeting place for North Enders of all generations.

DON'T MISS

➡ Elaborate brass chandeliers lit with candles

➡ The decorated Bay Pew

➡ Behind the Scenes tour into the belfry and crypt

➡ Lovely 18th-century gardens behind the church

PRACTICALITIES

➡ Map p248
➡ www.oldnorth.com
➡ 193 Salem St
➡ donation $1
➡ ⊘9am-5pm Mar-Oct, 10am-4pm Tue-Sun Nov-Feb
➡ Ⓜ Haymarket or North Station

⊙ **West End**

MUSEUM OF SCIENCE   MUSEUM
See p54.

OTIS HOUSE   HISTORIC HOUSE
Map p246 (www.historicnewengland.org; 141 Cambridge St; adult/child/senior $8/4/7; ⊘11am-5pm Wed-Sun; MCharles/MGH) This stern, Federal brick building was the first of three houses designed by Charles Bulfinch for Mr Harrison Gray Otis at the end of the 18th century. These days it is the headquarters of Historic New England, a preservation society that has recreated the interior of Otis' day, complete with flashy wallpaper and exquisite period furnishings.

A real-estate developer, congressman and mayor of Boston, Otis and his wife Sally were renowned entertainers who hosted many lavish parties here. Since then the house has had quite a history, serving as a women's bath and rooming house.

FREE WEST END MUSEUM   MUSEUM
Map p246 (www.thewestendmuseum.org; 150 Staniford St; ⊘11am-5pm Tue-Fri, 11am-4pm Sat; MNorth Station) This little neighborhood museum is dedicated to preserving the memory of the West End and educating the public about the ramifications of unchecked urban development. The main exhibit *The Last Tenement* traces the history of the neighborhood from 1850 to 1958, highlighting its immigrant populations, economic evolution and eventual destruction.

Additional space is devoted to temporary exhibits that highlight former residents, neighborhood architecture and broader issues of historic preservation. The museum also hosts occasional concerts, book talks and guided tours.

NEW ENGLAND SPORTS MUSEUM   MUSEUM
Map p246 (www.sportsmuseum.org; TD Banknorth Garden; adult/child $10/5; ⊘10am-4pm except event days; MNorth Station) Nobody can say that Bostonians are not passionate about their sports teams. The New England Sports Museum is not the best place to witness this deep-rooted devotion (try Fenway Park for that), but sports fans might enjoy the photographs, jerseys and other items from Boston sports history.

The highlight is the penalty box from the old Boston Garden – gifted to Bruin Terry O'Reiley because he had spent so much time in there. Also on display are Larry Bird's locker, Adam Vinatieri's shoes and Tony Conigliaro's baseball (yes, the one that landed on his left eye and derailed his career). Other interesting exhibits showcase the development of women's basketball, the history of football before the Patriots and – of course – a century in Red Sox nation.

This museum is actually in the concourse area of the Garden's box seats. The good news is that if you go on a game day, you may see the Celtics or the Bruins warming up. The bad news is that it often closes for special events at the Garden; closing days are posted in advance on the website.

FREE ETHER DOME   HISTORIC SITE
Map p246 (Mass General Hospital, 4th fl; ⊘9am-8pm; P; MCharles/MGH) On October 16, 1846, Thomas WG Morton administered ether to the patient Gilbert Abbott, while Dr John Collins Warren cut a tumor from his neck. It was the first use of anesthesia in a surgical procedure and it happened in this domed operating room in Mass General Hospital.

The Ether Dome looks like a typical old-fashioned hall used for medical lectures and demonstrations, up to and including the skeleton hanging in the corner. The dome is still used today for meetings and lectures, so it is sometimes closed to the public.

⊙ **North End**

OLD NORTH CHURCH   CHURCH
See p55.

PAUL REVERE HOUSE   HISTORIC HOUSE
Map p248 (☏617-523-2338; www.paulreverehouse.org; 19 North Sq; adult/child/senior & student $3.50/1/3; ⊘9:30am-5:15pm, shorter hours Nov-Apr; ♿; MHaymarket) When silversmith Paul Revere rode to warn patriots of the British march to Lexington and Concord, he set out from his home on North Sq. This small clapboard house was built in 1680, making it the oldest house in Boston. A self-guided tour through the house and courtyard gives a glimpse of what life was

NOT SO SLOW

For years Boston was a leader in the production and export of rum, made from West Indian sugar cane. Near the water's edge in the North End stood a storage tank for the Purity Distilling Company. On a January morning in 1919, the large tank, filled to the brim with brown molasses, suddenly began shuddering and rumbling as its bindings came undone.

The pressure caused the tank to explode, spewing 2 million gallons of molasses into the city like a volcano. The sweet explosion leveled surrounding tenements, knocked buildings off their foundations and wiped out a loaded freight train. Panic-stricken, man and beast fled the deadly ooze. A molasses wave surged down the streets drowning all in its sticky path. The Great Molasses Flood killed a dozen horses and 21 people, and injured more than 100. The clean-up lasted nearly six months. *Dark Tide*, by journalist Stephen Puleo, provides a fascinating account of the causes and controversy surrounding this devastating explosion.

like for the Revere family (which included 16 children!).

Also on display are some examples of his silversmithing and engraving talents, as well as an impressive bell that was forged in his foundry. The Freedom Trail ticket (which includes entry to the Paul Revere House, the Old State House and the Old South Meeting House) is $13.

The adjacent Pierce-Hichborn House, built in 1710, is a fine example of an English Renaissance brick house. It is also maintained by the Paul Revere Memorial Association, but you can visit it by guided tour (appointment only).

ALL SAINTS WAY SHRINE

Map p248 (4 Battery St; M Haymarket) 'Mock all and sundry things, but leave the saints alone.' So goes an old Italian saying that is now posted on the wall of this tiny alleyway off Battery St. The sign is surrounded by thousands of images of saints. The shrine is the pet project of North End resident Peter Baldassari, who has been collecting holy cards since his childhood.

COPP'S HILL BURYING GROUND CEMETERY

Map p248 (Hull St; ⊙dawn-dusk; M North Station) The city's second-oldest cemetery – dating to 1660 – is the final resting place for an estimated 10,000 souls. It is named for William Copp, who originally owned this land. While the oldest graves belong to Copp's children, there are several other noteworthy residents.

Near the Charter St gate you'll find the graves of the Mather family – Increase, Cotton and Samuel – all of whom were politically powerful religious leaders in the colonial community. Front and center is the grave of Daniel Malcolm, whose headstone commemorates his rebel activism. British soldiers apparently took offense at this claim and used the headstone for target practice. The small plot of land also contains more than a thousand free blacks, many of whom lived in the North End.

NARROWEST HOUSE HISTORIC HOUSE

Map p248 (44 Hull St; M North Station) Across the street from Copp's Hill Burying Ground, this is Boston's narrowest house, measuring a whopping 9½ft wide. It's sometimes called a 'spite house' – the c 1800 house was reportedly built to block light from the neighbor's house and to obliterate the view of the house behind it.

EATING

West End

After the massive redevelopment of the 1950s and more recent construction related to the Big Dig, the West End is suffering from a shortage of eating options. If you are looking for someplace to chow down before an event at TD Banknorth Garden, head to the Bulfinch Triangle, southeast of the arena.

SCAMPO ITALIAN $$$

Map p246 (✆617-536-2100; www.scampoboston.com; 215 Charles St; lunch $10-18, dinner $25-38; ⊙lunch & dinner; ✐; M Charles/MGH) Celeb chef Lydia Shire has done it again. This masterpiece – on the ground floor of the Liberty Hotel – is a trendy and tantalizing restaurant buzzing with energy. The wide variety of delectable handmade pastas and the region's finest freshest seafood are to be expected; the mozzarella bar is a delightful and delicious surprise.

It seems sinful to order pizza at such a fine restaurant, but Shire makes it easy to justify, by offering irresistible and unusual combinations of toppings.

CAFE RUSTICO
ITALIAN $

Map p246 (www.caferusticoboston.com; 85 Canal St; mains $7-10; ⏱11am-6pm Mon-Sat; 🔊🖊📶; Ⓜ️North Station) This family-run Italian joint is one of Boston's best-kept secrets. But those in the know keep coming back for more – staff seem to know everyone by name, or at least by favorite sandwich. Seating is in short supply, but everything is available for take-out. Pizza, salads and subs are all recommended, but the gnocchi is the hands-down favorite.

CLINK
MODERN AMERICAN $$$

Map p246 (www.libertyhotel.com; 215 Charles St, Liberty Hotel; lunch $12-24, dinner $20-30; Ⓜ️Charles/MGH) Set under the soaring ceiling of the lobby of the Liberty Hotel (formerly the Charles St Jail), Clink offers a gorgeous setting for a casual drink, while dinner guests will appreciate the privacy of the 'jail cells' in the enclosed dining area. Reliably good food includes a raw bar and a selection of cheese and charcuterie, in addition to modern preparations of pasta and meat dishes.

✖ North End

The streets of the North End are lined with *salumerie* and *pasticcerie* (pastry stores) and more *ristoranti* per block than anywhere else in Boston. Hanover St is the main drag, but the southern end of Salem St is loaded too. Many places do not take reservations, so arrive early or be prepared to wait.

TOP CHOICE POMODORO
ITALIAN $$

Map p248 (📞617-367-4348; www.pomodorosboston.com; 319 Hanover St; mains $15-25; ⏱dinner Tue-Sun; Ⓜ️Haymarket) This hole-in-the-wall eatery on Hanover is one of the North End's most romantic settings for delectable Italian. The food is simply but perfectly

MIKE'S VS MODERN

Only slightly less tempestuous than the rivalry between the Red Sox and the Yankees, is the rivalry between Mike's Pastry and Modern Pastry, which face off across Hanover St (Mike's is at number 300, Modern at number 257). If you have time to wait in line, you might as well sample both and decide for yourself. If you don't have time to wait in line, go to Maria's.

prepared: fresh pasta, spicy tomato sauce, grilled fish and meats, and wine by the glass. Credit cards are not accepted and the bathroom is smaller than your closet, but that's all part of the charm.

TOP CHOICE NEPTUNE OYSTER
SEAFOOD $$$

Map p248 (📞617-742-3474; www.neptuneoyster.com; 63 Salem St; mains $25-35; ⏱lunch & dinner; Ⓜ️Haymarket) Neptune's menu hints at Italian, but you'll also find elements of Mexican, French and old-fashioned New England. The daily seafood specials and impressive raw bar (featuring several kinds of oysters, plus littlenecks, cherrystones, crabs and mussels) confirm that this is not your traditional North End eatery.

The retro interior offers a convivial – if crowded – setting, with an excellent option for solo diners at the marble bar.

MARIA'S PASTRY
BAKERY $

Map p248 (www.mariaspastry.com; 46 Cross St; ⏱7am-7pm; 🖊; Ⓜ️Haymarket) Three generations of Merola women are now working to bring you Boston's most authentic Italian pastries. Many claim that Maria makes the best cannoli in the North End, but you'll also find more elaborate concoctions like *sfogliatelle* (layered, shell-shaped pastry filled with ricotta) and *aragosta* (cream-filled 'lobster tail' pastry). Note the early closing time: eat dessert first!

MARCO
ITALIAN $$

Map p248 (📞617-742-1276; www.marcoboston.com; 253 Hanover St; mains $22-26; ⏱dinner; 🖊; Ⓜ️Haymarket) Tucked into a tiny 2nd-floor space, Marc Orfaly's North End establishment feels intimate and inviting – like a true secret spot. The menu's focus is simplicity and freshness: homemade pasta; grilled fish, poultry and meats; seasonal vegetables. Perfect preparations of classic dishes and impeccable service ensure an exquisite dining experience.

VOLLE NOLLE   SANDWICHES $
Map p248 (351 Hanover St; sandwiches $8-12; ☺breakfast & lunch; ⌚; Ⓜ Haymarket) Apparently, *volle nolle* is Latin for 'willy-nilly,' but there is nothing haphazard about this much-beloved North End sandwich shop. Black-slate tables and pressed-tin walls adorn the simple, small space. The chalkboard menu features fresh salads, delicious flatbread sandwiches and dark rich coffee. A perfect lunchtime stop along the Freedom Trail.

🌱 TARANTA   FUSION $$$
Map p248 (☎617-720-0052; www.tarantarist. com; 210 Hanover St; mains $25-35; ☺dinner; Ⓜ Haymarket) Europe meets South America at this Italian restaurant with a Peruvian twist. So, for example, gnocchi is made from yucca and served with a spicy lamb ragout; salmon filet is encrusted with macadamia nuts, and filet mignon with crushed espresso beans. There's an incredible selection of Italian, Chilean and Argentinean wines, all of which are organic or biodynamic. Taranta is a Certified Green Restaurant.

CARMEN   ITALIAN $$$
Map p248 (☎617-742-6421; www.carmenboston. com; 33 North Sq; mains $25-35; ☺lunch Wed-Sat, dinner Tue-Sun; Ⓜ Haymarket) Exposed brick walls and candlelit tables are good for romance; interesting and exotic menu combinations are good for culinary indulgence. The innovative menu offers a selection of small plates providing a fresh take on traditional fare; mains such as pork roast and seared tuna sit alongside classic pasta dishes.

GALLERIA UMBERTO   PIZZERIA $
Map p248 (289 Hanover St; mains $2-6; ☺lunch Mon-Sat; ⌚🚻; Ⓜ Haymarket) Paper plates, cans of soda, Sicilian pizza: can't beat it. This lunchtime legend closes as soon as the slices are gone. And considering their thick and chewy goodness, that's often before the official 2:30pm closing time. Loyal patrons line up early so they are sure to get theirs.

DAILY CATCH   SEAFOOD $$
Map p248 (www.dailycatch.com; 323 Hanover St; mains $18-26; ☺lunch & dinner; Ⓜ Haymarket) Although owner Paul Freddura long ago added a few tables and an open kitchen, this shoebox fish joint still retains the atmosphere of a retail fish market (complete with wine served in plastic cups). Fortunately, it also retains the freshness of the fish. The specialty is calamari, fried to tender perfection. Cash only.

GIACOMO'S RISTORANTE   ITALIAN $$
Map p248 (www.giacomosblog-boston.blogspot. com; 355 Hanover St; mains $14-18; ☺dinner; ⌚; Ⓜ Haymarket) Customers line up before the doors open so they can guarantee themselves a spot in the first round of seating at this North End favorite. Enthusiastic and entertaining waiters, plus cramped quarters, ensure that you get to know your neighbors. The cuisine is no-frills southern Italian fare, served in unbelievable portions.

The specialty of the house is *zuppa di pesce* ($55 for two), chock-full of shrimp, scallops, calamari, mussels and lobster. Cash only.

PIZZERIA REGINA   PIZZERIA $
Map p248 (www.pizzeriaregina.com; 11½ Thatcher St; pizzas $14-20; ☺lunch & dinner; ⌚; Ⓜ Haymarket) The queen of North End pizzerias is the legendary Pizzeria Regina, famous for brusque but endearing waitresses and crispy, thin-crust pizza. Thanks to the slightly spicy sauce (flavored with aged romano) Regina repeatedly wins accolades for her pies. Reservations are not accepted, so be prepared to wait.

RISTORANTE DAMIANO   ITALIAN $$
Map p248 (www.ristorantedamiano.com; 307 Hanover St; small plates $10-18; ☺lunch Sat & Sun, dinner Tue-Sun; ⌚; Ⓜ Haymarket) If you can't stomach the thought of a huge plate of pasta and a bottle of wine, head to this contemporary Sicilian cafe for *piattini* (small plates) and wine by the glass. It's a small space, but large windows and open kitchen make it modern and welcoming (though slack service sometimes counters this atmosphere).

J PACE & SON   ITALIAN, DELI $
Map p248 (42 Cross St; mains $8-12; ☺7am-7pm; ⌚; Ⓜ Haymarket) For fresh cheese, olives, pasta and meats, stop in to see the neighborhood Italian grocer at J Pace & Son. Order your sandwiches, salads, soups or calzone at the counter and take your lunch to the pleasant plaza.

LULU'S SWEET SHOPPE   DESSERTS $

Map p248 (www.luluboston.com; 57 Salem St; ⊘11am-7pm; ⓂHaymarket) If you prefer cupcakes over cannolis. Red velvet? Boston cream cupcake? Salted caramel? Yes please. Formerly a 'bake shoppe,' this place has reopened as a 'sweet shoppe,' which means they now have old-fashioned candies and homemade chocolates. We don't know whether to be happy or sad that this cutesy place has reopened on the site of the former Dairy Fresh Candies.

DRINKING & NIGHTLIFE

West End

When the city fathers bulldozed and re-built this area in the 1950s and 1960s, one casualty that never recovered was nightlife. However, several of the city's most popular rowdy sports bars are clustered near TD Banknorth Garden, home of the Bruins and Celtics. Canal St and gritty Friend St are the best bets. At the other end of the neighborhood, the Liberty Hotel offers some upscale places to drink and be seen.

ALIBI   COCKTAIL BAR

Map p246 (www.alibiboston.com; ⊘5pm-2am; ⓂCharles/MGH) There are actually two hot-to-trot drinking venues in the Liberty Hotel, both architecturally impressive and socially oh-so-trendy. Downstairs, Alibi is set in the former 'drunk tank' of the Charles St Jail. The prison theme is played up, with mugshots hanging on the brick walls and iron bars on the doors and windows. Upstairs, Clink is the opposite, set under the soaring ceiling of the hotel's lobby. Both places are absurdly popular, so you'd best come early if you care to sit down.

WEST END JOHNNIES   SPORTS BAR

Map p246 (www.johnniesontheside.com; 138 Portland St; ⊘noon-midnight Mon-Thu, to 2am Fri & Sat, 11am-4pm Sun brunch; ⓂNorth Station) Despite the black leather furniture and big picture windows, this West End venue cannot escape the fact that it's a sports bar, with flatscreen TVs and sports paraphernalia adorning the walls. But it's a sports bar for grown-ups, with a good wine list and cocktail selection and tasty food.

Attention brunchies: JC's corned-beef hash and eggs and live reggae music make for an excellent way to recover from your Saturday night.

EQUAL EXCHANGE CAFE   CAFE

Map p246 (www.equalexchangecafe.com; 226 Causeway St; ⊘7am-7pm Mon-Fri, 9am-5pm Sat; @; ⓂNorth Station) Just by drinking rich delicious coffee and eating dark sweet chocolate, you are doing a good deed. All the coffees and cocoas are organically grown, fairly traded and locally roasted. You should really feel good about yourself. The cafe has also received the city's green business award, thanks to its comprehensive recycling program.

WORTH A DETOUR

EASTIE
....

People are passionate about pizza in the North End, home to Boston's oldest and most beloved pizzerias. But if you are serious about sampling the city's best slices, you'll have to wander far away from the Freedom Trail to edgy East Boston.

East Boston is a blue-collar, rough-and-tumble part of town. On the east side of the Boston Harbor, it's the site of Logan Airport, and also the setting for much of the Academy Award–winning movie *Mystic River*. But most importantly, Eastie is the home of **Santarpio's** (www.santarpiospizza.com; 111 Chelsea St, East Boston; ⊘11:30am-midnight; ⚲⏵; ⓂAirport), the pizza place that constantly tops the lists of Boston's best pizza pies.

Boston Bruins posters and neon beer signs constitute the decor here. A wood counter gives a glimpse into the kitchen, where the pizza chefs work their magic. A gruff waitress might offer a menu, but there is really no point. You come here for the thin-crust pizza – unique for its extra crispy, crunchy texture. This well-done crust is topped with slightly sweet sauce, plenty of pepperoni and not too much cheese.

Divey decor, rough service and delectable pizza. It's all part of the chaaaahm.

BOSTON BEER WORKS
BREWERY

Map p246 (www.beerworks.net; 112 Canal St; ⏱11:30am-midnight; Ⓜ North Station) Boston Beer Works is a solid option for beer lovers and sports lovers (conveniently located near the city's major sporting venues). The excellent selection of microbrews offers something for everyone, including plenty of seasonal specialties. Fruity brews like blueberry ale get rave reviews, with tasty sweet-potato fries as the perfect accompaniment. A few tables and plenty of TVs keep the troops entertained.

FOURS
SPORTS BAR

Map p246 (www.thefours.com; 166 Canal St; ⏱11am-1am; ☎; Ⓜ North Station) Boasting all sports, all the time, the Fours makes a great place to appreciate Bostonians' near-fanatical obsession with sporting events. The large two-level bar was established in 1976 and retains a dash of character from that period. In addition to the game of your choice, admire a jersey collection and loads of pictures depicting legendary events in Boston's sporting past.

📍 North End

Despite the vibrancy of Hanover St, the colorful North End is devoid of proper bars. If you weave your way through all the late-night bakeries and restaurants, you'll find a handful of cafes where you can drink in Italian-American style.

CAFFÉ VITTORIA
CAFE

Map p248 (www.vittoriacaffe.com; 290-296 Hanover St; ⏱7am-midnight; Ⓜ Haymarket) A delightful destination for dessert or aperitifs. The frilly parlor displays antique espresso machines and black-and-white photos, with a pressed-tin ceiling reminiscent of the era. Grab a marble-topped table, order a cappuccino and live it up in Victorian pleasure. Cash only, just like the olden days.

CAFFÉ DELLO SPORT
SPORTS BAR, CAFE

Map p248 (www.caffedellosport.us; 308 Hanover St; ⏱6am-midnight; Ⓜ Haymarket) An informal crowd of thick-accented guys from the 'hood sit at glass-topped tables and drink coffee and Campari. The cappuccinos and other espresso drinks are excellent. This is a great place to watch a football game (yes, we mean soccer), and watching the other patrons is equally entertaining. Cash only.

ITALIAN FESTIVALS

In July and August, the North End takes on a celebratory air, as old-timer Italians host festivals to honor their patron saints. The streets fill with local residents listening to music, playing games and – of course – eating. The highlight of every festival is the saint's parade, which features local marching bands and social clubs and the star participant, a statue of the patron saint. The lifesize likeness is hoisted onto a wooden platform and carried through the streets, while residents cheer and toss confetti. Banners stream behind the statue so that believers can pin on their dollar bills, thus earning the protection of the saint's watchful eye. While the saints' festivals occur throughout the summer, the biggest events are the **Fisherman's Feast** (www.fishermansfeast.com) and **St Anthony's Feast** (www.stanthonys feast.com), both in late August.

CAFFÉ PARADISO
BAR

Map p248 (255 Hanover St; ⏱7am-11pm; ☎; Ⓜ Haymarket) The Saturday-morning regulars are so dedicated that some painstakingly organize their business calendars so they don't miss their spot at the counter. As he has for years, Luigi masterfully attends to the espresso machine and pours neat cognacs with efficient and understated flourish. It's a good spot to watch overseas soccer matches. Excellent desserts.

☆ ENTERTAINMENT

TD BANKNORTH GARDEN
BASKETBALL, HOCKEY

Map p246 (ℹinformation 617-523-3030, tickets 617-931-2000; www.tdgarden.com; 150 Causeway St; Ⓜ North Station) Back in the day, the Boston Garden was the home of the Bruins and the Celtics. In 1997, that storied sports arena was destroyed and replaced by the current facility, which went through a slew of name changes before arriving at – you guessed it – 'the Garden.' Of course, now there is a corporate sponsor, so it's officially the TD Banknorth Garden.

It's still home to the Bruins, who play hockey here from September to June, and the Celtics, who play basketball from October to April. It's the city's largest venue so big-name musicians perform here too.

MUGAR OMNI IMAX THEATER   CINEMA

Map p246 (www.mos.org; Science Museum, Charles River Dam; adult/senior/child $10/8/9; ♿; Ⓜ Science Park) For total IMAX immersion, check out the space-themed and natural–science–oriented flicks at the Museum of Science's theater. A stellar sound system will help you believe that you're roving around Mars.

IMPROV ASYLUM   COMEDY

Map p248 (www.improvasylum.com; 216 Hanover St; tickets $20-25; ☺ shows 8pm Tue-Sun, plus 10pm Fri & Sat, 4pm Sat & Sun; Ⓜ Haymarket) This North End theater is a little dingy but somehow it enhances the dark and sometimes dirty humor spewing from the mouths of this offbeat crew. No topic is too touchy, no politics too correct. The show redefines itself with every fast-paced performance.

🔒 SHOPPING

Every visitor to Boston goes to the North End to savor the flavors of Italian cooking. But as a local community directory points out: 'Where do you think the chefs get their food from?' These tradition-steeped streets are filled with specialty markets selling wine, spices, fresh produce, meats and seafood. The constant flow of foot traffic has started to attract funky boutiques and galleries, too. There's not much in the way of shopping in the West End, so mosey across North End Park to spend your money.

SALUMERIA ITALIANA   FOOD & DRINK

Map p248 (www.salumeriaitaliana.com; 151 Richmond St; ☺ 7am-6pm Mon-Thu, to 7pm Fri & Sat; Ⓜ Haymarket) Shelves stocked with extra-virgin olive oil and aged balsamic vinegar; cases crammed with cured meats, hard cheeses and olives of all shapes and sizes; boxes of pasta; jars of sauce: this little store is the archetypal North End specialty shop.

POLCARI'S COFFEE   FOOD & DRINK

Map p248 (polcariscoffee.com; 105 Salem St; ☺ 9:30am-6pm Mon-Sat; Ⓜ Haymarket) Since 1932, this corner shop is where North Enders stock up on their beans. Look for 27 kinds of imported coffee, over 150 spices and an impressive selection of legumes, grains, flours and loose teas. Don't bypass the chance to indulge in a fresh Italian ice.

IN-JEAN-IUS   CLOTHING

Map p248 (www.injeanius.com; 441 Hanover St; Ⓜ Haymarket) You know what you're getting when you waltz into this denim haven. Offerings from over 30 designers include tried-and-true favorites and little-known gems, and staff are on hand to help you find the pair that fits you perfectly. Warning: the surgeon general has determined that it is not healthy to try on jeans after a gigantic plate of pasta; come here before dinner.

SHAKE THE TREE   CLOTHING, ACCESSORIES, JEWELRY, GIFTS

Map p248 (www.shakethetreeboston.com; 67 Salem St; ☺ 11am-7pm; Ⓜ Haymarket) You can't know what you will find at this sweet boutique, but it's bound to be good. The little shop carries a wonderful, eclectic assortment of jewelry by local artisans, interesting stationery, designer handbags and clothing and unique housewares.

DEPASQUALE'S HOMEMADE PASTA SHOPPE   FOOD & DRINK

Map p248 (66a Cross St; ☺ 10am-8pm Sun-Thu, 10am-10pm Fri & Sat; Ⓜ Haymarket) Peek into this little storefront to catch a glimpse of the pasta maker working her magic, crafting pasta in various shapes, sizes and flavors. The store carries more than 50 fresh varieties, including specialty ravioli and tortellini with mouthwatering fillings. If you can't decide, browse the recipe cards for ideas.

NORTH BENNET STREET SCHOOL   HANDICRAFTS

Map p248 (www.nbss.org; 39 North Bennet St; ☺ 10am-2pm Mon-Thu, 10am-3pm Sat; Ⓜ North Station) The North Bennet Street School has been training craftspeople since 1885, offering courses in traditional skills like bookbinding, woodworking and locksmithing. The on-site gallery sells hand-crafted works by students and alumni: unique jewelry, handmade journals and exquisite wood furniture and musical instruments.

SEDURRE   CLOTHING

Map p248 (www.sedurreboston.com; 281/2 Prince St; ☺ noon-8pm Mon-Sat, noon-6pm Sun; Ⓜ Haymarket) If you can speak Italian, you'll know that Sedurre's thing is sexy and stylish. (It means 'seduce.') The shop started with fine lingerie – beautiful lacy nightgowns and underthings for special occasions. Sisters Robyn and Daria were so good at that, they created an additional space next door for dresses and evening wear (for other kinds of special occasions).

TWILIGHT
CLOTHING

Map p248 (www.twilightboston.com; 12 Fleet St; [M]Haymarket) Alison Barnard proved that she could do jeans, when she opened In-jean-ius on Hanover St. She then proceeded to get her girls dressed up, opening a slick dress shop around the corner. The purple velvet drapes and black chandeliers create an elegant atmosphere to browse the racks and racks of fancy wear, featuring Nicole Miller, BCBG and other high-style designers.

FRESH CHEESE DELI
FOOD & DRINK

Map p248 (20 Fleet St; ⊙variable; Haymarket) The local cheesemonger has a tempting selection of Italian deliciousness – not only cheese, but also deli meats, olive oil, vinegar and other imported products. If you don't know what you want, the gentleman behind the counter will have suggestions. He'll also whip up an amazing sandwich that many claim is the best in the 'hood.

WINE BOTTEGA
FOOD & DRINK

Map p248 (www.thewinebottega.com; 341 Hanover St; ⊙11am-9pm; [M]Haymarket) With a large choice of wines packed into a small space, this is a delightful place to browse, though you'll face a challenge if you're looking for something specific. The ownership is enthusiastic about educating their customers, so they will love to help you find something you love too.

V CIRACE & SON, INC
FOOD & DRINK

Map p248 (www.vcirace.com; 127 North St; ⊙wine tastings 5-7pm Fri; [M]Haymarket) The third generation of the Cirace family now runs this North End institution. The store, established in 1906, carries a fine selection of Italian wines, grappa and spirits. Other specialties include artisanal pasta and olive oil, Italian sweets and honey, and imported ceramics.

LIT BOUTIQUE
CLOTHING

Map p248 (www.litboutique.com; 236 Hanover St; [M]Haymarket) The North End is going all stylish on us, with sharp, fashion-forward boutiques opening up and down Hanover St. Case in point: LIT Boutique, a shop

SECRET INGREDIENT

Inquire at the Salumeria Italiana (p62) about the Rubio aged balsamic vinegar, produced exclusively for this shop by an artisan in Modena, Italy. Made from Trebbiano grapes and aged in oak barrels, this is the secret ingredient of many North End chefs.

crowded with sexy city-wear. The clothing here is eclectic, featuring lace and leather, flowy skirts and shorty shorts.

BLING! OF BOSTON
JEWELRY

Map p248 (www.blingofboston.com; 236A Hanover St; [M]Haymarket) This sparkly store has garnered much success from a simple but clever concept: producing affordable replicas of the dazzling jewels worn by the likes of Marilyn Monroe, Audrey Hepburn and contemporary stars. It's not just bling, but *celebrity* bling. The Jackie O collection includes hundreds of pieces copied from the former first lady's personal collection.

🏃 SPORTS & ACTIVITIES

OLD BOSTON ORIGINAL SECRET TOUR
WALKING TOUR

Map p248 (☑617-756-1059; www.oldbostontours.com; 11 North Sq; tours $30; ⊙tours 10am Mon-Sat, plus 3pm Fri & Sat) Spend two hours on this excellent walking tour and learn all the sordid secrets about the North End, one of Boston's oldest and most enigmatic neighborhoods. Strange and startling stories focus on the influence of the various immigrant groups, including 'secret tunnels, anarchists and hidden loot.' Are you intrigued yet?

NORTH END MARKET TOUR
WALKING TOUR

(☑617-523-6032; www.bostonfoodtours.com; tours $55; ⊙10am & 2pm Wed & Sat, 10am & 3pm Fri) This three-hour tour around the North End includes shopping in a *salumeria*, sampling pastries at the local *pasticceria*, smelling the herbs and spices that flavor Italian cooking, and sampling spirits at an *enoteca* (wine bar). Guests have the opportunity to chat with local shopkeepers and other long-time North End residents about eating and living in this food-rich neighborhood.

1. Patriot's Day Parade (p20)
On the third Monday in April, Bostonians proudly commemorate the start of the American Revolution with marches and reenactments.

2. Polcari's Coffee (p62)
North Enders have stocked up on beans from this corner coffee shop since 1932.

3. Charlestown (p44)
Classic wooden town houses line the streets surrounding Bunker Hill.

4. Liberty Hotel (p186)
The West End's Charles St Jail has been converted – with due irony – into a luxury hotel.

Beacon Hill & Boston Common

Neighborhood Top Five

1 Breathing in the sweet smell of flowering trees and blooming beds, as you admire the seasonal display in the **Public Garden** (p70). A ride in a swan boat on the lagoon completes an idyllic outing.

2 Exploring the **Massachusetts State House**(p71) in search of the Sacred Cod and the Holy Mackerel.

3 Packing a picnic for an evening of **Shakespeare on the Common** (p75).

4 Browsing for trash and treasures in the antique shops that line **Charles St** (p75).

5 Following the **Black Heritage Trail** (p77) to learn about the early African American settlement on Beacon Hill.

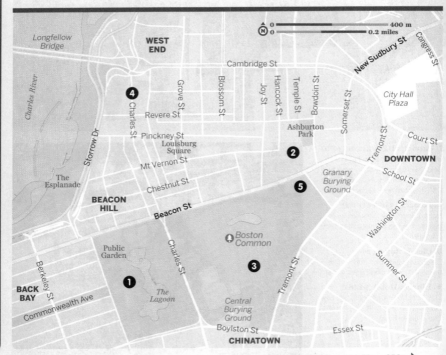

For more details of this area, see Map p250 ➡

Explore Beacon Hill & Boston Common

The Boston Common is the starting point for the Freedom Trail and, as such, the starting point for many visitors' exploration of Boston. Whether or not it is the first place you visit in Boston, it is a central meeting point, a jumping-off point for several neighborhoods and an always-enjoyable place for a picnic lunch. You'll likely find yourself passing through more than once.

Besides the Common, several other Freedom Trail sights lie within the borders of Beacon Hill, including the impressive gold-domed Massachusetts State House. This building is the focal point of politics in the Commonwealth – it was famously dubbed 'the hub of the solar system' – and the neighborhood buzzes with the business of local politicos and State House staffers.

But the appeal of this neighborhood lies behind the landmarks, along the narrow cobblestone streets that crisscross the hill. Lined with brick townhouses and lit by gas lanterns, these streets are a delightful setting to spend an afternoon – whether browsing boutiques and haggling for antiques, or just sipping a cappuccino and admiring the quintessentially Bostonian landscape.

Local Life

➡ **Book Nook** Local writers and bibliophiles enjoy the artistic atmosphere and historic setting at the Boston Athenaeum (p72).

➡ **Local Politics** State House staffers hang out across the street at the 21st Amendment (p74) when their working day is through.

➡ **Secret Spot** Escape the crowds on Charles St and retreat to 75 Chestnut (p73) to hobnob with the locals.

Getting There & Away

➡ **Metro** At the junction of the red and green lines, Park St T-station services the Boston Common and sights in the southeastern part of Beacon Hill. Also on the red line, Charles/MGH T station is convenient to Beacon Hill's Charles and Cambridge Sts, as well as the Charles River Esplanade. The blue-line Bowdoin T station is a less-used stop convenient to the eastern end of Cambridge St.

Lonely Planet's Top Tip

Get a great view of Boston's skyline from the Longfellow Bridge, also known as the 'salt and pepper bridge,' which crosses the river at the top of Charles St.

✖ Best Places to Eat

➡ Paramount (p73)
➡ Grotto (p73)
➡ 75 Chestnut (p73)
➡ No 9 Park (p73)

For reviews, see p73

🍷 Best Places to Drink

➡ 21st Amendment (p74)
➡ Bin 26 Enoteca (p75)

For reviews, see p74

🔒 Best Boutiques & Antiques

➡ Artifaktori Vintage (p75)
➡ Crush Boutique (p75)
➡ Ruby Door (p76)
➡ Eugene Galleries (p76)
➡ Marika's Antique Shop (p76)
➡ Moxie (p77)

For reviews, see p74 ➡

TOP SIGHTS
BOSTON COMMON

The 50-acre Boston Common is the country's oldest public park. If you have any doubt, refer to the plaque emblazoned with the words of the treaty between Governor Winthrop and William Blaxton, who sold the land for £30 in 1634. The Common has served many purposes over the years, including as a campground for British troops during the Revolutionary War and as green grass for cattle grazing until the 1830s. Although there is still a grazing ordinance on the books, the Common today serves picnickers, sunbathers and people-watchers.

Bostonians hustle to and from the nearby T stations; others stroll leisurely, enjoying the fresh air or engaging in any number of Common activities, from free concerts to political rallies to seasonal festivities. In winter, the Frog Pond (p77) attracts ice-skaters, while summer draws theater-lovers for Shakespeare on the Common (p75). This is the first link in the **Emerald Necklace** (p165) and the starting point for the Freedom Trail.

DON'T MISS

➡ Blaxton Plaque
➡ Robert Gould Shaw Memorial
➡ Boston Massacre Monument

PRACTICALITIES

➡ Map p250
➡ btwn Tremont, Charles, Beacon & Park Sts
➡ ⊙6am-midnight
➡ MPark St

Robert Gould Shaw Memorial

The magnificent bas-relief memorial (Map p251) sculpted by Augustus Saint-Gaudens honors the 54th Massachusetts Regiment of the Union Army, the nation's first all-black Civil War regiment (depicted in the 1989 film *Glory*). The soldiers, led by 26-year-old Shaw, steadfastly refused their monthly stipend for two years, until Congress increased it to match the amount that white regiments received. Shaw (the son of a wealthy Brahmin family) and half his men were killed in a battle at Fort Wagner, South Carolina. The National Park Service (NPS) tour of the Black Heritage Trail (p77) departs from here.

Brewer Fountain

This bronze beauty dates to 1868, when it was gifted to the city of Boston by wealthy merchant Gardner Brewer. The fountain (Map p251) was unveiled in 2011 after an extensive restoration, rendering the four Classical deities in their full splendor: the Roman god of water, Neptune; the Greek sea goddess, Amphitrite; and the spirit Acis and sea nymph Galatea, both from Ovid's *Metamorphoses*. The design won a gold medal at the 1855 World's Fair.

Boston Massacre Monument

This 25ft monument (Map p250) commemorates the five victims of the Boston Massacre, replicating Paul Revere's famous engraving of the event. Revere's interpretation depicts the soldiers shooting defenseless colonists in cold blood, when in reality they were reacting to the aggressive crowd in self-defense.

Soldiers & Sailors Monument

This massive 1877 monument (Map p250) pays tribute to the soldiers and sailors who died in the Civil War. The four bronze statues represent Peace (the female figure looking to the South), the Sailor (the seaman facing the ocean), History (the Greek figure looking to heaven) and the Soldier (an infantryman standing at ease). See if you can recognize the many historical figures in the elaborate bronze reliefs.

Great Elm Site

A plaque marks the site of the Old Elm (Map p250) that stood here for over two centuries. Ann Hibbens was hanged from its branches for witchery in 1656, and Mary Dyer for religious heresy in 1660. On a gentler note, the Sons of Liberty hung lanterns here to symbolize unity. Boston's 'oldest inhabitant' was damaged in a 1869 storm and destroyed by a storm in 1876.

Central Burying Ground

Dating to 1756, the Central Burying Ground (Map p250) is the least celebrated of the old cemeteries, as it was the burial ground of the down-and-out (according to Edwin Bacon's *Boston Illustrated*, it was used for 'Roman Catholics and strangers dying in the town'). Some reports indicate that it contains an unmarked mass grave for British soldiers who died in the Battle of Bunker Hill. The most recognized name here is artist-in-residence Gilbert Stuart.

Parkman Bandstand

The site of concerts and rabble-rousing activities, Parkman Bandstand (Map p250) has been a landmark on the Boston Common since 1912.

The Boston Common is often called 'the Common' in local parlance, but never 'the Commons.' Use the singular or risk ridicule by locals!

AFFORDABLE PARKING

After 4pm you can park in the lot under the Common for $10.

The Common is a primo hunting ground for red-tailed hawks, which are often spotted terrorizing the pigeons.

THE BARD

Every summer the Commonwealth Shakespeare Company hosts the free Shakespeare on the Common (p75) for picnic-packing theater-lovers.

Dating to 1897, Park St station is the oldest subway station in America.

BEACON HILL & BOSTON COMMON BOSTON COMMON

TOP SIGHTS
BOSTON COMMON

TOP SIGHTS
PUBLIC GARDEN

The Public Garden is a 24-acre oasis of Victorian flowerbeds, verdant grasses and willow trees shading a tranquil lagoon. Until it was filled in the early 19th century, it was (like Back Bay) a tidal salt marsh. Now, at any time of year, it is an island of loveliness, awash in spring blooms, gold-toned leaves or fields of snow.

Monuments

At the main (Arlington St) entrance, visitors are met by a **statue of George Washington** (Map p250) mounted nobly on his horse. Other pieces of public art are more whimsical. The most endearing is **Make Way for Ducklings** (Map p250), always a favorite with tiny tots who can climb and sit on the bronze ducks. The sculpture depicts Mrs Mallard and her ducklings, characters in Robert McCloskey's beloved book. As the story goes, Mrs Mallard and her brood are helped across the busy street by a friendly Boston policeman.

On the lagoon's northwest side, the **Ether Monument** (Map p250) commemorates the first use – in Boston – of anesthesia for medical purposes (see the Ether Dome, p56).

Swan Boats

If the slow-going **swan boats** (Map p250; www.swanboats.com; Public Garden; adult/child/senior $2.75/1.50/2; ☉10am-4pm daily mid-Apr–mid-Jun, 10am-5pm daily mid-Jun–Aug, 10am-4pm Sat & Sun, noon-4pm Mon-Fri Sep–mid-Oct; ⓂArlington) seem out of place in today's fast-paced city setting, they are. The story of the swan boats (pictured above) goes back to 1877, when Robert Paget developed a catamaran with a pedal-propelled paddlewheel. Inspired by the opera *Lohengrin*, in which a knight crosses a river in a swan-drawn boat, Paget designed a graceful swan to hide the boat captain. Today's swan boats are larger than the 1877 original, but still use the same technology and they are still managed by Paget's descendants.

DON'T MISS

➡ Make Way for Ducklings statue
➡ Swan Boats
➡ Rose Gardens

PRACTICALITIES

➡ Map p250
➡ www.friendsofthe publicgarden.org
➡ btwn Charles, Beacon, Boylston & Arlington Sts
➡ ☉6am-midnight
➡ ⓂArlington

TOP SIGHTS
MASSACHUSETTS STATE HOUSE

High atop Beacon Hill, Massachusetts' leaders and legislators attempt to turn their ideals into concrete policies and State practices. Charles Bulfinch designed the commanding state capitol, but it was Oliver Wendell Holmes who called it 'the hub of the solar system' (thus earning Boston the nickname 'the Hub').

For most of the 18th century, the seat of the Massachusetts government was the Old State House. After the revolution, when state leaders decided they needed an upgrade, they chose the city's highest peak – land that was previously part of John Hancock's cow pasture.

Tours

A free 40-minute tour of the State House covers its history, artwork, architecture and political personalities. Knowledgeable 'Doric Docents' provide details about the many statues, flags and murals that decorate the various halls.

Tours start in the Doric Hall, the columned reception area directly below the dome. Once the main entryway to the State House, these front doors are now used only by a visiting US president or by a departing governor taking 'the long walk' on his last day in office.

Visitors can see both legislative chambers: the House of Representatives, also house of the famous Sacred Cod; and the Senate Chamber, residence of the Holy Mackerel.

DON'T MISS

➡ Hall of Flags
➡ Sacred Cod & Holy Mackerel
➡ Robert Reid's murals in Nurses Hall
➡ The clock in the Great Hall

PRACTICALITIES

➡ Map p250
➡ www.sec.state.ma.us
➡ cnr Beacon & Bowdoin Sts
➡ admission free
➡ ⊙9am-5pm, tours 10am-4pm Mon-Fri
➡ 🚻
➡ Ⓜ Park St

State House Lawn

Statues on the front lawn honor notable Massachusetts figures, including Daniel Webster, religious martyrs Anne Hutchinson and Mary Dyer, and John F Kennedy. These lovely grounds are closed to the public, however, so you'll have to peek through the iron fence.

◉ SIGHTS

BOSTON COMMON   PARK
See p68.

PUBLIC GARDEN   GARDENS
See p70.

MASSACHUSETTS STATE
HOUSE   NOTABLE BUILDING
See p71.

PARK STREET CHURCH   CHURCH
Map p250 (www.parkstreet.org; 1 Park St; ⏱9am-4pm Tue-Sat mid-Jun–Aug; MPark St) Shortly after the construction of Park St Church, powder for the War of 1812 was stored in the basement, earning this location the moniker 'Brimstone Corner.' But that was hardly the most inflammatory event that took place here. Noted for its graceful, 217ft steeple, this Boston landmark has been hosting historic lectures and musical performances since its founding.

In 1829 William Lloyd Garrison railed against slavery from the church's pulpit. And on Independence Day in 1831, Samuel Francis Smith's hymn 'America' ('My Country 'Tis of Thee') was first sung. These days, Park St is a conservative congregational church.

GRANARY BURYING GROUND   CEMETERY
Map p250 (Tremont St; ⏱9am-5pm; MPark St) Dating to 1660, this atmospheric atoll is crammed with historic headstones, many with evocative (and creepy) carvings. This is the final resting place of all your favorite revolutionary heroes including Paul Revere, Samuel Adams, John Hancock and James Otis. Benjamin Franklin is buried in Philadelphia, but the Franklin family plot contains his parents.

The five victims of the Boston Massacre share a common grave, though the only name you are likely to recognize is that of Crispus Attucks, the freed slave who is considered the first person to lose his life in the struggle for American independence. Other noteworthy permanent residents include Peter Faneuil, of Faneuil Hall fame, and Judge Sewall, the only magistrate to denounce the hanging of the so-called Salem witches.

The location of Park Street Church was once the site of the town granary: as the burying ground predates the church, it is named after the grain storage facility instead. While it is sometimes called the Old Granary Burying Ground, it's not the oldest; King's Chapel and Copp's Hill date back even further.

FREE BOSTON ATHENAEUM   CULTURAL BUILDING
Map p250 (☎617-227-0270; www.bostonathenaeum.org; 10½ Beacon St; donation $5; ⏱8:30am-8pm Mon-Wed, 9am-4pm Thu-Sat; MPark St) Founded in 1807, the Boston Athenaeum is an old and distinguished private library, having hosted the likes of Ralph Waldo Emerson and Nathaniel Hawthorne, as well as less traditional members like Amy Lowell.

Its collection has over half a million volumes, including an impressive selection of art, which is showcased in the on-site gallery. Unfortunately, the library itself is open to members only, but tourists can visit the gallery. Tours of the whole library are conducted at 3pm on Tuesday and Thursday, but you must reserve your spot in advance.

MUSEUM OF AFRO-AMERICAN
HISTORY   MUSEUM
Map p250 (www.afroammuseum.org; 46 Joy St; adult/senior/child $5/3/free; ⏱10am-4pm Mon-Sat; MPark St or Bowdoin) Beacon Hill was never the exclusive domain of blue-blood Brahmins. In the 19th century, freed African Americans settled on the back side of the hill. The Museum of Afro-American History occupies two adjacent historic buildings: the African Meeting House, the country's oldest black church and meeting house; and Abiel Smith School, the country's first school for blacks.

Within these walls William Lloyd Garrison began the New England Anti-Slavery Society, which later expanded to become the American Anti-Slavery Society. Here, Maria Stewart became the first American woman – a black woman, no less – to speak before a mixed-gender audience. Frederick Douglass delivered stirring calls to action within this hall, and Robert Gould Shaw recruited black soldiers for the Civil War effort.

Today the Museum of Afro-American History offers rotating exhibits about these historic events. The galleries are located in the Abiel Smith School, while the African Meeting House is undergoing extensive preservation work to return the building to its 19th-century appearance. The museum is also a source of information about – and the final destination of – the Black Heritage Trail (p77).

NICHOLS HOUSE MUSEUM
MUSEUM

Map p250 (www.nicholshousemuseum.org; 55 Mt Vernon St; adult/child $7/free; ⊙11am-4pm Tue-Sat Apr-Oct, Thu-Sat Nov-Mar; MPark St) This 1804 town house might be your only opportunity to peek inside one of these classic Beacon Hill beauties. Attributed to Charles Bulfinch, it is unique in its merger of Federal and Greek Revival architectural styles.

Equally impressive is the story told inside the museum – that of the day-to-day life of Miss Rose Standish Nichols, who lived here from 1885 to 1960. Miss Rose was an author, pacifist and suffragette. The museum has reconstructed her home, furnished with art and antiques from all over the world, as well as some impressive examples of her own needlepoint and woodwork.

LOUISBURG SQUARE
STREET

Map p250 (Louisburg Sq; MCharles/MGH) There is no more prestigious address than this lane, a cluster of stately brick row houses facing a private park. After she gained literary success, Louisa May Alcott's home was at No 10; at the northern corner of the square is the home of Senator John Kerry and his wife Teresa Heinz.

ACORN STREET
STREET

Map p250 (Acorn St; MCharles/MGH) Boston's oft-photographed narrowest street. This cobblestone alleyway was once home to artisans and to the service people who worked for the adjacent mansion dwellers. The brick walls on the north side of the street enclose examples of Beacon Hill's hidden gardens.

EATING

TOP CHOICE PARAMOUNT
CAFETERIA $$

Map p250 (www.paramountboston.com; 44 Charles St; breakfast & lunch $8-12, dinner $15-30; ⊙breakfast, lunch & dinner; ⌨ ☗; MCharles/MGH) This old-fashioned cafeteria is a neighborhood favorite. Basic diner fare includes pancakes, steak and eggs, burgers and sandwiches, and big, hearty salads. For dinner, add table service and candlelight, and the place goes upscale without losing its down-home charm. The menu is enhanced by homemade pastas, a selection of meat and fish dishes and an impressive roster of daily specials.

GROTTO
ITALIAN $$

Map p250 (☎617-227-3434; www.grottores taurant.com; 37 Bowdoin St; mains $21, prix fixe $36; ⊙lunch Mon-Fri, dinner daily; MBowdoin) Tucked into a basement on the back side of Beacon Hill, this cozy, cavelike place lives up to its name. The funky decor – exposed brick walls decked with rotating art – reflects the innovative menu (which also changes frequently). Reservations recommended.

75 CHESTNUT
AMERICAN $$

Map p250 (www.75chestnut.com; 75 Chestnut St; mains $15-25; ⊙brunch Sat & Sun, dinner daily; MCharles/MGH) You might not think to take a peek around the corner, away from the well-trod sidewalks of Charles St. But locals know that Chestnut St is the place to go for tried-and-true steaks and seafood and a genuine warm welcome.

It's a perfect place to stop for a drink, but you'll probably end up staying for dinner because the place is that comfy-cozy. And once you catch a glimpse of the signature desserts, you'll certainly want to stay for wild berry crumble or Swiss chocolate almond soup.

NO 9 PARK
EUROPEAN $$$

Map p250 (☎617-742-9991; www.no9park. com; 9 Park St; lunch $40, dinner $60; ⊙lunch Mon-Fri, dinner Mon-Sat; MPark St) Set in a 19th-century mansion opposite the State House, this swanky place tops many fine-dining lists. Chef-owner Barbara Lynch has been lauded by food and wine magazines for her delectable French and Italian culinary masterpieces and her first-rate wine list. She has now cast her celebrity-chef spell all around town, but this is the place that made her famous. Reservations recommended.

LALA ROKH
PERSIAN $$

Map p250 (☎617-720-5511; www.lalarokh.com; 97 Mt Vernon St; meals $20-30; ⊙lunch Mon-Fri, dinner daily; MCharles/MGH) Lala Rokh is a beautiful Persian princess, the protagonist of an epic romance by poet Thomas Moore. The tale evokes the exotic East, as does the flavorful food served at this Beacon Hill gem. While the ingredients are standard to Persian cuisine, the subtle innovations – an aromatic spice here or savory herb there – set this cooking apart. Reservations recommended.

LOCAL KNOWLEDGE

BARBARA LYNCH

Barbara Lynch is a Southie native and Boston celebrity chef. She is the owner of fabulous food venues like No 9 Park (p73), B&G Oysters (p98), Sportello (p139) and Drink (p140).

➧ **How Boston dining has changed in recent years** More fine dining, more bistro food, vast improvements in wine, service and hospitality.

➧ **Favorite holdovers from yesteryear** Snap dogs from Sullivan's (p139) at Castle Island, fried clams from clam shacks in Ipswich.

➧ **What is unique about Boston cuisine** Seafood!

➧ **Where to sample seafood** B&G Oysters (p98) and Summer Shack (p118).

➧ **New trends in Boston dining** Bakeries and cafes like Volle Nolle (p59). Also, the revival of the art of the cocktail, like we are doing at Drink (p140).

➧ **Best places for foodies to shop** South End Formaggio (p106), Butcher Shop (p99) and Salumeria Italiana (p62). Louis Boston (p141) is good for gifts and kitchenware.

➧ **Best time of year to eat in Boston** Summertime is best for fresh produce, rooftop barbecues and picnics on the Esplanade (p115).

FIGS PIZZERIA $$

Map p250 (www.toddenglish.com; 42 Charles St; mains $10-20; ☺lunch & dinner; ⎘; MᴄCharles/MGH) The brainchild of celebrity chef Todd English, Figs rakes 'em in with its innovative whisper-thin pizzas. For a real treat, order the signature fig and prosciutto pizza with gorgonzola. Equally delish are the sandwiches, salads and pastas.

MOOO... STEAKHOUSE $$$

Map p250 (☏617-670-2515; www.mooorestaurant.com; 15 Beacon St; lunch $20-30, dinner $60; ☺breakfast, lunch & dinner; MᴄPark St) This super-cool, modern steakhouse presents a challenge: don't fill up on the irresistible rolls before your food arrives. You'll be glad you saved room for the meaty specialties like Kobe beef dumplings and steak tartare. For an extra decadent, carnivorous touch, steaks are served with bone-marrow butter.

SCOLLAY SQUARE AMERICAN $$

Map p250 (www.scollaysquare.com; 21 Beacon St; lunch mains $10-16, dinner mains $17-23; ☺lunch Mon-Fri, brunch Sun, dinner daily; MᴄPark St) Down the road from the former Scollay Sq, this retro restaurant hearkens back to the glory days of its namesake. Old photos and memorabilia adorn the walls, while suits sip martinis to big-band music. The classic American fare is reliably good, with the lobster mac and cheese as the perennial favorite.

ZEN SUSHI BAR & GRILL JAPANESE, SUSHI $$

Map p250 (www.zensushibar.com; 21A Beacon St; lunch mains $8-12, dinner mains $15-20; ☺lunch Mon-Sat, dinner daily; MᴄPark St) Affordable lunch specials make this a popular spot for State House staffers and other professional types. The minimalist decor and extensive menu are typical sushi-bar stuff, but the menu also features mains such as rack of lamb and soft-shell crab, as well as items cooked on the authentic Japanese stone grill.

DRINKING & NIGHTLIFE

21ST AMENDMENT PUB

Map p250 (www.21stboston.com; 150 Bowdoin St; ☺11:30am-10pm Sun-Thu, to 11pm Fri & Sat; MᴄPark St) Named for one of the most important amendments to the US Constitution, this quintessential tavern has been an ever-popular haunt for overeducated and underpaid statehouse workers to whinge about the wheels of government. The place feels especially cozy in the winter, when you'll feel pretty good about yourself as you drink a stout near the copper-hooded fireplace.

6B LOUNGE COCKTAIL BAR, CLUB

Map p250 (www.6blounge.com; 6 Beacon St; cover $5 Fri after 9:30pm; ☺dance party from 10pm Fri & Sat; MᴄPark St) Most nights of the week, this is a pleasant but innocuous cocktail bar with forgettable food. But come Friday night, the bar morphs into a wildly popular 1990s dance party, featuring the local spinning legend DJ T-Rex. Saturdays are fun too (and free), with all your favorite pop tunes from Madonna, Rick James, Michael Jackson and Wham!

BIN 26 ENOTECA   WINE BAR
Map p250 (☑617-723-5939; www.bin26.com; 26 Charles St; ◷noon-10pm; MCharles/MGH) If you are into your wine, you'll be into the Bin. Big windows overlook Charles St and wine bottles line the walls. The 60-page wine list spans the globe, including a moderately priced house wine that is bottled in Italy just for the restaurant. Staff will insist you order food (due to licensing requirements) but you won't regret sampling the simple, seasonal menu.

SEVENS   PUB
Map p250 (www.sevensalehouse.com; 77 Charles St; ◷noon-1am; MCharles/MGH) Beacon Hill's longstanding favorite neighborhood joint looks old school, with its wooden bar placed under hanging glasses, and a few comfortable booths. Service is brusque but endearing. The place serves only wine and beer, including a house brew from Harpoon. Darts, chess and sports on the tube provide the entertainment.

CHEERS   PUB
Map p250 (www.cheersboston.com; 84 Beacon St; ◷11am-1am; MArlington) We understand that this is a mandatory pilgrimage place for fans of the TV show. But be aware that the bar doesn't look like its famous TV alter ego, nor is it charming or local or 'Boston' in any way. In short, nobody knows your name. The fact that there is another outlet in Quincy Market proves our point.

⭐ ENTERTAINMENT

TOP CHOICE SHAKESPEARE ON THE COMMON   THEATER
Map p250 (www.commshakes.org; Boston Common; admission free; ◷8pm Tue-Sat, 7pm Sun Jul & Aug; MPark St) Each summer, the Commonwealth Shakespeare Company stages a major production on the Boston Common, drawing crowds for Shakespeare under the stars. Productions often appeal to the masses with a populist twist. Thus *The Taming of the Shrew*, set in a North End restaurant.

🔒 SHOPPING

There was a time when Charles St was lined with antique shops and nothing else: some historians claim that the country's antique trade began right here on Beacon Hill. There are still enough antique shops to thrill the Antiques Roadshow lover in you, but you'll also find plenty of contemporary galleries, preppy boutiques and practical shops to go along with all that old stuff.

TOP CHOICE ARTIFAKTORI VINTAGE   CLOTHING
Map p250 (www.artifaktori.com; 121 Charles St; ◷Tue-Sun; MCharles/MGH) Vintage meets Beacon Hill. Stop by this sweet spot for a choice selection of oldies-but-goodies, as well as fantastic retro-inspired designs that are brand new. The eye-popping colors and bold patterns cater to dapper men and women who are passionate about fashion from any era.

But here's a modern concept: Artifaktori combines style-conscious with eco-conscious, featuring ethically produced clothing (fairly traded or locally made with all-natural materials).

CRUSH BOUTIQUE   CLOTHING
Map p250 (www.shopcrushboutique.com; 131 Charles St; MCharles/MGH) Fashion mavens rave about this cute basement boutique on Charles St, which features both well-loved designers and up-and-coming talents. The selection of clothing is excellent, but it's the expert advice that makes this place so popular. Co-owners (and childhood BFFs) Rebecca and Laura would love to help you find something that makes you look fabulous.

BLACKSTONE'S OF BEACON HILL   GIFTS, ACCESSORIES
Map p250 (www.blackstonesbeaconhill.com; 46 Charles St; MCharles/MGH) Here's a guarantee: you will find the perfect gift for that certain someone at Blackstone's. This tiny place is crammed with classy, clever and otherwise unusual items. Highlights include the custom-designed stationary, locally made handicrafts and quirky themed souvenirs like clocks and coasters.

If none of that fits your fancy, there's always a Vera Bradley handbag.

RUBY DOOR
JEWELRY

Map p250 (www.therubydoor.com; 15 Charles St; ☺11am-5pm Mon-Sat; ⓜCharles/MGH) What will you find behind the ruby door? Gorgeous, hand-crafted jewelry, much of it featuring intriguing gemstones and unique vintage elements. Designer and owner Tracy Weiss reworks antique and vintage jewels into thoroughly modern pieces of art. There is also plenty of more affordable costume jewelry for bauble lovers. Great for browsing with no pressure to buy.

GOOD
JEWELRY, GIFTS

Map p250 (www.shopatgood.com; 88 Charles St; ⓜCharles/MGH) This tiny boutique might be intimidating, but call up your courage and go on inside. The custom-designed jewelry is nothing short of exquisite, while other gift items range from extraneous (agarwood-scented votive candle, $38) to exotic (embossed lizard handbag, $395). And one other ex- word springs to mind. Browsing is encouraged.

BEACON HILL CHOCOLATES
FOOD & DRINK

Map p250 (www.beaconhillchocolates.com; 91 Charles St; ⓜCharles/MGH) This artisanal chocolatier puts equal effort into selecting fine chocolates from around the world and designing beautiful keepsake boxes to contain them. Using decoupage to affix old postcards, photos and illustrations, the boxes are works of art even before they are filled with truffles. Pick out an image of Historic Boston as a souvenir for the sweet tooth in your life.

CIBELINE
CLOTHING, ACCESSORIES

Map p250 (www.cibelinesariano.com; 120 Charles St; ⓜCharles/MGH) Cibeline Sariano's Hepburn-inspired styles – 'classic, tailored, with a feminine twist' – include gorgeous gowns, trim jackets, fun and fresh skirts and slacks. She produces a very limited number of garments in each size, so women can enjoy wearing 'exclusive' designs. Cibeline's styles are complemented with a selection of vintage pieces and accessories by other local designers.

CORE DE VIE
CLOTHING

Map p250 (www.coredevie.com; 40 Charles St; ⓜCharles/MGH) Work that thing in the onsite studio, then reward yourself with a new outfit to show off your fit self. The main rea-

son to come to Core de Vie is its excellent, ever-renewing selection of active wear, but you'll also find versatile, comfortable clothing that you can wear in your everyday life.

EUGENE GALLERIES
ANTIQUES

Map p250 (www.eugenegalleries.com; 76 Charles St; ☺11am-6pm Mon-Sat, noon-6pm Sun; ⓜCharles/MGH) This tiny shop has a remarkable selection of antique prints and maps, especially focusing on old Boston. Follow the history of the city's development by examining 18th- and 19th-century maps; witness the filling-in of Back Bay and the greening of the city. Historic prints highlight Boston landmarks, making for excellent old-fashioned gifts.

HELEN'S LEATHER
SHOES, ACESSORIES

Map p250 (www.helensleather.com; 110 Charles St; ⓜCharles/MGH) You probably didn't realize that you would need your cowboy boots in Boston. Never fear, you can pick up a slick pair right here on Beacon Hill. (Indeed, this is the number one distributor of cowboy boots in New England.) Helen also carries stylish dress boots and work boots, as well as gorgeous jackets, classy handbags and sharp wallets and belts.

FOUR PREPPY PAWS
PET BOUTIQUE

Map p250 (www.fourpreppypaws.com; 103 Charles St; ⓜCharles/MGH) 'Chuchufli is a preppy dog... and should be dressed accordingly.' That is a real quote from Preppy Paws owner Heidi Barraza, explaining why she decided to open this upscale pet boutique. Now Chuchufli and other classy canines can choose from plaid, gingham, seersucker or solids for their collars and leashes. Also available: a handy waterproof tote bag that doubles as a doggy drink dish.

FRENCH DRESSING
LINGERIE

Map p250 (www.frenchdressinglingerie.com; 49 River St; ☺Tue-Sun; ⓜCharles/MGH) Crystal chandeliers, paisley prints and soft pink and blue hues make shopping for underwear the romantic affair that it should be. Putting the French accent in 'lingerie,' this boutique features light and lacy underthings, as well as luxurious loungewear. Great gift idea: membership in the thong-of-the-month club. (Now *that's* the gift that keeps on giving.)

MARIKA'S ANTIQUE SHOP
ANTIQUES

Map p250 (130 Charles St; ⓜCharles/MGH) More than 50 years ago, a Hungarian immigrant opened this treasure trove in Boston's antique central. Today, it is run by her grandson, who is extremely knowledgeable about his inventory. And the place still holds an excellent selection of fine collectibles – most notably jewelry, silver and porcelain.

MOXIE
SHOES, ACESSORIES

Map p250 (www.moxieboston.com; 51 Charles St; [M]Charles/MGH) 'No outfit is complete without that perfect pair of shoes.' And 'Why have one bag when you can have a collection?' These bits of wisdom are what inspired avid shopper Karen Fabbri to open a store dedicated to shoes, handbags and other accessories. She pulls it off with much aplomb, enticing shoppers with unique styles, designer labels and top-notch service.

RED WAGON & PIXIE STIX
CHILDREN

Map p250 (www.theredwagon.com; 69 Charles St; [M]Charles/MGH) If you want your little tykes to look as good as you do, stop by the Red Wagon for unique, stylish kids' clothing. Upstairs, Pixie Stix caters to 'tweens' – that awkward age between kid and teenager – doing so with cuteness *and* coolness. With bright colors and bold patterns, these fun fashions will appeal to both parent and child.

TWENTIETH CENTURY LTD
JEWELRY

Map p250 (www.boston-vintagejewelry.com; 73 Charles St; [M]Charles/MGH) Not just jewelry, but vintage jewelry, especially Bakelite, silver and art-deco designs... costume jewelry made by the great designers of yesteryear. The selection is overwhelming, with something to fit everybody's price range (eg the $10 bin for the budget-conscious). This is where to come, princess, if you need a tiara for that upcoming ball.

DEVONIA ANTIQUES
ANTIQUES

Map p250 (www.devonia-antiques.com; 15 Charles St; [M]Charles/MGH) This one-of-a-kind antique shop specializes in china and stemware from the Gilded Age (1880–1920), an era that was characterized by luxury and lavishness in dinnerware. The place is a veritable museum of hand-painted porcelain, engraved glass and gold-plated glitz.

WISH
CLOTHING

Map p250 (www.wishboston.com; 49 Charles St; [M]Charles/MGH) Some skeptics complain about the more-fashionable-than-thou attitude, but others argue that it does not detract from the way-cool women's wear at Wish. Snazzy suits and sweaters by top-end designers have price tags to match; the dress selection is superb, so it's a nice place to splurge on a special-occasion gown.

SPORTS & ACTIVITIES

TOP CHOICE **BOSTON COMMON**

FROG POND
SKATING

Map p250 (www.bostonfrogpond.com; Boston Common; adult/child admission $5/free, rental $9/5; 10am-4pm Mon, to 9pm Tue-Thu & Sun, to 10pm Fri & Sat mid-Nov–mid-Mar; [+]; [M]Park St) When temperatures drop, the Boston Common becomes an urban winter wonderland, with slipping and sliding, swirling and twirling on the Frog Pond. Skate rental, lockers and restrooms are available. Weekends are often crowded, as are weekdays around noon, as local skate fiends spend their lunch break on the ice.

FREE **BLACK HERITAGE TRAIL**
WALKING TOUR

Map p250 (www.nps.gov/boaf; tours 2pm Mon-Sat, more frequently in summer; [M]Park St) This free 1.6-mile walking tour explores the history of the abolitionist movement and African American settlement on Beacon Hill. The NPS conducts guided tours, but maps and descriptions for self-guided tours are available at the Museum of Afro-American History. Departs from the Robert Gould Shaw memorial.

GONDOLA DI VENEZIA
CRUISE

Map p250 (617-876-2800; www.bostongondolas.com; Community Boating, Charles River Esplanade; tours per couple $99-229; 2-11pm Fri-Sun Jun-Oct; [M]Charles/MGH) Make no mistake about it – the Charles River is not the Grand Canal. However, the gondolier's technique and the craftsmanship of the boat make these private gondola rides a romantic treat. Advanced reservations required.

Downtown & Waterfront

FANEUIL HALL & QUINCY MARKET & AROUND | DOWNTOWN CROSSING & FINANCIAL DISTRICT | WATERFRONT

Neighborhood Top Five

1 Soaking up the sun, exploring an old fort, splashing in the sea, munching on wild berries, spying on the resident birds and bunnies, and enjoying the seascape from the **Boston Harbor Islands** (p80).

2 Taking a **whale-watching boat** (p92) out to Stellwagen Bank to spy on whales, dolphins and other sea life.

3 Remembering the first violent confrontation of the American Revolution at the **site of the Boston Massacre** (p84).

4 Frolicking with the fish at the **New England Aquarium** (p83).

5 Eating, drinking, shopping and general merry-making at **Faneuil Hall & Quincy Market** (p85, p88), Boston's oldest marketplace.

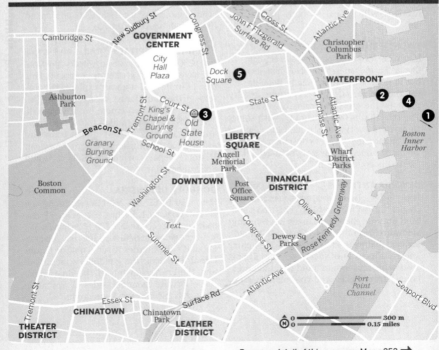

For more detail of this area, see Map p252 ➡

Explore Downtown & Waterfront

Almost every visitor will visit this neighborhood while walking the Freedom Trail, from King's Chapel to the Old South Meeting House, from the Old State House to Faneuil Hall & Quincy Market. Indeed, the marketplace is one of the most visited tourist sites in the country. Even though it's basically a shopping mall (but a *historic* shopping mall!), it's a fun stop to admire the public art, cheer on the street performers and soak up the festive atmosphere.

The marketplace is in stark contrast to the neighborhood's interior streets around Downtown Crossing and the Financial District. This is the Boston of the work-a-day world: old-fashioned shops have been displaced by national chains and luxury hotels cater to business travelers. White-collar workers take lunch breaks at speedy sandwich shops, but after hours the streets are eerily empty.

Along the waterfront, the dismantling of the Central Artery has meant that the call of seagulls and the lapping of waves no longer compete with the roar of the cars. Instead, pedestrians can stroll across the Wharf District parks to the harbor, enjoying the greenery and admiring the Rings Fountain along the way. The focal point of the waterfront is the excellent New England Aquarium. From Long Wharf, you can catch the ferry out to the Boston Harbor Islands for a day of berry picking, beachcombing or sunbathing. Harbor cruises and trolley tours also depart from these docks, while seafood restaurants and outdoor cafes line the shore.

It's basically tourist central, and with good reason. With the sun sparkling off the water and the boats bobbing at their moorings, it's hard to resist this city by the sea.

Local Life

→ **Lunch Break** Working Boston's favorite lunch spots are Chacarero and Sam La Grassa's (p89). If you don't mind the grit, Falafel King (p89) is a winner.

→ **Happy Hour** There are still a few downtown bars that feel like neighborhood places, mainly Mr Dooley's Boston Tavern and Silvertone (p90).

Getting There & Away

→ **Metro** To reach Faneuil Hall & Quincy Market, take the green, orange or blue line to Haymarket, Government Center or State. The Aquarium (blue) and State (orange or blue) stops have waterfront access. Downtown Crossing is at the junction of the red and orange lines; Park St Station, just west of here, sit on both red and green.

→ **Boat** City Water Taxi stops at Long Wharf on the waterfront, while the MBTA water shuttle runs from Long Wharf to Charlestown Navy Yard.

Lonely Planet's Top Tip

If you are following the red brick road, consider purchasing the Freedom Trail Ticket (adult/child $13/3), which includes admission to the Old State House, the Old South Meeting House and the Paul Revere House.

Best Places to Eat

→ Chacarero (p89)
→ Casa Razdora (p89)
→ Marliave (p89)

For reviews, see p88 →

Best Places to Drink

→ Woodward (p90)
→ Silvertone (p90)
→ Thinking Cup (p90)
→ RumBa (p90)

For reviews, see p89 →

Best Historic Buildings

→ Old State House (p84)
→ Faneuil Hall (p85)
→ Custom House (p87)

For reviews, see p85 →

TOP SIGHTS
BOSTON HARBOR ISLANDS

Boston Harbor is sprinkled with 34 islands, many of which are open for trail walking, bird-watching, fishing and swimming. The Boston Harbor Islands offer a range of ecosystems – sandy beaches, rocky cliffs, fresh and saltwater marshes and forested trails – only 45 minutes from downtown Boston. Since the massive, multimillion-dollar cleanup of Boston Harbor in the mid-1990s, the islands are one of the city's most magnificent natural assets.

A Day on the Harbor Islands

Hop on the first ferry at 9am to Georges Island, where you can spend about two hours exploring Fort Warren. After lunch, take the shuttle to Lovells Island to catch some rays on the otherwise empty beach and cool off in the refreshing Atlantic waters. Spend a few hours on Lovells' rocky shores, but don't miss the afternoon shuttle to Grape Island. Here you can tag along on the ranger-led 'wild edibles' tour, or find your own stash of wild berries. Take the last shuttle (around 4:30pm) back to Georges Island to catch the ferry to the mainland. Don't try to visit more than two or three islands in one day: you'll end up spending all your time riding on or waiting for boats.

Georges Island

Georges Island is the transportation hub for the islands, as the inter-island shuttle leaves from here. It is also the site of Fort Warren, a 19th-century fort and Civil War prison. While National Park Service (NPS) rangers give guided tours of the fort and there is a small museum, it is largely abandoned, with many dark tunnels, creepy corners and magnificent lookouts to discover. The extensive picnic area attracts large groups of kids, as do the fam-

DON'T MISS

➡ Exploring Fort Warren

➡ Hiking the trails on Spectacle Island

➡ Swimming and sunning at Lovells or Bumpkin Beaches

➡ Climbing to the top of First Light

PRACTICALITIES

➡ www.bostonislands. com

➡ admission free

➡ 🚢 Boston's Best Cruises from Long Wharf

ily programs like children's theater and family fun days. This is one of the only islands with facilities like a snack bar and rest rooms.

Spectacle Island

A Harbor Island hub, Spectacle Island has a large marina, a solar-powered visitors center, a healthy snack bar and supervised beaches. Five miles of walking trails provide access to a 157ft peak overlooking the harbor. Special events include live music on weekend afternoons and weekly clam bakes on the beach, hosted by Jasper White's Summer Shack (p118). Spectacle Island is relatively close to the city and a ferry runs here directly from Long Wharf (hourly 9am-5pm daily, to 6pm Saturday and Sunday early May to early September).

Lovells Island

Two deadly shipwrecks may bode badly for seafarers, but that doesn't seem to stop recreational boaters, swimmers and sunbathers from lounging on Lovells' long rocky beach. Some of the former uses of Lovells are evident: European settlers used the island as a rabbit run, and descendent bunnies are still running this place; Fort Standish dates from WWI but has yet to be excavated. With facilities for camping and picnicking, Lovells is one of the most popular Harbor Island destinations.

Bumpkin Island

This small island has served many purposes over the years, first farming then fish drying and smelting. In 1900 it was the site of a children's hospital, but it was taken over for navy training during WWI. You can still explore the remains of a stone farmhouse and the hospital. The beaches are not the best for swimming, as they are slate and seashell. A network of trails leads through fields overgrown with wildflowers. It's one of three islands with camping facilities.

Grape Island

Grape Island is rich with fruity goodness – not grapes, but raspberries, bayberries and elderberries, all growing wild amid the scrubby wooded trails. The wild fruit attracts abundant bird life. Park rangers lead an interesting 'wild edibles' tour highlighting the fruits of the earth. Grape Island is also the starting point for twice-daily sea-kayak outings led by park rangers. Unlike many of the Harbor Islands, Grape Island has no remains of forts or military prisons; but during the Revolutionary War, it was the site of a skirmish over hay, known as the Battle of Grape Island.

TRANSPORT

Boston's Best Cruises (p175) offers a seasonal ferry service from Long Wharf, which reaches most of the islands. Purchase a round-trip ticket to Georges Island or Spectacle Island (adult/child $14/8), where you catch the interisland water shuttle to the smaller islands. The interisland shuttle runs several times a day, but not every hour. Make sure you check the schedule in advance and plan your day accordingly.

Boston Logan Airport sits on land that used to be four islands in Boston Harbor: Apple, Bird, Governors and Noodles Islands.

EATING & DRINKING

Georges and Spectacle Islands have snack shacks (10am-5pm) but there is no food or water on the other islands. Pack a picnic!

Fort Warren is one of the most important Civil War sites in New England. See www.bostonharborislands.org/civil-war to find out about special events commemorating the 150th anniversary.

Peddocks Island

One of the largest Harbor Islands, Peddocks consists of four headlands connected by sandbars. Hiking trails wander through marsh, pond and coastal environs. But the dominant feature of Peddocks Island is the remains of Fort Andrews, a large facility with more than 20 buildings. Peddocks' proximity to the mainland ensured its use as a military stronghold, from the Revolutionary War right through WWII. In 2011 the ferry service to Peddocks was suspended due to damage from Hurricane Irene, but it's expected to resume when the dock is repaired.

Little Brewster Island

Little Brewster is the country's oldest light station and site of the iconic Boston Light (pictured on p80). Although the first lighthouse was built on this spot in 1715, it was demolished by the British in the revolution; today's lighthouse dates from 1783. To visit **Little Brewster** (☑617-223-8666; www.bostonharborislands.org/tour-lighthouse; adult/child/senior $39/29/35; ⊙10am & 1:30pm Fri-Sun late Jun–mid-Oct; ☒Fan Pier), you must take an organized tour (reservations recommended). Learn about Boston's maritime history during a one-hour sail around the harbor, then spend two hours exploring the island. Adventurous travelers can climb the 76 steps to the top of the light for a close-up view of the rotating light and a far-off view of the city skyline. Tours depart from Moakley Courthouse Dock in the Seaport District.

Deer Island

Funny thing about **Deer Island** (☑617-660-7607; www.mwra.com; ⊙dawn-dusk): it's not technically an island. A hurricane in 1938 created the causeway that now connects the 'island' to the mainland, so the Harbor Express boats do not go here (it's accessible only by car). The other funny thing about Deer Island is that it is dominated by a gigantic sewage treatment plant, which is one of the key factors in the clean-up of Boston Harbor. The facility is surrounded by 60 acres of parkland, with 5 miles of trails. Tours of the waste water treatment facility are also available, with advance arrangements.

Thompson Island

Thompson Island was settled as early as 1626 by a Scotsman, David Thompson, who set up a trading post to do business with the Neponset Indians. Today the island is privately owned and inhabited by **Thompson Island Outward Bound** (☑617-328-3900; www.thompsonisland.org; ⊙noon-5pm Sun Jun-Aug), a nonprofit organization that develops fun and challenging physical adventures, especially for training and developing leadership skills. As such, the public can explore its 200-plus acres only on Sunday, when it's wonderful for walking, fishing and birding. A dedicated ferry leaves from EDIC Pier in the Seaport District; see the website for details.

World's End

Not exactly an island, **World's End** (www.thetrustees.org; 250 Martin's Lane, Hingham; adult/child $5/free; ⊙8am-dusk year-round) is a 251-acre peninsula that was originally designed by Frederick Law Olmsted for residential development in 1889. Carriage paths were laid out and trees were planted, but the houses were never built. Instead, wide grassy meadows attract butterflies and grass-nesting birds. Over the years the area escaped proposals for development as a UN headquarters and a nuclear power plant, and today it is managed by the Trustees of Reservations, which guarantees continued serenity and beauty. The four-plus miles of tree-lined carriage paths are perfect for walking, mountain-biking or cross-country skiing – download a map from the Trustees website. It is accessible by car from Hingham.

TOP SIGHTS
NEW ENGLAND AQUARIUM

This giant fishbowl, teeming with sea creatures of all sizes, shapes and colors, was the first step Boston took to reconnecting the city and the sea. The main attraction is a three-story cylindrical saltwater tank, which swirls with more than 600 species great and small, including turtles, sharks and eels. At the base of the tank the penguin pool is home to three species of fun-loving penguins. Side exhibits explore the lives and habitats of other underwater oddities, including exhibits on ethereal jellyfish and exotic sea dragons.

The 3-D Simons IMAX Theater (p91) features films with aquatic themes. The aquarium also organizes whale-watching (p92) cruises. Combination tickets are available.

Most of the aquarium's 1st floor is occupied by an enormous penguin exhibit, home to more than 80 birds. Throughout the day, visitors can see live demonstrations and feedings.

Harbor seals frolic in a large observation tank near the aquarium entrance, while the inside facility is home to northern fur seals. Both groups of pinnipeds put on an entertaining show without much prodding. The open-air Marine Mammal Center is set up for daily training demonstrations, when the fur seals show off their skills in shaking hands, rolling over and playing dead.

The awesome Shark & Ray Touch Tank recreates a mangrove swamp teeming with Atlantic rays, cownose rays, bonnethead sharks and epaulette sharks. The huge tank is at waist-level, which allows visitors to dip a hand in and feel the smooth skin of the sea creatures sliding past.

DON'T MISS

➡ The magical Leafy Sea Dragon
➡ The ethereal Moon Jelly
➡ Shark & Ray Touch Tank
➡ Training demonstration at the Marine Mammal Center

PRACTICALITIES

➡ Map p252
➡ www.neaq.org
➡ Central Wharf
➡ adult/child/senior $23/16/21
➡ ⊙9am-5pm Mon-Thu, to 6pm Fri-Sun, open 1hr later Jul & Aug
➡ P
➡ M Aquarium

TOP SIGHTS
OLD STATE HOUSE & BOSTON MASSACRE SITE

Dating to 1713, making it Boston's oldest surviving public building, the Old State House is where the Massachusetts Assembly used to debate the issues of the day before the revolution. It occupies a once prominent spot at the top of State St (then known as King St), which was Boston's main thoroughfare. The building is best known for its balcony, from where the Declaration of Independence was first read to Bostonians in 1776.

Inside, the Old State House contains a small museum of revolutionary memorabilia, with videos and multimedia presentations about the Boston Massacre. An informative exhibit *From Colony to Commonwealth* utilizes audio presentations and items from the Bostonian Society's collection to trace the most important events of the independence movement. Upstairs, a hands-on interactive exhibit is designed for children.

Directly in front of the Old State House, encircled by cobblestones, the **Boston Massacre Site** (Map p252; cnr State & Devonshire Sts; Ⓜ State) marks the spot where the first blood was shed for the American independence movement. On March 5, 1770, an angry mob of colonists swarmed the British soldiers guarding the State House. Samuel Adams, John Hancock and about 40 other protesters hurled snow-balls, rocks and insults. Thus provoked, the soldiers fired into the crowd and killed five townspeople, including Crispus Attucks, a former slave. The incident sparked enormous anti-British sentiment. Paul Revere helped fan the flames by widely disseminating an engraving that depicted the scene as an unmitigated slaughter. Interestingly, John Adams and Josiah Quincy – both of whom opposed the heavy-handed authoritarian British rule – defended the accused soldiers in court, and seven of the nine were acquitted.

DON'T MISS

→ *From Colony to Commonwealth* audio tour

→ Paul Revere's engraving of the Boston Massacre

→ Boston Massacre Site

PRACTICALITIES

→ Map p252

→ www.boston history.org

→ 206 Washington St

→ adult/child/senior & student $7.50/3/6

→ ◷9am-5pm

→ Ⓜ State

◉ SIGHTS

◉ Faneuil Hall & Quincy Market & Around

Historic Faneuil Hall, along with the three long granite buildings that make up Quincy Market, served as the center of the city's produce and meat industry for almost 150 years. In the 1970s the old buildings were redeveloped into today's touristy, festive shopping and eating center, so it still serves its original purpose, albeit with all the modern trappings.

OLD STATE HOUSE   HISTORIC BUILDING
See p84.

FREE **FANEUIL HALL**   HISTORIC BUILDING
Map p252 (www.faneuilhall.com; Congress St; admission free; ◷9am-5pm; ⓂHaymarket or Aquarium) 'Those who cannot bear free speech had best go home,' said Wendell Phillips. 'Faneuil Hall is no place for slavish hearts.' Indeed, this public meeting place was the site of so much rabble-rousing that it earned the nickname the 'Cradle of Liberty.'

Although Faneuil Hall was supposed to be exclusively for local issues, the Sons of Liberty called many meetings here, informing public opinion about their objections to British taxation without representation. In December of 1773 meetings concerning the controversial consignment of tea that had recently arrived in Boston Harbor were drawing so many townspeople that they had to move to the larger Old South Meeting House (p87). In later years Faneuil Hall was a forum for meetings about abolition, women's suffrage and war.

The brick colonial building – topped with the beloved grasshopper weather vane – was constructed in 1740 at the urging of Boston benefactor and merchant Peter Faneuil. In 1805 Charles Bulfinch enlarged the building enclosed the 1st-floor market and designed the 2nd-floor meeting space, where public ceremonies are still held today. It's normally open to the public, who can hear about the building's history from NPS rangers. On the 3rd floor the Ancient & Honorable Artillery Co of Massachusetts, which was chartered in 1638, maintains a peculiar collection of antique firearms, political mementos and curious artifacts.

BLACKSTONE BLOCK   HISTORIC STREET
Map p252 (cnr Union & Hanover Sts; ⓂHaymarket) Bounded by Union, Hanover, Blackstone and North Sts, and named after Boston's first settler, this tiny warren of streets dates back to the 17th and 18th centuries.

Established in 1826, the Union Oyster House (p88) is Boston's oldest restaurant. Around the corner in Creek Sq, the c 1767 **Ebenezer Hancock House** was the home of John Hancock's brother. At the base of the shop next door, the 1737 **Boston Stone** served as the terminus for measuring distances to and from 'the Hub.' (The State House dome now serves this purpose.)

NEW ENGLAND HOLOCAUST MEMORIAL   MEMORIAL
Map p248 (www.nehm.org; btwn Union & Congress Sts; ⓂHaymarket) Constructed in 1995, the six luminescent glass columns of the New England Holocaust Memorial are engraved with six million numbers, representing those killed in the Holocaust. Each tower – with smoldering coals sending plumes of steam up through the glass corridors – represents a different Nazi death camp. The memorial sits along the Freedom Trail, a sobering reminder of its larger meaning.

CITY HALL PLAZA   SQUARE
Map p252 (City Hall Plaza; ⓂGovernment Center) City Hall Plaza is a cold 56-acre concrete plaza surrounded by government office buildings. Occupying the site of the former Scollay Square, the urban focal point was supposed to be a model of innovation and modernization when it was built in the 1960s. But it has been much maligned in recent years, topping at least one list of the world's ugliest buildings.

Designed by IM Pei (who also designed the Kennedy Library), City Hall Plaza is home to the fortress-like Boston City Hall and the twin towers of the John F Kennedy Federal Building. The plaza's high points are the gracefully curved brick **Sears Crescent** (Map p252; cnr Court & Tremont Sts), one of the few buildings that remains from the Scollay Sq days, and the sweeping curve of the modern **Center Plaza** (Map p252; Cambridge St), which mirrors Sears Crescent. The plaza sometimes hosts public gatherings and summertime performances.

STEAMING TEA KETTLE

The steaming kettle on Sears Crescent has been a Boston landmark since 1873, when it was hung over the door of the Oriental Tea Co at 57 Court St. The teashop held a contest to determine how much tea the giant kettle might hold. The answer – awarded with a chest of premium tea – was 227 gallons, two quarts, one pint and three gills.

The tea kettle was relocated to its current location on the western tip of the Sears Crescent building in 1967, when 'urban renewal' swept this neighborhood. Tea drinkers are grateful that this icon of old Boston was saved, although many are miffed that it now marks the spot of a Starbucks.

⊙ Downtown Crossing & Financial District

KING'S CHAPEL & BURYING GROUND
CHURCH, CEMETERY

Map p252 (www.kings-chapel.org; 58 Tremont St; self-guided tour $2 donation, Bells & Bones tours $5-8; ☉10am-4pm Mon-Sat & 1:30pm-4pm Sun Jun-Aug, Sat & Sun only Sep-May; Ⓜ Park St) Bostonians were not pleased when the original Anglican church was erected on this site in 1688. (Remember, it was the Anglicans – the Church of England – whom the Puritans were fleeing.) The granite chapel standing today was built in 1754, while the adjacent burying ground is the oldest in the city.

King's Chapel features some unusual architectural features, or non-features as it were. Most notably, funds ran out before a spire could be added. So if the church seems to be missing something, it is. The chapel houses the largest bell ever made by Paul Revere, as well as a historic organ.

Request a brochure to take a self-guided tour of the church's architectural and historical highlights. In addition to the self-guided tour, visitors are invited on the Bells & Bones tour, which ascends into the bell tower to admire Paul Revere's work and descends into the crypt to wander among 250-year-old remains.

Besides the bi-weekly services (Wednesday and Sunday), recitals are held here every week (Tuesday at 12:15pm).

The church was built on a corner of the city cemetery because the Puritans refused to allow the Anglicans to use any other land. As a result, these are some of the city's oldest headstones, including one that dates to 1623. Famous graves include John Winthrop, the first governor of the fledgling Massachusetts Bay Colony; William Dawes, who rode with Paul Revere; and Mary Chilton, the first European woman to set foot in Plymouth.

OLD CITY HALL
HISTORIC SITE

Map p252 (www.oldcityhall.com; 45 School St; Ⓜ State) This monumental French Second Empire building occupies a historic spot. Out front, a plaque commemorates the site of the first public school, Boston Latin, founded in 1635 and still operational in Fenway. The hopscotch sidewalk mosaic, *City Carpet,* marks the spot where Benjamin Franklin, Ralph Waldo Emerson and Charles Bulfinch were educated.

Statues of Benjamin Franklin, founding father, and Josiah Quincy, second mayor of Boston, stand inside the courtyard. They are accompanied by a life-sized replica of a donkey, symbol of the Democratic Party. ('Why the donkey?' you wonder. Read the plaque to find out.) Two bronze footprints 'stand in opposition.'

The building is now office space with one fancy restaurant.

OLD CORNER BOOKSTORE
HISTORIC BUILDING

Map p252 (cnr School & Washington Sts; Ⓜ Downtown Crossing) In the 19th century, this historic house was leased to a bookseller, Carter & Hendlee. This was the first of nine bookshops and publishing companies that would occupy the spot, making it a breeding ground for literary and philosophical ideas. The most illustrious was Ticknor & Fields, publisher of books by Thoreau, Emerson, Hawthorne, Longfellow and Harriet Beecher Stowe.

In the earliest days of Boston history, this was the site of the home of Anne Hutchinson, the religious dissident who was expelled from the Massachusetts Bay colony and co-founded the Rhode Island colony. The current brick building dates to 1718, when it served as a pharmacy and residence. Today the storefront houses a fast food restaurant, which seems somewhat less lofty than its earlier incarnations.

OLD SOUTH
MEETING HOUSE
HISTORIC BUILDING

Map p252 (www.oldsouthmeetinghouse.org; 310 Washington St; adult/child/senior & student $6/1/5; ☺9:30am-5pm Apr-Oct, 10am-4pm Nov-Mar; ⓘ; ⓜDowntown Crossing) 'No tax on tea!' That was the decision on December 16, 1773, when 5000 angry colonists gathered here to protest British taxes, leading to the Boston Tea Party. The graceful meeting house is still a gathering place for discussion, although there's less rabble-rousing now. Instead, it hosts concert and lecture series, as well as reenactments and other historical programs.

This brick meeting house, with its soaring steeple, was also used as a church house back in the day. In fact, Ben Franklin was baptized here. Which is why he found it so abhorrent when – after the Tea Party – British soldiers used the building for a stable and riding practice. The Old South congregation moved to a new building in Back Bay in 1875, when Ralph Waldo Emerson and Julia Ward Howe gathered support to convert the church into a museum.

When you visit today, you can check out an exhibit about the history of the building and listen to an audio of the historic pre–Tea Party meeting. Kids will be engaged by activity kits and scavenger hunts designed for their age groups.

◉ Waterfront

BOSTON HARBOR ISLANDS
PARK

See p80.

NEW ENGLAND AQUARIUM
AQUARIUM

See p83.

CUSTOM HOUSE
MUSEUM

Map p252 (www.marriott.com; 3 McKinley Sq; observation deck $2; ☺observation deck 2pm Sat-Thu; ⓜAquarium) Begun in 1837, the lower portion of the Custom House resembles a Greek temple. But the federal government wanted something grander, so in 1913 it exempted itself from local height restrictions and financed a 500ft tower. Nowadays there are many taller buildings, but the 22ft illuminated clock makes this gem the most recognizable part of the city skyline.

One of Boston's first skyscrapers, the Custom House now houses a Marriott hotel. But that doesn't mean you have to dole out big

DOWNTOWN & WATERFRONT SIGHTS

WORTH A DETOUR

ROSE KENNEDY GREENWAY

Now that the Big Dig is complete, Bostonians have something new to talk about. The infamous underground construction project has had major implications for the city above ground, reclaiming about 27 acres of industrial wasteland for parks and civic plazas. Where the hulking Central Artery once created barriers and shadows, Bostonians are now enjoying a tree-lined open space, known as the **Rose Kennedy Greenway** (www.rosekennedygreenway.org).

➡ **North End Parks** A portion of this park is being redeveloped by the Armenian Heritage Foundation to pay tribute to the immigrant experience.

➡ **Boston Museum** The city had to scrap plans to build a museum on the Greenway itself (apparently it's tricky to balance fancy architecture above eight lanes of moving traffic), but there is still a movement to build this state-of-the-art museum on Parcel 9, adjacent to Blackstone Block and overlooking the North End Parks.

➡ **Custom Carousel** Coming soon: a one-of-a-kind carousel designed by local artist Jeffrey Briggs, with help from local school children.

➡ **Boston Harbor Islands Pavilion** Want more information about the Boston Harbor Islands? Stop by this seasonal information center (p228).

➡ **Wharf District Parks** Between Atlantic Ave and High St, these parks define the landscape where the city meets the sea. The highlight is the light-enhanced Ring Fountains, while the 'Great Room' is an open-air gathering space,

➡ **Dewey Sq Parks** Between Oliver St and Summer St, these parks host food vendors and farmers markets, making them a popular lunch spot for the working world.

➡ **Chinatown Park** Between Chinatown and the Leather District, this new Asian-accented park was the first section of the Greenway to open in 2007.

bucks to stay here or to appreciate the building's history and aesthetics. The 1st-floor rotunda, a work of art in itself, also houses a small exhibit of maritime art and artifacts from Salem's Peabody Essex Museum (p175). Even better, the public is welcome to enjoy the spectacular views from the 26th-floor **observation deck** when weather permits.

EATING

✗ Fanueil Hall & Quincy Markets & Around

Faneuil Hall and its environs are packed with touristy places touting baked beans, live lobsters and other Boston specialties. It's hard to get off the beaten track, but that doesn't mean you won't find some fun, funky and delicious places to eat.

QUINCY MARKET
FOOD COURT $

Map p252 (off Congress & North Sts; ⊘10am-9pm Mon-Sat, noon-6pm Sun; ⚡♿; ⓂHaymarket) Northeast of the intersection of Congress and State Sts, this food hall offers a variety of places under one roof: the place is packed with about 20 restaurants and 40 food stalls. Choose from chowder, bagels, Indian, Greek,

baked goods and ice cream, and take a seat at one of the tables in the central rotunda.

UNION OYSTER HOUSE
SEAFOOD $$

Map p252 (www.unionoysterhouse.com; 41 Union St; ⊘lunch & dinner; ⓂHaymarket) Ye olde Union Oyster House, the oldest restaurant in Boston, has been serving seafood in this historic red-brick building since 1826. Countless history-makers have propped themselves up at this bar, including Daniel Webster and John F Kennedy. Apparently JFK used to order the lobster bisque, but the raw bar is the real draw here. Order a dozen on the half-shell and watch the shucker work his magic.

DURGIN PARK
AMERICAN $$

Map p252 (www.durgin-park.com; North Market, Faneuil Hall; lunch mains $9-15, dinner mains $15-30; ⊘lunch & dinner; ♿; ⓂHaymarket) Known for no-nonsense service and sawdust on the floorboards, Durgin Park hasn't changed much since it opened in 1827. Nor has the menu, which features New England standards like prime rib, fish chowder, chicken pot pie and Boston baked beans. Be prepared to make friends with the other parties seated at your table.

BERTUCCI'S
PIZZERIA $$

Map p252 (www.bertuccis.com; 22 Merchants Row; mains $8-18; ⊘lunch & dinner; ⚡♿; ⓂAquarium or State) Despite its nationwide expansion, Ber-

---

LOCAL KNOWLEDGE

TO MARKET, TO MARKET

➡ Touch the produce at **Haymarket** (Map p252; Blackstone & Hanover Sts; ⊘7am-5pm Fri & Sat) and you risk the wrath of the vendors ('They're a friggin' dollar – quit looking at the strawberries and just buy 'em!'). But nowhere in the city matches these prices on ripe-and-ready fruits and vegetables. And nowhere matches Haymarket for local charm. Operated by the Haymarket Vendors Association, this outdoor market is an outlet for discount produce that was purchased from wholesalers.

➡ With the growth of the locavore movement, there has been a push for a daily farmers market that would give shoppers access to fresh locally grown produce. As it is envisioned, the **Boston Public Market** (www.bostonpublicmarket.org) will offer seasonal produce, fresh seafood, meats and poultry from local farms, artisan cheeses and dairy products, maple syrup and other sweets. The goal is to create a market where restaurateurs, residents and tourists can shop every day and be assured of finding fresh, high-quality items made right here in New England.

➡ After years of planning, the conversion of Parcel 7 – a currently vacant building that sits between Blackstone Block and the Rose Kennedy Greenway – is just started to come to fruition. The location is just a few steps from Haymarket, which will continue to operate, and a few more steps from Faneuil Hall and Quincy Market, which is the city's historic marketplace. As such, the new public market will anchor a vibrant 'market district.' Work on Parcel 7 is supposed to begin in 2012.

tucci's remains a Boston favorite for brick-oven pizza. The location near Faneuil Hall Marketplace is one of several in the Boston area. Lunch is a real bargain: all mains come with unlimited salad and fresh, hot rolls.

✖ Downtown Crossing & Financial District

CHACARERO
SANDWICHES $

Map p252 (www.chacarero.com; 101 Arch St; breakfast $4-6, lunch $7-10; ☺8am-6pm; ⓂDowntown Crossing) A *chacarero* is a traditional Chilean sandwich made with grilled chicken or beef, Muenster cheese, fresh tomatoes, guacamole and the surprise ingredient – steamed green beans. Stuffed into homemade bread, the sandwiches are the hands-down favorite for lunch around Downtown.

CASA RAZDORA
ITALIAN $

Map p252 (www.casarazdora.com; 115 Water St; mains $6-10; ☺lunch Mon-Fri; ✉; ⓂState) The line is usually out the door, but it's worth the wait for amazing Italian food, just like your nonna made. Pick a pasta (all made fresh on the premises) and top it with the delicious sauce of your choosing. Or select one of the chef's mouthwatering daily specials. Seats are limited, so snag one if you can!

MARLIAVE
AMERICAN, FRENCH $$

Map p252 (www.marliave.com; 10 Bosworth St; sandwiches $12-15, mains $18-28; ☺lunch & dinner; ✉; ⓂPark St) A French immigrant, Henry Marliave first opened this restaurant way back in 1885. After a recent rehab, the Marliave has reopened with all of its vintage architectural quirks still intact, from the mosaic floor to the tin ceilings. The black-and-white photos on the wall add to the old-Boston ambience, as do the cleverly named drinks (Molasses Flood, anyone?).

Note that the downstairs area feels more historically authentic, but the glass-enclosed upstairs has a unique view of the surrounding neighborhood.

SAM LA GRASSA'S
DELI $

Map p252 (www.samlagrassas.com; 44 Province St; sandwiches $11; ☺lunch Mon-Fri; ♿; ⓂDowntown Crossing) Step up to the counter and place your order for one of Sam La Grassa's signature sandwiches, then find a spot at the crowded communal table. You won't be disappointed by the famous Romanian pastrami or the 'fresh from the pot' corned beef. All of the sandwiches are so well stuffed that they can be tricky to eat, which is part of the fun.

FALAFEL KING
MIDDLE EASTERN $

Map p252 (http://falafelkingwinterstreet.com; 48 Winter St; mains $5-7; ☺11am-8pm Mon-Fri, 11am-4pm Sat; ✉; ⓂDowntown Crossing) Two words: free falafels. That's right, everyone gets a little free sample before ordering. There is no disputing that this carry-out spot is indeed the falafel king of Boston. The sandwiches are fast, delicious and cheap. Besides the namesake falafel, the King sells *shawarma* and shish kebab made from the meat of your choice, as well as many vegetarian delights.

KO PRIME
STEAKHOUSE $$$

Map p252 (✆617-772-5821; www.koprimeboston.com; 90 Tremont St; mains $26-40; ☺lunch Mon-Fri, dinner daily; ⓂPark St) If you are not getting enough red meat in your diet, Ken Oringer has come to the rescue with this too-cool-for-cow steak house, featuring 10 different kinds of steak, plus other meaty delights such as bone marrow, seared foie gras and Kobe beef tartare, all of which seem to leave the guests craving more.

With slick leather furniture and hip Holstein-print details, this is a sophisticated, stylish (and sustainable!) take on a steak house.

✖ Waterfront

LEGAL SEA FOODS
SEAFOOD $$

Map p252 (www.legalseafoods.com; 255 State St; lunch $8-15, dinner $16-24; ☺lunch & dinner; ♿; ⓂAquarium) Running with the motto 'If it isn't fresh, it isn't Legal,' this Boston establishment indeed serves top-of-the-line seafood – broiled, grilled or fried – and invariably draws a satisfied crowd.

🍷 DRINKING & NIGHTLIFE

After the department store at Downtown Crossing locks up for the night, the street life quiets considerably. There are a cluster of bars around Faneuil Hall and Blackstone Block but most of them actively cater to the tourist crowd and

have an underwhelming, generic vibe. Embedded nearby are some perennial favorites, some of them quite crowded on weekends.

♥ Faneuil Hall & Quincy Market & Around

WOODWARD   COCKTAIL BAR

Map p252 (www.woodwardatames.com; 1 Court; Ⓜ State) See and be seen at this 'modern tavern' in the luxurious Ames Hotel. Choose from a long list of fancy cocktails, many of which are custom-designed by in-house cocktail experts. Thus, the Tea Party (vodka, Earl Grey, ginger beer, lemon) and other unique concoctions. The food here is also rather sophisticated, with lots of seafood and seasonal vegetables.

♥ Downtown Crossing & Financial District

🍴THINKING CUP   CAFE

Map p252 (www.thinkingcup.com; 165 Tremont St; ⊘7am-10pm Mon-Thu, to 11pm Fri-Sun; Ⓜ Boylston) There are a few things that make the Thinking Cup special. One is the French hot chocolate – ooh la la. Another is the Stumptown Coffee, the Portland brew that has earned accolades from coffee-drinkers around the country. But the best thing? It's across from the Boston Common, making it a perfect stop for a post-skating warm-up.

SILVERTONE   BAR

Map p252 (www.silvertonedowntown.com; 69 Bromfield St; ⊘11:30am-midnight; Ⓜ Park St) Black-and-white photos and retro advertising posters create a nostalgic atmosphere at this still-trendy pub and grill. The old-fashioned comfort food is always satisfying (the mac and cheese comes highly recommended), as is the cold beer drawn from the tap. The only downside is that the service suffers when the place gets crowded – and it does get crowded.

GOOD LIFE   NIGHTCLUB

Map p252 (www.goodlifebar.com; 28 Kingston St; cover $5; ⊘11:30am-2am Mon-Fri, 6pm-2am Sat; Ⓜ Boylston) The Good Life means a lot of things to a lot of people - solid lunch option, after-work hangout etc. But the top reason to come to the Good Life is to get your groove on. Two bars on two floors, and

great DJs spinning the tunes. Don't miss the monthly Middle School Dance; it's guaranteed to bring back memories.

MR DOOLEY'S BOSTON TAVERN   IRISH PUB

Map p252 (www.somerspubs.com; 77 Broad St; ⊘11:30am-2am; Ⓜ State) With Irish bands playing traditional tunes from Friday to Sunday and a decent list of appropriate beers, this cozy bar is one of the best bets in the area. Sit in a booth and linger over a copy of the *Irish Immigrant* or *Boston Irish Reporter* to learn about current events on the other side of the Atlantic.

LAST HURRAH   HOTEL BAR

Map p252 (www.omnihotels.com; 60 School St; ⊘11:30am-12:30am Mon-Fri, 4:30-11:30pm Sat; Ⓜ Park St) It's now named for the 1956 novel about former Boston mayor James Michael Curley, but the beautiful lobby bar of the Omni Parker House hotel was a hallowed haunt for Boston's 19th-century intelligentsia and politicians. Enjoy a dish of hot nuts and drink a bourbon at this throwback to Old Boston.

ALLEY BAR   GAY BAR

Map p252 (www.thealleybar.com; 275 Washington St; Ⓜ Downtown Crossing) If you can find this secret spot, you will be welcomed in, no matter if you are petite, effeminate (or female) or even straight. This place is known as a 'bear bar,' but most of these big gruff guys are friendly – very friendly. Enjoy the cheap beer and laidback atmosphere (which sometimes translates into slow service).

UMBRIA PRIME   NIGHTCLUB

Map p252 (www.umbriaristorante.com; 295 Franklin St; cover $20; ⊘10pm-2am Fri-Sat; Ⓜ State) On weekends, the upper floors of this Italian restaurant are transformed into a swank nightclub, featuring plush couches, crowded dance floors, a vodka lounge and a great line-up of DJs. An international designer crowd lines up, starting around midnight. Go online to get yourself on the guestlist and look sharp. Free admission if you eat at the restaurant.

♥ Waterfront

🍴RUMBA   COCKTAIL LOUNGE

Map p252 (www.intercontinentalboston.com; 501 Atlantic Ave; Ⓜ South Station) Not *Rum*-ba (the Latin dance) but Rum *Bah* ('Rum Bar' with a Boston accent). The classy cocktail lounge at the Intercontinental Hotel is a tribute to the days when Boston was at the center of a thriving rum trade (even Paul Revere stopped off for a nip, they claim).

Fun rum drinks, a tempting raw bar and Latin grooves attract a crowd of creatives and international types. For special occasions, slip into the swanky champagne lounge.

⭐ ENTERTAINMENT

OPERA HOUSE
LIVE PERFORMANCE

Map p252 (www.bostonoperahouse.com; 539 Washington St; ⓜDowntown Crossing) This lavish theater has been restored to its 1928 glory, complete with mural-painted ceiling, gilded molding and plush velvet curtains. The glitzy venue regularly hosts productions from the Broadway Across America series, and is also the main performance space for the Boston Ballet.

PARAMOUNT CENTER
DANCE, THEATER

Map p252 (www.artsemerson.org; 559 Washington St; ⓜDowntown Crossing) This art-deco masterpiece, restored by Emerson College, re-opened in 2010. Originally a 1700-seat, single-screen cinema, it was owned by Paramount Pictures (thus the name). The new facility includes a cinema and a black-box stage, as well as the more traditional but still grand theater space.

SIMONS IMAX THEATRE
CINEMA

Map p252 (www.neaq.org; Central Wharf; adult/senior & child $10/8; ⓒ10am-10pm; 🚼; ⓜAquarium) At the New England Aquarium, this IMAX bad boy plays lots of educational films on a six-story screen, in 3D. That way, when you have a gander at *Sharks,* you'll actually feel like you're about to be eaten. It occasionally plays IMAX versions of popular fare.

MODERN THEATRE
CINEMA, THEATER

Map p252 (www.moderntheatre.blogs.suffolk.edu; 525 Washington St; ⓜDowntown Crossing) The Modern Theatre dates to 1876 and showed Boston's first 'talkie' in 1928. Nearly a century later, the theater has opened its doors again as a venue for Suffolk University. Only the facade remains from the original building, but it looks stellar – another step in the revival of a mini theater district on lower Washington St.

🛍 SHOPPING

Downtown Crossing is an outdoor pedestrian mall. Many of the stores are outlets of national chains, although a few local yokels are still keeping it real. The Faneuil Hall and Quincy Market area is possibly Boston's most popular tourist shopping spot: upwards of 15 million people visit annually. The five buildings are filled with 100-plus tourist-oriented shops, pushcart vendors and national chain stores.

BRATTLE BOOK SHOP
BOOKS

Map p252 (www.brattlebookshop.com; 9 West St; ⓒ9am-5:30pm Mon-Sat; ⓜPark St) Since 1825, the Brattle Book Shop has catered to Boston's literati: it's a treasure trove crammed with out-of-print, rare and first-edition books. Ken Gloss – whose family has owned this gem since 1949 – is an expert on antiquarian books, moonlighting as a consultant and appraiser (see him on *Antiques Roadshow*!). Don't miss the bargains on the outside lot.

GREENWAY OPEN MARKET
ART MARKET

Map p252 (www.greenwayopenmarket.com; Surface Ave; ⓒ11am-5pm Sat Jun-Oct; ⓜAquarium) One of the newest features on the Greenway, the Saturday-only Open Market brings dozens of vendors to display their wares in the open air. Look for unique, handmade gifts, jewelry, bags, paintings, ceramics and other arts and crafts – most of which are locally and ethically made.

CITY SPORTS OUTLET
SPORTSWEAR

Map p252 (www.citysports.com; 11 Bromfield St; ⓒ9am-8pm Mon-Fri, 10am-8pm Sat, 11am-7pm Sun; ⓜDowntown Crossing) The outlet has the regular City Sports T-shirts and other stuff, but the basement is a treasure trove of factory seconds, irregular sizes and last year's models. It takes some patience to sift through the racks, but you're likely to find cool workout gear and specialty sports shoes at deep discounts.

FUNUSUAL
GIFTS, GAMES

Map p252 (www.funusual.com; 8 North Building, Faneuil Hall; ⓜGovernment Center) It's hard to describe this silly gift shop without using the obvious adjectives. It's filled with quirky, clever and crazy toys, games and knick-knacks. Shop here and you too can serve drinks in Matchbox-car shotglasses at your next party. Popular 'Life is Crap' T-shirts give 'Life is Good' a run for their money, and there are plenty of other funny T-shirts that are more optimistic.

LUCY'S LEAGUE
CLOTHING

Map p252 (North Building, Faneuil Hall; MGovernment Center) We're not advocating those pink Red Sox caps. But sometimes a girl wants to look good while she's supporting the team. At Lucy's League, fashionable sports fans will find shirts, jackets and other gear sporting the local teams' logos – but in super-cute styles designed to flatter the female figure.

JEWELERS EXCHANGE BUILDING
JEWELLERY

Map p252 (www.jewelersbuildingboston.com; 333 Washington St; ⊙8am-8pm Mon-Sat; MDowntown Crossing) With over 100 jewelers, this historic building is the first stop for many would-be grooms. Some jewelers have retail space on the 1st floor; other less conspicuous artisans work upstairs. If you're overwhelmed by too many options, go to BRAG on the 2nd floor. The Zargarian family has been designing and crafting the sparkly stuff for seven generations.

LOCAL CHARM
JEWELLERY

Map p252 (2 South Market; MState) These days, Quincy Market is packed with chain stores that you can find anywhere in America. Wouldn't it be nice to experience a little local charm? This tiny jewelry boutique delivers, offering up exquisite things with sterling silver and gemstones. The jewelry is tasteful yet artful, interesting yet unique. Best of all, it's handmade by local artisans.

GEOCLASSICS
JEWELLERY

Map p252 (www.geoclassics.com; 7 North Market; ⊙10am-9pm Mon-Sat, noon-6pm Sun; MState) Geoclassics showcases minerals, fossils and gemstones in jewelry and other decorative settings. The natural beauty of the stones is enhanced by their artistic presentation. The collection of fossils – from dinosaur eggs to dragonflies – is incredible.

BILL RODGERS RUNNING CENTER
SPORTSWEAR

Map p252 (www.billrodgersrunningcenter.com; 8 North Market, Faneuil Hall; MGovernment Center) Owned by champion marathoner Bill Rodgers and his two brothers, this is the place to go for expert advice on running shoes and other gear. The selection is not huge, but they will offer suggestions and place orders so you can get your perfect fit.

WINDSOR BUTTON
SEWING SUPPLIES

Map p252 (www.windsorbutton.com; 35 Temple Pl; ⊙10am-6pm Mon-Sat, to 7pm Thu; MPark St) Windsor Button has Boston's most extensive collection of buttons and yarn, as well as sewing and craft products. Designer buttons, hand-painted buttons, leather buttons, seashell buttons... not to mention a whole line of New England–themed buttons (lighthouses, lobsters, swan boats, etc) – the perfect souvenir for sewing enthusiasts.

🏃 SPORTS & ACTIVITIES

TOP CHOICE NEW ENGLAND AQUARIUM WHALE WATCH
WHALE-WATCHING

Map p252 (www.neaq.org; Central Wharf; adult/child/infant $40/32/15; ⊙10am Apr-Oct, additional cruises May-Sep; 👶; MAquarium) Board the Voyager III for the journey out to Stellwagen Bank, a rich feeding ground for whales, dolphins and marine birds. Onboard naturalists can answer all your questions; plus they have keen eyes. Whale sightings are guaranteed; otherwise, you receive a coupon for a free trip at a later date.

FREE NPS FREEDOM TRAIL TOUR
WALKING TOUR

Map p252 (www.nps.gov/bost; Faneuil Hall; ⊙10am & 2pm Apr-Nov; 👶; MState) Show up at least 30 minutes early to snag a spot on one of the free, ranger-led Freedom Trail tours provided by the National Park Service. Tours depart from the visitor center in Faneuil Hall, and follow a portion of the Freedom Trail (not including Charlestown), for a total of 90 minutes. Each tour is limited to 30 people.

LIBERTY CLIPPER
CRUISE

Map p252 (☎617-742-0333; www.libertyfleet.com; 67 Long Wharf, tickets; adult/child $30/15; ⊙noon, 3pm & 6pm Jun-Sep; MAquarium) This 125ft schooner takes a two-hour, 12-mile sail around the harbor several times a day. It is docked on Central Wharf, north of the Aquarium.

CODZILLA   BOATING

Map p252 (www.bostonharborcruises.com; 1 Long Wharf; adult/senior/child $27/23/25; ☻10am, noon, 2pm & 4pm May-Sep, plus 3pm, 5pm & 6pm Jul & Aug; ⓓ; ⓜAquarium) 'Boating' may not be the proper word to describe this activity, which takes place on a 2800HP speedboat that cruises through the waves at speeds of up to 40mph. Painted like a multicolored shark with a big toothy grin, the boat has a unique hull design that enables it to do the ocean version of doughnuts.

FOGSTOCK / ALAMY ©

1. **Faneuil Hall (p85)**
Once the 'cradle of liberty,' now a festive retail center.

2. **Waterfront (p78)**
City on the water: Boston Harbor and the Financial District skyline at dusk.

3. **Beacon Hill (p66)**
Cobblestones and lamplight: the quintessentially Bostonian streets of Beacon Hill.

4. **King's Chapel Burying Ground (p86)**
Flags and foliage surround a gravestone at this historic cemetery on the Freedom Trail.

VINCENT DEWITT / ALAMY ©

South End & Chinatown

SOUTH END | CHINATOWN | THEATER DISTRICT | LEATHER DISTRICT

Neighborhood Top Five

1 Dressing to the nines and going out for a night on the town, whether for comedy at the **Wilbur Theatre** (p105), opera at the **Shubert Theatre** (p105) or music or dance at the **Wang Theatre** (p105).

2 Browsing at the **South End Open Market** (p105) and **SoWa Vintage Market** (p106) followed by Sunday brunch on **Tremont St** (p98).

3 Packing into **Wally's Café** (p104) for old-time jazz and blues.

4 Sampling the stylish vintage threads at **Bobby from Boston** (p106).

5 Club-hopping in the **Theater District** (p103) and post-club noshing in **Chinatown** (p100).

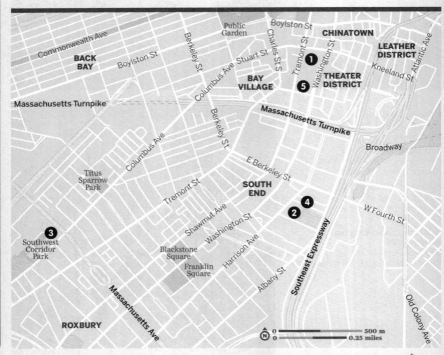

For more detail of this area, see Maps p256 & p258 ➡

Explore South End & Chinatown

Four side-by-side neighborhoods are home to Boston's lively theater scene, its most hip-hop-happening night-clubs and its best international and contemporary dining. Ethnically and economically diverse, these districts border Downtown and Back Bay, but they are edgier and artier.

The edgiest (and artiest) is the South End. Once downtrodden, it was claimed and cleaned up by the gay community, and now everyone wants to live there. And why not? The South End boasts the country's largest concentration of Victorian row houses; it offers Boston's most innovative and exciting options for dining out; and the artistic community has moved into the area south of Washington St (now known as SoWa), converting old warehouses into studio and gallery space.

Although tiny by New York standards, Boston's Theater District has long served as a pre-Broadway staging area. It's also Boston's club hub, with many late-night hotspots clustered along Boylston St and surrounding streets.

Nearby, Chinatown is overflowing with multicultural restaurants, live-poultry and fresh-produce markets, tea-houses and textile shops. This tight-knit community also includes Cambodians, Vietnamese and Laotians.

East of Chinatown, the Leather District is a pocket of uniform brick buildings that shelter some fine restaurants and a few funky clubs.

Essentially, these aren't districts to visit for traditional 'sights,' but for their abundant eating and entertainment options. You could go out every night for months on end, and never run out of trendy restaurants, innovative theater and electrifying nightlife.

Local Life

➡ **First Fridays** On the first Friday of the month, get thee to the open studios at SoWa Artists Guild (p98) to chat with the resident creatives.

➡ **Hang-outs** Southenders hang out at Delux Café (p102) while the Corner Pub (p104) is the Leather District local.

Getting There & Away

➡ **Metro** For the South End, take the orange line to Back Bay station for Tremont St or to Tufts Medical Center station for SoWa. Chinatown is served by the station of the same name, also on the orange line. The green-line Boylston station is closest to the Theater District, though Chinatown station is also nearby. The Leather District is easiest to access from the red-line South Station.

➡ **Bus** Good for the South End, the silver-line bus runs down Washington St from South Station (SL4) or Downtown Crossing (SL5).

Lonely Planet's Top Tip

If you plan to hit any night-clubs in the Theater District (or anywhere), definitely go online and get yourself on the guest list. This normally will ensure entry (instead of leaving it to the whims of the bouncer) and sometimes will get you a reduced cover charge.

 Best Places to Eat

➡ O Ya (p102)
➡ Coppa (p98)
➡ Gourmet Dumpling House (p100)
➡ B&G Oysters (p98)

For reviews, see p100 ➡

🍷 Best Places to Drink

➡ Delux Café (p102)
➡ The Gallows (p103)
➡ Les Zygomates (p104)
➡ Beehive (p103)

For reviews, see p102 ➡

☆ Best Places to Dance

➡ Bijou (p103)
➡ District (p104)
➡ Underbar (p103)

For reviews, see p102 ➡

SOUTH END & CHINATOWN

⊙ SIGHTS

⊙ South End

SOWA ARTISTS GUILD   GALLERY

Map p256 (www.sowaartistsguild.com; 450 Harrison Ave; ⊘5-9pm first Fri; MTufts Medical Center, ⊡SL4 or SL5) From the former warehouses and factories on Harrison Ave, artists have carved out studios and gallery space. The center of the action is the SoWa Artists Guild, which hosts an Open Studios event on the first Friday of every month. During daytime hours, you can see the goods at **Bromfield Art Gallery** (Map p256; www.bromfieldgallery.com; 450 Harrison Ave; ⊘noon-5pm Wed-Sat; MTufts Medical Center) and other on-site venues.

MILLS GALLERY   GALLERY

Map p256 (www.bcaonline.org; 539 Tremont St; ⊘noon-5pm Wed & Sun, noon-9pm Thu-Sat; MBack Bay) Besides several performance spaces, the main venue for visual arts at the Boston Center for the Arts is the Mills Gallery, which hosts cutting-edge art exhibits, as well as opportunities to interact with the artists (eg artist and curator talks). The gallery features established and emerging artists from Boston and around the country, who put on shows appropriate to this trendsetting neighborhood.

CATHEDRAL OF THE HOLY CROSS   CHURCH

Map p256 (www.holycrossboston.com; 1400 Washington St; ⊘service 9am Mon-Sat, 8am & 11:30am Sun; MBack Bay, ⊡SL4 or SL5) When this neo-Gothic cathedral was built in 1875, it was America's largest Catholic cathedral, as big as London's Westminster Abbey. It serves as the main cathedral for the archdiocese of Boston and the seat of the archbishop. The exquisite rose window features King David playing his harp, while the rest of the cross-shaped building is peppered with stained-glass windows and traditional church art.

⊙ Chinatown

CHINATOWN GATE   LANDMARK

Map p258 (cnr Beach St & Surface Rd; MChinatown) The official entrance to Chinatown is the decorative gate, or *paifong*, a gift from the city of Taipei. It is symbolic – not only as an entryway for guests visiting Chinatown,

but also as an entryway for immigrants who are still settling here, as they come to establish relationships and roots in their newly claimed home.

Surrounding the gate and anchoring the southern end of the Rose Kennedy Greenway is the new **Chinatown Park**. The park design, which incorporates elements of feng shui, is inspired by the many generations of Asian immigrants that have passed through this gate.

✕ EATING

✕ South End

Much like the neighborhood itself – where the up-and-coming live next door to the down-and-out – the South End boasts an eclectic mix of trendy, high-end eateries and old-school neighborhood cafes.

⌐TOP⌐CHOICE⌐ COPPA   ITALIAN $$

Map p256 (☑617-391-0902; www.coppaboston.com; 253 Shawmut Ave; dishes $14-22; ⊘lunch Mon-Fri, brunch Sun, dinner daily; MBack Bay, ⊡SL4 or SL5) Ken Oringer and Jamie Bissonette have a knack for recreating dining experiences from around the world with authenticity and innovation. This South End *enoteca* (wine bar) is no exception, serving up *salumi* (cured meats), antipasti, pasta and other delicious Italian small plates. Wash down with an Aperol spritz and you might be tricked into thinking you're in Venice.

The setting is delightfully informal and small.

B&G OYSTERS   SEAFOOD $$$

Map p256 (☑617-423-0550; www.bandgoysters.com; 550 Tremont St; oysters $3 each, mains $25-30; ⊘lunch & dinner; MBack Bay) Patrons flock to this casually cool oyster bar to get in on the raw delicacies offered by chef Barbara Lynch. Sit inside at the marble bar or outside on the peaceful terrace, and indulge in the freshest oysters from local waters. An extensive list of wines and a modest menu of mains and appetizers (mostly seafood) are ample accompaniment for the oysters.

MYERS & CHANG   ASIAN $$

Map p256 (☑617-542-5200; www.myersandchang.com; 1145 Washington St; small plates $10-

COMBAT ZONE

With the demolition of Scollay Sq in the 1960s, the city's go-go dancers, strippers and prostitutes – as well as their clientele – made their way to the blocks wedged between the Theater District and Chinatown. The city administration supported this move, believing that it could concentrate the city's sleaze into a sort of red-light district (although prostitution was technically illegal), and free the rest of the city of riff-raff.

Washington St – between Boylston and Kneeland Sts – became the center of all skankiness in Boston. Lined with clubs like the Teddy Bare Lounge and the Naked I, this was the place to come for adult bookstores and X-rated movie theaters. Prostitutes congregated along LaGrange St. Local reporters dubbed it the 'Combat Zone.'

Residents were generally poor immigrants. They had little voice in local government and were unable to change official policy. The Combat Zone flourished.

The heyday of the Combat Zone has passed (although there are still a few strip clubs in this area). Due to rising real-estate values, this area attracted the attention of developers in the 1980s: the Four Seasons Hotel and the State Transportation Building were built on Park Sq; Emerson College moved its campus here; other development followed suit.

City officials cracked down on street crime, forcing the Combat Zone clientele to stay home and surf the internet. Many of the old theaters – such as the Opera House and the Paramount – were revamped for Broadway shows and upscale nightclubs.

Chinatown residents also engaged in grassroots efforts to shut down the Combat Zone, and for the most part they succeeded. Unfortunately, even as the neighborhood is enjoying revitalization, this ethnic enclave continues to be jeopardized – not by peep shows and porn theaters but by skyrocketing rents.

15; ⊙lunch & dinner; ⏩; Ⓜ Tufts Medical Center, ⬚SL4 or SL5) This super-hip Asian spot blends Thai, Chinese and Vietnamese cuisines, which means delicious dumplings, spicy stir-fries and oodles of noodles. The kitchen staff does amazing things with a wok, and the menu of small plates allows you to sample a wide selection of dishes. The vibe is casual but cool, international and independent.

⏩ TORO   TAPAS $$

Map p256 (☎617-536-4300; www.toro-res taurant.com; 1704 Washington St; tapas $6-15; ⊙lunch Mon-Sat, brunch Sun, dinner daily; ⏩; Ⓜ Massachusetts Ave, ⬚SL4 or SL5) This much lauded tapas bar is one of many success stories by celebrity chef Ken Oringer. True to its Spanish spirit, the place is bursting with energy, from the open kitchen to the lively bar to the communal butcher-block tables. The menu features sublime yet simple tapas – grilled chilies with sea salt, corn on the cob dripping with lemon and butter, and delectable, garlicky shrimp.

For accompaniment, take your pick from rioja, sangria or any number of spiced-up mojitos and margaritas.

PICCO   PIZZERIA $$

Map p256 (www.piccorestaurant.com; 513 Tremont St; mains $10-20; ⊙lunch & dinner; ⏩⏩⏩; Ⓜ Back Bay) The crust of a Picco pizza undergoes a two-day process of cold fermentation before it goes into the oven and then into your mouth. The result is a thin crust with substantial texture and rich flavor. You can add toppings to create your own pie, or try the specialty Alsatian (sautéed onions, shallots, garlic, sour cream, bacon and Gruyère cheese).

The menu also features sandwiches, salads and delectable homemade ice cream. The breezy decor and free wi-fi access lure those who might like to linger.

BUTCHER SHOP   FRENCH, ITALIAN $$

Map p256 (☎617-423-4800; www.thebutcher shopboston.com; 552 Tremont St; petite charcuterie $15; ⊙lunch & dinner; Ⓜ Back Bay) Only in the South End does the neighborhood butcher shop double as an elegant eatery and wine bar. The cases filled with tantalizing cuts of meat, fresh foie gras and homemade sausages give you a glimpse of the ingredients and provide the decoration at this bistro.

The menu is short and sweet, offering charcuterie and antipasti that highlight the butcher shop's products (not a good place for vegetarians). A nice selection of artisanal wines accompanies the food.

FRANKLIN CAFÉ
AMERICAN **$$**

Map p256 (www.franklincafe.com; 278 Shawmut Ave; mains $15-20; ⊙5:30pm-1:30am; ⚡; Ⓜ Back Bay, 🚇 SL4 or SL5) The Franklin is probably the South End's longest-standing favorite neighborhood joint – and that's saying something in this restaurant-rich neighborhood. It's still friendly and hip – a fantastic spot for people-watching (especially the beautiful boys in the 'hood).

The menu is New American comfort food prepared by a gourmet chef: duck pot pie with root vegetables and cranberry jam or oyster-mushroom ravioli in sage brown butter.

GASLIGHT, BRASSERIE DU COIN
FRENCH **$$**

Map p256 (📞617-422-0224; www.gaslight560.com; 560 Harrison Ave; mains $17-27; ⊙brunch Sat & Sun, dinner daily; ⚡; Ⓜ Back Bay, 🚇 SL4 or SL5) Gaslight is the friendly and affordable 'brasserie on the corner' that we all wish we had in our own neighborhood. Mosaic tiles, wood-beam ceilings and comfy cozy booths set up the comfortable, convivial atmosphere, which is enhanced by classic French fare and an excellent selection of wines by the glass.

UNION BAR & GRILLE
AMERICAN **$$**

Map p256 (📞617-423-0555; www.unionrestaurant.com; 1357 Washington St; mains $16-24; ⊙brunch Sat & Sun, dinner daily; Ⓜ Back Bay, 🚇 SL4 or SL5) Union has transformed a warehouse in trendy SoWa into a cool, comfortable bar and grill, a big light-filled space that retains its postindustrial atmosphere in the steel and brick walls. Sidle up to the bar for your $5 cocktail or sink into a plush leather booth for a delicious dinner. The menu presents traditional American fare with an eye to innovation.

MIKE'S CITY DINER
DINER **$**

Map p256 (www.mikescitydiner.com; 1714 Washington St; meals $10-15; ⊙breakfast & lunch; 🚼; Ⓜ Massachusetts Ave, 🚇 SL4 or SL5) Start the day with a big breakfast of eggs, bacon, toast and other old-fashioned goodness, topped with a bottomless cup of coffee. If you need to refuel at lunchtime, go for classics such as meatloaf and mashed potatoes or fried chicken and biscuits. The service is friendly and fast. Your server will probably call you 'hon.' Cash only.

ADDIS RED SEA
ETHIOPIAN **$**

Map p256 (📞617-426-8727; www.addisredsea.com; 544 Tremont St; mains $8-12; ⊙lunch Sat & Sun, dinner daily; ⚡; Ⓜ Back Bay) An excellent introduction to Ethiopian food. Take a seat at a tiny table and soak up the exotic ambience at this authentic African eatery. Most entrées are served atop a spongy bread; tear off a piece and use it to scoop up the spicy beef, lamb, chicken and veggie stews. Finish off your meal with honey wine.

The warm and welcoming staff will offer recommendations if you don't know how to order.

🍴 SOUTH END BUTTERY
BAKERY, CAFE **$**

Map p256 (www.southendbuttery.com; 314 Shawmut Ave; meals $6-10; ⊙breakfast, lunch & dinner; ⚡🚼; Ⓜ Back Bay, 🚇 SL4 or SL5) A portion of the revenue from cupcake sales here goes to a local animal shelter. Coffee drinks feature shade-grown organic beans. Packaging materials are made from recycled paper. Now that your conscience is eased, you can really enjoy that chocolate-hazelnut cupcake. The brunch and dinner meals are simple, seasonal and delicious.

🍴 Chinatown

The most colorful part of Chinatown is overflowing with authentic restaurants (many open until 4am), bakeries and markets. It's not just Chinese, but also Vietnamese, Japanese, Korean, Thai, Malaysian and more. This is some of Boston's best budget eating.

🔝 TOP CHOICE GOURMET DUMPLING HOUSE
CHINESE, TAIWANESE **$**

Map p258 (www.gourmetdumpling.com; 52 Beach St; lunch $8, dinner mains $10-15; ⊙11am-1am; ⚡; Ⓜ Chinatown) *Xiao long bao.* That's all the Chinese you need to know to take advantage of the specialty at the Gourmet Dumpling House (or GDH, as it is fondly called). They are Shanghai soup dumplings, of course, and they are fresh, doughy and delicious. The menu offers plenty of other options, including scrumptious crispy scallion pancakes. Come early or be prepared to wait.

XINH XINH
VIETNAMESE **$$**

Map p258 (7 Beach St; mains $8-12; ⊙lunch & dinner; ⚡; Ⓜ Chinatown) Wins the award for Boston's favorite *pho* (pronounced 'fuh'), the sometimes exotic, always fragrant and flavorful Vietnamese noodle soup. These hot, hearty meals come in big bowls and warm you from the inside out. The lemongrass tofu is especially recommended, as are the roll-it-yourself spring rolls (work for your food!).

TAIWAN CAFE
TAIWANESE **$**

Map p258 (34 Oxford St; mains $8-12; ⊙11am-1am; ⊠; MChinatown) Chinatown regulars like to debate the merits of the neighborhood's various dumpling houses (GDH vs DC, etc). But there's a contingent that quietly bypasses the lines at these more popular joints, then sidles into Taiwan Cafe to feast on excellent *xiao long bao* and other Taiwanese specialties. Like most places in Chinatown, the decor is minimal and prices are cheap. Cash only.

KAZE SHABU SHABU
JAPANESE **$$**

Map p258 (www.kazeshabushabu.com; 1 Harrison Ave; mains $12-16; ⊙11:30am-1am Sun-Thu, to 3am Fri & Sat) Offering a hands-on approach to dinner, 'Shabu-shabu' is also known as hotpot cuisine, where you cook your meal at your table in a big family-style pot. Choose from a variety of seafood, poultry and meats, fresh vegetables and an array of homemade broths, then cook it up the way you like it. It's a divine sensory experience in a tranquil setting.

WINSOR DIM SUM CAFE
DIM SUM **$**

Map p258 (10 Tyler St; items $2-6; ⊙9am-10pm; ⊠; MChinatown) The downside is that there are no pushcarts to choose your food from – the place is tiny so the pushcarts would have nowhere to go. Instead you have to pre-order from a menu with photographs. The upside is that the food is freshly made to order and it is delish. Shrimp dumplings and steamed pork buns are highly recommended.

CAFÉ DE LULU
CHINESE **$**

Map p258 (www.cafedelulu.com; 42 Beach St; mains $6-10; ⊙breakChinatownfast, lunch & dinner; ☏; MChinatown) Tucked into a tiny basement. Food served on plastic dishes. Hong Kong soap operas on the tube. Eating at Lulu's feels like you're eating at a friend's house, as the servers and management go out of their way to make sure you are sated. And you will be sated. Look for the unusual but delectable Portuguese chicken or stir-fried ramen noodles.

MY THAI VEGAN CAFÉ
THAI **$**

Map p258 (3 Beach St; mains $8-12; ⊙lunch & dinner; ⊠; MChinatown) Formerly Buddha's

Delight, this welcoming cafe is tucked into a sunlit second-story space. It's still an animal-free zone – but good enough that meat-eaters will enjoy eating here too. The menu has a Thai twist, offering noodle soups, dumplings and pad thai. The bubble tea gets raves. Service can be slow, so bring a book.

PEACH FARM
CHINESE, SEAFOOD **$**

Map p258 (4 Tyler St; mains $7-18; ⊙11am-3am; ⊠; MChinatown) Popular wisdom says that if you don't know where to eat in Chinatown, you should ask some locals where *they* like to eat. Chances are they will direct you to the Peach Farm, a Chinatown haunt where the focus is on the food. It's not much to look at, but fried noodles and rice, *moo shi* (shredded pork pancakes) and Szechuan dishes are plentiful and cheap. This place is packed in the wee hours.

JADE GARDEN
CANTONESE **$**

Map p258 (18-20 Tyler St; lunch $4-6, dinner $10-15; ⊙noon-midnight, to 2am Fri & Sat; MChinatown) With lunch specials under $5 you really can't go wrong. The place is pretty plain, with mirrors and TVs for decor, but the food is anything but. The seafood dishes are the highlight, especially the ginger scallion lobster.

JUMBO SEAFOOD
CHINESE, SEAFOOD **$$**

Map p258 (www.newjumboseafoodrestaurant. com; 5 Hudson St; lunch $6-10, dinner mains $12-18; ⊙11am-1am Sun-Thu, 11am-4am Fri & Sat; ⊠; MChinatown) You know the seafood is fresh when you see the huge tanks of lobster, crabs and fish that constitute the decor at this Chinatown classic. But it's not only seafood on the menu, which represents the best of Hong Kong cuisine. Other specialties include braised duck with mushrooms and Szechuan-style shrimp. Lunch specials are a bargain.

EMPIRE GARDEN
DIM SUM **$$**

Map p258 (690 Washington St; mains $9-15, dim sum items $3-8; ⊙9am-9pm Sun-Thu, 9am-10pm Fri & Sat; MChinatown) Emperor's Garden (or Empire Garden, or whatever it is called) is one of a handful of places that are recommended for dim sum. This massive space was converted from an old theater, and now it is a vast dingy dining room that gets packed with Chinese patrons, feasting on pork buns and shrimp dumplings. If your Cantonese is not up to snuff, use the point-and-choose method (that's what the carts are for).

✖ Theater District

JACOB WIRTH GERMAN $$
Map p258 (☎617-338-8586; www.jacobwirth.com; 31-37 Stuart St; sandwiches $8-12, mains $16-22; ⊗lunch & dinner; ♿; ⓂBoylston) Boston's second-oldest eatery is this atmospheric Bavarian beer hall. The menu features Wiener schnitzel, sauerbraten, potato pancakes and pork chops, but the highlight is the beer – almost 30 different drafts, including Jake's House Lager and Jake's Special Dark. On Friday night (open until 1am), Jake hosts a sing-along that rouses the *haus*.

VIA MATTA ITALIAN $$$
Map p258 (☎617-422-0008; www.viamattaristaurant.com; 79 Park Plaza; caffe $13-17, mains $21-31; ⊗11:30am-1am; ⓂArlington) Via Matta tries to recreate your finest memories of Italy – the ambience, the romance and of course the flavors. Sample the chef's whims in the tastefully trendy dining room or, better yet, in the dark, sexy *caffe*. The latter serves pizzas, bruschettas and other small plates late into the night – a perfect place to stop for a bite after the theater.

MARKET BY JEAN-GEORGES MODERN AMERICAN $$$
Map p258 (☎617-310-6790; www.marketbyjgboston.com; 100 Stuart St; mains $25-35; ⊗breakfast Mon-Fri, brunch Sat & Sun, lunch & dinner daily; ⓂBoylston) You might want to fix your hair before you head out to this market. Set inside the W Hotel, it's a slick modern space heightened by tall ceilings and floor-to-ceiling windows. It's a perfect setting to sample Jean-Georges' delectable interpretations of American cuisine. A three-course, pre-theater prix-fixe is available for $55.

FINALE DESSERTERIE CAFE $$
Map p258 (www.finaledesserts.com; 1 Columbus Ave; desserts $9-14; ⊗lunch & dinner; ♿; ⓂArlington) Choose from a long list of tempting treats, from crème brûlée to chocolate soufflé, and enjoy them with coffee, wine or port. Mirrors over the pastry chefs' workstation allow patrons to watch their magic. There are also light soups, salads and sandwiches at lunchtime and appetizer-size din-

ner dishes so you don't have to eat sweets on an empty stomach.

✖ Leather District

O YA SUSHI $$$
Map p258 (☎617-654-9900; www.oyarestaurantboston.com; 9 East St; nigiri & sashimi pieces $12-24; ⊗dinner Tue-Sat; ♿; ⓂSouth Station) Boston's food community can't stop talking about this inspired sushi restaurant, which has even been lauded by the *New York Times* food critics. Who knew that raw fish could be so exciting? Each piece of nagiri or sashimi is dripped with something unexpected but exquisite, ranging from honey truffle sauce to banana pepper mousse.

Shrimp tempura is topped with a bacon truffle emulsion. Homemade soba noodles are chilled and served with sea urchin, nori and scallions. The service is impeccable, with knowledgeable waiters ready to offer advice and explanations.

SOUTH STREET DINER DINER $
Map p258 (www.southstreetdiner.com; 178 Kneeland St; mains $6-12; ⊗24hr; ⓂSouth Station) A divey diner that does what a diner is supposed to do – that is, serve bacon and eggs and burgers and fries, at any time of the day or night. Plonk yourself into a vinyl-upholstered booth and let the sass-talking waitstaff satisfy your midnight munchies.

Considering the location, this place is bound to attract some sketchy characters. But again, that's what a diner is supposed to do.

⬤ DRINKING & NIGHTLIFE

⬤ South End

This neighborhood contains some of Boston's hippest bars. As the South End serves as home base for much of Boston's gay community, you'll find plenty of spots catering to the fellas.

 DELUX CAFÉ DIVE BAR
Map p256 (☎617-338-5258; 100 Chandler St; ⊗5pm-1am Mon-Sat; ⓂBack Bay) If Boston has a laid-back hipster bar, this is it. The small

room on the 1st floor of a brownstone comes covered in knotty pine paneling, artwork from old LPs and Christmas lights. A small TV in the corner plays silent cartoons (not sports), and a noteworthy kitchen serves incredible grilled-cheese sandwiches and inspired comfort food.

TOP CHOICE BEEHIVE JAZZ

Map p256 (📞617-423-0069; www.beehiveboston. com; 541 Tremont St; ◷5pm-2am; Ⓜ Back Bay) The Beehive has transformed the basement of the Boston Center for the Arts into a 1920s Paris jazz club. This place is more about the scene than the music, which is often provided by students from Berklee College of Music. But the food is good and the vibe is definitely hip. Reservations required if you want a table.

THE GALLOWS BAR

Map p256 (www.thegallowsboston.com; 1395 Washington St; 🚇SL4 or SL5) It's hard to say whether this is a restaurant with amazing cocktails and a cozy, crowded, convivial atmosphere; or a bar with irresistible and innovative food. Either way, the dark woody interior is inviting and the bartenders are truly talented. The 'pub grub' includes such interesting fare as the 'carpet burger' topped with fried oysters and pickles, the enticing Scotch egg and scrumptious vegetarian poutine.

FRITZ GAY

Map p256 (www.fritzboston.com; 26 Chandler St; ◷noon-2am; Ⓜ Back Bay) Enjoy a long bar full of chatty men and lots of bottles of booze, all dimly lit by pink Christmas lights that enhance Fritz's atmosphere without it feeling kitschy. Indeed, the place veers toward romantic, with several breakaway spots. It's a comfortable, low-key spot to watch the boys play ball – or to watch the boys watching the boys playing ball.

28 DEGREES COCKTAIL BAR

Map p256 (www.28degrees-boston.com; 1 Appleton St; ◷5pm-midnight; Ⓜ Back Bay or Arlington) Twenty-eight degrees is the optimum temperature for a martini. Now, perhaps you're getting an idea about what to order at this this super-slick bar on the edge of the South End. The blue basil and cucumber martini is just an example from a long list of perfectly chilled treats, which change seasonally.

The uber-chic interior makes this a sweet spot to impress a date. Don't leave without checking out the loo.

🍴 Chinatown

INTERMISSION TAVERN PUB

Map p258 (www.intermissiontavern.com; 228 Tremont St; ◷10:30am-2am; Ⓜ Boylston) Enter beneath the masks of Comedy and Tragedy into the dimly lit interior, where show posters adorn the brick walls. This tiny, theatrically themed tavern is a cozy, casual spot for a drink or a bite to eat before or after a show. Reasonable prices and late-night dining (until 1am) attract clubbers, theatergoers and other night owls.

🍴 Theater District

TROQUET WINE BAR

Map p258 (📞617-695-9463; www.troquetboston. com; 140 Boylston St; Ⓜ Boylston) Overlooking the Boston Common, this simple and sophisticated French restaurant has an unbeatable location. The 1st-floor wine bar is an ideal place to nibble on delectable appetizers and sample the amazing menu of wines by the glass. Each menu item suggests a wine pairing to perfectly please your palate.

BIJOU CLUB

Map p258 (www.bijouboston.com; 51 Stuart St; Ⓜ Boylston) Named after the old Bijou Theater, which was the first electrically-lit playhouse back in 1882 (wired by Thomas Edison himself). Now the nightclub creates the same electric atmosphere for the sparkly set to drink and dance and see and be seen. The place has a super sexy vibe thanks to good-looking staff and loud music.

VENU & RUMOR CLUB

Map p258 (www.venuboston.com; 100 Warrenton St; cover $15-20; ◷11pm-2am Tue-Wed & Fri-Sat; Ⓜ Boylston) For a night of drinking and dancing, don your designer duds and head to tiny Stuart St, where there are two super-chic side-by-side clubs. If you don't like the vibe at one, just go next door. Of course, if you arrive after 11:30pm you'll have to join the line of good-looking, impeccably dressed types waiting to get in. (Caveat: Wednesday is Latin night at Rumor, but Venu is closed.)

UNDERBAR CLUB

Map p258 (www.underbaronline.com; 275 Tremont St; cover $10-20; ◷10pm-2am Fri-Sun; Ⓜ Tufts Medical Center) House music pounds out of the hard-working sound system and reverberates off the walls in this basement club. Unfortunately, the dance floor is small, but if you want to feel the beat – really feel it, because the bass is making your body throb – get down under. 'Hot Mess' Sunday is a crazy, non-stop boozing, cruising gay party.

ESTATE CLUB

Map p258 (www.theestateboston.com; 1 Boylston Pl; ⊙10:30pm-2am Thu-Sat; Ⓜ Boylston) Dress to impress if you want to get past the door attendant and into this luxury lounge, where sweaty bodies swarm together on the dance floor and move to the sounds of the latest spins. 'Glamlife Thursdays' are very hot, thanks to the gay clientele grooving to the tunes.

Leather District

LES ZYGOMATES WINE BAR

Map p258 (☑617-542-5108; www.winebar.com; 129 South St; lunch $15, dinner mains $24-32; ⊙lunch Mon-Fri, dinner to 1am Mon-Sat; Ⓜ South Station) This late-night Parisian bistro serves up live jazz music alongside classic but contemporary French cuisine. Daily prix-fixe menus and Tuesday-night wine tastings ($30; 7pm) attract a clientele that is sophisticated but not stuffy. Dinner is pricey, but the tempting selection of starters and cocktails make it a perfect pre- or post-theater spot.

DISTRICT CLUB

Map p258 (www.districtboston.com; 180 Lincoln St; ⊙10pm-2am Wed-Sat; Ⓜ South Station) It's worth a night at District to marvel at the funked-out decor, which combines bold-patterned tapestries, white leather booths and unexpected elements like faux birch trees. Eclectic is an understatement. The crowd and the vibe vary from night to night, as various promoters draw crowds with Classic Wednesdays (Top 40), In Thursdays (R&B), Latin Fridays and Clique Saturdays (Top 40). Dress sharp.

CORNER PUB DIVE BAR

Map p258 (www.cornerpubboston.com; 162 Lincoln St; Ⓜ South Station) This place will always be Weggie's to the devoted clientele. This loungie dive has been a neighborhood fixture for decades. The recent upgrade means that the counters are cleaner and the kitchen serves some seriously edible

grub. Three-dollar bottles of beer are still the drink of choice. We lament the name change but we appreciate the bathroom improvements.

⭐ ENTERTAINMENT

TOP CHOICE WALLY'S CAFÉ BLUES, JAZZ

Map p256 (http://wallyscafe.com; 427 Massachusetts Ave; ⊙2pm-2am; Ⓜ Massachusetts Ave) When Wally's opened in 1947, Barbadian immigrant Joseph Walcott became the first African American to own a nightclub in New England. Old-school, gritty and small, it still attracts a racially diverse crowd to hear jammin' jazz music 365 days a year. Wally's is the kind of place where someone on stage will recognize a high-caliber out-of-town musician in the crowd and convince them to play.

Berklee students love this place, especially the weekend jam sessions (6pm to 8pm Saturday and Sunday).

BOSTON CENTER FOR THE ARTS THEATER

Map p256 (www.bcaonline.org; 539 Tremont St; Ⓜ Back Bay) There's rarely a dull moment at the BCA, which serves as a nexus for excellent small theater productions. Each year over 20 companies present more than 45 separate productions, from comedies and drama to modern dance and musicals. The BCA occupies a complex comprising several buildings, including a cyclorama from 1884 built to display panoramic paintings, a former organ factory, and the Mills Gallery.

COMPANY ONE THEATER

Map p256 (www.companyone.org; 539 Tremont St; Ⓜ Back Bay) Company One strives for radical theater work, in an attempt to reach less traditional, younger, ethnically diverse audiences. Critics are crazy for C1, which has wracked up a slew of awards and nominations for its innovative productions. Most shows are performed in the Boston Center for the Arts (BCA) theaters.

CUTLER MAJESTIC THEATRE OPERA, DANCE

Map p258 (☑617-824-8000; www.maj.org; 219 Tremont St; Ⓜ Boylston) This beautiful beaux-arts-style opera house dates to 1903. One century after its construction, the theater was sumptuously renovated and reopened by Emerson College. Today, the performances that take place here are incredibly

SOUTH END & CHINATOWN ENTERTAINMENT

diverse, including shows by **Opera Boston** (Map p258), seasonal celebrations like the popular Celtic Christmas Sojourn, dance events such as the Flamenco Festival or Tango Stories, comedy, music and more.

DICK'S BEANTOWN COMEDY VAULT COMEDY
Map p258 (☑800-401-2221; www.dickdoherty.com; 124 Boylston St; admission $15-20; ☺shows 8:30pm Mon-Thu, 9pm Fri, 8pm & 10:15pm Sat, 9pm Sun; Ⓜ Boylston) In the basement of Remington's Restaurant, local comedian Dick Doherty and a collection of regular helpers work the room into painful howls with surgical precision. Sunday nights are open mic, and the pain you feel on such occasions might feel very different than on other days.

SHEAR MADNESS COMEDY
Map p258 (☑617-426-5255; www.shearmadness.com; 1 Shear Madness Alley; admission $50; ☺8pm Tue-Fri, 6pm & 9pm Sat, 3pm & 7pm Sun; Ⓜ Boylston) America's longest-running comedy theater operates out of the Charles Playhouse, in a former church situated on a sleazy street (don't worry, it adds to the ambience). An odd mix of murder mystery and improvisation, the show features an outrageous gay hairstylist and various freakshow characters. In the whodunnit-style performance, actors ad-lib the plot based on cues from the audience.

WILBUR THEATRE COMEDY
Map p258 (www.thewilburtheatre.com; 246 Tremont St; tickets $20-50; Ⓜ Boylston) The colonial Wilbur Theatre dates to 1914, and over the years has hosted many prominent theatrical productions. These days it is Boston's premier comedy club. Once known as the Comedy Connection (and located in Quincy Market), this long-running operation has hosted the likes of Chris Rock, Rosie O'Donnell and other nationally known cutups.

SHUBERT THEATRE OPERA
Map p258 (www.citicenter.org; 265 Tremont St; Ⓜ Boylston) With 1600 seats, the Shubert is smaller and more intimate than some of the other Theater District venues, thus earning the moniker the 'Little Princess' of the Theater District. The Shubert is the place to see the **Boston Lyric Opera** (Map p258; www.blo.org; tickets $33-112) and other musical theater.

CITI PERFORMING ARTS CENTER MUSIC, DANCE
Map p258 (☑617-482-9393; www.citicenter.org; 270 Tremont St; Ⓜ Boylston) Boston's biggest music and dance venue, the Citi Performing Arts Center is comprised of two theaters which face off across Tremont St. The opulent and enormous **Wang Theatre**, built in 1925, has one of the largest stages in the country. The Wang hosts extravagant music and modern dance productions, as well as occasional giant-screen movies (the center was originally built as a movie palace). The Citi Center also includes the more intimate Shubert Theatre (p105) across the street.

JACQUES CABARET GAY, CABARET
Map p258 (www.jacquescabaret.com; 79 Broadway; admission $6-10; ☺11am-midnight Mon-Sat, noon-midnight Sun; Ⓜ Arlington) Head to this dive on a dark side street to experience the gay culture of the South End before gentrification took over. A shaded-lamp and pool-table kind of place, Jacques hosts outstanding low-budget drag shows every night. We think Mizery is the cat's pyjamas.

🛍 SHOPPING

The South End is the only neighborhood in Boston that has more boutiques for men than women. If you are a straight guy in need of a queer eye (or any guy in need of knock-'em-dead duds), take a walk to the South End. SoWa – the area south of Washington St – is also home to Boston's edgiest, up-and-coming art scene.

TOP CHOICE SOUTH END OPEN MARKET HANDICRAFTS, MARKET
Map p256 (www.southendopenmarket.com; 540 Harrison Ave; ☺10am-4pm Sun May-Oct; Ⓜ Tufts Medical Center, ⓢSL4 or SL5) Part flea market and part artists' market, this weekly outdoor event is a fabulous opportunity for strolling, shopping and people-watching. More than 100 vendors set up shop under white tents. It's never the same two weeks in a row, but there's always plenty of arts and crafts, as well as edgier art, vintage clothing, jewelry, local farm produce and homemade sweets.

TOP CHOICE BOBBY FROM BOSTON
CLOTHING, VINTAGE

Map p256 (19 Thayer St; ⊘noon-6pm Mon-Sat; MTufts Medical Center, ⊡SL4 or SL5) Bobby is one of Boston's coolest cats. Men from all over the greater Boston area come to the South End to peruse Bobby's amazing selection of classic clothing from another era. This is stuff that your grandfather wore – if he was a very stylish man. Smoking jackets, bow ties, bomber jackets and more.

The women's section is smaller, but there is enough here to make sure the lady looks as good as her date.

MOTLEY
CLOTHING, GIFTS

Map p256 (www.shopmotley.com; 623 Tremont St; MBack Bay) This little shoebox of a store lives up to its name, offering a 'motley' array of hip clothing, funny books and novelty gift items. The ever-changing product line includes supercomfy, clever T-shirts and true-blue vintage Boston sports-fan gear. You absolutely do not need anything that is on offer at Motley, but you will absolutely find something that you *have* to own.

SAULT NEW ENGLAND
CLOTHING, GIFTS

Map p256 (www.saultne.com; 577 Tremont St; ⊘11am-7pm Tue-Sun; MBack Bay) Blending prepster and hipster, rustic and chic, this little basement boutique packs in a lot of intriguing stuff. The eclectic mix of merchandise runs the gamut from new and vintage clothing to coffee-table books and homemade terrariums. A New England theme runs through the store, with nods to the Kennedys, *Jaws* and LL Bean.

WILD INDIGO
CLOTHING, ACCESSORIES

Map p256 (www.wildindigoboston.com; 53 Dartmouth St; ⊘11:30am-7pm Wed-Sat, noon-5:30pm Sun; MBack Bay) Wild Indigo calls itself a neighborhood boutique, but it's almost like a gallery, featuring clothing and accessories (for the body and home) by more than 50 local artists and designers. Come here for really unique clothing – not to mention jewelry, handbags, belts and scarves – that are conceived from the heart and made by hand.

SOWA VINTAGE MARKET
MARKET, VINTAGE

Map p256 (www.sowavintagemarket.com; 460 Harrison Ave; ⊘10am-4pm Sun, 5-9pm first Fri; MTufts Medical Center, ⊡SL4 or SL5) Where the Open Market is for cool hand-made stuff, the Vintage Market is for cool old stuff. It's like an indoor flea market, with dozens of vendors selling clothes, furniture, posters, housewares and loads of other trash and treasures.

ARS LIBRI
BOOKS

Map p256 (www.arslibri.com; 500 Harrison Ave; ⊘9am-6pm Mon-Fri, 11am-5pm Sat; MNew England Medical Center, ⊡SL4 or SL5) You do have to ring the doorbell to get in, which is intimidating, but it's worth it. Ars Libri is an art bookstore extraordinaire, specializing in rare and out-of-print books. The former warehouse is filled from floor to ceiling with books on all aspects and eras of art, architecture and design. If you love books or art, and especially books about art, you'll love Ars Libri.

TADPOLE
CHILDREN

Map p256 (www.shoptadpole.com; 58 Clarendon St; MBack Bay) Shopper beware: enter this store and be tempted to play. Whether it's the reproduction Fisher-Price record player that you had as a kid, or the pint-size teepee where you can have your own powwow, Tadpole sells some serious fun. Fortunately, it doesn't discourage adults from 'testing' out the products.

GRACIE FINN
GIFTS

Map p256 (www.graciefinn.com; 18 Union Park St; MBack Bay) This is essentially a stationery store, with contemporary, cool, hand-pressed cards. But there is more to this little gift shop than fancy writing. There's the never-ending array of Aunt Sadie's scented candles (all-time bestseller: Tree in a Can), a great selection of tote bags, funny magnets, and other things you didn't know you needed.

SOUTH END FORMAGGIO
FOOD & DRINK

Map p256 (www.southendformaggio.com; 268 Shawmut Ave; ⊘9am-8pm Mon-Fri, to 7pm Sat, 11am-5pm Sun; MBack Bay, ⊡SL4 or SL5) Weave your way through this tiny store – past the shelves piled high with dry goods, past the eclectic selection of wines. Way in the back, you'll find what you're looking for: the cheese. The smallish case is practically overflowing with hard cheeses, soft cheeses, pungent cheeses, mild cheeses, spreadable cheeses, shredded cheeses.

To really get to know your cheeses, join the cheesemongers for a Sunday-night wine and cheese pairing (per person $35).

CALAMUS BOOKSTORE
BOOKS

Map p258 (www.calamusbooks.com; 92 South St; ⊘9am-7pm Mon-Sat, noon-6pm Sun; MSouth

Station) The Greek deity Calamus was transformed with grief into a reed when his lover drowned. The character inspired Walt Whitman's 'Calamus' poems, which celebrate gay love. And now, he has inspired Boston's biggest and best GLBT bookstore. With a full calendar of author talks and art exhibitions, as well as a regular electronic newsletter, Calamus is not only a bookstore but also a community center.

UNIFORM   CLOTHING
Map p256 (www.uniformboston.com; 511 Tremont St; MBack Bay) With its cool collection of men's casual wear, Uniform caters to all the metrosexuals in this hipster 'hood. Guys leave this place decked out in designers like Ben Sherman and Penguin, with Freitag bag slung over shoulder. Hot men looking good in hot fashions: it's very South End.

LEKKER HOME   HOMEWARES
Map p256 (www.lekkerhome.com; 1317 Washington St; ⊙10am-6pm Sun & Mon, to 7pm Tue-Sat; MTufts Medical Center, ⍰SL4 or SL5) If you are into Scandinavian design, get into Lekker. Look for crisp, clean lines, attractive yet practical gadgets, stainless steel and monochrome color patterns and plenty of modern chic. Gift idea for the Thurston Howell in your life: a set of eight whiskey stones, to chill a digestif without diluting.

TURTLE   CLOTHING
Map p256 (www.turtleboston.com; 619 Tremont St; ⊙11am-7pm Tue-Fri, 10am-6pm Sat, noon-5pm Sun; MBack Bay) Fashion is art, according to the ladies at Turtle. And this edgy urban boutique is a part of the exciting art scene in the South End, carrying jewelry, dresses and sweaters like you won't see anywhere else. Focusing on emerging designers from around the world, Turtle's collection is innovative, energetic and – well – expensive. Fortunately, it has great end-of-season sales: timing is everything.

COCO BABY   CHILDREN
Map p256 (www.cocobaby.co; 1636 Washington St; MMassachusetts Ave, ⍰SL4 or SL5) This South End newbie reflects the changing face of the neighborhood. Coco Baby caters to eco- and style-conscious families, with a great selection of baby clothes, toys and accessories. The unique selection of items means that your little friend won't receive a duplicate of your gift. The helpful staff members really know their stuff.

🏃 SPORTS & ACTIVITIES

CHINATOWN MARKET TOUR   WALKING TOUR
(www.bostonfoodtours.com; per person $65; ⊙9:30am-1pm Thu & Sat) Is it a walking tour or a cooking class? Let local chef Jim Becker guide you through the crowded, chaotic streets of Chinatown, with stops at a produce market, a Chinese bakery, an herbal pharmacy and a traditional teahouse, with plenty of shopping and cooking tips along the way. The tour ends with a dim sum feast.

KARMA YOGA STUDIO   YOGA
Map p256 (www.karmayogastudio.com; class $10-15; ⊙7:30am-7:30pm; MMassachusetts Ave, ⍰1) Yoga classes are offered in a lofty, light-filled space that is beautifully decorated and exudes positive vibes. Most of the classes are vinyasa and core power yoga. Get up for the sunrise class and get rewarded with free tea afterwards.

EXHALE SPA   DAY SPA, YOGA
Map p258 (☎617-532-7000; www.exhalespa.com; 28 Arlington St; ⊙6am-9pm Mon-Fri, 8am-8pm Sat & Sun; MArlington) If you are waiting to exhale, now you can do it at this spa for mind and body. Offering up to 10 classes a day, Exhale focuses on core fusion (like Pilates) and yoga basics. Exhale also offers acupuncture, nutrition consulting and other healing services, in addition to more traditional spa services. After your workout, treat yourself to a fusion massage.

GRUB STREET   WRITING COURSES
Map p258 (www.grubstreet.org; 160 Boylston St; one-day seminar $115; ⊙9am-5pm Mon-Fri; MBoylston) Designed to offer a supportive environment for would-be writers, Grub Street sponsors long-term writing workshops, evening and weekend seminars and countless readings and other events. Programs tend to focus on a genre (fiction, poetry, screenplays etc) and involve a lot of writing and rewriting.

BOSTON CENTER FOR ADULT EDUCATION   COURSES
Map p258 (www.bcae.org; 122 Arlington St; ⊙9am-5pm Mon-Fri; MArlington) The Boston Center for Adult Education offers everything from historical tours to writing classes to massage courses for couples.

2

1. The Back Bay Fens (p129)
A lush green link in Frederick Law Olmsted's Emerald Necklace.

2. Sign of an icon (p129)
Boston's beloved Citgo sign presides over Kenmore Sq.

3. Fan Pier (p135)
Visit the Seaport District for some of the city's best galleries, seafood, gardens and – of course – views.

Back Bay

Neighborhood Top Five

1 Admiring Boston's most evocative and archetypal architecture in Copley Sq, with **Trinity Church** (p114) reflecting in the facade of the **John Hancock Tower** (p116) at one end, and the **Boston Public Library** (p112) anchoring the other end.

2 Strolling, cycling or running along the **Charles River Esplanade** (p115).

3 Window shopping and gallery hopping on **Newbury St** (p120).

4 Feeling yourself at the center of the world in the unusual **Mapparium** (p116).

5 Locating the landmarks from the sky at the **Prudential Center Skywalk Observatory** (p116).

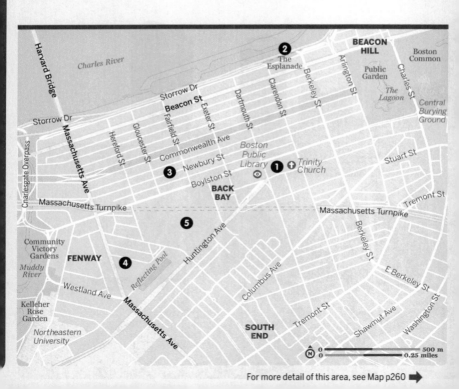

For more detail of this area, see Map p260 ➡

Explore Back Bay

Back Bay is not as old as some other Boston neighborhoods, nor is it as historically significant. But thanks to magnificent Victorian brownstones and high-minded civic plazas, it is certainly among the loveliest – and a required destination for all Boston visitors.

Copley Sq represents the best of Back Bay architecture, as it gracefully blends disparate elements like the Renaissance Revival Boston Public Library, the Richardsonian Romanesque Trinity Church and the modernist John Hancock Tower. Copley Sq should be your first stop in Back Bay, good for whiling away an hour or even a day.

After admiring the architecture and browsing the books, you are perfectly placed for an afternoon of window shopping or gallery hopping. Swanky Newbury St is famous among fashion mavens, art aficionados and music lovers, for it is lined with boutiques and galleries (and one legendary music store).

Not surprising, this bustling retail and residential center is also a drinking and dining wonderland, with sidewalk cafes, trendy bars and chic restaurants on nearly every block. It's not quite the same slick scene as the trendsetting South End, but there are still places to see and be seen in Back Bay.

Local Life

→ **Hang-outs** It doesn't get more local than the Corner Tavern (p118).
→ **Outdoors** Perfect for picnic lunches and summertime lounging, the Charles River Esplanade (p115) is Boston's backyard.

Getting There & Away

→ **Metro** The main branch of the green line runs the length of Boylston St, with stops at Arlington near the Public Garden, Copley at Copley Sq and Hynes at Mass Ave. The green E-line branch follows along Huntington Ave to Prudential and Symphony.

Lonely Planet's Top Tip

Visit BosTix (www.bostix.org; p34) on Copley Sq for same-day, half-price tickets to local theater, comedy and music events.

Best Places to Eat

→ Courtyard (p116)
→ Piattini (p116)
→ L'Espalier (p117)
→ Douzo (p117)
→ Parish Café (p117)

For reviews, see p116 →

Best Places to Drink

→ Flash's Cocktails (p118)
→ Corner Tavern (p118)
→ Bukowski Tavern (p118)
→ Minibar (p119)

For reviews, see p118 →

Best Galleries

→ Gallery Naga (p115)
→ Barbara Krakow Gallery (p115)
→ Copley Society of Art (p115)
→ Alpha Gallery (p115)
→ Society of Arts & Crafts (p121)

For reviews, see p115 →

BACK BAY

TOP SIGHTS
BOSTON PUBLIC LIBRARY

Dating from 1852, the esteemed Boston Public Library (BPL) was built as a 'shrine of letters,' lending credence to Boston's reputation as the Athens of America. The old McKim building is notable for its magnificent facade (inspired by Italian Renaissance palazzi) and exquisite interior art. Pick up a free brochure and take a self-guided tour; alternatively, free guided tours (times vary) depart from the entrance hall.

Puvis de Chavannes Gallery

From the main entrance, a marble staircase leads past Pierre Puvis de Chavannes' inspirational murals. The artist titled his composition *The Muses of Inspiration Hail the Spirit, the Harbinger of Light.* The mural depicts poetry, philosophy, history and science, which he considered 'the four great expressions of the human mind.'

Don't miss the mighty lions posed on their pedestals, carved by Saint-Gaudens to honor the Massachusetts Civil War infantries.

Upstairs, at the entrance to Bates Hall, there is another Puvis de Chavannes mural, also *The Muses*. Here, the nine muses from Greek mythology are honoring a male figure, the Genius of the Enlightenment.

Bates Hall

The staircase terminates at the splendid Bates Hall Reading Room (pictured above), where even mundane musings are elevated by the barrel-vaulted, 50ft coffered ceilings.

Bates Hall is named for Joshua Bates, the BPL's original benefactor in 1852. After spending his childhood browsing in bookstores, Bates

DON'T MISS...

➡ Mora and Saint-Gaudens' carving of Minerva, goddess of wisdom, on the central keystone on the facade

➡ *Frieze of the Prophets* by John Singer Sargent

➡ Peaceful Italianate courtyard

PRACTICALITIES

➡ Map p260

➡ www.bpl.org

➡ 700 Boylston St

➡ admission free

➡ ⊘9am-9pm Mon-Thu, 9am-5pm Fri & Sat year-round, 1-5pm Sun Oct-May

➡ 🛜

➡ Ⓜ Copley

appreciated the potential for and importance of self-education through reading. He donated $50,000 to the city of Boston, with the stipulations that 'the building shall be...an ornament to the city, that there shall be a room for 100 to 150 person to sit at reading tables, and that it be perfectly free to all.'

Abbey Room

The Abbey Room is among the library's most sumptuous, with its oak wainscoting, marble flooring and elaborate fireplace. The room is named for the author of the 1895 murals, which recount Sir Galahad's *Quest and Achievement of the Holy Grail*.

Elliott Room

The two 2nd-floor lobbies borrow their artistic elements from Pompeii and Venice, respectively. Off the Venetian lobby, the relatively plain study room is named for painter John Elliott, who did the ceiling mural. *The Triumph of Time* depicts 12 angelic figures, representing the 12 hours on the clock, while the male figure in the cart is Father Time. He is flanked on either side by the Hours of Life and Death. The 20 horses are the centuries since the birth of Christ.

Sargent Gallery

The pièce de résistance of the BPL artwork is on the 3rd floor, which features John Singer Sargent's unfinished Judaic and Christian murals entitled *The Triumph of Religion*.

The theme is surprising for an institution of secular learning. The mural traces the history of Western religion from the primitive worship of pagan gods to the foundation of the Law of Israel to the commencement of the Messianic Age with the birth of Christ. Some scholars argue that the sequence depicts a progression toward religious subjectivity and individualist spiritual pursuits. Others have interpreted that the artist portrayed Christianity as being more evolved than Judaism. Most controversial was Sargent's use of a strong and steadfast figure for *Church*, in contrast with the weak and blindfolded figure for *Synagogue*.

A final painting of the Sermon on the Mount was intended for the vacant space above the stairwell; the mural was never completed, due in part to the strong reaction from the Jewish community. When the installation was unveiled in 1919, critics called it anti-Semitic. Sargent (by all accounts, dismayed) was unable to appease his critics.

The murals were largely (and perhaps intentionally) forgotten for the remainder of the century. They were finally restored and unveiled in 1999.

BPL EVENTS

See the BPL website for a schedule of free events, which range from author talks to musical performances.

DID YOU KNOW?

The Boston Public Library was the first free municipal library in the world, as well as being the first library to allow its guests to borrow books and materials. The BPL was also the first library to establish a branch system, when it opened a branch in East Boston in 1870 (and 20 more in subsequent years). And in 1895, BPL became the first library with a designated children's area.

TOTS & TEENS & IN-BETWEENS

The BPL offers loads of entertaining and educational resources for kids and teenagers, including homework help, book lists, movie nights and even video games. Of course there is a dedicated children's area, but older kids will want to hang out in the fun and funky Teen Lounge.

BACK BAY BOSTON PUBLIC LIBRARY

TOP SIGHTS
BOSTON PUBLIC LIBRARY

TOP SIGHTS
TRINITY CHURCH

A masterpiece of American architecture, Trinity Church is the country's ultimate example of Richardsonian Romanesque. The granite exterior, with a massive portico and side cloister, uses sandstone in colorful patterns. The interior is an awe-striking array of vibrant murals and stained glass, most by artist John LaFarge, who cooperated closely with architect Henry Hobson Richardson to create an integrated composition of shapes, colors and textures. Free architectural tours are offered following Sunday service at 11:15am.

The footprint of Trinity Church is a Greek cross, with chancel, nave and transepts surrounding the central square. The wide-open interior was a radical departure from traditional Episcopal architecture, but it embodies the democratic spirit of the congregation in the 1870s.

The walls of the great central tower are covered by two tiers of **murals**, soaring more than 100ft. Prior to this commission, LaFarge did not have experience with mural painting on this scale. The result – thousands of square feet of exquisite, jewel-toned encaustic paintings – established his authority as the father of the American mural movement.

The 33 **stained-glass windows** in the church represent diverse styles: most of them were executed by different glass workshops. The jewels of the church are the work of La-Farge, who was not commissioned until 1883. His windows are distinctive for their use of layered opalescent glass, resulting in an unprecedented richness of shades and dimensions. LaFarge's first commission was *Christ in Majesty*, the three-panel clerestory window at the west end, now considered one of America's finest examples of stained-glass art.

DON'T MISS

➡ Sunlight streaming through John La-Farge's stained-glass windows

➡ Free concerts on the impressive pipe organ on Fridays at 12:15pm

➡ Reflection of Trinity Church in the facade of the John Hancock Tower

PRACTICALITIES

➡ Map p260

➡ www.trinitychurch boston.org

➡ 206 Clarendon St

➡ adult/child/senior & student $7/free/5

➡ ⊘10am-3:30pm Mon-Fri, 9am-4pm Sat, 1-5pm Sun

➡ Ⓜ Copley

 SIGHTS

BOSTON PUBLIC LIBRARY · LIBRARY
See p112.

TRINITY CHURCH · CHURCH
See p114.

COMMONWEALTH AVENUE · STREET
Map p260 (Commonwealth Ave; M Arlington, Copley or Hynes) The grandest of Back Bay's grand boulevards is Commonwealth Ave (more commonly Comm Ave). Boston's Champs Élysées, the dual-carriageway connects the Public Garden with the Back Bay Fens, a green link in Olmsted's Emerald Necklace. The grassy mall is dotted with grand elms and lined with stately brownstones.

The eclectic array of public art honors – among others – a Civil War hero, a First Lady, an abolitionist, a suffragist, a maritime historian, an Argentinian statesman and a Viking explorer.

CHARLES RIVER ESPLANADE · PARK
Map p261 (www.esplanadeassociation.org; M Charles/MGH or Kenmore) The southern bank of the Charles River Basin is an enticing urban escape, with grassy knolls and cooling waterways, all designed by Frederick Law Olmsted. The park is dotted with public art, including an oversized bust of Arthur Fiedler, long-time conductor of the Boston Pops. Paths along the river are ideal for bicycling, jogging or walking.

The Esplanade stretches almost 3 miles along the Boston shore of the Charles River, from the Museum of Science to BU Bridge.

GIBSON HOUSE MUSEUM · HISTORIC BUILDING
Map p260 (www.thegibsonhouse.org; 137 Beacon St; tours adult/child/senior & student $9/3/6; ☺tours 1pm, 2pm & 3pm Wed-Sun; M Arlington) Catherine Hammond Gibson was considered quite the pioneer when she moved to this Italian Renaissance row house in 1860 (that she was a female homeowner in this 'New Land' was even more unusual). The Gibson House attempts to preserve a piece of Victorian-era Boston, showcasing antique furniture and art that was collected by the Gibson family.

ARLINGTON STREET CHURCH · CHURCH
Map p260 (www.ascboston.org; 351 Boylston St; ☺noon-6pm Wed-Sun May-Oct; M Arlington) The first public building erected in Back Bay in 1861, this graceful church features extraordinary Tiffany windows and 16 bells in its steeple. The church's Unitarian Universalist ministry is purely progressive, as it has been since Rev William Ellery Channing preached here in the early 19th century. (A statue in his honor is across the street in the Public Garden.)

BARBARA KRAKOW GALLERY · GALLERY
Map p260 (www.barbarakrakowgallery.com; 10 Newbury St; ☺10am-5:30pm Tue-Sat; M Arlington) The catalogue of artists represented by this older gallery (established in 1964) reads like something you'd expect from a major museum. Among the famous are Josef Albers, Ellsworth Kelly, Sol LeWitt and Jasper Johns. Though it's very much a house of the modernists, the gallery sometimes displays the work of an emerging artist.

COPLEY SOCIETY OF ART · GALLERY
Map p260 (www.copleysociety.org; 158 Newbury St; ☺11am-6pm Mon-Sat, noon-5pm Sun; M Copley) Dating to 1879, CoSo is the country's oldest non-profit art association in the country. With more than 500 members, the showings in the three exhibit spaces are rich and varied. There are usually 15 to 20 exhibits each year, including annual shows featuring new members, small works and Boston-themed pieces.

ALPHA GALLERY · GALLERY
Map p260 (www.alphagallery.com; 38 Newbury St; ☺10am-5:30pm Tue-Sat, 11am-5:30pm Sun; M Arlington) Presenting the work of some headline-grabbing artists (sometimes local, sometimes international), this starkly minimalist gallery mostly shows oils (some figurative, some abstract), though occasionally you'll see sculpture, mixed media and prints. It hosts an annual new-talent exhibition and intermittently has special shows of masters such as Max Beckmann and Milton Avery.

GALLERY NAGA · GALLERY
Map p260 (www.gallerynaga.com; 67 Newbury St; ☺10am-5pm Tue-Sat; M Arlington) Inside the Gothic digs of the Church of the Covenant, Gallery Naga exhibits contemporary painters, featuring many highly-regarded local and regional artists. You can also see varied prints, photographs and sculpture, as well as some impressive examples of holography. Naga has a warm place in many hearts for specializing in unique and limited-edition furniture.

JOHN HANCOCK TOWER · NOTABLE BUILDING

Map p260 (200 Clarendon St; MCopley) Constructed with more than 10,000 panels of mirrored glass, the 62-story John Hancock Tower was designed in 1976 by Henry Cobb. It is the tallest and most beloved skyscraper on the Boston skyline – despite the precarious falling panes of glass when it was first built. The Hancock offers an amazing perspective on Trinity Church, reflected in its facade.

NEW OLD SOUTH CHURCH · CHURCH

Map p260 (www.oldsouth.org; 645 Boylston St; ☺9am-7pm Mon-Fri, 10am-4pm Sat & Sun; MCopley) This magnificent puddingstone Venetian Gothic church on Copley Sq is called the 'new' Old South because up until 1875, the congregation worshiped in the Old South Church on Milk St (now the **Old South Meeting House**). The Congregational church has an impressive collection of stained-glass windows, all shipped from London, and an organ that was rescued from a Minneapolis church just before demolition.

PRUDENTIAL CENTER SKYWALK OBSERVATORY · LOOKOUT

Map p260 (www.prudentialcenter.com; 800 Boylston St; adult/child/senior & student $13/9/11; ☺10am-10pm Mar-Oct, to 8pm Nov-Feb; P ⛤; MPrudential) Technically called the Shops at Prudential Center, this landmark Boston building is not much more than a fancy shopping mall. But it does provide a bird's-eye view of Boston from its 50th-floor skywalk. Completely enclosed by glass, the skywalk offers spectacular 360-degree views of Boston and Cambridge, accompanied by an entertaining audio tour (with a special version catering to kids).

If these soaring heights aren't enough for you, catch the fun film called *Wings over Boston* (not for acrophobes). Also included in the price of admission is *Dreams of Freedom*, an exhibit that explores the role that immigrants have played in the history of Boston. Read first-hand accounts of immigrants' experiences and see if you could pass the citizenship test. Alternatively, enjoy the same view from Top of the Hub (p119) for the price of a drink.

MARY BAKER EDDY LIBRARY & MAPPARIUM · LIBRARY

Map p260 (www.marybakereddylibrary.org; 200 Massachusetts Ave; adult/child, senior & student $6/4; ☺10am-4pm Tue-Sun; ⛤; MSymphony)

The Mary Baker Eddy Library houses one of Boston's hidden treasures, the intriguing Mapparium. The Mapparium is a room-size, stained-glass globe that visitors walk through on a glass bridge. It was created in 1935, which is reflected in the globe's geopolitical boundaries. The acoustics, which surprised even the designer, allow everyone in the room to hear even the tiniest whisper.

Besides the Mapparium, the library has an odd amalgam of exhibits related to its full name, the MBE Library for the Betterment of Humanity. Second-floor galleries deal with the 'search for the meaning of life,' both on a personal and global level. The heart of the library's collections, Eddy's papers and transcripts, are on the top floors and accessible by permission.

CHRISTIAN SCIENCE CHURCH · CHURCH

Map p260 (www.tfccs.com; 175 Huntington Ave; ☺noon-4pm Tue, 1-4pm Wed, noon-5pm Thu-Sat, 11am-3pm Sun, service 10am Sun; MSymphony) Known to adherents as the 'Mother Church,' this is the international home base for the Church of Christ, Scientist (Christian Science), founded by Mary Baker Eddy in 1866. Tour the grand classical revival basilica, which can seat 3000 worshippers, listen to the 14,000-pipe organ, and linger on the expansive plaza with its 670ft-long reflecting pool.

✖ EATING

COURTYARD · MODERN AMERICAN $$

Map p260 (www.thecateredaffair.com/bpl/courtyard; 700 Boylston St; mains $12-17; ☺lunch Mon-Fri; ✐; MCopley) The perfect destination for an elegant luncheon with artfully prepared food is – believe it or not – the Boston Public Library. Overlooking the beautiful Italianate courtyard, this grown-up restaurant serves seasonal, innovative and exotic dishes (along with a few standards). The only downside is the lack of alcohol, but we understand the concern about drinking and reading.

PIATTINI · ITALIAN $$

Map p260 (www.piattini.com; 226 Newbury St; mains $18-25; ☺lunch Mon-Fri, dinner daily; ✐; MCopley) If you have trouble deciding what to order, Piattini can help. The name means 'small plates,' so you don't have to choose just one. The list of wines by the glass is extensive, each accompanied by tasting

WEATHER OR NOT

Steady blue, clear view
Flashing blue, clouds are due
Steady red, rain ahead
Flashing red, snow instead
Since 1950, Bostonians have used this simple rhyme and the weather beacon atop the old Hancock tower (next to the new John Hancock Tower) to determine if they need to take their umbrella when they leave the house. And yes, the beacon has been known to flash red in midsummer. But that is not a warning of some extremely inclement New England weather, but rather an indication that the Red Sox game has been canceled for the night.

notes and fun facts. This intimate *enoteca* (wine bar) is a delightful setting to sample the flavors of Italy, and you might just learn something while you're there.

L'ESPALIER FRENCH **$$$**
Map p260 (☏617-262-3023; www.lespalier.com; 774 Boylston St; lunch $40, dinner $85; ☺lunch & dinner Mon-Sat; ⓂPrudential) This tried-and-true favorite remains the crème de la crème of Boston's culinary scene, thanks to impeccable service and a variety of prix-fixe and tasting menus. The menus change daily, but usually include a degustation of caviar, a degustation of seasonal vegetables and recommended wine pairings.

DOUZO SUSHI **$$**
Map p260 (☏617-859-8886; www.douzosushi.com; 131 Dartmouth St; sushi & sashimi $4-10, dinner platters $20-28; ☺lunch & dinner; ⓂBack Bay) Easy on the eyes, easy on the palate. Douzo fills its loungey interior with attractive urbanites sipping fancy cocktails and feasting on fresh raw fish. The place buzzes with an atmosphere of see-and-be-seen, but attentive eaters are also paying close attention to the mini masterpieces coming from the sushi bar.

PARISH CAFÉ SANDWICHES **$**
Map p260 (www.parishcafe.com; 361 Boylston St; mains $8-15; ☺noon-2am; ☒; ⓂArlington) Sample the creations of Boston's most famous chefs without exhausting your expense account. The menu at Parish features a rotating roster of salads and sandwiches, each designed by

a local celebrity chef, including Lydia Shire, Ken Oringer and Barbara Lynch.

Despite the creative fare, this place feels more 'pub' than 'cafe.' The long bar – backed by big TVs and mirrors – attracts a lively after-work crowd.

TRIDENT BOOKSELLERS & CAFÉ INTERNATIONAL **$**
Map p260 (www.tridentbookscafe.com; 338 Newbury St; mains $8-15; ☺9am-midnight; ☖☒; ⓂHynes) Is Trident a bookstore with an amazingly eclectic menu or a cafe with a super selection of reading material? The collection of books is wide but leans toward political and New Age themes. The food menu is equally varied, ranging from the comforting (muffins, soups, smoothies) to the daring (spinach *arancini* or rice balls, Tibetan dumplings). Vegetarians rejoice over the vegan cashew chili.

ATLANTIC FISH CO SEAFOOD **$$**
Map p260 (www.atlanticfishco.com; 761 Boylston St; mains $17-27; ☺lunch & dinner; ⓂCopley) New England clam chowder in a bread bowl. For a perfect lunch at Atlantic Fish Co, that's all you need to know. For the nonbelievers, we will add Maine lobster pot pie, lobster ravioli and jumbo lump crabcakes. There's more, of course, and the menu is printed daily to showcase the freshest ingredients. Enjoy it in the seafaring dining room or the flower-filled sidewalk patio.

CASA ROMERO MEXICAN **$$**
Map p260 (☏617-536-4341; www.casaromero.com; 30 Gloucester St; mains $17-28; ☺dinner; ☒; ⓂHynes) The entrance to this hidden treasure is in the public alley off Gloucester St. Step inside and find yourself in a cozy casa – filled with folk art and Talavera tiles – which is wonderful and warm during winter months. In pleasant weather, dine under the stars on the delightful patio.

This is not your average *taqueria* – be prepared to pay for the experience (unless you arrive before 6pm, in which case you can take advantage of the early bird special, a three-course meal for $22).

BAR LOLA TAPAS **$$**
Map p260 (www.barlola.com; 160 Commonwealth Ave; tapas $6-12; ☺brunch Sat & Sun, dinner daily to 1am; ⓂCopley) This authentic Spanish eatery is tucked into a subterranean space on residential Commonwealth Ave. The menu is exclusively tapas, prepared by a team of

chefs trained in España. Mural-painted walls and flamenco music create an inviting old-world ambience; the lively, Spanish-speaking crowd and pitchers of sangria add to it. Live flamenco dancing Sundays at 8pm.

VLORA MEDITERRANEAN **$$**

Map p260 (www.vloraboston.com; 545 Boylston St; mains $15-25; ⏰lunch & dinner; 🍷; Ⓜ Copley) Tucked in below street level, Vlora is a hidden blue gem with a chic, modern Mediterranean ambience. The chef/owner is actually Albanian (Vlora is his hometown) but the menu hints of Greece and southern Italy, with plenty of healthy, delicious vegetarian options. Food preparation is simple and fresh; the service is attentive; and the vibe is cool but not cold. 'Eat better, live better' indeed!

BRASSERIE JO FRENCH **$$**

Map p260 (www.brasseriejoboston.com; 120 Huntington Ave; mains $12-20; ⏰breakfast, lunch & dinner, to 1:30am Fri & Sat; Ⓜ Prudential) Both classy and convivial, this French brasserie is a prime place to catch a bite before the symphony. The kitchen stays open late, so you can also stop by afterwards for classic French fare such as steak frites, mussels *marinière* and *croque monsieur*. Regulars crow about the coq au vin.

SONSIE INTERNATIONAL **$$**

Map p260 (www.sonsieboston.com; 327 Newbury St; mains $18-25; ⏰breakfast, lunch & dinner; 📶; Ⓜ Hynes) Upstairs, Sonsie is a trendy spot that continues to attract devotees with its interesting, eclectic menu, not to mention the eye candy that patronizes the place. Tiny, cafe-style tables are crammed into the front of the restaurant, offering a fabulous view through French windows onto Newbury St.

If you're not into the scene, descend into the Wine Room @ Sonsie for a wonderful selection of wine, and bartenders that really know their stuff.

SUMMER SHACK SEAFOOD **$$**

Map p260 (☎617-867-9955; 50 Dalton St; lunch $12-18, dinner $18-28; ⏰lunch & dinner; 👪; Ⓜ Hynes) This Back Bay outlet of Jasper White's famous restaurant is as big and noisy as the lobster is delectable. Portions are large and preparations are straightforward: specialties include traditional lobster rolls, steamed clams and a magnificently huge raw bar.

DRINKING & NIGHTLIFE

FLASH'S COCKTAILS COCKTAIL BAR

Map p260 (www.flashscocktails.com; 312 Stuart St; ⏰11:30am-midnight Mon-Sat, 5pm-midnight Sun; 📶; Ⓜ Arlington) With its old-fashioned neon sign shining bright across Back Bay, Flash's offers an awesome balance between retro and right-now. The menu includes classic cocktails known as 'Flashbacks' and contemporary concoctions, dubbed 'Flash Forward.' Garlic fries are the perfect munchy accompaniment. Considering the fancy-pants drinks, Flash's does an admirable job of preserving a neighborhood atmosphere.

CORNER TAVERN PUB

Map p260 (www.thecornerboston.com; 421 Marlborough St; Ⓜ Hynes) A true neighborhood bar, the Corner Tavern has a decent beer selection, satisfying food and a welcoming laid-back atmosphere. It's convivial but not overly crowded. The Sox are on the TVs (lots of TVs) but the volume is down. What more do you want from your local watering hole?

L'AROMA CAFE CAFE

Map p260 (www.laromacafe.com; 85 Newbury St; Ⓜ Copley) Crowded with sleepy guests lining up for their morning brew, L'Aroma perks them up with specialty teas, artful lattes and other fancy coffee drinks. The selection of pastries is hard to resist, so go for a crumbly buttery scone with your cup o' joe. Sandwiches and salads make this a good lunch stop, too.

CITY BAR HOTEL BAR

Map p260 (www.citybarboston.com; 710 Boylston St; Ⓜ Copley) For an intimate atmosphere and sweet selection of cocktails, you can't go wrong at this swish bar in the Lenox Hotel. It's not exactly a destination in and of itself, but it's ideal for after-work or early-evening drinks. Sink into the leather couch or sidle up to the polished bar for a fancy martini, and amuse yourself observing the clientele giving each other the eye.

BUKOWSKI TAVERN DIVE BAR

Map p260 (www.bukowskitavern.net; 50 Dalton St; ⏰11am-2am; Ⓜ Hynes) This sweet bar lies inside a parking garage next to the canyon of the Mass Pike. Expect sticky wooden tables, loud rock, lots of black hoodies, a dozen different burgers and dogs and more than 100 kinds of beer. In God we trust; all others pay cash.

CLUB CAFÉ
GAY, CLUB

Map p260 (www.clubcafe.com; 209 Columbus Ave; ☺Wed-Sat; ⓜBack Bay) For a glossy gay dance club, stop in this Boston mainstay where you see Kelly Clarkson on the big screen and admire the fellas in person. There is live cabaret in the Napoleon Room four nights a week, while the main dance and lounge area has tea parties, salsa dancing, trivia competitions, karaoke and good old-fashioned dance parties, depending on the night.

Bonus: excellent food. Double bonus: bartenders might be imported from a place that animates Greek statuary.

MINIBAR
COCKTAIL BAR

Map p260 (www.minibarboston.com; 51 Huntington Ave; ⓜCopley) Located in the posh Copley Square Hotel (in the lounge, not in the rooms), Minibar is much more enticing than your typical hotel bar. It's a swank space with cushy couches, sexy people and good vibes. Most importantly, the bartenders mix deadly delicious cocktails. Come for happy hour (5pm to 7pm Monday to Thursday) and feast on juicy $2 sliders.

STORYVILLE
CLUB

Map p260 (www.storyvilleboston.com; 90 Exeter St; ⓜCopley) The legendary Storyville jazz club occupied this same spot in the 1940s, when it hosted the likes of Dave Brubeck and Billie Holiday (who even recorded an album here). The contemporary nightclub recalls that era with its loungey atmosphere and sexy New Orleans–inspired vibe. One room is reserved for dancing, with live music on Wednesday nights.

Along with potent drinks, the place serves excellent modern New England fare well into the night.

RISE
CLUB

Map p260 (www.riseclub.us; 306 Stuart St; cover $20, students $10; ☺1-6am Fri & Sat; ⓜArlington) The clubs are closing and you still want more – that's when you head to RISE. The black light and trance music create an otherworldly atmosphere, where you'll see all kinds of people getting jiggy with it on the dance floor. There is no alcohol; in fact, even a bottle of water is pretty pricey.

TOP OF THE HUB
BAR

Map p260 (☑617-536-1775; www.topofthehub.net; 800 Boylston St; ☺11:30am-1am; ☎; ⓜPrudential) Yes, it's touristy. And overpriced. And a little bit snooty. But the head-spinning city view makes it worthwhile to ride the elevator up to the 52nd floor of the Prudential Center. Come for spectacular sunset drinks and stay for free live jazz. Beware the $24 per person minimum after 8pm.

POUR HOUSE
BAR

Map p260 (907 Boylston St; ⓜHynes) For years, young college students have introduced themselves to urban nightlife by enjoying cheap drinks and cheaper patty burgers in this pleasantly ratty bar. At least one of the TVs is playing Kino, not the Sox game.

⭐ ENTERTAINMENT

TOP CHOICE CAFÉ 939
LIVE MUSIC

Map p260 (Red Room @ 939; www.cafe939.com; 939 Boylston St; ⓜHynes) Run by Berklee students, the Red Room @ 939 is emerging as one of Boston's best music venues. The place has an excellent sound system and a baby grand piano; most importantly, it books interesting, eclectic up-and-coming musicians. This is where you'll see that band that's about to make it big.

And you can probably chat them up after the show, as the place is intimate that way. The only downside is the flat floor, which means short people may wish to arrive early and stand close to the stage. Buy tickets in advance at the Berklee Performance Center.

BERKLEE PERFORMANCE CENTER
BLUES, JAZZ

Map p260 (www.berkleebpc.com; 136 Massachusetts Ave; ⓜHynes) For high-energy jazz recitals, smoky-throated vocalists and oddball sets by keyboard-playing guys who look like they dabble at being dungeon masters, the performance hall at this notable music college hosts a wide variety of performers. Depending on the night, you'll hear student recitals, invited musicians, instructors or the Ultra Sonic Rock Orchestra.

HATCH MEMORIAL SHELL
CONCERT VENUE

(www.hatchshell.com; Charles River Esplanade; ⓜCharles/MGH or Arlington) Free summer concerts take place at this outdoor bandstand on the banks of the Charles River. Most famously, there's Boston's biggest annual music event, the Boston Pops' July 4 concert. But throughout the summer, there are Friday-night movies, Wednesday-night orchestral ensembles and the occasional oldies concert.

🛍 SHOPPING

BLUES JEAN BAR   CLOTHING
Map p260 (www.thebluesjeanbar.com; 85 Newbury St; ⊘11am-7pm Mon-Sat, noon-6pm Sun; ⓂArlington) If you get the blues when it comes to jeans and the way they fit your bod, prop yourself up at this bar and see what they can do for you. 'Jeantenders' are on hand to help you find something to make you look fabulous.

You'll pay big bucks for them, but you'll swear it's worth it when you see your stylin' self in these skinny, straight-leg and bootcut denims.

CLOSET, INC   CLOTHING
Map p260 (www.closetboston.com; 175 Newbury St; ⓂCopley) For shoppers with an eye for fashion but without a pocketbook to match. Closet, Inc (and it does feel like some fashion maven's overstuffed closet) is a secondhand clothing store that carries high-quality suits, sweaters, jackets, jeans, gowns and other garb by acclaimed designers. Most items are less than two years old and in excellent condition.

LUNARIK FASHIONS   ACCESSORIES
Map p260 (279 Newbury St; ⓂHynes) Lunarik is like a modern woman's handbag, with so much useful stuff packed into a small space. And isn't that appropriate, since the 'stuff' packed into Lunrik is – well – handbags. Purses and packs in all shapes and sizes, from funky to formal, from functional to ornamental.

Don't miss the richly colored leather bags designed by local artist Saya Cullinan. Who wouldn't want to pack their stuff into that!

CONDOM WORLD   ACCESSORIES
Map p260 (www.condomworldboston.com; 332 Newbury St; ⓂHynes) Boston's best selection of condoms can be found here, in all sizes, colors and textures. Cinnamon-flavored condoms are not the only way to spice up your sex life, however. Friendly staff can also help you pick out lubricants, adult toys

and other sex paraphernalia. And for the easily amused: provocatively shaped ice-cube trays, pasta and straws; X-rated fortune cookies, etc.

CONVERSE   SHOES, CLOTHING
Map p260 (www.converse.com; 348 Newbury St; ⊘10am-8pm Mon-Sat, 11am-7pm Sun; ⓂHynes) Converse started making shoes right up the road in Malden, Massachusetts way back in 1908. Chuck Taylor joined the 'team' in the 1920s and the rest is history. This retail store (one of three in the country) has an incredible selection of sneakers, denim and other gear.

The iconic shoes come in all colors and patterns; you can make them uniquely your own at the in-store customization area.

COPLEY PLACE   MALL
Map p260 (www.simon.com; 100 Huntington Ave; ⊘10am-8pm Mon-Sat, noon-6pm Sun; ⓂBack Bay) Half the fun of Back Bay shopping is the unique boutiques and local shops that line Newbury St. The other half is the super-swank designer stores that populate Copley Place. This urban mall includes 75 shops, most of them with big names like Neiman Marcus, Barneys New York, Tiffany & Co, Jimmy Choo, A/X Armani Exchange, Christian Dior etc.

EASTERN MOUNTAIN
SPORTS   SPORTS, OUTDOOR EQUIPMENT
Map p260 (www.ems.com; 855 Boylston St; ⊘10am-8pm Mon-Sat, noon-6pm Sun; ⓂHynes) EMS is all over the East Coast, but it began right here in Boston, when a couple of rock climbers started selling equipment they couldn't buy elsewhere. Now this tree-hugger retailer sells not only rock-climbing equipment, but also camping gear, kayaks, snowboards and all the special apparel you need to engage in the aforementioned activities.

FAIRY SHOP   GIFTS
Map p260 (www.thefairyshop.com; 272 Newbury St; ⓂHynes) No, it's not a shop catering to gay men. This place really sells fairies – yes, we mean Tinker Bell – in every shape and size imaginable. That little gnome from the French film Amélie is here too, many times over. So if you'd rather be 'chillin' with your gnomies,' here's where you can do it.

Also: crystals, magic potions, tarot cards, incense, jewelry and comic books.

HEMPEST
CLOTHING, HOMEWARES

Map p260 (www.hempest.com; 207 Newbury St;
⊙11am-8pm Mon-Sat, noon-6pm Sun; Ⓜ Copley)
All of the products at the Hempest are made
from cannabis hemp, the botanical cousin
of marijuana. It's all on the up and up: men's
and women's clothing, organic soaps and lo-
tions, and fun home-furnishing items.

These folks argue that hemp is a rapidly
renewable and versatile resource that is
economically and environmentally benefi-
cial...if only it were legal to grow it in the
United States.

IBEX
CLOTHING

Map p260 (www.retail.ibex.com/boston; 303
Newbury St; Ⓜ Hynes) Based in snowy, cold
Vermont, Ibex makes outdoor clothing
from soft, warm, breathable merino wool.
It's not the itchy stuff you remember – this
wool is plush and pleasurable, thanks to the
fineness of the fiber. Categorized as base
layer, midlayer or outerlayer, the clothing is
guaranteed to keep you cozy, even through
the coldest, snowiest Vermont winter. Bonus: it looks good too.

LIFE IS GOOD
CLOTHING, GIFTS

Map p260 (www.lifeisgood.com; 285 Newbury
St; Ⓜ Hynes) Life *is* good for this locally designed brand of T-shirts, backpacks and
other gear. Styles depict the fun-loving stick
figure Jake engaged in guitar playing, dog
walking, coffee drinking, mountain climbing and just about every other good-vibe di-
version you might enjoy. Jake's activity may
vary, but his 'life is good' theme is constant.

MARATHON SPORTS
SPORTS

Map p260 (www.marathonsports.com; 671 Boylston St; ⊙10:30am-7:30pm Mon-Fri, 10am-6pm
Sat, noon-6pm Sun; Ⓜ Copley) Specializing in
running gear, this place could not have a
better location: it overlooks the finish line
of the Boston Marathon. It's known for attentive customer service, as staff work hard
to make sure you are getting a shoe that fits.
Besides the latest styles and technologies,
Marathon also carries a line of retro running shoes.

NEWBURY COMICS
MUSIC

Map p260 (www.newburycomics.com; 332 Newbury St; Ⓜ Hynes) Any outlet of this local
chain is usually jam-packed with teenagers
clad in black and sporting multiple pierc-
ings. Apparently these kids know where to
find cheap CDs and DVDs. The newest alt-
rock and the latest movies are on sale here,
along with comic books, rock posters and
other silly gags. No wonder everyone is having such a wicked good time.

SECOND TIME AROUND
CLOTHING

Map p260 (www.secondtimearound.net; 176 Newbury St; ⊙10am-8pm Mon-Sat, 11am-7pm Sun;
Ⓜ Copley) This contemporary used-clothing
shop is a gold mine of barely worn designer
clothing (including lots of denim). Merchandise is all in perfect condition and no
more than two years old. Come early and
come often, because you never know what
you're going to find, but you can be sure it
will have a designer label.

Nowadays, Second Time Around has
shops up and down the East Coast, but this
is the flagship store. There are two more
outlets right here on Newbury St.

NEWBURY YARNS
HANDICRAFTS

Map p260 (www.newburyyarns.com; 164 Newbury
St; Ⓜ Copley) Aldrich Robinson is a fashion
designer, a store owner and – of course – a
knitter. She loves her craft and she loves her
customers, which means she offers super
service and plenty of helpful hints to her
fellow knitters.

SHOPS AT PRUDENTIAL CENTER
MALL

Map p260 (www.prudentialcenter.com; 800 Boylston St; ⊙10am-9pm; 🛈; Ⓜ Prudential) One of
Boston's most distinctive landmarks, the
Prudential Center has something for everyone: shops, restaurants, hotel, a chapel and
an amazing 360-degree city view from the
top-floor Skywalk (p116). The main department stores are Saks and Lord & Taylor, but
there are about 75 other vendors.

SOCIETY OF ARTS & CRAFTS
HANDICRAFTS

Map p260 (www.societyofcrafts.org; 175 Newbury
St; ⊙10am-6pm Mon-Sat, noon-5pm Sun; Ⓜ Copley) This prestigious nonprofit gallery was
founded in 1897. With retail space downstairs and exhibit space upstairs, the society
promotes emerging and established artists
and encourages innovative handicrafts. The
collection changes constantly, but you'll find
weaving, leather, ceramics, glassware, furniture and other hand-crafted items.

TRIDENT BOOKSELLERS & CAFÉ
BOOKS

Map p260 (www.tridentbookscafe.com; 338 Newbury St; ⊙9am-midnight; Ⓜ Hynes) Pick out a
pile of books and retreat to a quiet corner
of the cafe to decide which ones you really

want to buy. You'll come away enriched, as Trident's stock tends toward New Age titles. But there's a little bit of everything here, as the 'hippie turned back-to-the-lander, turned Buddhist, turned entrepreneur' owners know how to keep their customers happy.

🏃 SPORTS & ACTIVITIES

BACK BAY YOGA STUDIO　　　　YOGA
Map p260 (www.backbayyoga.com; 364 Boylston St; yoga class $15; ⊘variable; ⓂArlington) Services from massage to meditation, as well as all forms of yoga. Four to nine classes are offered daily, with a particularly full schedule on Monday. Daytime classes are $10, and there are daily community classes for only $5. With three studios painted in jewel tones, it's a warm and attractive space for your sun salutations.

EMERGE SPA　　　　DAY SPA
Map p260 (✉617-437-0006; www.emergespasalon.com; 275 Newbury St; ⓂHynes) Occupying a gorgeous 19th-century town house on swanky Newbury St, this day spa tempts both men and women. The mahogany Men's Club offers not only a shave and a haircut, but also manicures, pedicures, waxing and sports massage – everything the metrosexual in you might desire. Women are not neglected, of course, and there's a whole host of treatments (mostly massage) available for couples.

SOUTHWEST CORRIDOR　　　　CYCLING
(ⓂBack Bay) Extending for almost 5 miles, the Southwest Corridor is a beautiful paved and landscaped walkway, running between and parallel to Columbus and Huntington Aves. It's an ideal urban cycling route, leading from Back Bay, through the South End and Roxbury, to Forest Hills in Jamaica Plain. If you are beat when you get to the other end, you can return on the T (but you can't take bikes on the T during rush hour). Borrow a bike from the **bike-share program** (p222) or rent one at **Community Bicycle Supply** (www.communitybicycle.com; 496 Tremont St; per day $25-35; ⊘10am-6pm Mon-Sat year-round, noon-5pm Sun Apr-Sep; ⓂBack Bay).

KINGS　　　　BOWLING
Map p260 (www.kingsbackbay.com; 50 Dalton St; bowling per person per game $5.50-7, shoe rental $4; ⊘5pm-2am Mon, 11:30am-2am Tue-Sun; 🛜; ⓂHynes) For an over-the-top tenpin experience, roll a few at Kings, where high-tech lanes are lined with neon lights and surrounded by trippy graphics. Behind deck is an enormous cocktail lounge done up in a style reminiscent of *The Jetsons*. If bowling is not your game, there is also billiards, shuffleboard and skeeball.

Contrary to that, this is not the Jersey Shore: mind the dress code. Also, you must be 21 or older after 6pm.

Kenmore Square & Fenway

Neighborhood Top Five

① Spending a day at the **Museum of Fine Arts** (p125), immersing yourself in the Art of the Americas and lunching at the New American Cafe. Dedicate the afternoon to exploring other treasures, especially the Impressionist and post-Impressionist paintings.

② Watching the home-town team whip their opponents at **Fenway Park** (p133).

③ Venerating the artistic, aesthetic and cultural legacy of **Isabella Stewart Gardner** (p127) at her namesake museum.

④ Hearing the world-renowned **Boston Symphony Orchestra** (p132) play in the acoustically perfect Symphony Hall.

⑤ Hitting **Lansdowne St** (p132) for a night of drinking, music and merry-making.

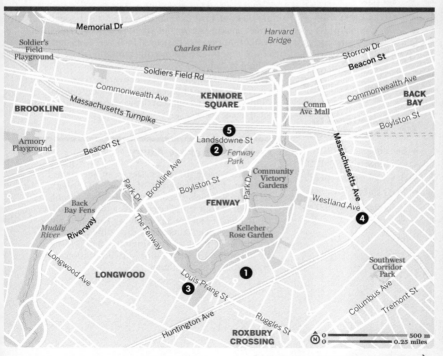

For more detail of this area, see Map p264 ➡

Lonely Planet's Top Tip

If you can't score tickets to the baseball game, you can still watch the action and soak up the atmosphere at one of the bars on Lansdowne St (they all definitely have TVs). You can even hear the cheers and the gasps from the fans inside the ballpark.

✖ Best Places to Eat

➜ Audubon Circle (p130)
➜ El Pelon (p130)
➜ Trattoria Toscana (p130)
➜ Citizen Public House (p130)

For reviews, see p130 ➜

🍷 Best Places to Drink

➜ Bleacher Bar (p131)
➜ Lower Depths (p131)
➜ Pavement Coffeehouse (p131)
➜ Eastern Standard (p131)

For reviews, see p131 ➜

👁 Best Places to Watch the Game

➜ Bleacher Bar (p131)
➜ Lansdowne Pub (p131)
➜ Baseball Tavern (p132)
➜ Tasty Burger (p130)

For reviews, see p131 ➜

Explore Kenmore Square & Fenway

Kenmore Sq is the epicenter of student life in Boston. In addition to the Boston University behemoth, there are more than a half-dozen colleges in the area. As such, Kenmore Sq has a disproportionate share of nightlife, inexpensive but nondescript eateries and dormitories disguised as brownstones.

Come to Kenmore Sq to cavort at cool clubs and to devour cheap food. If you get the timing right, you can do so before or after the Red Sox game. Watch the boys battle it out from your perch at one of the local sports bars or, if you're lucky, at Fenway Park

While Kenmore Sq is best for baseball and beer, the southern part of this neighborhood is dedicated to more high-minded pursuits. Dubbed 'Ave of the Arts,' Huntington Ave represents a concentrated area of major and minor artistic and cultural venues, including Symphony Hall, two universities and two museums. Art-lovers should devote a day to exploring one of Boston's celebrated art venues (although deciding which one will be a challenge).

Local Life

➜ **Cheap Grub** Locals know that Peterborough St (p129) is a hub for affordable eating. International eateries and take-out joints line the little residential street, making it a sort of urban food court. This mini restaurant row was destroyed by fire in 2008, but some of the local faves have recently reopened, much to the delight of Fenway residents and regulars.

➜ **Music Scene** Buy tickets in advance to see national acts at the House of Blues (p132), but hang out at Church (p132) any night of the week for a glimpse of the local music scene.

Getting There & Away

➜ **Metro** West of the center, the green line of the T forks into four branches, all of which run through Kenmore Sq. So you have to pay attention not only to the color of your train, but also its letter (B, C, D or E). To reach Kenmore Sq or Fenway Park, take any of the green-line trains except the E-line to Kenmore T station. Sights along Huntington Ave in Fenway are accessible from the E-line Museum station or the orange-line Ruggles station.

CHUCK CHOI ©

Since 1876, the Museum of Fine Arts has been Boston's premier venue for showcasing art by local, national and international artists. Nowadays the museum's holdings encompass all eras, from the ancient world to contemporary times, and all areas of the globe, making it truly encyclopedic in scope. With the recent opening of new wings dedicated to the Art of the Americas and to contemporary art, the museum has significantly increased its exhibition space and broadened its focus, contributing to Boston's emergence as an art center in the 21st century.

Art of the Americas

The centerpiece of the newly renovated MFA is the four-story Americas wing, which includes 53 galleries exhibiting art from the pre-Columbian era up through the 20th century.

Some of the newest acquisitions are on the lower level, which houses the Pre-Columbian and Native American artwork. There are also a few rooms dedicated to colonial America and the maritime trade, with a wonderful collection of model ships.

Level 1 is dedicated to 18th- and 19th-century art, with several rooms dedicated to Neoclassicism and revolutionary Boston. Thomas Sully's depiction of Washington's *Passage of the Delaware* is a highlight. The MFA has the world's largest holding of Copley paintings. Don't miss the alarming *Watson and the Shark*.

The second level is, perhaps, the richest part of the wing. An entire gallery is dedicated to John Singer Sargent, including his iconic painting *The Daughters of Edward Darley*

DON'T MISS

➡ *The Daughters of Edward Darley Boit* by John Singer Sargent

➡ *Boston Common at Twilight* by Childe Hassam

➡ *Where Do We Come From?* by Paul Gauguin

➡ Buddhist Temple room

PRACTICALITIES

➡ MFA

➡ Map p264

➡ www.mfa.org

➡ 465 Huntington Ave

➡ adult/child/senior & student $22/10/20

➡ ◷10am-5pm Sat-Tue, 10am-10pm Wed-Fri

➡ Ⓜ Museum or Ruggles

FOR KIDS

Children under the age of 17 are admitted free after 3pm on weekdays and all day on weekends – a fantastic family bargain.

DID YOU KNOW?

The murals in the rotunda and above the main staircase were painted by John Singer Sargent in the 1920s. The main rotunda painting depicts the Greek goddess of wisdom, Athena, turning back Time.

GET A GUIDE

For a guided tour in one of seven languages, rent the museum's multimedia guide (adult/child $6/4), which uses video, audio and animation to provide extra insight on the highlights of the MFA collection.

DINING AT THE MFA

The Linde wing features upscale dining at the restaurant Bravo, as well as a cafe and cafeteria. In the Shapiro Courtyard, sample Ken Oringer's menu of modern American cuisine at the New American Café.

Boit. Several highlights in the American Impressionism galleries include pieces by Mary Cassat and the perennial local favorite, *Boston Common at Twilight* by Childe Hassam.

The top floor is devoted to modernism, with wonderful pieces by Alexander Calder, Frank Stella and Georgia O'Keefe. There are also impressive additions by Latin American artists.

Art of Europe

The MFA's collection of European art spans the centuries from the Middle Ages to the 20th century. Art of the Italian Renaissance is well represented, with gilded icons and paintings by Botticelli, Titian and Tintoretto. Also in the house is the Golden Age of Dutch painting, with five paintings by Rembrandt. The highlight of the European exhibit is no doubt the Impressionists and post-Impressionists, with masterpieces by Degas, Gauguin, Renoir and Van Gogh, as well as the largest collection of Monets outside Paris.

Art of Asia, Oceania & Africa

One of the MFA's strongest areas, the collection of Asian art is located in the southwestern wing, along with art from the South Pacific and Africa. The centerpiece of the exhibit is the serene Buddhist Temple room on the 2nd floor, just one exhibit in a vast array of Japanese art, including prints and metal works. There is an extensive display of Chinese paintings, calligraphy and ceramics.

Art of the Ancient World

In the southeastern part of the museum, the MFA's ancient-art collection dates from 6000 BC to AD 600 and covers a huge geographic spectrum. The highlight is certainly the Egyptian galleries, especially the two rooms of mummies. The Etruscan painted tombs are also impressive. Greek, Roman and Nubian occupy the second level, with plenty of perfectly sculpted Greek gods and Roman emperors.

Linde Wing for Contemporary Art

Opened in 2011, this is the newest part of the 'new' MFA. The renovation of the west wing – originally designed by IM Pei – has nearly tripled the exhibition space for contemporary art. There are galleries dedicated to video, multimedia art and decorative arts in addition to the more traditional media.

The darling of museum patrons is *Black River*, a woven tapestry of discarded bottle caps, by Ghanaian artist El Anatsui. But the most compelling piece is perhaps the blue neon sign by Maurizio Nannucci, which spells out 'All Art Has Been Contemporary.'

TOP SIGHTS
ISABELLA STEWART GARDNER MUSEUM

The magnificent Venetian-style palazzo that houses this museum was home to 'Mrs Jack' Gardner herself until her death in 1924. A monument to one woman's taste for acquiring exquisite art, the Gardner is filled with almost 2000 priceless objects, primarily European, including outstanding tapestries and Italian Renaissance and 17th-century Dutch paintings. The four-story greenhouse courtyard is a masterpiece and a tranquil oasis that alone is worth the price of admission.

Art Heist

On March 18, 1990, two thieves disguised as police officers broke into the Isabella Stewart Gardner Museum, escaping with nearly $200 million worth of artwork. The most famous painting stolen was Vermeer's *The Concert,* but the loot also included works by Rembrandt, Manet and Degas, as well as French and Chinese artifacts. The crime was never solved.

Piano Building

In 2012, the Gardner Museum opened the doors of a greatly anticipated, hotly contested new building, designed by architect Renzo Piano. Mrs Jack's will stipulated that her palazzo never be altered, so the project required much negotiation (and approval from the Supreme Court of Massachusetts).

The end result allows the palazzo to better serve its originally intended purpose, which is to share Isabella's love for art and culture with the community. The new space includes a spectacular concert hall and a newly refurbished Tapestry Hall. There is also new exhibit space devoted to contemporary art, supporting the museum's vibrant artist-in-residency program.

DON'T MISS

➡ Ancient art and seasonal landscaping in the courtyard

➡ *Portrait of Isabella Stewart Gardner* by John Singer Sargent

➡ *Rape of Europa* by Titian

➡ Newly restored Tapestry Room

PRACTICALITIES

➡ Map p264

➡ www.gardner museum.org

➡ 280 The Fenway

➡ adult/child/student/senior $15/free/5/12

➡ ⊙11am-5pm Tue-Sun

➡ Ⓜ Museum

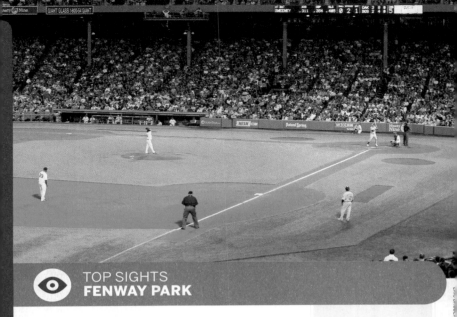

TOP SIGHTS
FENWAY PARK

What is it that makes Fenway Park 'America's Most Beloved Ballpark'? It's not just that it's the home of the Boston Red Sox. Open since 1912, it is the oldest operating baseball park in the country. As such, the park has many quirks that make for a unique experience at Fenway Park.

The **Green Monster**, the 37ft-high wall in left field, is Fenway Park's most famous feature. It's only 310ft away from home plate (compared to the standard 325ft). That makes it a popular target for right-handed hitters, who can score an easy home run with a high hit to left field. On the other hand, a powerful line drive – which might normally be a home run – bounces off the Monster for a double. As all Red Sox fans know, 'the wall giveth and the wall taketh away.'

The Green Monster was painted green only in 1947. But since then, it has become a patented part of the Fenway experience. Literally. The color is officially known as Fence Green and the supplier will not share the recipe.

The **Pesky Pole**, Fenway's right-field foul pole, is named for former shortstop Johnny Pesky. 'Mr Red Sox' Johnny Pesky has been associated with the team for 15 years as a player and 45 as a manager or coach.

The **Triangle**, in the deepest darkest corner of centre field where the walls form a triangle, is – at 425ft – the furthest distance from home plate.

The bleachers at Fenway Park are green, except for the **lone red seat**: seat 21 at section 42, row 37. This is supposedly the longest home run ever hit at Fenway Park – officially 502ft, hit by Ted Williams in 1946.

Tours normally allow you inside the press box and up on top of the Monster. Avoid afternoon tours on game days; crowds are huge and tours shortened.

DON'T MISS

➡ Sitting atop the Green Monster

➡ Original seats that are more than a century old

➡ Fenway's beloved manual scoreboard

PRACTICALITIES

➡ Map p264

➡ www.redsox.com

➡ 4 Yawkey Way

➡ adult/child/senior $12/10/11

➡ ⊘9am-4pm Apr-Oct, 10am-2pm Nov-Mar

➡ 🚹

➡ Ⓜ Kenmore

SIGN OF THE TIMES

'London has Big Ben, Paris has the Eiffel Tower, and Boston has the Citgo sign.' It's an unlikely landmark in this high-minded city, but Bostonians love the bright-blinking 'trimark' that has towered over Kenmore Sq since 1965.

For some, the Citgo sign means baseball: every time the Red Sox hit a home run over the leftfield wall at Fenway Park, Citgo's colorful logo is seen by thousands of fans. For others, it symbolizes the end of the Boston Marathon, as it falls at mile 25 in the race.

For whatever reason, Bostonians have claimed these neon lights as their own. The sign was turned off in 1979 to conserve energy; four years, later Citgo decided to dismantle the deteriorating sign. But local residents rallied, arguing it is a prime example of urban neon art. They fought to bestow landmark status on the sign to preserve it.

The sign was renovated in 2005, replacing the neon lights with LEDs (which are more durable, more energy-efficient and easier to maintain). Indeed, the previous version of the sign required more than 5 miles of neon tubing to light its 60ft-by-60ft face. Featured in film, photographs and song, the Citgo sign continues to shine.

◉ SIGHTS

◉ Kenmore Square

FENWAY PARK BASEBALL PARK
See p128.

FREE **MUGAR MEMORIAL LIBRARY** LIBRARY
Map p264 (www.bu.edu/archives; 771 Commonwealth Ave; admission free; ⏲9am-5pm Mon-Fri; ⓂBU Central) The special collections of BU's Mugar Memorial Library are housed in the Howard Gotlieb Archival Research Center, a 20th-century archive that balances pop culture and scholarly appeal. Rotating exhibits showcase holdings including papers from Arthur Fiedler's collection, Douglas Fairbanks, Jr's archives or the correspondence of BU alumnus Dr Martin Luther King, Jr.

Hours posted are for the archives; exhibit hours may vary depending on their exact location in the library.

◉ Fenway

MUSEUM OF FINE ARTS MUSEUM
See p125.

ISABELLA STEWART GARDNER MUSEUM MUSEUM
See p127.

BACK BAY FENS PARK
Map p264 (Park Dr at Jersey St; ⏲dawn-dusk; ⓂMuseum) The Back Bay Fens, or the Fenway, follows the Muddy River, an aptly named creek choked with reeds. The Fens features tended community gardens, the Kelleher Rose Garden, and plenty of space to toss a Frisbee, play pick-up basketball or lie in the sun. It isn't advisable to linger after dark.

FREE **MASSART** GALLERY
Map p264 (Massachusetts College of Art; www.massart.edu; 621 Huntington Ave, South Bldg; admission free; ⏲noon-6pm Mon-Sat; ⓂLongwood Ave) This is the country's first and only four-year independent public art college. It is one of the country's oldest art schools and as such was the first to grant an art degree. Originally the Massachusetts Normal Art School, the institution was part of a civic plan to promote fine arts and technology, to ensure the state's continued economic growth.

Other parts of this plan included establishing the Museum of Fine Arts (founded in 1870) and Massachusetts Institute of Technology (1860).

There are always thought-provoking or sense-stimulating exhibits to see at MassArt. The Bakalar and Paine galleries host nationally and internationally known artists, as well as emerging talent, as a complement to the school's curricula. Other campus galleries showcase student and faculty work.

✘ EATING

✘ Kenmore Square

Most places in Kenmore Sq target the large local student population, meaning cheap ethnic eats and divey sandwich shops, but a few upscale restaurants have found their way here too.

AUDUBON CIRCLE
MODERN AMERICAN **$$**

Map p264 (www.auduboncircle.us; 838 Beacon St; sandwiches $10-11, mains $15-22; ⏰11:30am-1am; 🛜🅿; Ⓜ️St Mary's) The long black bar, wood floors and high ceilings lend an industrial feel to this lively pub and restaurant. It exudes a good vibe for catching a bite, watching the game or both. Pressed sandwiches are highly recommended (including veggie options), as is the more sophisticated fare, which changes seasonally.

INDIA QUALITY
INDIAN **$**

Map p264 (www.indiaquality.com; 484 Commonwealth Ave; lunch mains $8, dinner mains $12-15; ⏰lunch & dinner; 🅿🚻; Ⓜ️Kenmore) India Quality has been serving chicken curry and lamb *saag* to hungry students, daytime professionals and baseball fans since 1983 – and it repeatedly tops the lists of Boston's best Indian food. The place is rather nondescript, but the food is anything but, especially considering the reasonable prices (look for lunch specials under $10). Service is reliably fast and friendly.

UBURGER
BURGERS **$**

Map p264 (www.uburgerboston.com; 636 Beacon St; ⏰lunch & dinner; Ⓜ️Kenmore) The way burgers were meant to be. The beef is ground fresh daily on the premises and burgers are made to order, with fancy (grilled mushrooms and Swiss cheese) or basic (American cheese and pickles) toppings. The french fries and onion rings are hand-cut and crispy-crunchy good. Also available: chicken sandwiches, hot dogs and salads, but why would you do that?

PETIT ROBERT BISTRO
FRENCH **$$**

Map p264 (📞617-375-0699; www.petitrobertbis tro.com; 468 Commonwealth Ave; lunch $10-15, dinner $20-30; ⏰lunch & dinner; Ⓜ️Kenmore) Once upon a time the legendary Maison Robert represented the finest dining in Boston. The ultrachic institution has now closed, but chef Jacky Robert has reapplied his talents to this welcoming, working-class bistro. The French fare is straightforward and hearty, with daily specials posted on the blackboard. The surroundings are casual-chic but crowded, including a tiny patio.

Service can be slow at peak times, but perhaps that makes it more *authentique*?

🍴 Fenway

The quiet streets between the Back Bay Fens and Fenway Park are home to a few neighborhood favorites. Sadly, a fire in 2008 destroyed all of the restaurants on Peterborough St, but some of these venues have started to reopen.

TOP CHOICE/ EL PELON
TAQUERIA **$**

Map p264 (www.elpelon.com; 92 Peterborough St; tacos $3-6; 🅿🚻; Ⓜ️Museum) If your budget is tight, don't miss this chance to fill up on Boston's best burritos, tacos and tortas, made with the freshest ingredients. The tacos de la casa are highly recommended, especially the *pescado*, made with Icelandic cod and topped with chili mayo. Plates are paper and cutlery is plastic.

TRATTORIA TOSCANA
ITALIAN **$$**

Map p264 (130 Jersey St; mains $15-25; ⏰dinner Mon-Sat; Ⓜ️Museum) On a residential street in the heart of the Fenway, this tiny Old World trattoria welcomes all comers as if they are old friends, serving up Tuscan wines, rich soups and delicious pastas, with gnocchi a particular highlight. The tantalizing aromas and intimate atmosphere delight the neighborhood crowd at this hidden gem.

It's a small place that does not take reservations, but your patience will be rewarded.

CITIZEN PUBLIC HOUSE
MODERN AMERICAN **$$**

Map p264 (📞617-450-9000; www.citizenpub. com; 1310 Boylston St; oysters $2-3, mains $18-22; ⏰dinner daily, brunch Sun; Ⓜ️Fenway) Long overdue on this side of Fenway Park, this is a modern, urban gastropub with food and drinks for a sophisticated palate. There is an eye-catching and daily-changing raw bar, while the selective list of main dishes focuses on roasts and grills. The food is top-notch and it's all complemented by an extensive bar menu, featuring 75 varieties of whisky.

Sample the award-winning Ideal Manhattan, if you dare.

TASTY BURGER
BURGERS **$**

Map p264 (www.tastyburger.com; 1301 Boylston St; burgers $4-6; ⏰11am-2am; 🚻; Ⓜ️Hynes) This ex-Mobile station is now a retro burger joint, replete with pool table. Its name (and poster of Samuel L Jackson) is a nod to *Pulp Fiction*. You won't find a half-pound of Kobe beef on your bun, but you will have to agree 'That's a tasty burger.' And it's a fun place to drink cheap beer and watch sports on TV.

🍷 DRINKING & NIGHTLIFE
⚓

Most bars in the vicinity of mecca (aka Fenway Park) cater to sports fans. While many are forgettable, a few complement and enhance the hysteria.

🍷 Kenmore Square

TOP CHOICE BLEACHER BAR   SPORTS BAR

Map p264 (www.bleacherbarboston.com; 82A Lansdowne St; MKenmore) Tucked under the bleachers at Fenway Park, this classy bar offers a view onto center field (go Jacoby baby!). It's not the best place to watch the game, as the place gets packed, but it's an awesome way to experience America's oldest ballpark, even when the Sox are not playing.

If you want a seat in front of the window, get your name on the waiting list an hour or two before game time; diners then have 45 minutes in the hot seat.

LOWER DEPTHS   BEER BAR

Map p264 (476 Commonwealth Ave; MKenmore) This subterranean space is a beer-lovers' paradise and a welcome addition to Kenmore Sq. It has all the atmosphere (and beer knowledge) of its sister establishment, Bukowski Tavern, but the Lower Depths classes it up. Besides the impressive beer selection, the kitchen turns out excellent comfort food, including one-dollar Fenway Franks with exotic one-dollar toppings. Cash only.

EASTERN STANDARD   COCKTAIL BAR

Map p264 (www.easternstandardboston.com; 528 Commonwealth Ave; mains $15-25; ⏰lunch Mon-Fri, brunch Sat & Sun, dinner daily; MKenmore) Whether you choose the sophisticated, brassy interior or the heated patio (open year-round), you're sure to enjoy the upscale atmosphere at this Kenmore Sq favorite. French bistro fare, with a hint of New American panache, caters to a pregame crowd that prefers wine and cheese to peanuts and crackerjacks. Great people-watching on game nights.

CORNWALL'S   PUB

Map p264 (www.cornwalls.com; 654 Beacon St; ⏰closed Sun; MKenmore) For an extensive list of English and Scottish beers plus a few interesting local brews (Tuckerman's Pale Ale), stop by this family-owned pub. If you need more convincing, the bartenders commonly pour samples should you be curious about an unknown ale. Board games, darts and pool tables keep the drinkers entertained.

LANSDOWNE PUB   IRISH PUB

Map p264 (www.lansdownepubboston.com; 9 Lansdowne St; ⏰4pm-2am Mon-Sat, 10am-2am Sun; MKenmore) Disclaimer: this place gets packed on weekends and on game nights. If you can stand the happy, sweaty people, it's a great vibe, especially if the Sox are winning. If you're not into baseball, maybe you'll like the live-band karaoke (9pm Thursday) or Sunday brunch accompanied by Irish folk music (from 1pm Sunday).

The last best reason to come to Lansdowne Pub is the Irish-cheddar grilled cheese with your pint of Guinness.

BOSTON BEER WORKS   BREWERY

Map p264 (www.beerworks.net; 61 Brookline Ave; ⏰11:30am-1am; MKenmore) Decked out with scads of TVs, which form a ring around the bar, this place is in a prime location – directly across the street from all the action at Fenway Park. Most importantly, there is a rotating menu of 15-plus delicious beer flavors. The slick, modern room uses blond-wood tones and simple trim stools to create an appealing design effect.

BILL'S BAR   CLUB

Map p264 (5½ Lansdowne St; ⏰10pm-2am; MKenmore) The self-dubbed Dirty Rock Club is an obligatory stop if you're clubbing on Lansdowne St. Not your first stop, though, as the scene only starts to pick up around 11pm. With live music and DJs on Friday and Saturday nights, the scrubby joint is reminiscent of the Lansdowne St of bygone days – a contrast to the glossier venues on this stretch.

⚓ Fenway

PAVEMENT COFFEEHOUSE   CAFE

Map p264 (www.pavementcoffeehouseboston. com; 1096 Boylston St; ⏰7am-10pm Mon-Fri, 8am-10pm Sat-Sun; 📶) Exposed brick walls hung with art create an arty atmosphere at this coffee-lovers' dream. Berklee students and other hipsters congregate for fair-trade coffee, free wi-fi and bagel sandwiches, with many veg-friendly options on the menu (eg vegan cream cheese).

MACHINE
GAY CLUB

Map p264 (Ramrod; www.machine-boston. com; 1256 Boylston St; ☉10pm-2am Wed-Mon; Ⓜ Hynes) This long-standing gay favorite practically guarantees a fun night out, thanks to strong drinks, a crowded dance floor and shirtless men. The big night is Dirty Sexy Monday, when guest DJs engage in a 'spin-off.' Other events include karaoke, gay comedy, drag night and a hot dyke night (second Saturday of every month).

BASEBALL TAVERN
SPORTS BAR

Map p264 (www.thebaseballtavern.com; 1270 Boylston St; Ⓜ Hynes) Two words: roof deck. When weather is fine, the Baseball Tavern's roof deck is Fenway's primo spot for pre- and post-game drinking. That said, with bars on three levels and dozens of big-screen TVs, the Baseball Tavern is not just for baseball, but any sport – including out-of-state college football games.

☆ ENTERTAINMENT

⎣TOP CHOICE⎦ BOSTON SYMPHONY ORCHESTRA
CLASSICAL MUSIC

Map p264 (BSO; ☏617-266-1200; www.bso.org; 301 Massachusetts Ave; tickets $30-115; Ⓜ Symphony) Near-perfect acoustics match the ambitious programs of the world-renowned Boston Symphony Orchestra. From September to April, the BSO performs in the beauteous Symphony Hall, featuring an ornamental high-relief ceiling and attracting a fancy-dress crowd. The building was designed in 1861 with the help of a Harvard physicist who pledged to make the building acoustically perfect (he succeeded).

In summer months, the BSO retreats to Tanglewood in Western Massachusetts.

BOSTON POPS
CLASSICAL MUSIC

Map p264 (☏617-266-1200; www.bostonpops.org; 301 Massachusetts Ave; tickets $30-111; Ⓜ Symphony) Also playing out of the auditorily and visually delightful Symphony Hall, the Boston Pops arranges crowd-pleasers for the orchestra to tackle. Usually this means seasonal fare such as Christmas carols, movie scores and thematic mischief. The business is conducted by the dashing Keith Lockhart, making Boston hearts swoon since 1995.

In recent years, real live pop stars have fronted the Pops, included Amy Mann, My Morning Jacket and Elvis Costello. Tickets are booked out far in advance, especially for shows during the winter holidays.

HUNTINGTON THEATRE COMPANY
DRAMA THEATER

Map p264 (Boston University Theatre; www.huntingtontheatre.org; 264 Huntington Ave; Ⓜ Symphony) Boston's leading award-winning theater company, the Huntington specializes in developing new plays, staging many shows before they're transferred to Broadway (several of which have won Tonys). Seven major works by August Wilson were performed by the Huntington before going on to fame in New York. The company's credentials also include more than 50 world premieres of works by playwrights such as Tom Stoppard and Christopher Durang.

The Huntington usually stages its shows at the Boston University Theatre (built in 1925), but its secondary venue is the Calderwood Pavilion at the Boston Center for the Arts (p104) (built in 2004).

CHURCH
LIVE MUSIC

Map p264 (www.churchofboston.com; 69 Kilmarnock St; cover $10-12; ☉5pm-2am; Ⓜ Museum or Kenmore) Say a prayer of thanks for this neighborhood music venue. It books cool bands nightly, which is the most important thing. But it's also stylish, with pool tables, a pretty slick restaurant and attractive people. And plasma TVs, of course. Music starts most nights at 9pm.

HOUSE OF BLUES
LIVE MUSIC

Map p264 (www.hob.com/boston; 15 Lansdowne St; Ⓜ Kenmore) The HOB is bigger and better than ever. Well, it's bigger. Ridiculously tight security measures aside, this is the place to see national acts play when they can't fill the Garden (eg, the reunited J Geils Band, Lady Gaga, Dropkick Murphys). The balcony offers an excellent view of the stage, while fighting the crowds on the mezzanine can be brutal.

MUSEUM OF FINE ARTS
CINEMA

Map p264 (www.mfa.org; 365 Huntington Ave; adult/student & senior $11/9; Ⓜ Museum or Ruggles) If you packed your thinking cap, the MFA screens highbrow film events where visiting artists often attend screenings to discuss their work. The MFA also hosts film festivals dedicated to every ethnicity on the planet (Jewish, Iranian, African, French, etc) as well as a gay and lesbian film festival and the Human Rights Watch film festival.

FREE NEW ENGLAND CONSERVATORY
CLASSICAL MUSIC

Map p264 (Jordan Hall; www.newenglandconserv atory.edu; Jordan Hall, 30 Gainsborough St; admission usually free; Ⓜ Northeastern or Symphony) Founded in 1867, the NEC is the country's oldest music school. The conservatory hosts professional and student chamber and orchestral concerts in the acoustically superlative Jordan Hall, which dates from 1904.

🛍 SHOPPING

Because of the proximity of the Berklee School of Music, loads of stores are selling new and used records and CDs, musical instruments and other noisemakers in Kenmore Sq. In the streets surrounding Fenway Park, there is no shortage of souvenir stalls, just in case you have not yet bought your very own Red Sox cap.

MASSART MADE
HANDICRAFTS

Map p264 (www.massartmade.com; 625 Huntington Ave; ⊙10am-7pm Mon-Sat; Ⓜ Longwood) This is the retail outlet of MassArt, exhibiting (and selling) jewelry, photography, paintings and other items of loveliness, all made by the students, profs and alums of the design school. Proceeds benefit a college scholarship program. The merchandise is absolutely unique and relatively affordable, and each purchase comes with a bio of the artist who created it.

LOONEY TUNES
MUSIC

Map p264 (1106 Boylston St; ⊙10am-9:30pm Mon-Sat, noon-8pm Sun; Ⓜ Hynes) Looney Tunes claims a rotating collection of hundreds of thousands of records. They are not all packed into this tiny store near Berklee School of Music (though it feels like it) – it has a huge stock of items in storage. All records are graded, so you know the condition of the product. Also carries CDs and DVDs.

NUGGETS
MUSIC

Map p264 (www.nuggetsrecords.com; 486 Commonwealth Ave; ⊙Tue-Sun; Ⓜ Kenmore) A little slice of 'old' Kenmore Sq. With a constantly shifting collection of vinyl, CDs and DVDs, Nuggets is a great place to browse. Many a Red Sox fan has popped in on the way to Fenway and ended up carting a sack of albums to the baseball game.

CLASSIC ON THE CHEAP

The BSO often offers various discounted ticket schemes, which can let you hear classical music on the cheap:

➡ Same-day 'rush' tickets ($9) are available for Tuesday, Thursday, and Friday evening performances (on sale starting at 5pm) as well as Friday afternoon performances (on sale starting at 10am).

➡ Check the schedule for occasional Open Rehearsals, which usually take place in the afternoon midweek. General admittance tickets are $20.

➡ Occasionally, discounted tickets are offered for certain segments of the population (eg, <40=$20).

🏃 SPORTS & ACTIVITIES

TOP CHOICE FENWAY PARK
BASEBALL

Map p264 (www.redsox.com; 4 Yawkey Way; tickets $25-125; Ⓜ Kenmore) From April to September you can watch the Red Sox play at Fenway Park, the nation's oldest and most storied ballpark. Unfortunately, it is also the most expensive – not that this stops the Fenway faithful from scooping up the tickets. There are sometimes game-day tickets on sale starting two hours before the opening pitch.

Arrive early at Gate E on Lansdowne St (but no earlier than five hours before game time) and be prepared to enter the ballpark as soon as you purchase your tickets. Otherwise, you can always get tickets in advance from online vendors or on game-day from scalpers around Kenmore Sq. If the Sox are doing well, expect to pay twice the face value (less if you wait until after the game starts).

JILLIAN'S & LUCKY STRIKE
BILLIARDS, BOWLING

Map p264 (www.jilliansboston.com; 145 Ipswich St; ⊙11am-2am Mon-Sat, noon-2am Sun; Ⓜ Kenmore) Bowling, billiards and gettin' jiggy with it. That's what you can do at this enormous, three-story entertainment complex, which also has seven bars and a full-service menu. Its 50 pool tables are in pristine condition; however, the high-tech bowling alley has only 16 flashy lanes, so it can be a long wait.

People also come here to play darts or table tennis and to ogle members of the opposite sex. After 8pm there's a strict no-sportswear dress code and a 21-and-over age limit.

Seaport District & South Boston

Neighborhood Top Five

① Spending an afternoon at the striking waterfront site of the **Institute of Contemporary Art** (p136), contemplating the artistic curiosities on display within and admiring the stunning harbor and city views without.

② Boarding the **Boston Tea Party Ships** (p137) and tossing crates of tea overboard.

③ Admiring the view and catching a breeze while feasting on the creatures of the sea at **Legal Harborside** (p139).

④ Wriggling, crawling and climbing on the three-story climbing structure at the **Boston Children's Museum** (p137).

⑤ Sidling up to the bar at **Drink** (p140) for some serious cocktail swilling.

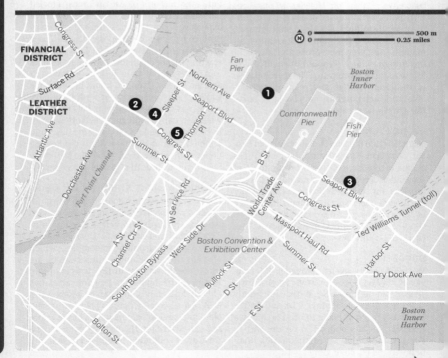

For more detail of this area, see Map p255 ➡

Explore Seaport District & South Boston

Separated from Boston proper by the jellyfish-laden Fort Point Channel, the Seaport District has always afforded a spectacular vista of the Boston Harbor and downtown Boston. Now this up-and-coming district offers all kinds of opportunities to see and savor it.

Following the HarborWalk, it's a pleasant stroll across the Northern Ave Bridge. Once across Fort Point Channel, walk around the Moakley Federal Courthouse to enjoy the landscaped parks and fantastic views from Fan Pier, eventually ending up at the Institute of Contemporary Art (ICA). Spend an afternoon admiring contemporary art and feasting on fish and you've got a pretty good sense of what the Seaport District is all about.

Further east, the wharves are dominated by fish-processing facilities and a marine industrial center. But change is afoot, as restaurants, bars and retail open in the new buildings. It's worth visiting the Fish Pier to catch a whiff of what this area used to be, and what it's becoming.

Meanwhile, the rest of South Boston remains well off the beaten path. Former stomping ground of Whitey Bulger and preferred setting for Boston-based mafia movies, 'Southie' lives large in local and national lore.

Despite its reputation, South Boston has its own charm. The waterside community offers great harbor views, as well as Boston's best city beaches. On a hot summer day, Castle Island is a windy, welcoming waterside playspace for families and outdoorsy types.

The 'hood is packed with Irish pubs, but there are also a few notable 'New American' restaurants, should you care to drink something other than Guinness or PBR. This area is getting a glimpse of the gentrification that has transformed other parts of the city, but Southie is still unapologetically old-school.

Local Life

➡ **Drinking joint 1** You know it's a local when they don't even put a sign outside. Such is Lucky's Lounge (p140).

➡ **Drinking joint 2** For a singular picture of local Southie, visit the regulars at (signless) Croke Park Whitey's (p140).

Getting There & Away

➡ **Metro** to The Seaport District is a 10-minute walk from South Station (red line), and Broadway Station (also red line) sits at the top of South Boston's main street.

➡ **Bus** The silver line bus (SL1 or SL2) runs from South Station through the Seaport District, stopping at Courthouse, the World Trade Center and Silver Line Way.

Thursday nights are free at the ICA while Friday nights at the Boston Children's Museum are only $1. The reduced admission is from 5pm to 9pm, in both cases.

 **Best Places to Eat**

➡ Sportello (p139)
➡ Yankee Lobster Fish Co (p139)
➡ Sam's (p139)
➡ Channel Café (p139)

For reviews, see p138 ➡

Best Places to Drink

➡ Drink (p140)
➡ Lucky's Lounge (p140)
➡ Croke Park Whitey's (p140)

For reviews, see p140 ➡

 Best Lookout Points

➡ Founder's Gallery in the ICA (p136)
➡ Sam's (p139)
➡ Legal Harborside (p139)

For reviews, see p136 ➡

SEAPORT DISTRICT & SOUTH BOSTON

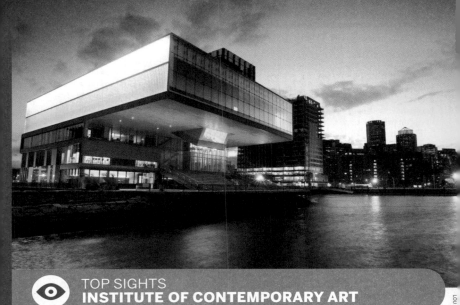

TOP SIGHTS
INSTITUTE OF CONTEMPORARY ART

Boston is poised to become a focal point for contemporary art in the 21st century, as hundreds of thousands of visitors flock to the dramatic quarters of the Institute of Contemporary Art. The building is a work of art in itself: a glass structure cantilevered over a waterside plaza. The vast light-filled interior allows for multimedia presentations, educational programs and studio space. More importantly, it allows for the development of the ICA's permanent collection.

Arguably, the ICA building, opened in 2006, is as much an attraction as the art; the structure skillfully incorporates its environs into the architecture. In the Founders Gallery, which spans the width of the building, a glass wall virtually removes any barrier between viewer and seascape.

The Mediatheque is the museum's digital media center, where visitors can use the computer stations to learn more about featured art and artists. The terraced room also has a wall of windows at the front, but the room's unique perspective shows only the dancing and rippling of water, with no horizon in sight.

The ICA began in 2000 to develop a permanent collection. Its primary strategy has been to acquire pieces by artists featured in its exhibits. More than a decade later, the ICA now has the space to display its growing collection. It showcases both national and international artists, including the likes of graffiti-artist Shepard Fairey; video artist Christian Jankowski; photographer Boris Mikhailov; local boy Josiah McElhany; and sculptors Tara Donovan, Mona Hatoum and Cornelia Parker. Look for all manner of art, from painting to video to multi-dimensional mixed-media mash-ups.

DON'T MISS

➡ Fineberg Art Wall in the lobby

➡ *Peace Goddess* and other powerful pieces by Shepard Fairey

➡ *Hanging Fire* by Cornelia Parker

➡ View from the Foundation Gallery

PRACTICALITIES

➡ ICA

➡ Map p255

➡ www.icaboston.org

➡ 100 Northern Ave

➡ adult/child/student/senior $15/free/10/13

➡ ⊙10am-5pm Tue-Wed & Sat-Sun, to 9pm Thu-Fri

➡ Ⓟ 🚻

➡ Ⓜ South Station, 🚊 SL1 or SL2

◉ SIGHTS

◉ Seaport District

**INSTITUTE OF
CONTEMPORARY ART** MUSEUM
See p136.

BOSTON CHILDREN'S MUSEUM MUSEUM
Map p255 (www.bostonchildrensmuseum.org; 300 Congress St; admission $12, Fri evenings $1; ☺10am-5pm Sat-Thu, 10am-9pm Fri; Ⓜ South Station) The interactive, educational exhibits at the delightful Children's Museum keep kids entertained for hours. Highlights include a bubble exhibit, rock-climbing walls, a hands-on construction site and intercultural immersion experiences. The museum underwent major expansion in 2006, with the addition of a new light-filled atrium featuring an amazing three-story climbing structure, bridges and glass elevators.

The new building utilizes loads of green technology, including salvaged and recycled construction materials and a fuel-efficient heating system that incorporates a green roof. Rain water run-off is collected and used for irrigation and plumbing.

In nice weather kids can enjoy outdoor eating and playing in the waterside park. Look for the iconic Hood milk bottle on Fort Point Channel.

**BOSTON TEA PARTY SHIPS
& MUSEUM** MUSEUM
Map p255 (www.bostonteapartyship.com; Congress St Bridge; Ⓜ South Station) After years of anticipation and restoration, the Tea Party Ships are moored at the reconstructed Griffin's Wharf, alongside a shiny new museum dedicated to the revolution's most catalytic event. Interactive exhibits allows visitors to meet re-enactors in period costume, explore the ships, learn about contemporary popular perceptions through multimedia presentations and even participate in the protest.

At the time of opening in 2012, visitors can board the fully-rigged *Eleanor* and the whaler *Beaver* to experience life aboard an 18th-century vessel. (*The Dartmouth* is expected to be built later.) Would-be rebels can throw crates of tea into the harbor, in solidarity with their fiery forebears.

Using re-enactments, multimedia and other fun exhibits, the museum addresses all aspects of the Boston Tea Party, as well as

the events that followed. To hear both sides of the story, visitors can witness a virtual debate between Sam Adams and King George III (though in reality they never met). The museum's one actual artifact – a tea crate known as the Robinson Half Chest – is highlighted with an audio presentation.

FORT POINT ARTS COMMUNITY GALLERY
Map p255 (FPAC; www.fortpointarts.org; 300 Summer St; ☺9am-3pm Mon, 9am-9pm Tue-Fri; Ⓜ South Station) This refurbished big-windowed warehouse is the hub of the Fort Point Arts Community, which contains a gallery featuring work from the talented collective. See huge psychedelic oils, prints inspired by 14th-century Venetian laces, lampshades made from birch and mixed-media films. Several times a year, FPAC hosts popular open-studio events that allow you to see the artists' living and working spaces as well as their creations.

◉ South Boston

**CASTLE ISLAND &
FORT INDEPENDENCE** PARK, FORTRESS
(Marine Park; ☺dawn-dusk May-Sep; P🚻; Ⓜ Broadway, ☐11) The 19th-century Fort Independence sits on 22 acres of parkland called Castle Island (a misnomer, as it's connected to the mainland). A paved pathway follows the perimeter of the peninsula – good for strolling or cycling – and there is a small swimming beach.

GOT MILK?

Up there with the Citgo sign and the Steaming Kettle, the giant Hood milk bottle is emblematic of Boston. Towering 40ft over Fort Point Channel, it would hold 50,000 gallons of milk if it could hold a drop (that's 800,000 glasses of milk, if anybody's counting). This unlikely wooden milk bottle was built in 1934 to house an ice-cream stand, which it did for 30-odd years before it was abandoned. The milk bottle was finally purchased by Hood Milk, New England's largest and oldest dairy, and moved to its current location in 1977. It's now back in business (during summer months) selling sandwiches and ice cream.

WORTH A DETOUR

COLUMBIA POINT

Columbia Point juts into the harbor south of the city center in Dorchester, one of Boston's rougher neighborhoods. The location is unexpected, but it does offer dramatic views of the sea. It's a four-mile stroll or ride along the HarborWalk between Columbia Point and Castle Island. Otherwise, take the red line to JFK/UMass and catch a free shuttle bus (departures every 20 minutes) to Columbia Point.

➜ The legacy of JFK is ubiquitous in Boston, but the official memorial to the 35th president is the **John F Kennedy Library & Museum** (www.jfklibrary.org; Columbia Point; adult/child/senior & student $12/9/10; ◉9am-5pm; P; MJFK/UMass), a striking modern marble building designed by IM Pei. The architectural centerpiece is the glass pavilion, with soaring 115ft ceilings and floor-to-ceiling windows overlooking Boston Harbor. The museum is a fitting tribute to JFK's life and legacy. The effective use of video recreates history for visitors who may or may not remember the early 1960s. A highlight is the museum's treatment of the Cuban Missile Crisis: a short film explores the dilemmas and decisions that the president faced, while an archival exhibit displays actual documents and correspondence from these gripping 13 days.

➜ The **Commonwealth Museum** (☏617-727-9268; www.commonwealthmuseum.org; 220 Morrissey Blvd, Columbia Point; admission free; ◉9am-5pm Mon-Fri; P; MJFK/UMass) exhibits documents dating to the early days of colonization. The permanent exhibit, *Our Common Wealth*, uses interactive multimedia technologies to trace the history of the colony and state using the rich materials from the on-site Massachusetts Archives. One unique element, *Tracing our Roots*, explores the state's heritage following four families: Native American, English, African American and Irish.

➜ In 2011, public officials joined the Kennedy clan in celebrating the groundbreaking for the **Edward Kennedy Institute for the US Senate** (www.emkinstitute.org; Columbia Point; MJKF/UMass). A striking building designed to complement the JFK Library, the institute will use high-tech exhibits to educate about the legislative process, highlighting history-making senators and legislative initiatives. Stay tuned.

Since 1634, eight different fortresses have occupied this strategic spot at the entrance to the Inner Harbor. Fort Independence – the five-point granite fort that stands here today – was built between 1834 and 1851. From the Seaport District, walk south on Summer St for about a half-mile, then turn left on E 1st St and continue to the waterfront. Alternatively, take bus 11 from Broadway station.

DORCHESTER HEIGHTS MONUMENT
(btwn G & Old Harbor Sts; ◉dawn-dusk; MBroadway, ☐11) High above the Boston Harbor, this strategic spot played a crucial role in overcoming the British occupation. The Georgian revival tower that stands today was built in 1898.

In the winter of 1776, rebel troops dragged 59 heavy cannons to Boston from Fort Ticonderoga in upstate New York. On the night of March 4, they perched them high atop Dorchester Heights, from where the British warships in the Harbor were at their mercy. The move caught the British completely by surprise, and ultimately convinced them to abandon Boston. To reach the Dorchester Heights Monument, walk east along West Broadway from the T station, turn right onto Dorchester St and head up any of the little streets. (Or take bus 11 and get off near Dorchester St.)

EATING

Seaport District

There was a time when hanging around the Seaport District meant you were eating seafood, because there was no other reason to be here. With the opening of the convention center and the Institute of Contemporary Art, this district is quickly developing as a hotspot for new restaurants.

YANKEE LOBSTER FISH CO
SEAFOOD **$$**

Map p255 (www.yankeelobstercompany.com; 300 Northern Ave; mains $10-18; ☺10am-8pm Mon-Sat, 11am-5pm Sun; Ⓜ South Station, ⧉ SL1 or SL2) The Zanti family has been fishing for three generations, so they definitely know their stuff. A relatively recent addition is this retail fish market, scattered with a few tables in case you want to dine in. And you do... Order something simple like clam chowder or a lobster roll, accompany it with a cold beer, and you will not be disappointed.

SPORTELLO
ITALIAN **$$**

Map p255 (✆617-737-1234; www.sportelloboston. com; 348 Congress St; mains $12-25; ☺lunch & dinner; Ⓜ South Station, ⧉ SL1 or SL2) Modern and minimalist, this brainchild of Barbara Lynch fits right into this up-and-coming urban 'hood. At the *sportello*, or lunch counter, suited yuppies indulge in sophisticated soups and salads and decadent polenta and pasta dishes. It's a popular spot, which means it's usually a tight squeeze, but the attentive waitstaff ensure that everybody is comfortable and contented.

SAM'S
MODERN AMERICAN **$$$**

Map p255 (✆617-295-0191; www.samsatlouis. com; 60 Northern Ave, Louis Boston; sandwiches $13-16, mains $25-30; ☺lunch & dinner Mon-Sat, brunch Sun; 🛜🚲; Ⓜ South Station, ⧉ SL1 or SL2) Unarguably, the highlight of Sam's is the three walls of windows, yielding a 180-degree view of city and sea. Chrome and leather, post-industrial decor complements this spectacular view. It's a delightfully casual-chic place, with an interesting, innovative menu to match. Live music on Friday nights.

🖊 CHANNEL CAFÉ
AMERICAN **$$**

Map p255 (www.channel-cafe.com; 300 Summer St; lunch mains $8-12, dinner mains $18-24; ☺7am-3pm Mon, 7am-10pm Tue-Fri; 🛜🚲; Ⓜ South Station) This café is tucked into the lower level of the Fort Point Arts Community, right next to the gallery space. Two-story ceilings and funky paintings on the walls give this place a sufficiently arty feel. The creative menu offers traditional comfort food with a modern twist (eg BL&FGT = bacon, lettuce and fried green tomato), including some intriguing vegetarian options.

🖊 FLOUR
BAKERY, CAFÉ **$**

Map p255 (www.flourbakery.com; 12 Farnsworth St; ☺7am-7pm Mon-Fri, 8am-6pm Sat, 9am-3pm Sun; 🚲🚶; Ⓜ South Station, ⧉ SL1 or SL2) Flour implores patrons to 'make life sweeter... eat dessert first!' It's hard to resist at this pastry-lover's paradise. If you can't decide – and it can be a challenge – go for the melt-in-your-mouth sticky buns. But dessert is not all: delicious sandwiches, soups, salads and pizzas are also available. The original Flour Bakery is in the South End; both are Certified Green Restaurants.

LEGAL HARBORSIDE
SEAFOOD **$$**

Map p255 (www.legalseafoods.com; 270 Northern Ave; mains $18-28; ☺lunch & dinner; 🚶; Ⓜ South Station, ⧉ SL1 or SL2) On the forefront of the development in the up-and-coming Seaport District, this new waterfront outlet brings Legal Seafood into the 21st century. The vast glass-fronted complex includes a casual restaurant and fish market on the 1st floor, fine dining on the 2nd floor and a slick all-season rooftop bar.

The old menu favorites have been updated to include simple seasonal preparations, more local fish and plenty of international influences (including sushi). There's outdoor seating in the summer months. (This concept has been a long time coming.)

BARKING CRAB
SEAFOOD **$$**

Map p255 (www.barkingcrab.com; 88 Sleeper St; mains $12-30; ☺lunch & dinner; Ⓜ South Station, ⧉ SL1 or SL2) Big buckets of crabs (Jonah, blue, snow, Alaskan etc), steamers dripping in lemon and butter, paper plates piled high with all things fried... The food is plentiful and cheap, and you eat it at communal picnic tables overlooking the water. Beer flows freely. Service is slack, but the atmosphere is jovial. Be prepared to wait for a table if the weather is warm.

✖ South Boston

SULLIVAN'S
SNACK BAR **$**

(www.sullivanscastleisland.com; 1080 Day Blvd; mains $3-10; ☺8:30am-10pm Mar-Nov; 🚶; Ⓜ Broadway, ⧉ 11) A Southie tradition since 1951, Sullivan's is beloved for hotdogs in their casing, known as 'Sully's snap dogs.' In 60-plus years of business, the price of those dogs has increased by more than 10 times – making them a whopping $1.60.

SEAPORT DISTRICT & SOUTH BOSTON EATING

Fried seafood, burgers and soft-serve ice cream round out the menu. You can't miss Sullivan's at the entrance to Castle Island.

FRANKLIN SOUTHIE MODERN AMERICAN **$$**
(www.franklincafe.com; 152 Dorchester Ave; mains $14-20; ⊘brunch Sat-Sun, dinner daily; ⓂBroadway) Where do you go when you find yourself in Southie with a hankering for tuna tartare or duck confit? There is only one answer. Franklin Southie is the younger brother of the South End hipster foodie favorite. It's every bit as hip and delicious as the original, with a little Southie charm to boot. Located one block south of Broadway station.

LOCAL 149 MODERN AMERICAN **$$**
(www.local149.com; 149 P St; mains $15-19; ⊘brunch Sat-Sun, dinner nightly; ⓂBroadway, ⓺11) What does it mean when an old-time South Boston Irish bar gets replaced with a modern tavern serving fried Brussels sprouts and chorizo cassoulet? It means Southie foodies have something to celebrate. Besides the interesting, southern-influenced menu, there is an incredible beer list, including over 20 selections on draft, most of which you have not heard of. Walk about one mile south from Castle Island along the shoreline.

 DRINKING & NIGHTLIFE

Seaport District

The Seaport District isn't oozing with hot spots, but it does contain a few throwbacks for the lounge lizard.

TOP CHOICE DRINK COCKTAIL LOUNGE
Map p255 (www.drinkfortpoint.com; 348 Congress St S; ⊘4pm-1am; ⓂSouth Station, ⓺SL1 or SL2) There is no cocktail menu at Drink. Instead you have a little chat with the bartender, and he or she will whip something up according to your specifications. The bar takes seriously the art of drink mixology – and you will too, after you sample one of its concoctions. The subterranean space creates a dark, sexy atmosphere, which makes for a great date destination.

LUCKY'S LOUNGE COCKTAIL BAR
Map p255 (www.luckyslounge.com; 355 Congress St S; ⊘11am-2am Sun-Fri, 6pm-2am Sat; ⓂSouth Station, ⓺SL1 or SL2) One of Boston's top-notch bars, Lucky's earns street cred by having no sign. Step inside and you'll return to a delightfully gritty lounge that looks like it's straight from 1959. Enjoy well-priced drinks, excellent martinis and Motown-inspired bands playing tunes to which people actually dance (Thursday to Sunday). Sinatra Sunday Brunch remains a perpetual favorite, and the after-work scene is one of the liveliest around.

FREE HARPOON BREWERY BREWERY
Map p255 (www.harpoonbrewery.com; 306 Northern Ave; ⊘tastings 2pm & 4pm Mon-Fri, tours 10:30am-5pm Sat & 11:30am-3pm Sun; ⓂSouth Station, ⓺SL1 or SL2) This brewery is the state's largest beer facility. Free tastings take place in a newly renovated room overlooking the brewery, while the tours provide an overview of the brewing process (also with samples). Tours last about one hour and they often sell out, so don't come too late in the day.

South Boston

Head deeper into South Boston for an authentic Boston Irish experience. Pubs galore line E and W Broadway.

CROKE PARK WHITEY'S DIVE BAR
(268 W Broadway; ⓂBroadway) Whitey's is everything a dive bar is supposed to be, with cheap beer, free pool and a cast of colorful local characters propping up the bar. This is old-school Southie, and it's not nearly as scary as it's made out to be in the movies. Potent mixed drinks are served in pint glasses ($5), as are PBRs ($1.50). Walk a half-mile south from Broadway station.

⭐ ENTERTAINMENT

INSTITUTE OF CONTEMPORARY ART FILM, PERFORMING ARTS
Map p255 (ICA; www.icaboston.org; 100 Northern Ave; ⓂSouth Station, ⓺SL1 or SL2) The Barbara Lee Family Foundation Theater is one of the ICA's coolest features. With wooden floor and ceiling and glass walls, the two-

story venue is an extension of the board-walk outside. It's a remarkable backdrop for edgy theater, dance, music and other performance art. The ICA also hosts occasional film festivals and screenings of offbeat and arty cinema.

BANK OF AMERICA PAVILION LIVE MUSIC
Map p255 (www.livenation.com; 290 Northern Ave; Ⓜ South Station, 🚌 SL1 or SL2) A white sail-like tent with sweeping harbor views, this is a great venue for summer concerts. It seats about 5000 people, so you can actually see the smiling faces of the performers on stage.

Boston, Louis is not pronounced the way you expect: it's *Loo*-eeez with a zed.)

MADE IN FORT POINT HANDICRAFTS
Map p255 (www.fortpointarts.org; 12 Farnsworth St; ⊙11am-6pm Mon-Fri, 10am-5pm Sat-Sun; Ⓜ South Station, 🚌 SL1 or SL2) This little boutique is the retail outlet for the Fort Point Arts Community (p137). Not exactly a gallery, it is more like a gift shop, featuring jewelry, prints, photographs, T-shirts, pottery, housewares and other cool, creative stuff. Shopping doesn't get more local than this, as most of this stuff was made around the corner at FPAC.

 SHOPPING

LOUIS BOSTON CLOTHING & ACCESSORIES
Map p255 (www.louisboston.com; 60 Northern Ave; Ⓜ South Station, 🚌 SL1 or SL2) It was big news when this high-class fashion icon moved shop from its fancy Back Bay quarters to the gritty Seaport District, but the influential designer is clearly at the forefront of something. Now in slick new digs with wall-to-ceiling windows, Louis inhabits a space that matches its trendy, on-point designs. (By the way, this being

SPORTS & ACTIVITIES

FREE **CARSON BEACH** BEACH
(Day Blvd; ⊙dawn-dusk; 🚻; Ⓜ Broadway, 🚌 11) West of Castle Island, 3 miles of beaches offer opportunities for urban swimming. L and M St beaches lie along Day Blvd; Carson Beach is further west. All have smooth sand, harbor views and decent facilities, but these are city beaches, so are not the most pristine setting to soak in.

LOU JONES / LONELY PLANET IMAGES ©

RICHARD CUMMINS / LONELY PLANET IMAGES ©

LOU JONES / LONELY PLANET IMAGES ©

1. Newbury St (p120)
Back Bay's swanky shopping strip is renowned among fashionistas, art aficionados and music buffs – and for good reason.

2. Wally's Café (p104)
Old-school jazz and blues at a historic South End institution.

3. South End Formaggio (p106)
Here it's all about cheese, wine and pairing wine with cheese.

4. Lisa Hoang mural in Chinatown (p96)
Vibrant Chinatown teems with restaurants, teahouses and fresh-produce markets.

Cambridge

HARVARD SQUARE | CENTRAL & KENDALL SQUARES

Neighborhood Top Five

1 Browsing the bookstores, rifling through the records and trying on vintage clothing in **Harvard Square** (p148), then camping out in a local cafe (preferably with sidewalk seating) to watch the world go by.

2 Cycling the **Minuteman Bikeway** (p159) from urban Cambridge to idyllic Bedford.

3 Getting the inside scoop from savvy students on the unofficial **Harvard Tour** (p160).

4 Exploring the **MIT campus** (p147) and discovering its fantastic, eclectic collection of public art.

5 Strolling around the **Mount Auburn Cemetery** (p149) in search of famous gravestones, impressive artwork and elusive birds.

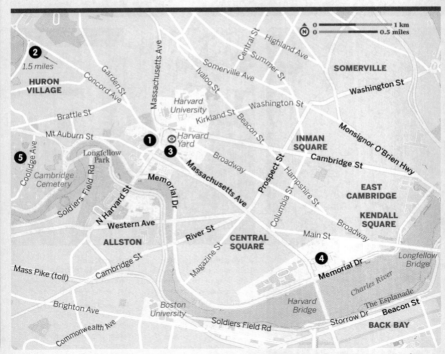

For more detail of this area, see Maps p266 and p268 ➡

Explore Cambridge

While we count Cambridge as one among many 'neighborhoods' in Boston, truth be told, this independent town has the historical and cultural offerings to rival many major cities. It matches Boston for quality (if not quantity) and diversity of drinking, dining and entertainment options, and with its array of museums, historic sites and university landmarks, you as easily spend a day as spend a year.

But you probably don't have a year. Too bad.

Much of life in Cambridge is centered on the universities – Harvard and MIT – each of which occupies its respective corner of town, with restaurants, shops and clubs clustered around each campus. If you have limited time in Cambridge, you'll probably want to choose one or the other, as there is plenty of activity around either campus to fill a day. (Harvard or MIT...? Harvard or MIT...? Now you know what it's like for the brainiacs who have to decide where they want to go to school.)

Both universities offer excellent (free) campus tours – Harvard is packed with history, while MIT boasts a wealth of public art and innovative architecture. Both universities have interesting and unusual museums showcasing cutting-edge art and science. Both universities have excellent dining and entertainment options in their vicinities. So take your pick.

That said, only Harvard has Harvard Sq. Overflowing with coffee houses and pubs, bookstores and record stores, street musicians and sidewalk artists, panhandlers and professors, Harvard Sq exudes energy, creativity and nonconformity – and it's all packed into a handful of streets between the university and the river. Even if you have your heart set on exploring MIT and its environs, it's worth setting aside a few hours to spend up the road in Harvard Sq.

Local Life

➡ **Student bars** Local life is student life. To see it in action go to Shay's Pub & Wine Bar (p153) (Harvard) or Miracle of Science (p152) (MIT).

➡ **Campus corners** JFK Park is a favorite local spot for picnics, dogs and frisbee, while the area outside the MIT Stratton Center attracts students and pigeons.

➡ **Sidewalk seating** The sidewalk cafe at Holyoke Center gives a front-row seat to watch the buskers, beggers, chess-players, good-deed-doers and other Harvard-Sq hullabaloo.

Getting There & Away

➡ **Metro** Take the red line to Harvard station for Harvard Sq, Central station for Central Sq and Kendall/MIT for Kendall Sq.

Lonely Planet's Top Tip

The Harvard Bookstore (p157) hosts lectures, author talks and book readings almost every night, Monday to Friday, presenting a cool opportunity to hobnob with local writers and scholars.

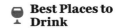 **Best Places to Eat**

➡ Cambridge, 1 (p150)
➡ Hungry Mother (p151)
➡ Christina's (p151)
➡ Russell House Tavern (p150)
➡ Clover Food Lab (p150)

For reviews, see p150 ➡

Best Places to Drink

➡ Casablanca (p152)
➡ Café Pamplona (p152)
➡ Voltage Coffee & Art (p153)
➡ LA Burdick (p152)
➡ Plough & Stars (p153)

For reviews, see p152 ➡

CAMBRIDGE

Best University Museums

➡ Harvard Art Museum (p148)
➡ MIT Museum (p147)
➡ Harvard Museum of Natural History (p149)
➡ Peabody Museum of Archaeology & Ethnology (p149)

For reviews, see p148 ➡

TOP SIGHTS
HARVARD YARD

Founded in 1636 to educate men for the ministry, Harvard is America's oldest college. The original Ivy League school has eight graduates who went on to be US presidents, not to mention dozens of Nobel Laureates and Pulitzer Prize winners. It educates 6500 undergraduates and about 12,000 graduates yearly in 10 professional schools. The geographic heart of Harvard University – where red-brick buildings and leaf-covered paths exude academia – is Harvard Yard.

Massachusetts Hall & Harvard Hall

Flanking Johnston Gate are the two oldest buildings on campus. South of the gate, **Massachusetts Hall** (Map p266) houses the offices of the President of the University. Dating to 1720, it is the oldest building at Harvard and the oldest academic building in the country. North is **Harvard Hall** (Map p266), which dates to 1766 and originally housed the library.

John Harvard Statue

The focal point of the yard is the **John Harvard Statue** (Map p266), where every Harvard hopeful has a photo taken (and touches the statue's shiny shoe for good luck). Daniel Chester French's sculpture, inscribed 'John Harvard, Founder of Harvard College, 1638,' is known as the statue of three lies: it does not actually depict Harvard (since no image of him exists), but a random student; John Harvard was not the founder of the college, but its first benefactor in 1638; and the college was actually founded in 1636, two years earlier. The Harvard symbol hardly lives up to the university's motto, Veritas, or 'truth.'

DON'T MISS

➜ Free campus tours, departing at 10am, noon and 2pm Monday through Saturday, from the **Harvard Information Center** (☎617-495-1573; www.harvard.edu/visitors; 1350 Massachusetts Ave) inside Holyoke Center.

PRACTICALITIES

➜ Map p266
➜ www.harvard.edu
➜ Massachusetts Ave
➜ tours free
➜ Ⓜ Harvard

TOP SIGHTS
MASSACHUSETTS INSTITUTE OF TECHNOLOGY

The Massachusetts Institute of Technology (MIT) offers a completely novel perspective on Cambridge academia: proudly nerdy, but not quite as tweedy as Harvard. A recent frenzy of building has resulted in some of the most architecturally intriguing structures you'll find on either side of the river.

Leave it to the mischievous brainiacs at MIT to come up with the city's quirkiest museum – the **MIT Museum** (Map p268; museum.mit.edu; 265 Massachusetts Ave; adult/child $8.50/4; ⊙10am-5pm; Ⓟ ♿; ⓂCentral). You can meet humanoid robots like observant Cog and personable Kismet and decide for yourself if they are smarter than humans. Another highlight: the fantastic Light Fantastic, the world's largest exhibit of holograms.

The stated goal of the **List Visual Arts Center** (Map p268; listart.mit.edu; 20 Ames St, Weisner Bldg; donation $5; ⊙noon-6pm Tue-Sun, to 8pm Thu; Ⓟ; ⓂKendall/MIT) is to explore the boundaries of artistic inquiry – to use art to ask questions about culture, society and science. Rotating exhibits push the contemporary art envelope in painting, sculpture, photography and video. This is also where you can pick up a map of MIT's public art, proof enough that this university supports artistic as well as technological innovation. If you want a professional opinion, book a free tour.

Of all the funky buildings on the MIT campus, none has received more attention than the **Stata Center** (CSAIL; Map p268; csail.mit.edu; 32 Vassar St; ⓂKendall/MIT), an avant-garde edifice (pictured above) that was designed by architectural legend Frank Gehry.

DON'T MISS
....
➡ *La Grande Voile* by Alexander Calder
➡ Henry Moore's bronze reclining figures
➡ Stata Center
➡ *Light Fantastic* in the MIT Museum

PRACTICALITIES
....
➡ MIT
➡ Map p268
➡ www.mit.edu
➡ 77 Massachusetts Ave
➡ ⓂKendall/MIT

⊙ SIGHTS

⊙ Harvard Square

HARVARD YARD   UNIVERSITY
See p146.

CHRIST CHURCH   CHURCH
Map p266 (www.cccambridge.org; 0 Garden St;
⊙services 7:45am & 10:15am Sun; MHarvard)
Cambridge's oldest church was designed in
1761 by America's first formally trained architect, Peter Harrison (who also did King's
Chapel in Boston). Washington's troops
used it as a barracks after its Tory congregation fled.

Christ Church's favorite son is Teddy
Roosevelt, who taught Sunday school here
when he was a student at Harvard. An interesting addendum to that story is that the
future president was actually discharged
because he refused to convert to Episcopa-
lianism but chose to remain a member of
the Dutch Reformed Church. Adjacent to
the church, the Old Burying Ground is a
tranquil revolutionary-era cemetery, where
Harvard's first eight presidents are buried.

CAMBRIDGE COMMON   PARK
Map p266 (cnr Massachusetts Ave & Garden St;
MHarvard) Opposite the main entrance to
Harvard Yard, Cambridge Common is the
village green where General Washington
took command of the Continental Army on
July 3, 1775. The traffic island at the south
end, known as Dawes Island, pays tribute
to the 'other rider' William Dawes, who
rode through here on April 18, 1775, to warn
that the British were coming (look for the
bronze hoofprints embedded in the sidewalk).

HARVARD ART MUSEUM   MUSEUM
Map p266 (www.harvardartmuseum.org; 32 Quincy St; MHarvard) Architect extraordinaire
Renzo Piano has overseen a renovation and
expansion of Harvard's art museum, allowing the university's massive 250,000-piece
collection to come together under one very
stylish roof. Harvard's art spans the globe,
with separate collections devoted to Asian
and Islamic cultures, Northern European
and Germanic cultures and other Western
art, especially European modernism. It
should be on full display starting in 2013.

CAR TALK

Here's a puzzler. How does a struggling auto-repair-shop owner parlay a brief spot on
local public radio into national fame and fortune? Answer: he is one of the Magliozzi
Brothers.

It helped, of course, to be invited back, which Tom Magliozzi was in 1977, when he
first accepted the invitation of radio station WBUR in hopes of drumming up free pub-
licity for his small Cambridge shop, the Good News Garage. It helped even more that
Tom brought his wise-cracking younger brother Ray to his next radio gig.

The Magliozzi Brothers were not your typical auto-repair guys, nor were they
your typical public radio fare. The East Cambridge natives and MIT graduates were
adept at leading listeners under the hood and unraveling the mysteries of internal
gas combustion, while engaging in nonstop playful banter and sibling rivalry. They
also offered insightful and unfiltered opinions of the auto-repair profession, the auto
industry as a whole and America's car culture.

The audience quickly grew beyond the do-it-yourself set as the Car Talk guys developed a local cult following. They were no longer the Magliozzi Brothers, humble
garage technicians, they were now the Marx Brothers of auto repair, starring in their
own weekly version of Grease Monkey Business.

In 1987 'Click and Clack, the Tappett Brothers,' took their show on the road, via
National Public Radio's nationwide network of affiliates. Today, Car Talk is heard by
more than four million listeners on over 500 radio stations each week. The brothers also have a syndicated automotive advice column that runs in 350 newspapers.
Their production company, Dewey, Cheetham & Howe, is located in Harvard Sq (cnr
Brattle & John F Kennedy Sts) and their shop, the Good News Garage, still operates
in Cambridge.

'Don't drive like my brother. Don't drive like my brother.'

ARTHUR M SACKLER MUSEUM   MUSEUM
Map p266 (www.harvardartmuseum.org; 485 Broadway; adult/child/senior/student $9/free/7/6; ⊘9am-5pm Tue-Sat; MHarvard) While Harvard's main art museum is under scaffolding (until 2013), the university is exhibiting a selection of works from its collections at the Sackler. *Re-View* includes some of the most acclaimed pieces from the university's three collections: the Fogg collection of Western art; the Busch-Reisinger collection of Germanic art; and the Sackler collection of ancient, Asian, Islamic and Indian art. Think of it as a sort of Greatest Hits.

HARVARD MUSEUM OF
NATURAL HISTORY   MUSEUM
Map p266 (www.hmnh.harvard.edu; 26 Oxford St; adult/child/senior & student $9/6/7; ⊘9am-5pm; ⊞; MHarvard, ⊑86) This esteemed institution is famed for its botanical galleries, featuring more than 3000 lifelike pieces of handblown glass flowers and plants. At the intersection of art and science, the collection of intricately crafted flora is truly amazing. The zoological galleries house an unbelievable number of stuffed animals and reassembled skeletons, as well as an impressive fossil collection.

The mineralogical and geological galleries contain sparkling gemstones from all over the world, including some found right here in New England. The museum sponsors loads of special programs for kids, so it's worth checking the website when planning your visit. The price of admission includes entry into the Peabody Museum of Archaeology & Ethnology, which is in the same building.

PEABODY MUSEUM OF
ARCHAEOLOGY & ETHNOLOGY   MUSEUM
Map p266 (www.peabody.harvard.edu; 11 Divinity Ave; adult/child/senior & student $9/6/7; ⊘9am-5pm; ⊞; MHarvard, ⊑86) The centerpiece of the Peabody is the impressive Hall of the North American Indian, which traces how native peoples responded to the arrival of Europeans from the 15th to the 18th centuries. Other exhibits examine indigenous cultures throughout the Americas, including a fantastic comparison of cave paintings and murals of the Awatovi (New Mexico), the Maya (Guatemala) and the Moche (Peru).

Founded in 1866, the Peabody Museum is one of the world's oldest museums devoted to anthropology. The price of admission includes entry to the neighboring Harvard Museum of Natural History.

FREE LONGFELLOW NATIONAL
HISTORIC SITE   HISTORIC HOUSE
Map p266 (www.nps.gov/long; 105 Brattle St; ⊘tours 10:30am-4pm Wed-Sun May-Oct, grounds dawn-dusk year-round; MHarvard, ⊑71 or 73) Brattle St's most famous resident was Henry Wadsworth Longfellow, whose stately manor is now a National Historic Site. The poet lived and wrote here for 45 years, from 1837 to 1882, writing many of his most famous poems including *Evangeline* and *Hiawatha*. Accessible by guided tour, the Georgian mansion contains many of Longfellow's belongings, as well as lush period gardens.

Incidentally, one reason Longfellow was so taken with this house was its historical significance. During the Revolutionary War, General Washington appropriated this beauty from its absent Loyalist owner and used it as his headquarters.

HOOPER-LEE-
NICHOLS HOUSE   HISTORIC HOUSE
(www.cambridgehistory.org; 159 Brattle St; admission $5; ⊘1-5pm Mon & Wed; MHarvard, ⊑71 or 73) Now the headquarters of the Cambridge Historical Society, this c 1685 Georgian mansion is open for architectural tours, which show off the massive stone fireplace in the Chandler room and hand-painted wallpaper in the Bosphorous room. This is just one of many spectacular colonial-era residences on Brattle St. Lined with mansions that were once home to royal sympathizers, the street earned the nickname Tory Row.

MOUNT AUBURN CEMETERY   CEMETERY
(www.mountauburn.org; 580 Mt Auburn St; admission free, guided tour $5; ⊘8am-5pm Oct-Apr, to 7pm May-Sep; P; MHarvard, ⊑71 or 73) On a sunny day, this delightful spot at the end of Brattle St is worth the 30-minute walk west from Harvard Sq. Developed in 1831, it was the first 'garden cemetery' in the US. Maps pinpoint the rare botanical specimens and notable burial plots.

Famous long-term residents include Mary Baker Eddy (founder of the Christian Science Church), Isabella Stewart Gardner (socialite and art collector), Winslow Homer (19th-century American painter), Oliver Wendell Holmes (US Supreme Court Justice) and Henry W Longfellow (19th-century writer).

⊙ Central & Kendall Squares

MASSACHUSETTS INSTITUTE OF TECHNOLOGY
UNIVERSITY
See p147.

EATING

🍴 Harvard Square

Harvard Sq has coffeehouses, sandwich shops, ethnic eateries and upscale restaurants to suit every budget and taste. There is also a decent food court in the mini-mall known as the Garage (p158).

CAMBRIDGE, 1
PIZZERIA **$$**
Map p266 (www.cambridge1.us; 27 Church St; pizzas $15-20; ⊙lunch & dinner; ✍; Ⓜ Harvard) Set in the old fire station, this pizzeria's name comes from the sign chiseled into the stonework out front. The interior is sleek, sparse and industrial, with big windows overlooking the Old Burying Ground in the back. The menu is equally simple: pizza, soup, salad, dessert. These oddly-shaped pizzas are delectable, with crispy crusts and creative topping combos.

RUSSELL HOUSE TAVERN
MODERN AMERICAN **$$**
Map p266 (www.russellhousecambridge.com; 14 John F Kennedy St; mains $12-24; ⊙lunch Mon-Fri, brunch Sat-Sun, dinner daily; Ⓜ Harvard) Smack dab in the middle of Harvard Sq, this attractive gastropub has a classy, classic atmosphere, enhanced by good-looking, effervescent patrons. The menu – with hints of Southern goodness – includes a raw bar and a list of intriguing but irresistible small plates, not to mention a well-selected all-American wine list and killer cocktails.

📷 CLOVER FOOD LAB
VEGETARIAN **$**
Map p266 (www.cloverfoodlab.com; 7 Holyoke St; mains $2-6; ⊙7am-midnight; ✍🚻; Ⓜ Harvard) Clover is on the cutting edge. It's all high-tech with its 'live' menu updates and electronic ordering system. But it's really about the food – local, seasonal, vegetarian food – which is cheap, delicious and fast. How fast? Check the menu. Interesting tidbit:

Clover started as a food truck (and still has a few trucks making the rounds).

DARWIN'S LTD
SANDWICHES **$**
Map p266 (www.darwinsltd.com; 148 Mt Auburn St; mains $8-12; ⊙8am-5pm; 📶✍🚻; Ⓜ Harvard) Punky staff serve fat sandwiches, fresh soup and salads, and delicious coffee and pastries, all with a generous helping of attitude. The limited seating is often occupied by students who are in for the long haul (thanks to wireless access). So unless you intend to surf, take your lunch to enjoy at JFK Park or Radcliffe Yard.

VEGGIE PLANET
VEGETARIAN **$**
Map p266 (www.veggieplanet.net; 47 Palmer St; mains $6-12; ⊙lunch & dinner; ✍🚻; Ⓜ Harvard) Vegetarians and vegans can go nuts on creative interpretations of pizza (literally nuts: try the peanut curry pizza with tofu and broccoli). Stirfries and oddly shaped pies call on all the ethnic cuisines – but none of the animals – for their tantalizing tastes. By night, these basement digs double as the famous folk music venue, Club Passim (p154).

MR BARTLEY'S BURGER COTTAGE
BURGERS **$**
Map p266 (www.mrbartley.com; 1246 Massachusetts Ave; burgers $9-13; ⊙11am-9pm Mon-Sat; 🚻; Ⓜ Harvard) Packed with small tables and hungry college students, this burger joint has been a Harvard Sq institution for more than 50 years. Bartley's offers at least 40 different burgers; if none of these suit your fancy, create your own 7oz juicy masterpiece with the toppings of your choice. Sweet potato fries, onion rings, thick frappes and raspberry-lime rickeys complete the classic American meal.

RED HOUSE
MODERN AMERICAN **$$**
Map p266 (📞617-576-0605; www.redhouse.com; 98 Winthrop St; mains $15-25; ⊙lunch & dinner Tue-Sun, to 1am Fri & Sat; ✍; Ⓜ Harvard) Formerly known as the Cox-Hicks House, this quaint clapboard house dates to 1802. Reminiscent of an old-fashioned inn, it retains its historic charm with its wide-plank wood floors, cozy layout and functioning fireplace. The menu is varied and variable: it always includes a good selection of seafood and pasta, though preparations are not as consistent as they could be.

In summer, the draw is the patio overlooking a quiet corner of Harvard Sq.

FULL MOON FUSION $$

(www.fullmoonrestaurant.com; 344 Huron Ave; mains lunch $10-12, dinner $15-20; ☺lunch & dinner; ⚡📶; 📖72 or 75) Families adore Full Moon for its interesting, eclectic menu, arty atmosphere and family-friendly facilities. We're not talking about the kids' menu and the coloring books – although there's that – but rather the full-scale play area that truly welcomes your children. There's probably no reason to trek out here if you don't have kids, but Mom and Dad will love this place.

MARKET IN THE SQUARE CAFETERIA $

Map p266 (60 Church St; per pound $11; ☺24hr; ⚡📶; MHarvard) For families, students and professionals on-the-go, this glorified convenience store fills a niche. The self-service cafeteria is well stocked with all kinds of fresh salads, soups, sandwiches and hot dishes, so there is something for everyone. Importantly, it's open around the clock – the only option in Harvard Sq for a late-night study break or a postdrinking snack attack.

✖ Central & Kendall Squares

TOP CHOICE **HUNGRY MOTHER** SOUTHERN $$$

Map p268 (☎617-499-0090; www.hungrymother cambridge.com; 233 Cardinal Medeiros Ave; mains $21-26; ☺dinner Tue-Sun; MKendall/MIT) Who knew that Bostonians would take so well to grits? No wonder, Hungry Mother does Southern fare right, using fresh local ingredients and classic French cooking techniques. It's a cozy crowded space that feels like somebody's country house, with lots of little rooms and eclectic art and photos on the wall. Early bird special: show up before 6pm and get discounted movie tickets.

CHRISTINA'S ICE CREAM $

Map p268 (www.christinasicecream.com; 1255 Cambridge St; ice cream from $3; ☺11:30am-10:30pm; MCentral, 📖91) It's a bit of a hike from Central Sq, but it's worth it to sample Christina's eclectic ice cream flavors such as adzuki bean or ginger molasses. There is always a selection of seasonal flavors such as fresh mint in summer and pumpkin in fall. All-time favorite flavor: coconut almond chip. Most unusual: fresh rose.

EMMA'S PIZZA PIZZERIA $$

Map p268 (www.emmaspizza.com; 40 Hampshire St; sandwiches $6-9, pizzas $12-20; ☺lunch & dinner Mon-Sat; ⚡📶; MKendall/MIT) Before or after a flick at the nearby Kendall Sq Cinema, make a point of stopping at this friendly neighborhood pizzeria, which instills a maniacal devotion in its customers. Crispy thin crust and creative topping combinations cause Emma's to be consistently rated among the city's best pizza. Slices and salads are sold from the front window.

🍃**LIFE ALIVE** VEGETARIAN $

Map p268 (www.lifealive.com; 765 Massachusetts Ave; mains $8-10; ☺8am-10pm Mon-Sat, 11am-7pm Sun; ⚡📶; MCentral) Life Alive offers a joyful, healthful, purposeful approach to fast food. The unusual combinations of ingredients yield delicious results, most of which come in a bowl (like a salad) or in a wrap (like a sandwich). There are also soups, sides and smoothies, all served in a funky, colorful, light-filled space.

BONDIR FRENCH $$$

Map p268 (☎617-661-0009; www.bondircam bridge.com; 279 Broadway; mains $28-30; ☺dinner Wed-Mon; ⚡; MCentral or Kendall/MIT) A tiny hole in the wall in an out-of-the-way location, this feels like a secret spot, except that everyone keeps talking about it. The daily-changing menu is not extensive, but carefully conceived to present local ingredients in fresh, exciting ways. Every meal starts with a basket of fresh-baked, heaven-on-earth breads, and the meal just gets better after that.

Most entrées come in half-sizes, which means more opportunities to sample!

CRAIGIE ON MAIN FRENCH $$$

Map p268 (☎617-497-5511; www.craigieonmain. com; 853 Main St; mains $37, three-course prix-fixe $65; ☺dinner Tue-Sun; MCentral) French foodies absolutely adore Tony Maws' rustic fare and intimate atmosphere at Craigie. The menu changes daily, depending on fresh, seasonal ingredients; there is also an excellent bar with an intriguing selection of cocktails and interesting bar food to go along with it. Creativity and energy exude from the open kitchen, along with the wonderful aromas.

GREEN STREET GRILL MODERN AMERICAN $$

Map p268 (☎617-876-1655; www.greenstreetgrill. com; 280 Green St; mains $17-24; ☺dinner; MCentral) Gritty on the outside, cozy on the inside, the Green Street Grill is a longstanding neighborhood joint that still manages to be thoroughly up to date. The urban bar and grill hints at upscale, but keeps it real with affordable prices and tried-and-true American fare. Killer cocktails make it a great place to drink, too.

MIRACLE OF SCIENCE
BAR & GRILL   AMERICAN $$

Map p268 (www.miracleofscience.us; 321 Massachusetts Ave; mains $10-14; ⊗breakfast, lunch & dinner; Central) With all the decor of your high school science lab, this bar and grill is still pretty hip and is popular among MIT student types. Join them for burgers, kebabs and other tasty grilled fare, as well as a choice selection of beers on tap. (It looks like the periodic table on the wall, but it's really the menu.)

FRIENDLY TOAST   DINER $

Map p268 (www.thefriendlytoast.net; 1 Kendall Sq; mains $8-12; ⊗8am-10pm Sun-Thu, 8am-1am Fri-Sat; ⌨; MKendall/MIT) Some people think that this retro funky diner is one of the best places to eat breakfast *in the country*. (Yes, the toast really is that friendly.) Decadent delights like Almond Joy pancakes and loads of vegetarian and vegan options have hungry folks lining up out the door for weekend brunch.

But here's the bonus: breakfast isn't just for breakfast anymore. At the Friendly Toast, it's served all day long, along with burgers, burritos and more.

BARAKA CAFÉ   NORTH AFRICAN $$

Map p268 (www.barakacafe.com; 801/2 Pearl St; mains $12-16; ⊗lunch & dinner Tue-Sat; ⌨; MCentral) This tiny storefront entices the adventurous eater to sample exotic flavors in a setting reminiscent of a Mediterranean kitchen. The flavor-filled menu offers hot and cold *kemiette* (small plates), as well as classic North African dishes like couscous and bastilla. Vegetarians have no shortage of options, while meat-eaters might indulge in the M'Katef (lamb chops with an almond pastry).

There's no alcohol, but the lemonade – spiced with orange essence and rose water – quenches any thirst.

VEGGIE GALAXY   VEGITARIAN DINER $

Map p268 (www.veggiegalaxy.com; 450 Massachusetts Ave; mains $8-12; ⊗breakfast, lunch & dinner; ⌨⌨; MCentral) What does the word 'diner' mean to you? All-day breakfast? Check. Burgers and milkshakes? Check. Counter seating and comfy booths? Got

those too. A circular glass display case showing off desserts? Yes, complete with tangy, delicious lemon meringue pie. In short, Veggie Galaxy does everything that a diner is supposed to do, but they do it without meat.

There's also an amazing vegan bakery – now that's going above and beyond diner duty!

TOSCANINI'S   ICE CREAM $

Map p268 (www.tosci.com; 899 Main St; ice cream from $4; ⊗8am-11pm Mon-Sat, 10am-11pm Sun; ⌨; MCentral) People come from miles around for Tosci's burnt caramel ice cream, which apparently was invented as the result of an accident (you can imagine). Besides the dozens of delicious ice cream flavors, there is also excellent coffee.

⌨ DRINKING & NIGHTLIFE

⌨ Harvard Square

TOP | CASABLANCA   BAR
CHOICE

Map p266 (www.casablanca-restaurant.com; 40 Brattle St; ⊗5pm-1am or 2am Mon-Sat; MHarvard) Below the Brattle Theatre, this Harvard Sq classic has long been the hangout of film fans, local literati and other arty types. Regulars skip the formal dining room and slip in the back door to the boisterous bar. A colorful mural depicting Rick's Café sets the stage for innovative Mediterranean delights, including a wonderful wine list and great selection of meze.

TOP | CAFÉ PAMPLONA   CAFE
CHOICE

Map p266 (12 Bow St; mains $8-15; ⊗11am-midnight; MHarvard) Located in a cozy cellar on a backstreet, this no-frills European cafe is the choice among old-time Cantabridgians. In addition to tea and coffee drinks, Pamplona has light snacks such as gazpacho, sandwiches and biscotti. The tiny outdoor terrace is a delight in summer.

LA BURDICK   CAFE

Map p266 (www.burdickchocolate.com; 52D Brattle St; ⊗8am-9pm Sun-Thu, 8am-10pm Fri-Sat; MHarvard) This boutique chocolatier doubles as a cafe, usually packed full of happy patrons drinking hot cocoa. Whether you

FOOD TRUCKS

Like many US cities, Boston now has dozens of food trucks cruising its streets, serving up cheap, filling foods to hungry patrons who are short on time and/or money. Nowadays, it's not just ethnic eats, but also burgers and dogs, grilled cheese sandwiches, lobster rolls, vegetarian and more.

The food truck phenomenon got its start in Cambridge near MIT, where the trucks would park to cater to hungry students and scientists. They still park on Carleton St to feed the MIT students and staff.

➡ The best loved and best established food truck is the **Clover Food Lab** (p150). It's so well established that they now also have several brick and mortar restaurants, including one in Harvard Sq.

➡ Really hungry people eat at **Jose's Mexican Truck** (Map p268; Carleton St; mains $5; MKendall/MIT), where they can get a big burrito, chips and salsa and rice and beans, all for a measly $5. It's the cheapest, most filling lunch around, and it tastes good, too.

➡ If you're in the mood for noodles or rice, head to the pan-Asian truck, **Momo-goose** (Map p268; www.momogoose.com; Carleton St; mains $5; ⊗10am-3:30pm Mon-Fri; ☑; MKendall/MIT). They have healthy rice bowls or noodle bowls (with many veg options) for $5, as well as soup and sandwiches.

choose dark or milk, it's sure to be some of the best chocolate you'll drink in your lifetime. There are only a handful of tables, so it's hard to score a seat when temperatures are chilly.

SHAY'S PUB & WINE BAR   PUB
Map p266 (www.shayspubandwinebar.com; 58 John F Kennedy St; ⊗noon-1am; MHarvard) A charming basement-level bar, Shay's is a long-standing favorite among Harvard graduate students that has recently fancied itself up and expanded its wine list. Inside, it's a small wooden pub where you'll sit on a stool and pretend to look thoughtful. Out front is a small brick patio full of sunners and smokers jockeying for a table and watching the sidewalk goings-on.

ALGIERS COFFEE HOUSE   CAFE
Map p266 (40 Brattle St; ⊗8am-midnight; MHarvard) Although the pace of service can be glacial, the palatial Middle Eastern decor makes this an inviting rest spot. The one good thing about the relaxed service is that you won't be rushed to finish your pot of Arabic coffee or mint tea. Bonus: roof-deck seating.

CHARLIE'S KITCHEN   DIVE BAR
Map p266 (www.charlieskitchen.com; 10 Eliot St; MHarvard) Charlie's has two floors: downstairs is a tamer diner and upstairs is where the scene thrives. It's packed by 9:30pm on a Saturday night; come inside to hear the Cars, Descendants and Pixies played at inordinate volumes from a rock-oriented

jukebox. Otherwise drink Pabst and eat patty burgers and lobster rolls while bumping the tattooed elbows of your screaming neighbors.

UPSTAIRS ON THE SQUARE   TEAHOUSE
Map p266 (☎617-864-1933; www.upstairsonthesquare.com; 91 Winthrop St; ⊗afternoon tea 2-4pm Sat-Sun; MHarvard) Pink-and-gold hues, chandeliers and lots of glamor and glitz: such is the decor that defines this restaurant, the successor to once-renowned Upstairs at the Pudding. It's a romantic setting for afternoon tea and a bite of sweet – the perfect way to celebrate a special occasion or warm up on a winter afternoon.

📍 Central & Kendall Squares

VOLTAGE COFFEE & ART   CAFE
Map p268 (www.voltagecoffee.com; 295 Third St; ⊗7am-7pm Mon-Fri, 9am-7pm Sun; 🛜; MKendall/MIT) The place promises 'Coffee & Art' but we are left to wonder – what's the difference? The lattes are beautiful to look at and they inspire deep thoughts. The artwork is deliciously dark and it stimulates the brain. No matter, art afficionados and coffee drinkers, come to Voltage for a little of both.

PLOUGH & STARS   IRISH PUB
Map p268 (www.ploughandstars.com; 912 Massachusetts Ave; ⊗noon-2am; MCentral) The Plough & Stars is the real deal Irish, serving up bangers, eggs and gastro-pub fare

in a cozy wooden room with stout on tap and in bottles. Weekend soccer matches are on the telly and stringed bands play Irish tunes. Actually, there's music every night of the week – not only Irish, but also jazz, blues, rockabilly, funk and other undefineable genres.

BRICK & MORTAR
COCKTAIL BAR

Map p268 (569 Massachusetts Ave; ⊙from 5:30pm; ⓂCentral) Enter through the unmarked door (next to Central Kitchen) and climb the stairs to cool cocktail heaven. No pretenses here – just a pared down setting and a choice list of craft cocktails and beers. The staff is knowledgeable and friendly, so if you don't see something you like, ask for advice.

RIVER GODS
BAR

Map p268 (www.rivergodsonline.com; 125 River St; ⊙3pm-1am; ⓂCentral) The decor of this small, cramped room (max 45 people) leans towards kitsch with a cluttered assortment of sparkly leather stools and gothic red velvet chairs. Art-house movies and documentary footage project silently on the wall while DJs spin from a second-story alcove. The DJs work their magic every night, with a few sessions weekly dedicated to new music.

AREA FOUR
CAFE, BAR

Map p268 (www.areafour.com; 500 Technology Sq; ⊙7am-10pm Mon-Thu, to 11pm Fri, 9am-11pm Sat, 9am-5pm Sun; 🛜; ⓂKendall/MIT) The postindustrial vibe at Area Four is perfect for the high-tech block where it is located (and for which it is named). Doubling as a cool cafe and modern gastropub, Area Four offers strong coffee and fresh pastries by day, and local brews, sustainable wines and wood-fired pizzas by night. Eat and drink your way around the clock.

MIDDLESEX
CLUB

Map p268 (www.middlesexlounge.com; 315 Massachusetts Ave; cover $5 Fri & Sat; ⊙lunch & dinner, to 1am Mon-Wed, to 2am Thu-Sat; ⓂCentral) Sleek and sophisticated, Middlesex brings the fashionable crowd to the Cambridge side of town. Black modular furniture sits on heavy casters, allowing the cubes to be rolled aside when the place transforms from lounge to club, making space for the beautiful people to become entranced with DJs experimenting with hip hop and electronica.

CAMBRIDGE BREWING CO
BREWERY

Map p268 (www.cambrew.com; 1 Kendall Sq; ⊙11:30am-midnight; ⓂKendall/MIT) This jovial microbrewery is often crowded, as students and other beer-lovers like to imbibe fresh local beer. Flavors include Regatta Golden, Cambridge Amber and Charles River Porter (love that dirty water). CBC occasionally hosts a 'brewers' dinner,' which pairs special menu items with complementary beers.

☆ ENTERTAINMENT

☆ Harvard Square

⌖ CLUB PASSIM
LIVE MUSIC

Map p266 (www.clubpassim.org; 47 Palmer St; tickets $15-30; ⓂHarvard) Folk music in Boston seems to be endangered outside of Irish bars, but the legendary Club Passim does such a great job booking top-notch acts that it practically fills in the vacuum by itself. The colorful, intimate room is hidden off a side street in Harvard Sq, and those attending shows are welcome to order filling dinners from Veggie Planet, an incredibly good restaurant that shares the space.

⌖ LIZARD LOUNGE
LIVE MUSIC

(www.lizardloungeclub.com; 1667 Massachusetts Ave; cover $5-10; ⊙7:30pm-1am, to 2am Fri-Sat; ⓂHarvard) The underground Lizard Lounge doubles as a jazz and rock venue. The big drawcard is the Sunday night poetry slam, featuring music by the jazzy Jeff Robinson Trio. Also popular are the Monday open-mic challenge and Tuesday nights with Session Americana. The bar stocks an excellent list of New England beers, which are complemented by the sweet-potato fries.

Located a quarter-mile north of Cambridge Common (the park), below Cambridge Common (the restaurant).

⌖ COMEDY STUDIO
COMEDY

Map p266 (www.thecomedystudio.com; 1238 Massachusetts Ave; admission $8-12; ⊙show 8pm Tue-Sun; ⓂHarvard) The 3rd floor of the Hong Kong noodle house contains a low-budget comedy house with a reputation for hosting cutting-edge acts. This is where talented future stars (eg Brian Kiley, who became a writer for Conan O'Brien) refine their racy material. Each night has a different theme, eg on Tuesday you can usually see a weird magician show.

BRATTLE THEATRE   CINEMA

Map p266 (www.brattlefilm.org; 40 Brattle St; adult/child/senior/student \$10/7/7/8, matinee \$8; Ⓜ Harvard) The Brattle is a film lover's *cinema paradiso*. Film noir, independent films and series that celebrate directors or periods are shown regularly in this renovated 1890 repertory theater. Some famous (or infamous) special events include the annual Valentine's Day screening of *Casablanca* and occasional cartoon marathons.

AMERICAN REPERTORY

THEATER   PERFORMING ARTS

Map p266 (ART; ☑ 617-547-8300; www.amrep. org; 64 Brattle St; tickets \$40-75; Ⓜ Harvard) There isn't a bad seat in the house at Harvard University's Loeb Drama Theater, where the prestigious ART stages new plays and experimental interpretations of classics. Since 2008, Artistic Director Diane Paulus has encouraged a broad interpretation of 'theater,' staging an interactive murder mysteries (*Sleep No More*), readings of novels in their entirety (*Gatz*) and robot operas (*Death & the Powers*).

TOAD   LIVE MUSIC

(www.toadcambridge.com; 1912 Massachusetts Ave; Ⓜ Porter) This tiny, laid-back place is beloved for its excellent lineup of music (seven nights a week) and its no-cover-charge policy. (Ever. At all.) There are a dozen beers on tap and 'all sorts of booze available.' No food, but it's okay to bring something to nosh from next door.

Located about one mile north of Harvard Sq, across from the Porter Sq shopping plaza.

REGATTABAR   BLUES, JAZZ

Map p266 (www.regattabarjazz.com; 1 Bennett St; tickets \$15-35; Ⓜ Harvard) Why does Boston have such clean jazz clubs? Regattabar looks just like a conference room in a hotel – in this case the Charles Hotel. They get big enough names (Virginia Rodrigues, Keb Mo) to transcend the mediocre space, though. As it only has 225 seats, you're guaranteed a good view and the sound system is excellent.

CLUB OBERON   PERFORMING ARTS

Map p266 (www.cluboberon.com; 2 Arrow St; Ⓜ Havard) The second stage of the American Repertory Theater, this black box is ideally suited for flashy song and dance performances and interactive, acrobatic theater. The long-running favorite is the Shakespearean disco, *The Donkey Show*, but you might also see *Rocky Horror Live* or *Abbey Road: An Erotic, Thrilling Interpretation*. Indeed, 'erotic' and 'thrilling' seem to be consistent themes across performances.

HARVARD FILM

ARCHIVE CINEMATHEQUE   CINEMA

Map p266 (Carpenter Center for the Arts; http://hcl.harvard.edu/hfa; 24 Quincy St; adult/senior & student \$9/7; ⊘ Fri-Mon; Ⓜ Harvard) Four nights a week, the Cinematheque presents retrospectives of distinguished actors, screenings of rare films, thematic groupings and special events featuring the filmmakers themselves. The screenings – which often sell out – take place at the 200-seat theater in the esteemed Carpenter Center (designed by Le Corbusier). Tickets go on sale 45 minutes ahead of show times.

CAMBRIDGE FORUM   LECTURES

Map p266 (First Parish in Cambridge; www.cambridgeforum.org; 3 Church St; Ⓜ Harvard) This excellent series brings speakers on a weekly basis to speak in the meeting house at First Parish in Cambridge. Recent speakers have included luminaries like Nobel Prize-winning economist Paul Krugman, poet laureate Robert Pinsky, beloved biologist of the people EO Wilson and former Secretary of Labor Robert Reich. Events are often held in conjunction with the Harvard Bookstore.

FREE LONGY SCHOOL

OF MUSIC   CLASSICAL MUSIC

Map p266 (www.longy.edu; 27-33 Garden St; Ⓜ Harvard) George Longy was an oboist with the Boston Symphony Orchestra before he decided to found the Longy School of Music in 1915. Now more than a century old, Longy is a well-respected training ground for classical musicians. Students and faculty show off the goods on an almost daily basis, often free of charge. Longy is just northwest of the Cambridge Common.

SANDERS THEATRE AT

MEMORIAL HALL   CONCERT VENUE

Map p266 (www.harvard.edu/arts; 45 Quincy St; Ⓜ Harvard) Set inside the magnificent Memorial Hall, this beautiful, 1166-seat, wood-paneled theater is known for its acoustics. It is frequently used for classical musical performances by local chorales and ensembles, as well as occasional concerts by jazz and world musicians.

HASTY PUDDING THEATRICALS COMEDY

Map p266 (www.hastypudding.org; 12 Holyoke St; tickets $28-38; Ⓜ Harvard) The oldest theater company in the States, Harvard's undergraduate dramatic society was founded in 1795. While you can see several kinds of events, including the annual Hasty Pudding Awards, mostly it's all about musical comedy with guys in drag.

☆ Central & Kendall Squares

TOP CHOICE LILY PAD PERFORMING ARTS

Map p268 (www.lily-pad.net; 1353 Cambridge St; cover $10; Ⓜ Central, ☐71) Lily Pad is a tiny space that fills up with music and performance art, whether it's tango dancing, narrated jazz storytelling or a musical conversation between jazz piano and tap dance. You might also hear indie, avant-garde, folk and even chamber music. The space is stripped down – basically folding chairs in a room – which adds to the underground ambience.

Lily Pad is located in Inman Sq, a 15-minute walk north of Central Sq.

RYLES JAZZ CLUB JAZZ, CLUB

Map p268 (☎617-876-9330; www.rylesjazz.com; 212 Hampshire St; cover $8-15; Ⓜ Central) Bonus: Ryles is not in a hotel. It is a dark lounge with low lighting and big windows, offering an intimate atmosphere to hear great music. This includes the house band – Ryles Jazz Orchestra – which plays monthly, as well as other local talent and the occasional big name. The Sunday jazz brunch is super popular: reserve if possible.

No matter what's going down on the 1st floor, there is dancing upstairs. And it usually has a Latin beat. Salsa Sunday, Noche Latina Tuesday, Viernes de Vacilon... you get the idea. On Saturday, SuperShag mixes it up with salsa and swing – a fabulous combination for those with fancy toes.

LANDMARK KENDALL SQUARE CINEMA CINEMA

Map p268 (www.landmarktheatres.com; 1 Kendall Sq; adult/child $9.75/7.50; Ⓜ Kendall/MIT) This cinema screens popular foreign films and the usual collection of hits from the Sundance Festival. Seats are steeply sloped and the concession stand serves cappuccino. New releases definitely sell out on Friday nights, so buy your tickets before dinner.

MIDDLE EAST LIVE MUSIC

Map p268 (www.mideastclub.com; 472 Massachusetts Ave; cover $10-30; Ⓜ Central) The Middle East is as good as the bands it books, which means it varies wildly. This is the preferred venue for local garage bands (hit or miss, by definition), as well as 1980s rockers and fun Euro-pop artists.

In addition to the two stages, creatively known as 'Upstairs' and 'Downstairs,' there are two bar/restaurant areas serving decent Middle Eastern food (go figure). All four areas are venues for DJs and dance parties, depending on the night.

CANTAB LOUNGE LIVE MUSIC

Map p268 (www.cantab-lounge.com; 738 Massachusetts Ave; Ⓜ Central) The Cantab is one of the neighborhood's divier dives (and that's saying something in Central Sq). But the eclectic music line-up attracts an awesome mixed crowd that likes to get its groove on. Tuesday night is the area's best bluegrass night, Wednesday is the poetry slam, and Thursday to Friday is a get-down, old-timer sweaty dance party.

TT THE BEAR'S PLACE LIVE MUSIC

Map p268 (www.ttthebears.com; 10 Brookline St; cover $7-10; Ⓜ Central) A dirty dive with two bars in two rooms, one of which provides refuge for those who discover that not all local bands are actually worth listening to. (But some are, so choose wisely.) TT's Saturday-night new-wave dance party 'Heroes' is wildly popular with folks that can remember the 80s – and many who can't.

🛍 SHOPPING

🛍 Harvard Square

Harvard Sq is home to upwards of 150 shops, all within a few blocks of the university campus. The area used to boast an avant-garde sensibility and dozens of independent stores, and vestiges of this free spirit remain. Certainly, there are still more bookstores in Harvard Sq than anywhere else in the

SOMERVILLE THEATRE

A classic neighborhood movie house, the **Somerville Theatre** (📞617-625-5700; www.somervilletheatreonline.com; 55 Davis Sq; adult/senior/matinee $8/5/7; Ⓜ Davis) dates from 1914 and features plenty of well-preserved gilding and pastel murals of muses. On offer are first- and second-run Hollywood hits, live performances by chamber orchestras and world musicians and the Independent Film Festival of Boston screenings. The main theater is the biggest, best and oldest and has the added treat of a balcony. This gem is in Davis Sq, a hop, skip and a jump north from Cambridge.

Boston area. However, many of the funkier shops have been replaced by chains, leading critics to complain that the square has become an outdoor shopping mall.

TOP CHOICE **WARD MAPS** MAPS, SOUVENIRS

(www.wardmaps.com; 1735 Massachusetts Ave; ⊙10am-6pm Mon-Fri, noon-6pm Sat, noon-3pm Sun; Ⓜ Harvard or Porter) If you're into maps, you'll be into Ward Maps. They have an incredible collection of original antique and reproduction maps. What's more, they print the maps on coffee mugs, mouse pads, journals and greeting cards, creating unique and personal gifts. Some stuff is readymade, or you can custom order. Located about a half-mile north of Harvard Sq.

TOP CHOICE **TAYRONA** ACCESSORIES

Map p266 (www.tayrona1156.com; 1156 Massachusetts Ave; ⊙10am-7pm Mon-Sat; Ⓜ Harvard) Tayrona is named for an ancient indigenous culture that inhabited the mountains of Colombia. But the items that Tayrona carries are by no means limited to South American–influenced styles. The jewelry runs the gamut from clunky costume jewels to delicate gold and silver. Beaded handbags, batik scarves and handcrafted gift items reflect an exotic, international but thoroughly sophisticated style.

CAMBRIDGE ARTISTS'
COOPERATIVE HANDICRAFTS

Map p266 (www.cambridgeartistscoop.com; 59a Church St; ⊙10am-6pm Tue-Wed & Fri-Sat, to 8pm Thu, noon-5pm Sun; Ⓜ Harvard) Owned and operated by Cambridge artists, this three-floor gallery displays an ever-changing exhibit of their work. The pieces are crafty – handmade jewelry, woven scarves, leather products and pottery. The craftspeople double as sales staff, so you may get to meet the creative force behind your souvenir.

HARVARD BOOKSTORE BOOKS

Map p266 (www.harvard.com; 1256 Massachusetts Ave; ⊙9am-11pm Mon-Sat, 10am-10pm Sun; Ⓜ Harvard) Family-owned and operated since 1932, the Harvard Bookstore is not officially affiliated with the university, but it is the university community's favorite place to come to browse. While the shop maintains an academic focus, there is plenty of fiction for the less lofty, as well as used books and bargain books in the basement.

Harvard Bookstore hosts author talks and other interesting lectures, often in conjunction with Cambridge Forum.

RAVEN USED BOOKS BOOKS

Map p266 (www.ravencambridge.com; 52 John F Kennedy St; ⊙10am-9pm Mon-Sat, 11am-8pm Sun; Ⓜ Harvard) Tucked into a tiny basement, Raven knows its audience: its 14,000 books focus on scholarly titles, especially in the liberal arts. Bibliophiles agree that the quality and condition of books is top-notch.

BERK'S SHOES

Map p266 (www.berkshoes.com; 50 John F Kennedy St; ⊙10am-9pm Mon-Sat, 11am-7pm Sun; Ⓜ Harvard) Berk's is a little store with a great selection of shoes – half for your sensible feet and half for your fancy feet. Prices can be prohibitively high, unless you manage to strike the awesome end-of-season sales. You know they're going on when you see tables on the sidewalks piled high with shoes.

GROLIER POETRY BOOKSHOP BOOKS

Map p266 (www.grolierpoetrybookshop.org; 6 Plympton St; ⊙11am-7pm Tue & Wed, to 6pm Thu-Sat; Ⓜ Harvard) Founded in 1927, Grolier is the oldest – and perhaps the most famous – poetry bookstore in the USA. Through the years, TS Eliot, ee cummings, Marianne Moore and Allen Ginsberg all passed through these doors. Today, Grolier continues to foster young poets and poetry readers. Besides selling written poetry and recordings, the store hosts readings and festivals.

SCHOENHOF'S FOREIGN BOOKS BOOKS

Map p266 (www.schoenhofs.com; 76A Mt Auburn St; ⊙10am-8pm Mon-Sat, to 6pm Sun; ⓂHarvard) Since 1856, Schoenhof's has been providing Boston's foreign-language-speaking literati with reading material. Special booklists keep regulars abreast of new arrivals in their language of choice, whether it's scholarly or literary works, language instruction materials or children's books. If you are wondering which languages and dialects are available, the official count is over 700, so Schoenhof's probably has you covered.

OONA'S EXPERIENCED CLOTHING CLOTHING

Map p266 (www.oonasboston.com; 1210 Massachusetts Ave; ⓂHarvard) Oona's sells kitschy clothes from all eras. Dress-up dandies come here for Halloween costumes, drag wear, retro attire from any decade and outfits for every theme. Not that you need an excuse to go vintage: Oona's merchandise is cheap enough that you can buy it just for fun.

DICKSON BROS HARDWARE

Map p266 (www.dicksonbros.com; 26 Brattle St; ⊙8:30am-6pm Mon-Sat, 10am-4pm Sun; ⓂHarvard) Locals know that you can find just about anything you need for your home at this old-timer hardware store. From house paint to cleaning supplies, from kitchen accessories to storage bins, it's all crammed into this three-storey space in the heart of Harvard Sq.

COLONIAL DRUG PHARMACY

Map p266 (www.colonialdrug.com; 49 Brattle St; ⊙8am-7pm Mon-Fri, to 6pm Sat; ⓂHarvard) This old-time apothecary carries hundreds of scents, including many hard-to-find fragrances, which are its specialty. Besides cosmetics, colognes and soaps, it also stocks old-fashioned shaving kits – complete with razor, bowl and brush – like your grandfather used to use.

IN YOUR EAR MUSIC

Map p266 (www.iye.com; 72 Mt Auburn St; ⊙11am-8pm Mon-Sat, noon-6pm Sun; ⓂHarvard) In an out-of-the-way spot on the edge of the square, this underground (literally) record shop is everything it should be. Crammed with LPs and 45s, there's also a huge selection of CDs, DVDs and even eight-tracks. The albums on the wall will catch your eye, but they are expensive; look down below for unbelievable bargains.

The original 'Mothership' store is on Commonwealth Ave in Brighton, near the Paradise Rock Club.

CARDULLO'S GOURMET SHOP FOOD & DRINK

Map p266 (www.cardullos.com; 6 Brattle St; ⊙9am-9pm Mon-Sat, 10am-7pm Sun; ⓂHarvard) We've never seen so many goodies packed into such a small space. You'll find every sort of imported edible your heart desires, from caviar to chocolate. The excellent selection of New England products is a good source of souvenirs.

GARAGE MALL

Map p266 (36 John F Kennedy St; ⊙10am-9pm; ⓂHarvard) This gritty mini-mall in the midst of Harvard Sq houses an eclectic collection of shops. Highlights include an outlet of Newbury Comics, as well as the crazy costume store Hootenanny, and an edgy urban boutique and skate shop, Proletariat. Also, for hungry people, a sort of upscale food court.

🏠 Central & Kendall Squares

TOP CHOICE ⟩ WEIRDO RECORDS MUSIC

Map p268 (www.weirdorecords.com; 844 Massachusetts Ave; ⊙11am-9pm; ⓂCentral) Not to be confused with Cheapo Records up the street, this place is not particularly cheap, but it sure is weird. And we mean that in the best possible way. The shop is packed with thousands of records, most of which are out of print, from another country, or on obscure or defunct labels.

There are listening stations for your convenience and the Monday-night 'Series' has live performances by local weirdos.

NEW BALANCE FACTORY STORE

Run like the wind...to the **New Balance Factory Store** (40 Life St, Brighton; ☉9am-7pm Mon-Sat, 11am-6pm Sun; ⊟64) for the most comfortable, supportive running shoes at discounted prices. Runners rejoice over these shoes, but regular people wear them too. This warehouse-sized place also carries factory seconds and overruns of fleece jackets and synthetic clothing made by New Balance. You may have to search for your size, but you can easily save 50% or more off any given item. Unfortunately the store is not so easy to get to: take bus 64 from Central Sq (about 20 minutes).

CAMBRIDGE ANTIQUE MARKET MARKET

Map p268 (http://marketantique.com; 201 Monsignor O'Brien Hwy; ☉11am-6pm Tue-Sun; ⓂLechmere) This old brick warehouse in East Cambridge looks foreboding from the outside, but inside is an antiquer's paradise. With more than 150 dealers on five floors, Cambridge Antique Market is a trove of trash and treasures. The constant turnover of dealers lends a flea-market feel, guaranteeing that you never know what you will find.

LOREM IPSUM BOOKS

Map p268 (www.loremipsumbooks.com; 157 Hampshire St; ☉11am-9pm Sun-Wed, to 11pm Thu, to midnight Fri-Sat; ⓂCentral) Thanks to fancy inventory-tracing software developed in-house, you can browse Lorem Ipsum's extensive catalogue online. But why would you want to, if you can go to the brick and mortar bookstore and browse the old-fashioned way? Floor-to-ceiling shelves, hardwood floors and lots and lots of books.

STELLA BELLA TOYS

Map p268 (www.stellabellatoys.com; 1360 Cambridge St; ☉10am-6pm Mon-Sat, to 5pm Sun; ⓂCentral, ⊟69 or 91) If you let them, kids could play all day at Stella Bella. Aside from the toys that are for sale (many of which can also be played with), there is a train table, a toy kitchen and a ball pit that are open for business. Stella Bella is especially strong for creative and educational toys and games.

CHEAPO RECORDS MUSIC

Map p268 (www.cheaporecords.com; 538 Massachusetts Ave; ☉11am-7pm Mon-Wed & Sat, to 9pm Thu-Fri, to 5pm Sun; ⓂCentral) With tunes blasting out onto the sidewalk, Cheapo Records lures in music-lovers to browse through its huge selection of vinyl and decent selection of CDs. The staff knows their stuff, and the collection spans all genres, with a fun box of new arrivals for the regulars. And yes, they really are cheap-o.

GARMENT DISTRICT CLOTHING

Map p268 (www.garmentdistrict.com; 200 Broadway; ☉11am-7pm Sun-Tue, to 8pm Wed-Fri, 9am-7pm Sat; ⓂKendall/MIT) If your memories of

the fashion-conscious '60s and '70s have faded like an old pair of jeans, this store will bring it all back. Downstairs, Dollar-a-Pound offers piles of clothes that are priced by the pound. Also in the same location, **Boston Costume** (Map p268; www.bostoncostume.com) can dress you like your favorite superhero, sports mascot, literary character or historical figure.

🏃 SPORTS & ACTIVITIES

⬛ᵀᴼᴾ MINUTEMAN BIKEWAY CYCLING

(www.minutemanbikeway.org; ⓂAlewife or Davis) The best of Boston's bicycle trails starts near Alewife station and leads 5 miles to historic Lexington Center, then traverses an additional 4 miles of idyllic scenery and terminates in the rural suburb of Bedford. The wide, straight, paved path gets crowded on weekend. Rent a bike at the Bicycle Exchange (p222).

The Minuteman Bikeway is also accessible from Davis Sq in Somerville (Davis T station) via the 2-mile Community Path to Alewife.

⬛ᵀᴼᴾ KARMA YOGA STUDIO YOGA

Map p266 (www.karmayogastudio.com; 1120 Massachusetts Ave; yoga class before/after noon $10/20; ☉6am-10pm Mon-Fri, 8am-8pm Sat & Sun; ⓂHarvard) This studio offers 10 different types of yoga classes, including a range of physio yoga, heat yoga (takes place in a 90°F room) and Chi Kung (Chinese yoga). There is also a fully-equipped gym upstairs. This place is gorgeous, with hardwood floors and imported Indian art and furniture. The quaint cafe serves organic tea and vegan treats.

CHARLES RIVER CANOE
& KAYAK CENTER
CANOEING, KAYAKING

Map p268 (www.ski-paddle.com; 500 Broad Canal St; per hr canoe $16-28, kayak $15-28, kids' kayak $7; ☉noon-8pm Mon-Fri, 9am-8pm Sat-Sun; 👪; ⓂKendall/MIT) Besides canoe and kayak rental, Charles River Canoe & Kayak offers classes and organized outings. Experienced kayakers can venture out to the harbor, but the river and basin are lovely for skyline views and fall foliage. There is another outlet in Allston (near Harvard Sq), which allows for an excellent one-way five-mile trip between the two rental centers.

CHARLES RIVER BIKE PATH
CYCLING

(Storrow Dr & Memorial Dr; ⓂHarvard, Kendall/ MIT, Charles/MGH or Science Park) A popular cycling circuit runs along both sides of the Charles River between the Museum of Science and the Mt Auburn St Bridge in Watertown center (5 miles west of Cambridge). The round trip is 17 miles, but 10 bridges in between offer ample opportunities to turn around and shorten the trip. Rent a bike at Cambridge Bicycle (p222).

This trail is not particularly well maintained (watch for roots and narrow passes) and is often crowded with pedestrians.

HARVARD TOUR
WALKING TOUR

(Trademark Tours; www.trademarktours.com; $10; ⓂHarvard) This company was founded by a couple of Harvard students who shared the inside scoop on history and student life at The University. Now the company offers a whole menu of Boston tours, but the funny, offbeat Harvard Tour – still led by students – is the trademark. Tours depart from the Cambridge Visitor Information Kiosk in Harvard Sq; see the website for schedule details.

COMMUNITY ICE SKATING
@ KENDALL SQUARE
SKATING

Map p268 (www.ski-paddle.com; 300 Athenaeum St; adult/child $5/3, rental $8; ☉noon-8pm Mon-Fri, till 9pm Fri-Sat, 11am-6pm Sun; 👪; ⓂKendall/ MIT) This smallish rink is on par with Bos-

ton's other ice skating venues, but there are usually fewer people, which means more room for your pirouettes. The place is relatively new so the rental skates are in excellent condition.

CAMBRIDGE CENTER
FOR ADULT EDUCATION
COURSE

Map p266 (www.ccae.org; 42 Brattle St; ☉9am-9pm Mon-Thu, to 7pm Fri, to 2pm Sat; ⓂHarvard) The Cambridge Center for Adult Education offers everything from historical tours to writing classes to massage courses for couples.

RINK AT THE CHARLES
SKATING

Map p266 (www.charleshotel.com; 1 Bennett St; adult/child $5/3, skate rental $5/3; ☉4-8pm Mon-Fri, 10am-6pm Sat & Sun Dec-Mar; 👪; ⓂHarvard) The plaza in front of the Charles is a charming location for skating, with H-Square passers-by enjoying the music and admiring the talent on the ice. Again, it's a small rink, but not nearly as crowded as the Frog Pond. And there are many nearby options for post-skating hot chocolates.

FLAT TOP JOHNNY'S
BILLIARDS

Map p268 (www.flattopjohnnys.com; 1 Kendall Sq; ☉noon-1am Thu-Fri, 4pm-1am Sat-Wed; ⓂKendall/MIT) Twelve tournament tables are set in a tall-ceilinged space surrounded by brick walls and comic-book murals. The tables are in excellent condition and the beer selection is also good. Weekly tournaments are held on Sunday afternoons and Monday

---

WORTH A DETOUR

FLATBREAD CO & SACCO'S BOWL HAVEN

Founded in 1939, Sacco's Bowl Haven was a Somerville institution, featuring old-time candlepin bowling lanes that managed to survive into the 21st century. The place has been overtaken and updated by **Flatbread Co** (www.flatbreadcompany.com; 45 Day St, Somerville; per person per game $5; ☉10am-midnight Mon-Sat, noon-11:30pm Sun; 👪; ⓂDavis), who brightened the space and added clay ovens, but preserved most of the lanes and the good-time atmosphere. Now you can enjoy delicious organic pizzas and cold beers with your candlepins.

nights, while pool is free for all after 9pm on Wednesdays.

CAMBRIDGE SCHOOL OF CULINARY ARTS COURSE

(www.cambridgeculinary.com; 2020 Massachusetts Ave; MPorter) The recreation division of this professional school offers one-time courses focusing on seasonal meals such as 'An American Gathering' or on crucial cooking skills such as 'All You Knead' (basic breads). The most popular course, offered monthly, is based around cooking for cou-

ples. Located two blocks north of the Porter Sq T station.

FRESH POND GOLF COURSE GOLF COURSE

(617-349-6282; www.freshpondgolf.com; 691 Huron Ave; 71, 73 or 78) About 2 miles west of Harvard Sq, the Fresh Pond is a nine-hole public course that wraps around the city's reservoir. It's easily accessible but the setting is suburban. Drive west on Mt Auburn St and turn right on the Fresh Pond Parkway and left on Huron Ave.

Streetcar Suburbs

BROOKLINE | JAMAICA PLAIN

Neighborhood Top Five

❶ Taking a pilgrimage to the **birthplace of John F Kennedy** (p164), touring the home and listening to Rose Kennedy's reminiscence of her family's time, and then following the NPS walking tour to see the schools, churches and other places from Kennedy lore.

❷ Sitting in the balcony at the **Coolidge Corner Theatre** (p168) and catching an art-house flick.

❸ Enjoying an evening of delightful food, music and camaraderie at **Tres Gatos** (p166).

❹ Browsing the stacks, listening to a lecture or finding a bargain at the **Brookline Booksmith** (p168).

❺ Cycling along the **Emerald Necklace** (p165), from downtown Boston to Franklin Park.

For more detail of this area, see Maps p270 & p271 ➡

Explore Streetcar Suburbs

Brookline and Jamaica Plain (among others) are streetcar suburbs, residential areas that developed around Boston in the late 19th century. They are geographically isolated from other parts of Boston, though transitionally connected, yes, by streetcar (or metro now). Both JP and Brookline maintain distinct identities and unique 'neighborhood' atmospheres that make them attractive, off-the-beaten-path destinations for travelers.

Brookline was built as a modest, middle-income neighborhood, suitable for young families, which explains the draw to Joseph and Rose Kennedy, who moved here in 1914. Today, JFK admirers and history buffs make the pilgrimage to Beals St to see the birthplace of the United States' 35th president. The tour only takes an hour, but it's easy to while away the rest of the afternoon lunching at Jewish delis and browsing boutiques and bookshops.

By day, Coolidge Corner is a hub of shopping and eating. After dark, things quiet down, although the local cinema – a retro movie house – draws crowds for its international films and balcony seating. For a more raucous good time, check out the music clubs in nearby Allston and Brighton.

Further south, Jamaica Plain was actually a summertime retreat for wealthy Bostonians who built stately homes overlooking the quaint glacial pond. JP's open spaces are still part of this outer neighborhood's appeal: the cooling breezes off Jamaica Pond, the diverse flora at Arnold Arboretum, the solemn landscaping of Forest Hills Cemetery and the extensive recreational facilities at Franklin Park. If you want to enjoy the great outdoors but you can't leave the city, head to Jamaica Plain instead.

Downtown JP is Centre St – that's where you'll find an eclectic assortment of eateries for lunch or dinner and delightful neighborhood shopping, as well as some drinking options if you are in the mood for Guinness.

Local Life

➡ **Brookline Local** Shop at Rubin's Kosher Deli (p166); get a bite to eat at the Regal Beagle (p166).

➡ **JP Local** Go jogging around Jamaica Pond (p170); take your dog for a drink at Brendan Behan Pub (p168).

Getting There & Away

➡ **Metro** Two branches of the green line traverse Brookline. Take the C-line to Coolidge Corner or the D-line to Brookline Village. Travelling to Jamaica Plain, orange-line stations Green St and Stony Brook provide the easiest access to Centre St and Jamaica Pond. Use Forest Hills station to reach JP's major sights, which are further out.

Lonely Planet's Top Tip

The Coolidge Corner Theatre is not just a cinema. The theater offers a wide variety of programming for all segments of the population, including: @fter Midnite (horror and comedy for the late-night set); Europe's Grand Operas (high-def screenings straight from the best opera houses on the continent); Off the Couch (film accompanied by psychoanalytic discussion); and Sounds of Silents (silent-film classics accompanied by live music performance.

 ### Best Places to Eat

➡ Ten Tables (p166)

➡ Tres Gatos (p166)

➡ Zaftigs Delicatessen (p165)

➡ Zenna Noodle Bar (p166)

➡ Kookoo Café (p166)

For reviews, see p165

 ### Best Places to Drink

➡ Brendan Behan Pub (p168)

➡ Publick House (p168)

➡ The Haven (p168)

➡ Samuel Adams Brewery (p168)

For reviews, see p168 ➡

Best Urban Oases

➡ Arnold Arboretum (p164)

➡ Forest Hills Cemetery (p164)

➡ Frederick Law Olmsted National Historic Site (p164)

➡ Jamaica Pond (p170)

➡ Franklin Park (p165)

For reviews, see p164

STREETCAR SUBURBS

◉ SIGHTS

◉ Brookline

PHOTOGRAPHIC RESOURCE
CENTER
GALLERY

Map p270 (PRC; ☑617-975-0600; www.bu.edu/prc; 832 Commonwealth Ave; adult/child/senior & student $4/free/2; ☺10am-5pm Tue-Fri, noon-4pm Sat; ⓂBU West) The independent Photographic Resource Center is one of the few centers in the US devoted exclusively to this art form. The PRC's rotating exhibits lean toward the modern and experimental, often featuring work by amateur members. Other resources include educational programs, online exhibits, a well-stocked library and unique events.

FREE JOHN F KENNEDY
NATIONAL HISTORIC SITE
HISTORIC HOUSE

Map p270 (www.nps.gov/jofi; 83 Beals St; admission free; ☺9:30am-5pm Wed-Sun May-Oct; ⓂCoolidge Corner) In 1914 newlyweds Joseph and Rose Kennedy moved into this modest three-story house. Four of their nine children would be born and raised here, including Jack, who was born in the master bedroom in 1917. Matriarch Rose Kennedy oversaw the restoration of the house in the late 1960s; today her narrative sheds light on the Kennedys' family life.

Guided tours allow visitors to see furnishings, photographs and mementos that have been preserved from the time the family lived here. A self-guided walking tour of the surrounding neighborhood sets the scene for the Kennedy family's day-to-day life, including church, school and shopping.

LARZ ANDERSON AUTO MUSEUM
& PARK
MUSEUM

(www.larzanderson.org; 15 Newton St; adult/senior, student & child $10/5; ☺10am-4pm Tue-Sun; ⓂForest Hill or Reservoir, ☐51) Larz and Isabel Anderson, a high-society couple, bought their first automobile in 1899: a Winton Runabout. It was the first of 32 autos that they would purchase over the next 50 years. 'America's oldest motorcar collection' is now on display in the carriage house on the grounds of the estate (now Larz Anderson Park). Take bus 51 from Forest Hill (orange) or Reservoir (green D-line).

FREE FREDERICK LAW OLMSTED
NATIONAL HISTORIC SITE
HISTORIC HOUSE

(☑617-566-1689; www.nps.gov/frla; 99 Warren St; admission free; ☺tours 9am, 11am & 2pm Mon, Wed & Fri, 11am, 1pm & 3pm Sun; Ⓜ Brookline Hills, ☐60) Widely considered the father of landscape design architecture, Frederick Law Olmsted ran his operation from his home 'Fairsted,' where he established a full-scale landscape-design office. Olmsted made an indelible mark on Boston's urban landscape with the creation of the Emerald Necklace. He also was influential in the creation of the National Park Service, which manages the homestead as a historic site.

Visit Olmsted's office, which remains as it was a century ago, and peruse his designs for the country's most beloved green spaces, which include Central Park in New York City; Rock Creek Park in Washington, DC; national parks such as Acadia and the Great Smoky Mountains; and more. Reservations are required to tour the site. From Brookline Hills, walk two blocks south on Cypress St and a long three blocks west on Walnut St, then turn south on Warren.

◉ Jamaica Plain

FREE ARNOLD ARBORETUM
PARK

(www.arboretum.harvard.edu; 125 Arborway, Jamaica Plain; admission free; ☺dawn-dusk; ⓘ; ⓂForest Hills) Under a public/private partnership with Harvard University, the 265-acre Arnold Arboretum is planted with over 15,000 exotic trees and flowering shrubs. This gem is pleasant year-round, but it's particularly beautiful in the bloom of spring. Dog walking, Frisbee throwing, bicycling, sledding and general contemplation are encouraged (but picnicking is not allowed). The southern Forest Hills gate is located on the Arborway about 60ft west of the metro station.

A visitors center is located at the main gate, just south of the rotary at Rte 1 and Rte 203. Free one-hour walking tours are offered several times a week from April to November.

FOREST HILLS CEMETERY
CEMETERY

(www.foresthillstrust.com; 95 Forest Hills Ave; ☺7.30am-dusk; ⓟ; ⓂForest Hills) Dating to 1848, Forest Hills is a gorgeous, green cemetery that is filled with art and whimsy. It is still an active burial ground, but it also plays the role of open-air museum. The walking

EMERALD NECKLACE

The **Emerald Necklace** (www.emeraldnecklace.org) is an evocative name for the series of parks and green spaces that weave through Boston, some 7 miles from the Boston Common to Franklin Park. Designed by Frederick Law Olmsted in the late 19th century, the Emerald Necklace treats city residents to a bit of fresh air, green grass and flowing water, right within the city limits. It's particularly well suited for cycling, so hop on a bike and go for the green.

➡ Olmsted Park features a paved path that hugs the banks of Leverett Pond and Ward Pond in Jamaica Plain. The idyllic spring-fed Jamaica Pond, on the west side of the Jamaicaway, is more than 50ft deep and great for boating, fishing, jogging and picnicking. serene **Arnold Arboretum** (p164) will appeal not only to green thumbs and plant lovers, but also to anyone who takes time to smell the roses.

➡ Franklin Park, at 500-plus acres, is an underutilized resource – partly because it borders a sketchy neighborhood, and partly because it is so huge. Still, on weekend afternoons the park is full of families from the nearby neighborhoods of Jamaica Plain, Dorchester and Roxbury. The park also contains the **Franklin Park Zoo** (p165). Take the orange line to Stony Brook, Green St or Forest Hills and head east until you reach the park's western edge. The park is dangerous after dark, so don't linger longer than the sun.

➡ North of Jamaica Plain, other green links in the Emerald Necklace include the **Back Bay Fens** (p129); the **Commonwealth Ave Mall** (p115); and the **Public Garden** (p70), with the terminus at the **Boston Common** (p68).

---

paths are lined with sculptures paying tribute to individuals and causes from times past, while a contemporary sculpture path winds its way around the historic gravestones, connecting then and now.

Gravestones include such famous figures as revolutionary heroes William Dawes and Joseph Warren; abolitionist William Lloyd Garrison and suffragette Lucy Stone; poets ee cummings and Anne Sexton; sculptors Daniel Chester French and Martin Milmore; and playwright Eugene O'Neill. The on-site Forsyth Chapel is a spot for peaceful contemplation surrounded by vaulted wood ceilings and stained-glass windows, in the midst of the greenery. Concerts, poetry readings and other events are often held in this exquisite space. Walk east along the Arborway a half-mile from Forest Hills station.

FRANKLIN PARK ZOO   ZOO
(www.zoonewengland.com; 1 Franklin Park Rd; adult/child/senior $16/10/13; ⊙10am-5pm Mon-Fri Apr-Sep, 10am-4pm Oct-Mar; 🅿🚻; Ⓜ Forest Hills, 🚌16) Tucked into Franklin Park, the zoo features a half-dozen different habitats, as well as special exhibits devoted to birds and butterflies. The zoo's highlight is the well-designed Tropical Forest pavilion, complete with lush vegetation, waterfalls, lowland gorillas and over 30 species of free flight birds. The Australian Outback Trail

allows visitors to walk among red kangaroos and wallabies.

Several exhibits are devoted to life on the savannah, showcasing an African lion, as well as giraffes, zebras and wildebeests. The Franklin Farms lets kids get up close and personal with sheep and goats. Take bus 16 from Forest Hills station.

✖ EATING

✖ Brookline

Brookline is worth the trip for an eclectic assortment of dining options, including kosher delis, Russian restaurants and many other ethnic eats. Coolidge Corner, which is around the intersection of Harvard and Beacon Sts, is the hub for the Brookline dining scene. Brookline Village – about 1½ miles south – also hosts a cluster of restaurants and pubs.

ZAFTIGS DELICATESSEN   DELI, DINER $
Map p270 (www.zaftigs.com; 335 Harvard St; mains $10-15; ⊙breakfast, lunch & dinner; 🚻; Ⓜ Coolidge Corner) 'Let us be your Jewish mother,' Zaftigs implores. And on Saturday

and Sunday mornings, patrons craving potato pancakes with smoked salmon, challah French toast and cheese blintzes line up out the door to oblige. Fortunately, breakfast is served all day, so no one has to miss it. Otherwise, the deli turns out a huge selection of sandwiches, including classics like Reubens, egg salad and pastrami.

ZENNA NOODLE BAR
ASIAN FUSION $$

Map p270 (1374 Beacon St; mains $8-16; [M]Coolidge Corner) Fresh flowers and eager staff welcome you into this oasis of calm and loveliness. It's an irresistible setting for delicious noodle soups, spicy stir-fries and mango sticky rice. The signature dish – Zenna Noodle Soup – is a heartwarming bowl of organic, vegetarian goodness.

REGAL BEAGLE
MODERN AMERICAN $$

Map p270 (www.thebeaglebrookline.com; 308 Harvard St; mains $16-25; ⊘lunch & dinner; [M]Coolidge Corner) Coolidge Corner is packed with ethnic eateries and Jewish delis, but where do you go when you want good old-fashioned New American food? You go to the Regal Beagle, the 'neighborhood joint' with a comfortably chic interior, a generous barkeep and delectable food. The restaurant's only references to *Three's Company* are on the cocktail menu, which we regret. And appreciate.

KOOKOO CAFÉ
CAFÉ $

(www.kookoocafe.com; 7 Station St; meals $8-12; ⊘7am-6pm Mon-Fri, 8am-5pm Sat; ♪ ♿; [M]Brookline Village) Kookoo is a sooper-cute café serving delicious soups and salads – most with some hint of the magic of the Middle East. The sandwich rollups are all fresh, healthy and vegetarian, including the signature Kookoo rollup (parsley, spinach, coriander and minty yogurt). The tiny space is crowded with an eclectic display of knickknacks, with a quaint seating area in the back.

RUBIN'S KOSHER DELI
DELI $$

Map p270 (www.rubinskosher.com; 500 Harvard St; ⊘9am-9pm Sun-Thu, 9am-3pm Fri; [M]Coolidge Corner) Boston's favorite kosher deli is just north of Coolidge Corner, serving chewy bagels, flaky knishes and overstuffed sandwiches to Brookline's discerning Jewish community. All sandwiches come with a dill pickle straight from the barrel.

STOLI BAR
RUSSIAN $$

(✆617-731-5070; www.stolibar.com; 213 Washington St; mains $18-26; ⊘lunch & dinner Tue-Sat; [M]Brookline Village) Get a taste of Russian hospitality at this fancy Russian affair. You might think this place is named for Stolichnaya vodka, but actually a *stoli* is an old-fashioned Russian teapot. But don't worry, there is plenty of vodka here, some infused with tantalizing flavors. There is also borscht, beef stroganoff and live accordion music.

FUGAKYU
SUSHI $$

Map p270 (✆617-734-1268; www.fugakyu.net; 1280 Beacon St; mains $20-25; ⊘lunch, dinner to 1:30am; [M]Coolidge Corner) The name aptly translates as 'house of elegance.' Upscale and over-the-top, Fugakyu offers a gorgeous array of sushi and sashimi as well as traditional cooked meals, served by staff dressed in kimonos. The sushi bar features a water canal; watch for your order to arrive by boat.

✖ Jamaica Plain

Funky, progressive Jamaica Plain hosts an ever-growing restaurant scene. The neighborhood's diverse population enjoys a variety of spunky cafes and international eateries, with many veg-friendly options.

TOP CHOICE TRES GATOS
TAPAS $$

Map p271 (www.tresgatosjp.com; 470 Centre St; tapas $5-12; ⊘3pm-10pm Mon-Wed, 3pm-11pm Thu-Sun; ♪; [M]Stony Brook, ☐39) This small space is not only a tapas bar, but also a bookstore and a music store. It all feels like you are eating, browsing books and listening to music in somebody's living room; but that somebody is a gracious, fun host and somehow it works.

The menu features charcuterie, cheeses and a selection of authentic Spanish tapas and wine. Chef Marco is on hand to offer suggestions.

TEN TABLES
INTERNATIONAL $$$

Map p271 (✆617-524-8810; www.tentables.net; 597 Centre St; mains $21-28; ⊘dinner; ♪; [M]Green St) True to its name, this gem has only 10 tables (you'll need to reserve one of them). The emphasis here is on simplicity – appropriate for a restaurant that specializes in traditional cooking techniques. The menu is short but changes frequently to highlight local, organic produce, handmade pastas, fresh seafood and homemade sausages.

VEE VEE
INTERNATIONAL $$

(✆617-522-0145; www.veeveejp.com; 763 Centre St; mains $18-24; ⊘dinner Tue-Sun, brunch Sun;

ETHNIC EATING 101: ALLSTON

Ethnic food lovers take note: one segment of one Boston neighborhood packs in 40 ethnic restaurants spanning more than 20 different cuisines.

The crossroads of Harvard Ave and Brighton Ave in Allston is the city's epicenter of ethnic eating. In the surrounding 500yd radius, there's a choice of Afghan, Brazilian, Burmese, Cantonese, Colombian, Egyptian, Guatemalan, Indian, Israeli, Italian, Japanese, Korean, Lebanese, Mexican, Pakistani, Salvadoran, Shanghainese, Taiwanese, Thai, Turkish or Vietnamese.

This colorful neighborhood comprises a mélange of immigrants and students, a demographic formula resulting in an eating paradise. Here are five can't-miss options:

➡ When at **Cafe Brazil** (www.cafebrazilrestaurant.com; 421 Cambridge St; $10-18; ⊙lunch & dinner; ⬛66, Ⓜ Harvard Ave, B-line), do as the Brazilians do and order the feijoada, their country's national dish. Available only on weekends, this dish's familiar (and not-so-familiar) stewed meats are enough to make even the most ardent carnivore blush.

➡ The walls in **Color** (166 Harvard Ave; $8-12; ⊙lunch & dinner; ✍; ⬛66, Ⓜ Harvard Ave, B-line) are painted bright yellow, and the food emerges from the kitchen through a set of closet doors. For a twist on 'KFC,' try Color's Korean fried chicken, or clear your sinuses with the classic Korean stew, *kimchi chigae*.

➡ **Jo Jo TaiPei** (www.jojotaipeiboston.com; 103 Brighton Ave; $7-14; ⊙lunch & dinner; ✍; Ⓜ Harvard Ave, B-line) is the keystone of Boston's 'Little Taiwan' – a Taiwanese bakery and a bubble tea café are across the street. Try the three cups tofu and wonder how such a perfect combination of flavors can be made so simply.

➡ The menu at **Shanghai Gate** (www.shanghaigateboston.com; 204 Harvard Ave; $10-18; ⊙lunch & dinner Wed-Mon; ✍; ⬛66, Ⓜ Harvard Ave, B-line) offers regional dishes that will redefine your concept of Chinese food. Cold appetizers such as the five-spice tofu or the scallion jellyfish preface the meal like a perfect aperitif, and the 'lion's head' casserole elevates the modest meatball to new heights.

➡ Thanks to **Yoma Burmese Restaurant** (www.yomaboston.com; 5 North Beacon St; $7-12; ⊙lunch & dinner Thu-Tue; ✍; ⬛66, Ⓜ Harvard Ave, B-line), Boston is one of the few US cities that boasts a Burmese eatery. Yoma's *la phet thot* (green tea leaf salad) is rich in the hearty taste called *umami*. And the freshly ground, complexly flavored Burmese curry powder makes the chicken curry the best in town across all cuisines.

To reach this corner in Allston, take bus 66 from Harvard Sq, or walk a few blocks north from the B-line Harvard Ave T-stop.

Jason Beerman is a freelance writer who spent five years living in, and eating his way around, Allston.

✍; Ⓜ Green St) Vee Vee stands for Valachovic, the last name of the two creative genii behind this sweet spot on Centre St. The décor is minimalist and modern, but nothing too trendy for granola-loving Jamaica Plain. The menu is limited to seafood and vegetarian items, with the occasional meat special, but the focus is always on fresh and local.

Veggies: come on Wednesday for a $25 three-course prix-fixe bargain.

JP LICKS   ICE CREAM $

Map p271 (659 Centre St; ☎; Ⓜ Green St) 'JP' stands for Jamaica Plain: this is the flagship location of the ice-creamery that's now all over Boston. You can't miss the happy Holstein head looking down over Centre St.

And you shouldn't miss the white coffee ice cream either.

BELLA LUNA MILKY WAY   PIZZERIA $$

Map p271 (www.milkywayjp.com; 284 Amory St; ⊙dinner; ✍; Ⓜ Stony Brook) Now housed in an old brewery building, Bella Luna Milky Way is a neighborhood haunt that has long enticed JP residents with its colorfully painted walls and sci-fi decor. Regulars keep coming back, year after year, for crispy thin-crust pizza pies with interesting combinations of toppings, such as the all-time favorite Gipsy King, with spinach, ricotta and caramelized onions.

While waiting for pizza, regulars keep themselves entertained with pool, Connect

Four and vintage video games. There is no longer bowling here, but there is Wii bowling – somehow appropriate for this space-age place.

CENTRE STREET CAFÉ
FUSION $$

Map p271 (centrestcafe.com; 669 Centre St; mains $14-20; ☺lunch Mon-Fri, brunch Sat-Sun, dinner Mon-Sat; ✍; MGreen St) This artistic, eclectic restaurant embodies the essence of Jamaica Plain. Smart but idiosyncratic staff serve dishes that range from 'Shrimp Nirvana' to 'Danno's Szechwan Shaboom.' It's not particularly fancy fare, but ingredients are organic and locally grown, and the outcome is – as the menu promises – 'outrageously good!' A highlight is Sunday brunch, when patient would-be patrons wait in lines that stretch down the block.

DRINKING & NIGHTLIFE

 Brookline

PUBLICK HOUSE
BEER BAR

(www.eatgoodfooddrinkbetterbeer.com; 1648 Beacon St; ☺5pm-2am; MWashington Square) This loud, friendly pub is buzzing with good vibes, thanks to the superb selection of brews. The specialty is pints of the good stuff from Belgium, most of which seems to have a high alcohol content. The place gets crowded on weekends, so be prepared to wait if you want to sample the mussels or mac and cheese.

Jamaica Plain

BRENDAN BEHAN PUB
IRISH PUB

Map p271 (www.brendanbehanpub.com; 378 Centre St; ☺closed Sun; MStony Brook) Candle-lit tables, stained glass and old liquor cabinets make this dark den an attractive destination for regulars of all ages and origins. There are a few things that make this place unique: no food (but you can bring it in), no TVs, dogs at the bar.

THE HAVEN
PUB

Map p271 (www.thehavenjp.com; 2 Perkins St; ☎; MStony Brook) If you can't stand to drink in another Irish pub, this is your Haven: a Scottish pub. There are more than a dozen Scottish craft beers, haggis, and men in kilts. Trivia, movies and live music keep the troops entertained, and the food gets rave reviews, especially the burgers.

FREE SAMUEL ADAMS BREWERY
BREWERY

Map p271 (www.samueladamsbrewery.com; 30 Germania St; donation $2; ☺10am-3pm Mon-Sat, to 5:30pm Fri; MStony Brook) Learn about Sam Adams (the patriot and the beer). See how they make the ales and lagers, and sample a few too. Tours last about one hour and end at the gift shop and tour center (aka bar).

☆ ENTERTAINMENT

COOLIDGE CORNER THEATRE
CINEMA

Map p270 (www.coolidge.org; 290 Harvard St; MCoolidge Corner) An art-deco neighborhood palace, this old theater blazes with exterior neon. Inside, view select Hollywood hits, cult flicks, popular independent fare and special events such as 'open mic for movies' where you bring self-made masterpieces (less than 10 minutes in length) for a pastiche of amateur weirdness. Fifty cents of every ticket sale goes to the upkeep of the building.

MIDWAY CAFÉ
LIVE MUSIC

(www.midwaycafe.com; 3496 Washington St; cover $5; MGreen St) In addition to hosting a kick-ass dyke night (Thursday), this queer-friendly rock and punk bar books some of Boston's finest independent music, ranging from rockabilly to dub. Inside, find Pabst beer signs of antique vintage, some longhorn skulls, pinball and a genuinely friendly atmosphere.

SHOPPING

Centre St (JP) is edgy and urban, while Coolidge Corner (Brookline) is sophisticated and suburban.

BROOKLINE BOOKSMITH
BOOKSTORE

Map p270 (www.brooklinebooksmith.com; 279 Harvard St; ☺8:30am-10pm Mon-Thu, to 11pm Fri & Sat, 9am-9pm Sun; MCoolidge Corner) Year after year, this independent bookstore wins 'Best Bookstore in Boston.' Customers love the line-up of author talks and poetry read-

MUSIC THEORY 201: ALLSTON/BRIGHTON

If you care to sample the Boston music scene, venture west to Allston/Brighton, the gritty 'student ghetto.' Some of Boston's best music clubs are located in these innocuous alleys and subterranean spaces. This is where you can hear the future of music.

➡ The current 'it' place for rock and indie, **Great Scott** (Map p270; www.greatscott boston.com; 1222 Commonwealth Ave; cover $5-12; MHarvard Ave) is a music palace. Get up close and personal with the bands, hang out with them after the set and buy them some beers. On Friday nights, the place turns into a comedy club known as the Gas (7:30pm), after which it turns into an awesome indie dance club, aka the Pill (10pm). Both guarantee some thrills.

➡ A reincarnation of Harpers Ferry, **Brighton Music Hall** (Map p270; www.brighton musichall.com; 158 Brighton Ave; ticket $10-15; MHarvard Ave) is now owned and operated by Paradise Rock Club, which bodes well. The cavernous space attracts great local bands like Mission of Burma, cool world-music acts and touring national bands.The interior hasn't changed much from the HF days and thankfully the pool tables still stand.

➡ Top bands rock at the landmark **Paradise Rock Club** (Map p270; www.thedise. com; 967 Commonwealth Ave; cover $20-40; MPleasant St) – like U2, whose first gig in the USA was on this stage. Nowadays, you're more likely to hear the likes of the DelFuegos, Los Compesiños, Trombone Shorty, and plenty of Boston bands that made good but still come home to play the Dise.

➡ A more mature music experience, **Scullers Jazz Club** (617-642-4111; www. scullersjazz.com; 400 Soldiers Field Rd; tickets $20-45; MCentral, 47 or 70) books big names (Dave Brubeck, Dr John, Michael Franks) in a small room. Though it enjoys impressive views over the Charles, the room itself lacks the grit you might hanker for in a jazz club. It feels like it's inside a Doubletree Hotel (which it is). Book in advance.

ings, the emphasis on local writers and the Used Book Cellar in the basement. Extra-long hours are also a perk.

TOP CHOICE SALMAGUNDI — ACCESSORIES

(www.salmagundiboston.com; 765 Centre St; ⊙noon-8pm Tue-Sat, 11am-6pm Sun; MGreen St) In our humble opinion, every man should own at least one fedora. And if not a fedora, some other fun and functional head-topper. If you are intrigued by this idea, head to Salmagundi, where style mavens Jessen and Andria can help you find a hat that was made for your head, whether you are male or female.

KITCHENWITCH — HOUSEWARES

Map p271 (671 Centre St; 10:30am-6pm Mon-Sat, noon-5pm; MGreen St) For the modern cook, the 'witch' is a culinary treasure trove, crammed with everything but the kitchen sink. (Actually, you might find that too.) This place carries all kinds of gadgets and appliances – from the absolutely necessary to the practically playful. Find what you need or need what you find!

EUREKA PUZZLES — GAMES

Map p270 (www.eurekapuzzles.com; 1349 Beacon St; ; MCoolidge Corner) Puzzles, of course. But even better, this place has board games. And card games. And many, many other kinds of games (but no role-playing games, for better or for worse). The folks who work here know and love games so much that they will scour their shop to find a game that you will love too.

BOING! — TOYS

Map p271 (www.boingtoys.com; 667 Centre St; ⊙Tue-Sun; MGreen St) Boing! is fun. It's fun that they have an exclamation point at the end of their name and crazy colorful creatures adorning their facade. And it's really fun inside, where kids and parents can find educational, age-appropriate toys, games and activities with the help of knowledgeable, caring staff. Favorite aunts love this place.

ON CENTRE — GIFTS, JEWELRY

Map p271 (636 Centre St; ; MGreen St) The friendly folks at this little gift boutique can help you find the perfect gift. The jewelry is inexpensive and highly original; much of it designed by local artists. But if your person is not into origami earrings, never fear, there are funky reusable shopping bags, designer T-shirts, as well as cool, colorful glassware, rugs and other stuff for the home.

MAGIC BEANS   TOYS

Map p270 (www.mbeans.com; 312 Harvard St; ⚲; Ⓜ Coolidge Corner) Both kids and parents agree that Magic Beans is a well-stocked, super-fun toy store. Both kids and parents appreciate the selection of wooden toys, educational toys and creative toys. Both kids and parents like the designated play area. But only parents rave about the selection of strollers, which is apparently among the best in the city.

GOOD VIBRATIONS   SEX SHOP

Map p270 (www.goodvibes.com; 308A Harvard St; ⊙10am-8pm Sun-Thu, to 10pm Fri-Sat; Ⓜ Coolidge Corner) Down a narrow alley and marked by a discrete sign, this woman-focused sex shop is worth seeking out. This tasteful and tantalizing boutique offers sex-positive products, not to mention newsletters, workshops and pleasure parties. No question is too probing for the women at Good Vibes. And it would seem that no product is either.

MINT JULEP   CLOTHING & ACCESSORIES

Map p270 (www.shopmintjulep.com; 1302 Beacon St; ⊙10am-7pm; Ⓜ Coolidge Corner) Just like an actual mint julep, this little boutique is sweet, refreshing and a little bit intoxicating. It's filled with enough fabulous frocks, printed tops, flowing skirts and colorful jewelry to make a girl swoon, plus a few sophisticated hats, just in case you really are going to be drinking mint juleps.

HATCHED   CHILDREN

Map p271 (www.hatchedboston.com; 5 Green St; ⊙Tue-Sun; ⚲; Ⓜ Green St) A baby is surely one of nature's most incredible creations, so why muff it up with synthetic fabrics and toxic toys? If you prefer to dress your little bundle of natural goodness in unbleached cloth diapers and adorable organic clothing, you'll find an excellent selection at 'Boston's first ecobaby store' (but you can't buy an ecobaby here).

🏃 SPORTS & ACTIVITIES

JAMAICA POND   SAILING, FISHING

Map p271 (www.jamaicapond.com; 507 Jamaica Way; rowboat/sailboat $10/15; ⊙10am-6pm Jun-Aug; ⚲; Ⓜ Green St) Once a summer destination for city residents, Jamaica Pond is now a tranquil urban oasis, perfect for paddling or rather tame sailing. A 1.4-mile paved path circles the glacial kettlehole. Rowboats and sailboats are available for rental at the 1913 Tudor boat house. The pond is even stocked with fish, though you'll need your own equipment and a MA fishing license.

BROOKLINE GOLF CLUB AT PUTTERHAM   GOLF

(www.brooklinegolf.com; 1281 West Roxbury Pkwy; 18 holes weekday/weekend $30/41) You probably can't get on the famous Brookline Country Club, but you can play next door at Putterham, a less famed but perfectly pleasant public course. Wide fairways and a lack of water hazards make it a suitable course for all levels.

Take Huntington Ave west to Boylston St (Rte 9); turn left on Hammond St, then turn onto Newton St at the rotary.

Day Trips from Boston

Lexington & Concord p172
Now serene suburbs, these twin towns were the site of the dramatic kickoff to the War for Independence on April 19, 1775.

Salem p174
In addition to the many witchy sites in 'Witch City,' Salem showcases a proud maritime history and unique artistic legacy.

Plymouth p176
Settled by the Pilgrims in 1620, Plymouth is now home to *Mayflower II*, a replica of their ship, and Plimoth Plantation, a replica of their settlement.

Provincetown p178
Provincetown is a perfect summertime destination, with vast stretches of sandy beaches, miles of seaside bicycle trails, and an eclectic strip of art galleries and seafood restaurants.

Lexington & Concord

Explore

Students of history and lovers of liberty can trace the events of the fateful day that started a revolution – April 19, 1775. Follow in the footsteps of British troops and colonial Minutemen, who tromped out to Lexington to face off on the town green then continued on to Concord for the battle at the Old North Bridge. Concord is the bigger town, with many more sights to see, so don't dally in Lexington.

This day trip is an excellent bicycle outing: the paved Minuteman Bikeway covers the route from Cambridge to Lexington, while the more rugged Battle Rd (within the Minute National Historic Park) continues from Lexington to Concord. If you don't feel like pedaling back, you can take your bicycle on the commuter rail. Otherwise, you will probably need a car (or the Liberty Ride) to see both towns in one day.

The Best...

➡ **Sight** Walden Pond (p174)
➡ **Place to Eat** Country Kitchen (p174)
➡ **Place to Drink** 80 Thoreau (p174)

Top Tip

If you don't have your own wheels, consider catching the **Liberty Ride** (www.libertyride.us; adult/child $25/10; ☺10am-4pm Sat & Sun Apr-May, daily Jun-Oct), a hop-on hop-off trolley, which includes all of the major sites in both towns. Buy tickets at the Lexington Visitors Center.

Getting There & Away

Bicycle The Minuteman Bikeway runs for 6 miles from Alewife, in Cambridge, to Lexington. From Lexington you can follow the Battle Rd Trail to Concord.

Bus MBTA buses 62 and 76 run from the red-line T terminus at Alewife through to Lexington center hourly on weekdays, less frequently on Saturday, with no Sunday service.

Car Take Rte 2 west from Cambridge to Waltham St (exit 54) for Lexington and Walden St (Rte 126) for Concord.

Train MBTA commuter-rail trains ($6.25, 40 minutes, eight daily) run between Boston's North Station and the Concord Depot on the Fitchburg/South Acton line.

Need to Know

➡ **Area Codes** ☐781 (Lexington), ☐978 (Concord)
➡ **Locations** 12 miles west of Boston (Lexington), 18 miles west of Boston (Concord)
➡ **Tourist Offices** (Lexington Chamber of Commerce & Visitors Center; ☐862 2480; www.lexingtonchamber.org; 1875 Massachusetts Ave, Lexington; ☺9am-5pm Apr-Nov, 10am-4pm Dec-Mar), (Concord Chamber of Commerce & Visitors Center; ☐369 3120; www.concordchamberofcommerce.org; 58 Main St; ☺9:30am-4:30pm Apr-Oct)

◉ SIGHTS

Lexington

BATTLE GREEN   HISTORIC SITE

(Lexington center) The historic Battle Green is where the skirmish between patriots and British troops jumpstarted the War for Independence. The **Lexington Minuteman Statue** (crafted by Henry Hudson Kitson in 1900) stands guard at the southeast end of Battle Green, honoring the bravery of the 77 Minutemen who met the British here in 1775, and the eight who died.

The **Parker Boulder**, named for their commander, marks the spot where the Minuteman faced a force almost 10 times their strength. It is inscribed with Parker's instructions to his troops: 'Stand your ground. Don't fire unless fired upon. But if they mean to have a war, let it begin here.' Across the street, history buffs have preserved the **Old Belfry** that sounded the alarm signaling the start of the revolution.

BUCKMAN TAVERN   MUSEUM

(www.lexingtonhistory.org; 1 Bedford Rd; adult/child $7/5; ☺10am-4pm Apr-Oct) Facing the Battle Green, the 1709 Buckman Tavern was the headquarters of the Minutemen. Here, they spent the tense hours between the midnight call to arms and the dawn arrival of the Redcoats. Today, the tavern has been restored to its 18th-century appearance, complete with bar, fireplace and bullet holes resulting from British musket fire.

MINUTE MAN NATIONAL HISTORIC PARK   PARK
(www.nps.gov/mima; 250 North Great Rd, Lincoln; admission free; ⊙9am-5pm Apr-Oct) Two miles west of Lexington center, the route that British troops followed to Concord has been designated the Minute Man National Historic Park. The **visitors center** (www.nps. gov/mima; ⊙9am-5pm Apr-Oct) at the eastern end of the park shows an informative multimedia presentation depicting Paul Revere's ride and the ensuing battles.

Within the park, Battle Rd is a five-mile wooded trail that connects the historic sites related to the battles – from Meriam's Corner, where gunfire erupted while British soldiers were retreating, to the Paul Revere capture site.

Concord

OLD NORTH BRIDGE

(www.nps.org/mima; Minute Man National Historic Park, Monument St) A half-mile north of Memorial Sq in Concord center, the wooden span of Old North Bridge is the site of the 'shot heard around the world' (as Emerson wrote in his poem *Concord Hymn*). Daniel Chester French's first statue, *Minute Man*, presides over the park from the opposite side of the bridge.

On the far side of the bridge, the Buttrick mansion contains the **visitor center** (www. nps.gov/mima; Liberty St; ⊙9am-5pm Apr-Oct, 9am-4pm Nov-Mar), where you can see a video about the battle and admire the Revolutionary War brass cannon, the Hancock.

On your way up to Old North Bridge, look for the yellow **Bullet Hole House** (262 Monument St), at which British troops purportedly fired as they retreated from North Bridge.

OLD MANSE   HISTORIC HOUSE

(www.thetrustees.org; 269 Monument St; adult/ child/senior & student $8/5/7; ⊙10am-5pm Mon-Sat & noon-5pm Sun Apr-Oct, 12:30pm-4:30pm Sat & Sun Nov-Mar) Right next to Old North Bridge, the Old Manse was built in 1769 by Ralph Waldo's grandfather, the Reverend William Emerson. Today it's filled with mementos, including those of Nathaniel and Sophia Hawthorne, who lived here for a few years. The highlight of Old Manse is the gorgeously maintained grounds – the fabulous organic garden was planted by Henry Thoreau as a wedding gift to the Hawthornes.

CONCORD MUSEUM   MUSEUM

(www.concordmuseum.org; 200 Lexington Rd; adult/child/senior & student $10/5/8; ⊙9am-5pm Mon-Sat & noon-5pm Sun Apr-Dec, 11am-4pm Mon-Fri & 1-4pm Sun Jan-Mar) Concord Museum, located southeast of Monument Sq, brings the town's diverse history under one roof. The museum's prized possession is one of the 'two if by sea' lanterns that hung in the steeple of the Old North Church in Boston as a signal to Paul Revere. It also has the world's largest collection of Henry David Thoreau artifacts, including his writing desk from Walden Pond.

RALPH WALDO EMERSON MEMORIAL HOUSE   HISTORIC HOUSE

(28 Cambridge Turnpike; adult/child/senior & student $7/free/5; ⊙10am-4:30pm Thu-Sat, 1-4:30pm Sun mid-Apr–Oct) Here is where the paterfamilias of literary Concord lived for almost 50 years (1835–82). Ralph Waldo Emerson was one of the great literary figures of his age and the founding thinker of the Transcendentalist movement. This house once hosted his renowned circle of friends and still contains many original furnishings.

ORCHARD HOUSE   HISTORIC HOUSE

(www.louisamayalcott.org; 399 Lexington Rd; adult/child/senior & student $9/5/8; ⊙10am-4:30pm Mon-Sat, 1-4:30pm Sun Apr-Oct, 11am-3pm Mon-Fri, 10am-4:30pm Sat, 1-4:30pm Sun Nov-Mar) Louisa May Alcott (1832–88) was a junior member of Concord's august literary crowd, but her work proved durable: *Little Women* is among the most popular young-adult books ever written. The mostly autobiographical novel is set in Concord. Orchard House, her fully furnished childhood home, is across from the Emerson Memorial House and is open for guided tours.

SLEEPY HOLLOW CEMETERY   CEMETERY

(Bedford St; ⊙dawn-dusk) This is the final resting place for the most famous Concordians. Though the entrance is only a block east of Monument Sq, the most interesting

WORTH A DETOUR

DECORDOVA MUSEUM & SCULPTURE PARK

Located near Walden Pond, the magical **DeCordova Museum & Sculpture Park** (☎781-259-8355; w 51 Sandy Pond Rd; adult/senior, student & child $12/8; ⏱dawn-dusk) encompasses 35 acres of green hills, providing a spectacular natural environment for a constantly changing exhibit of outdoor artwork. As many as 75 pieces are on display at any given time. Inside the complex, a museum hosts rotating exhibits of sculpture, painting, photography and mixed media.

part, Authors' Ridge, is a 15-minute walk along Bedford St. You'll find Thoreau and his family buried here, as well as the Alcotts and the Hawthornes.

Emerson's tombstone is the large uncarved rock of New England marble, an appropriate Transcendentalist symbol.

WALDEN POND HISTORIC PARK

(www.mass.gov/dcr/parks/walden; 915 Walden St; admission free; ⏱dawn-dusk) Thoreau took the naturalist beliefs of Transcendentalism out of the realm of theory and into practice when he left the comforts of town and built a rustic cabin at Walden Pond. Now a state park, the glacial pond is surrounded by acres of forest preserved by the nonprofit Walden Woods project.

The site of Thoreau's cabin is on the northeast side, marked by a cairn and signs. Parking costs $5.

EATING & DRINKING

Lexington

VIA LAGO CAFÉ CAFE $

(www.vialagocatering.com; 1845 Massachusetts Ave; mains $5-8; ⏱breakfast, lunch & dinner Mon-Sat) This cafe has high ceilings, intimate tables, a scent of fresh-roasted coffee and a great deli case. You'll often see cyclists in here kicking back with the daily paper, a cup of exotic java or tea, and a sandwich of roasted turkey, Swiss and sprouts.

Concord

Myriad cafes and restaurants are located on the streets immediately surrounding Memorial Sq, but the really special places to eat are located slightly out of the center, near the train depot.

COUNTRY KITCHEN SANDWICHES $

(181 Sudbury Ave; sandwiches $5-10; ⏱breakfast & lunch Mon-Fri) At lunchtime, this little yellow house often has a line out the door, which is testament to its tiny size, as well as its amazing sandwiches. The Thanksgiving sandwich is the hands-down favorite, with roasted turkey carved straight off the bird. They don't accept credit cards and there's no seating, save the picnic table out front.

BEDFORD FARMS ICE CREAM $

(www.bedfordfarmsicecream.com; 68 Thoreau St; ⏱noon-9pm Mar-Nov) Dating to the 19th century, this local dairy specializes in delectable ice cream, and frozen yogurt that tastes like delectable ice cream. If prices seem a tad high, it's because the scoops are gigantic. Besides their trademark Moosetracks (vanilla ice cream, chocolate swirl, peanut-butter cups), most of the flavors are pretty standard. Conveniently located next to the train depot.

80 THOREAU MODERN AMERICAN $$

(☎978-318-0008; www.80thoreau.com; 80 Thoreau St; mains $18-29; ⏱dinner Mon-Sat) Understated and elegant, this modern restaurant is an anomaly in historic Concord – but that's a good thing. The menu – short but sweet – features deliciously unexpected combinations of flavors, mostly using seasonal, local ingredients. There's also a busy bar area, which offers a short selection of classic cocktails and long list of wines by the glass.

Salem

Explore

A lot of history is packed into this gritty city. There is much more than a day's worth of sights and activities, so be selective when planning your time here.

Your starting point should be the Salem Maritime National Historic Site, which includes a smattering of historic buildings and the impressive ship *Friendship*. This overview of the city's maritime exploits is the perfect introduction to the Peabody Essex Museum, which is Salem's unrivaled highlight.

Dubbed 'Witch City,' Salem is also infamous as the site of the witch trials in 1692, when 19 people were hanged as a result of witch-hunt hysteria. There are dozens of witch-themed sights, as well as an excellent trial re-enactment. Most of these destinations are more about fun than authenticity, so choose wisely.

The Best...

➡ **Sight** Peabody Essex Museum (p175)

➡ **Place to Eat** Old Spot (p176)

➡ **Place to Drink** Gulu-Gulu Café (p176)

Top Tip

During the month of October, the **Haunted Happenings** Halloween festival (www.haunted happenings.org) includes trick-or-treating, exhibits, parades, concerts, pumpkin carvings and costume parties.

Getting There & Away

Boat Boston's Best Cruises (📞617 770 0040; www.bostonsbestcruises.com; 1 Long Wharf; Ⓜ Aquarium) operates the ferry from Long Wharf to Salem (adult/child $10.50/9.50).

Bus MBTA buses 450 and 455 from Boston's Haymarket Sq are slower than the train.

Car Follow US 1 north across the Tobin Bridge and bear right onto MA 16 toward Revere Beach, then follow MA 1A (Shore Rd) to Salem.

Train Both the Newburyport and Rockport lines of the MBTA commuter rail ($5.25, 30 minutes) run from Boston's North Station to Salem Depot.

Need to Know

➡ **Area Code** 📞978

➡ **Location** 20 miles northeast of Boston

➡ **Tourist Office** (📞740 1650; 2 New Liberty St; ⊙9am-5pm)

◉ SIGHTS

FREE **SALEM MARITIME NATIONAL HISTORIC SITE** HISTORIC SITE
(www.nps.gov/sama; 193 Derby St; ⊙9am-5pm) The witch phenomenon obscures Salem's true claim to fame: its glory days as a center for clipper-ship trade with China, started by Elias Hasket Derby. The Salem Maritime National Historic Site comprises the customhouse, the ship *Friendship* and the wharves, as well as other buildings along Derby St that are remnants of the shipping industry once thriving along this stretch of Salem.

In all, the site comprises 10 different historic locations within a two-block area. Check in at the **visitor center** (www.nps.gov/ sama; 193 Derby St; ⊙9am-5pm) for a schedule of ranger-led tours.

PEABODY ESSEX MUSEUM MUSEUM
(www.pem.org; 161 Essex St; adult/child $15/free; ⊙10am-5pm Tue-Sun) Many Salem vessels followed Derby's ship *Grand Turk* around the Cape of Good Hope, and soon the merchants founded the East India Marine Society to provide warehousing services. The new company's charter required the establishment of a museum 'to house the natural and artificial curiosities' brought back by member ships. The collection was the basis for what is now the world-class Peabody Essex Museum.

Predictably, the collection of Asian art is particularly strong, and includes Yin Yu Tang, a house that was shipped from southeastern China. The museum also has extensive collections focusing on New England decorative arts and maritime history, and there is a fascinating exhibit dedicated to Native American art.

HOUSE OF THE SEVEN GABLES HISTORIC HOUSE
(www.7gables.org; 54 Turner St; adult/child/ senior $12.50/7.50/11.50; ⊙10am-5pm Nov-Jun, 10am-7pm Jul-Oct) The House of the Seven Gables was made famous in Nathaniel Hawthorne's 1851 novel of the same name. The novel brings to life the gloomy Puritan atmosphere of early New England and its effect on the psyches of the residents; the house does the same. Look for wonderful seaside gardens, many original furnishings and a mysterious secret staircase.

WITCH HOUSE
HISTORIC HOUSE

(www.salemweb.com/witchhouse; 310 Essex St; adult/child/senior $8.25/4.25/6.25, tour add $2; ☺10am-5pm May-Nov) The most authentic of more than a score of witchy sites is Witch House – once the home of Jonathan Corwin, a local magistrate who was called on to investigate witchcraft claims. He examined several accused witches, possibly in the 1st-floor rooms of this house. Open longer hours in October.

✖ EATING & DRINKING

OLD SPOT
PUB $$

(www.theoldspot.com; 121 Essex St; sandwiches $8-10, mains $15-18; ☺lunch Fri-Sun, dinner daily) It's pub food, to be sure, but so perfectly prepared that it becomes a dining experience – a meat pie with beef and lamb in a Guinness stew, a slow-roasted pork sammie where the pork melts in your mouth, irresistible sweet potato fries. Dim lighting and plush pillows make the place extra comfortable and cozy.

RED'S SANDWICH SHOP
DINER $

(www.redssandwichshop.com; 15 Central St; mains $5-8; ☺breakfast & lunch) This Salem institution has been serving eggs and sandwiches to faithful customers for over 50 years. The food is hearty and basic, but the real attraction is Red's old-school decor, complete with counter service and friendly faces. It's housed in the old London Coffee House building (around since 1698).

⌐TOP⌐ GULU-GULU CAFÉ
CHOICE
CAFE

(www.gulu-gulu.com; 247 Essex St; mains $6-8; ☺8am-11pm Sun-Tue, to 1am Wed-Sat; 🛜) Gulu-gulu means 'gulp, gulp' in French and it's named after a now-defunct cafe in Prague. That is an indication of how eclectic this place is, featuring (in no particular order) delicious coffee, art-adorned walls, sinful crêpes, live music, a great wine list and board games. Come for a snack but you might be tempted to stay all day.

IN A PIG'S EYE
PUB

(www.inapigseye.com; 148 Derby St; mains $8-13; ☺11:30am-midnight Wed-Sat, 11:30am-10pm Sun-Tue) This dark, friendly pub boasts an eclectic menu of burgers and beef stroganoff, homemade soups and tasty salads, and

'Pig's Eye Favorites' like steak tips or pork chops. Despite the small space, it has live music (usually acoustic) six nights a week.

Plymouth

Explore

Neatly contained and historically significant, Plymouth is the perfect day trip. Start the day at *Mayflower II* to experience life aboard the 17th-century sailing vessel. Make the obligatory stop at Plymouth Rock to see where the Pilgrims (might have) first stepped ashore. Then climb the hill into town, which is lined up along Main St. This is an opportunity to stop for lunch, before moving on to spend the afternoon at Plimoth Plantation to experience what life was like for the Pilgrims once they were settled here.

Not surprisingly, Plymouth has a handful of historic houses and other micro museums that are also open for visitors. The best is Pilgrim Hall (America's oldest museum!), which contains some cool artifacts and excellent educational exhibits.

The Best...

➡ **Sight** Plimoth Plantation (p177)

➡ **Place to Eat** Jubilee (p177)

➡ **Place to Drink** Blue-Eyed Crab (p177)

Top Tip

If you plan to visit both *Mayflower II* and Plimoth Plantation, consider purchasing a combination ticket, which is good for admission to Plimoth Plantation on two consecutive days and to *Mayflower II* for any one day within a year.

Getting There & Away

Boat The Plymouth-to-Provincetown Express Ferry (www.captjohn.com; State Pier; 90min round trip; adult/child/senior $42/32/37) departs Plymouth at 10am and leaves Provincetown at 4:30pm (once daily in July and August, weekends only in June and September).

Bus Plymouth & Brockton (P&B) buses (www.p-b.com) travel to South Station or Logan Airport in Boston (adult/child $14/7, hourly). Heading south, these buses continue as far as Provincetown. GATRA buses (www.gatra.org; one-way/day-pass $1/3) connect the P&B terminal and the train station at Cordage Park to the town center, while another link runs from the center to Plimoth Plantation.

Car Take I-93 South to MA 3.

Train MBTA commuter trains (www. mbta.com, $7.75, one hour, four daily) to Plymouth leave from South Station.

Need to Know

➡ **Area Code** ☑508
➡ **Location** 40 miles south of Boston
➡ **Tourist Office** (☑747 7533; www. seeplymouth.com; 130 Water St; 9am-5pm Apr-Nov, until 8pm Jun-Aug)

SIGHTS

PLYMOUTH ROCK   MONUMENT
(Water St) Historic Plymouth, 'America's Home Town,' is synonymous with Plymouth Rock. Thousands of visitors come here each year to look at this weathered granite ball and to consider what it was like for the Pilgrims, who stepped ashore on this strange land in the autumn of 1620.

We don't really know that the Pilgrims landed on Plymouth Rock, as it's not mentioned in any early written records, but it stands today as an enduring symbol of the quest for religious freedom.

MAYFLOWER II   HISTORIC SITE
(www.plimoth.org; State Pier, Water St; adult/child/ senior $10/7/9, with Plimoth Plantation $30/19/27; ⊙9am-5pm Apr-Nov) If Plymouth Rock tells us little about the Pilgrims, *Mayflower II* speaks volumes. Climb aboard this replica of the small ship in which they made the fateful voyage, where 102 people lived together for 66 days as the ship passed through stormy North Atlantic waters. Actors in period costume are often on board, recounting harrowing tales from the journey.

PLIMOTH PLANTATION   VILLAGE
(www.plimoth.org; MA 3A; adult/child/senior $26/15/23, with Mayflower II $30/19/27; ⊙9am-5:30pm Apr-Nov) The Plimoth Plantation, a mile or so south of Plymouth Rock, au-

thentically recreates the Pilgrims' 1627 settlement. Everything in the village – costumes, implements, vocabulary, artistry, recipes and crops – has been painstakingly researched and remade. Hobbamock's (Wampanoag) Homesite replicates the life of a Native American community in the area at the same time.

PILGRIM HALL MUSEUM   MUSEUM
(www.pilgrimhall.org; 75 Court St; adult/child/ senior $8/5/7; ⊙9:30am-4:30pm Feb-Dec) Claiming to be the oldest continually operating public museum in the country, Pilgrim Hall Museum was founded in 1824. Its exhibits are not reproductions, but real objects that the Pilgrims and their Wampanoag neighbors used in their daily lives – from Governor Bradford's chair to Constance Hopkins' beaver hat.

The exhibits are dedicated to correcting the misrepresentations about the Pilgrims that have been passed down through history.

✕ EATING

JUBILEE   CAFE $$
(22 Court St; mains $5-8; ⊙breakfast, lunch & dinner) Regulars keep coming back, over and over again, because Jubilee always has something different. Early birds crow about the breakfast sandwich. At other times of day, look for weekly specials, signature sandwiches and unusual but utterly delicious soups. The service comes with a smile.

ALL-AMERICAN DINER   DINER $
(60 Court St; mains $6-12; ⊙breakfast & lunch) You are here in America's Hometown, what better place to eat than the All-American Diner? It's a classic red-white-and-blue place, with a breakfast menu that reads like a novel. From corn-beef hash to eggs Benedict and amazing omelets, all of the breakfast items get rave reviews (especially the home fries). If you prefer lunch, try the Thanksgiving sandwich.

BLUE-EYED CRAB   SEAFOOD $$
(www.blue-eyedcrab.com; 170 Water St; sandwiches $10-12, dinner mains $20-25; ⊙lunch & dinner) There are a few tried-and-true seafood restaurants clustered around Town Wharf. But if you like a little innovation with your fish (and perhaps a cocktail or a glass of wine),

head a bit further east to this fun and funky joint, with sea-blue walls and fish floating from the ceiling.

You can still get clam chowder and lobster rolls, but you can also try shrimp and bacon tacos, pan-seared scallop salad or a crispy crab burger.

Provincetown

Explore

Provincetown is far out. We're not just talking geographically (though it does occupy the outermost point on Cape Cod). We're also talking about the flamboyant street scenes, brilliant art galleries and unbridled nightlife. Once a seaside outpost for fringe writers and artists, Provincetown has morphed into the hottest gay and lesbian destination in the Northeast.

Even if you're only in town for a day, you'll want to spend part of it admiring the art and watching the street life on Commercial St. If you are lucky enough to be here at night, you can also partake in some diverse dining, and singing and dancing until dawn.

But that's only half the show. As part of the Cape Cod National Seashore, Provincetown's untamed coastline and vast beaches beg exploring. A network of bicycle trails wind through picturesque sand dunes and a beach backed by sea and sky (and a lighthouse or two).

The Best

→ **Sight** Cape Cod National Seashore (p179)
→ **Place to Eat** Mews Restaurant & Cafe (p180)
→ **Place to Drink** Harbor Lounge (p180)

Top Tip

The best way to get around Provincetown is by bicycle (free parking everywhere you go). Bring a bicycle on the ferry from Boston for only $6, or rent one from Ptown Bikes.

Getting There & Away

Air Cape Air flies several times a day to Provincetown's Municipal Airport (one way/round trip $90/180, 25 minutes).

Boat Both Bay State Cruise Co (☑877-783-3779; www.boston-ptown.com; Com-

Provincetown

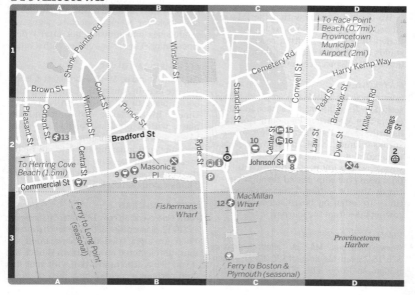

monwealth Pier, Seaport Blvd; Ⓜ South Station, ⬛SL1 or SL2; round trip adult/child $83/62) and Boston Harbor Cruises (☏877-733-9425; www.bostonharbor cruises.com; 1 Long Wharf; Ⓜ Aquarium; adult/child/senior $83/63/73) operate ferries between Boston and Provincetown. Both companies run the 90-minute trip three times a day.

Bus The Plymouth & Brocktown(P&B) bus (adult/child $29/15, 3½ hours), which terminates at the Chamber of Commerce, operates several times a day from Boston, stopping at other Cape towns along the way. From late May to mid-October, the shuttle buses (one-trip/day pass $1/3) travel up and down Bradford St, and to MacMillan Wharf, Herring Cove Beach and North Truro.

Car Allow 2½ hours to drive from Boston; weekend traffic can be brutal.

....

Need to Know

➡ **Area Code** ☏508

➡ **Location** 128 miles southeast of Boston

➡ **Tourist Office** (www.ptownchamber. com; 307 Commercial St; ⊙9am-5pm Jun-Aug, 10am-4pm Mon-Sat Sep May)

◉ SIGHTS

🏷CAPE COD NATIONAL SEASHORE   BEACH
(www.nps.gov/caco; Route 6; admission $3, parking $15; Ⓟ) Even with all the art and history, the main draw to Provincetown is the Cape Cod National Seashore, which includes eight miles of exhilarating mountain bike trails leading through sand dunes and coastal forest. Two spurs lead to the pounding surf at Race Point Beach and the calmer waters of Herring Cove. Rent bikes at **Ptown Bikes** (www.ptownbikes.com; 42 Bradford St; per 2/24hr $12/22; ⊙9am-6pm).

When the weather is fine, swimmers and sun-worshippers set up camp near the entrances at these two beaches. But the seashore stretches for miles and miles in either direction, so take a hike to find your own private patch of sea and sand.

COMMERCIAL STREET   STREET
(Commercial St) Walking down Commercial St, the main artery of the town, is a top

attraction in Provincetown. On any given day you may see cross-dressers, leather-clad motorcyclists, barely clad in-line skaters, same-sex couples strolling hand in hand and heterosexual tourists wondering what they've stumbled into on their way to a whale-watch.

PROVINCETOWN ART
ASSOCIATION & MUSEUM   GALLERY
(PAAM; www.paam.org; 460 Commercial St; adult/child $7/free; ⊙11am-8pm Mon-Fri, to 5pm Sat & Sun Jun-Sep, noon-5pm Thu-Sun Oct-May) Founded in 1914 to celebrate the town's thriving art community, this museum showcases the works of hundreds of artists who have found their inspiration on the Lower Cape. Chief among them are Charles Hawthorne, who led the early Provincetown art movement, and Edward Hopper, who had a home and gallery in the Truro dunes.

EATING & DRINKING

MEWS RESTAURANT
& CAFE   MODERN AMERICAN $$$
(☑508-487-1500; www.mews.com; 429 Commercial St; cafe mains $12-24, restaurant mains $26-33; ⊙dinner) A fantastic water view, the hottest martini bar in town and scrumptious food add up to Provincetown's finest dining scene. There are two sections. Opt to dine gourmet on tuna sushi and rack of lamb downstairs, where you're right on the sand, or go casual with a juicy Angus burger from the cafe menu upstairs. There's also a happening Sunday brunch.

ROSS' GRILL   AMERICAN, FRENCH $$$
(☑508-487-8878; www.rossgrillptown.com; 237 Commercial St; sandwiches $10-15, mains $15-30;

⊙lunch & dinner) A much beloved hideaway tucked above Whalers Wharf, this casual bar and grill has spectacular views of the harbor, an impressive wine list and impeccable, traditional steaks and seafood. Regulars rave about the French onion soup, which could be a meal in and of itself. Large portions make dessert a challenge but try to save room for banana-bread pudding.

FANIZZI'S BY THE SEA   SEAFOOD $$
(☑508-487-1964; www.fanizzisrestaurant.com; 539 Commercial St; mains lunch $10-17, dinner $18-22; ⊙lunch & dinner; 🖽) Consistent food, an amazing water view and reasonable prices make this restaurant a local favorite. The extensive menu has something for everyone, from fresh seafood and salads to comfort food; there's even a kids' menu. So why is it cheaper than the rest of the pack? It's less central – about a 15-minute walk northeast of the town center.

HARBOR LOUNGE   COCKTAIL BAR
(www.theharborlounge.com; 359 Commercial St; ⊙noon-10pm) The Harbor Lounge takes full advantage of its seaside setting, with floor-to-ceiling windows and a boardwalk stretching out into the bay. Candlelit tables and black leather sofas constitute the decor. The cocktails are surprisingly affordable, with many martini concoctions to sample.

AQUA BAR   BAR
(207 Commercial St; ⊙11am-midnight) Imagine a food court where the options include a raw bar, sushi, gelato and other global delights. Add a well-stocked bar with generous tenders pouring drinks. Now put the whole place in a gorgeous seaside setting, overlooking a beautiful harbor. Now, imagine this whole scene at sunset. That's no fantasy, that's Aqua Bar.

GLBTQ PROVINCETOWN

While other cities have their gay districts, in Provincetown the entire town is the gay district.

➡ **A-House** (Atlantic House; www.ahouse.com; 4 Masonic Pl) P-town's gay scene got its start here and it's still the leading bar in town. Includes an intimate 1st-floor pub with fireplace, as well as a dance club and cabaret through a separate entrance.

➡ **Boatslip Resort** (www.boatslipresort.com; 161 Commercial St; cover $5; ⊙4-7pm) Hosts wildly popular afternoon-tea dances, often packed with gorgeous guys.

➡ **Pied Bar** (www.piedbar.com; 193 Commercial St; ⊙6am-2am May-Oct) A popular waterfront lounge that attracts both lesbians and gay men. Particularly hot place to be around sunset.

SLEEPING IN PROVINCETOWN

Provincetown has a hundred delightful small inns and guesthouses lining Commercial St and the side roads. Most require reservations in summer, but inquire at the Chamber of Commerce if you arrive unannounced.

➡ **Carpe Diem** (☎508-487-0132; www.carpediemguesthouse.com; 12 Johnson St; r incl breakfast $159-259; 🛜) This is one classy place to rest your head. Sophisticated yet relaxed, each room has a theme inspired by a different writer and the corner of the world they hail from. It makes for a soothing mix of smiling Buddhas, orchid sprays and thoughtful decor.

➡ **Christopher's by the Bay** (☎508-476-9263; www.christophersbythebay.com; 8 Johnson St; r with shared/private bathroom from $105/155; 🛜) Tucked away on a side street with a backyard koi pond, this welcoming inn is top value. Local art on the walls and the afternoon wine and cheese reception add a homey Provincetown flavor.

➡ **Cape Codder** (☎508-487-0131; www.capecodderguests.com; 570 Commercial St; r $60-85; ☺Apr-Nov; 🐕) Definitely think budget – this is a very simple place that doesn't pretend to be anything more. The are four bathrooms shared between 14 rooms, no TVs or phones, and the occasional wall crack and threadbare bedspread. But for these prices in this town it's a steal. You can't beat the private beach and sundeck.

➡ **Surfside Hotel & Suites** (☎508 487 1726; www.surfsideinn.cc; 543 Commercial St; r incl breakfast from $209; ❄🛜🏊🐕) For those who prefer a hotel to a B&B, this locally owned establishment has an enviable beachfront location and a pool that the kids can splash in. The continental breakfast is nothing mind-blowing, but there are plenty of cafes and bakeries in the vicinity.

PURPLE FEATHER CAFE & TREATERY   CAFE
(www.thepurplefeather.com; 334 Commercial St; snacks $2-10; ☺8am-midnight; 🐕) Head to this stylish cafe for killer panini sandwiches, a rainbow of gelatos and decadent desserts all made from scratch. There's no better place in town for light eats and sweet treats. Good mocha lattes too.

🏃 ACTIVITIES

DOLPHIN FLEET WHALE WATCH   WHALE-WATCHING
(☎508-240-3636; www.whalewatch.com; MacMillan Wharf; adult/child $39/31; ☺Apr-Oct; 🐕) Offers up to nine tours daily in peak season, each lasting three to four hours.

Sleeping

Boston offers a complete range of accommodations, from dorms and hostels to inviting guesthouses in historic quarters and swanky hotels with all the amenities. Considering that Boston is a city filled with students, there are surprisingly few accommodation options targeting budget travelers and backpackers.

Rates

Most hotels, particularly chains, have no set rates. Instead, rates fluctuate seasonally, if not daily. This book quotes high-season rates, which is roughly defined as April through October, although prices are more accurately driven by occupancy and high-profile events. So holidays, university graduations, baseball games and pride parades all affect hotel prices. Often the most expensive period is from mid-September to mid-October.

Boutique Hotels

In recent years, Boston has become a hotspot for boutique hotels – small, stylish hotels, usually with personalized service and contemporary flair. The classier boutique hotels are not cheap, but most offer competitive rates to attract tourists and businesspeople.

Budget Lodging

Inexpensive accommodations are rare, but the savvy traveler should have no problem locating an acceptable option. Boston has only a few hostels catering to traditional backpacking budget travelers. Other budget options include guesthouses, offering simple accommodation and personal service and usually catering to international types, students and long-term guests.

B&Bs

Many B&Bs and inns are housed in historic or architecturally significant buildings. Contact B&Bs direct or, better yet, use an agency that will attempt to match your neighborhood desires with the thickness of your wallet. Note that that there's no room tax on B&Bs with fewer than three rooms.

➡ **B&B Agency of Boston** (Map p248; ☎617-720-3540, 800-248-9262, free from the UK 0800-89-5128; www.boston-bnbagency.com; r $120-200, 2-bedroom $200-350, 3-bedroom $300-400) Lists over 100 different properties, including B&Bs and furnished apartments, in Beacon Hill, Back Bay, North End and South End.

➡ **Bed & Breakfast Associates Bay Colony** (☎781-449-5302, 888-486-6018, from UK 08-234-7113; www.bnbboston.com) A huge database of furnished rooms and apartments in Boston, Brookline, Cambridge and the suburbs.

Longer-Term Rentals

With hordes of students and other transients moving around town, Boston, Brookline and Cambridge are full of summer sublets and longer-term apartments available to rent. Signs are often posted at coffee shops, bookstores and other student hang-outs. University housing offices are also good sources of information, as is good ol' Craig's List.

➡ **Boston Apartments** (www.boston apartments.com) Includes listings for long and short term, furnished and unfurnished, and a search by neighborhood.

➡ **Rental Beast** (www.rentalbeast.com) Rental properties all over town. Search by neighborhood or requirements (eg lead-free).

➡ **Rent.com** (www.rent.com) Though this site is operated by eBay, you don't have to bid on the properties. Search by neighborhood, amenity and pet policy.

Lonely Planet's Top Choices

Liberty Hotel (p185) You'll want to throw away the key to your 'cell' at this luxury hotel.

Green Turtle (p185) Let the gentle waves rock you to sleep.

Gryphon House (p191) Indulge your senses at this gorgeous riverside brownstone.

Kendall Hotel (p192) The old Cambridge firehouse is now a charmingly nostalgic boutique hotel.

Inn @ St Botolph (p189) Enjoy affordable luxury and artful design on the edge of Back Bay.

Harding House (p192) This comfy, cozy B&B goes above and beyond to make you feel at home.

Best by Budget

$

Longwood Inn (p193)

463 Beacon Street Guest House (p190)

New HI Boston (p188)

Commonwealth Court Guest House (p190)

$$

Newbury Guest House (p189)

Harborside Inn (p187)

Charlesmark Hotel (p189)

Chandler Inn (p188)

$$$

XV Beacon (p186)

Nine Zero (p187)

Hotel Veritas (p192)

Hotel Commonwealth (p191)

Best Green Hotels

Seaport Boston Hotel (p191)

Lenox Hotel (p189)

Hotel Marlowe (p192)

New HI Boston (p188)

Irving House (p192)

Best for Families

Seaport Boston Hotel (p191)

Charles Hotel (p192)

Midtown Hotel (p190)

Colonnade (p189)

Royal Sonesta (p193)

Best Gay Stays

Chandler Inn (p188)

Clarendon Square Inn (p188)

Encore (p188)

Taylor House (p193)

Best for Baseball Fans

Hotel Buckminster (p191)

Hotel Commonwealth (p191)

Gryphon House (p191)

Best Hostels

40 Berkeley (p188)

New HI Boston (p188)

Friend Street Hostel (p185)

Best B&Bs

Clarendon Square Inn (p188)

Taylor House (p193)

La Cappella Suites (p185)

Encore (p188)

Best Boutique Hotels

Nine Zero (p187)

Ames Hotel (p187)

Hotel Veritas (p192)

XV Beacon (p186)

Hotel Marlowe (p192)

NEED TO KNOW

Price Guide

$	less than $125
$$	$125 to $250
$$$	over $250

Taxes

All accommodations (except B&Bs) are subject to a 12.45% lodging tax, comprising the 9.7% tax and a 2.75% convention-center fee. Rates quoted here don't include taxes.

Miscellany

Reviews indicate rates for single occupancy (s), double occupancy (d) or simply a room (r) if there is no appreciable difference in the rate for one or two people. Unless otherwise noted, breakfast is not included, bathrooms are private and lodging is open year-round.

Accommodation Websites

Even the highest-end hotels post promotions and off-season sales on their websites. While rack rates are quoted in this book, cheaper rates are often available, especially using online booking sites.

➡ **LonelyPlanet.com** Includes reviews and booking service.

➡ **Hotels.com** Guarantees to match any other site's rates.

➡ **Booking.com** Promises rock-bottom prices, and usually delivers.

➡ **Priceline.com** Includes user reviews and a sorting-by-neighborhood feature.

➡ **HostelZ.com** The world's largest hostel database, with private and dorm-style lodging.

SLEEPING

Where to Stay

Neighborhood	For	Against
Charlestown	Relatively affordable; neighborhood charm; great skyline views; close to some sights but removed from city center	Removed from city center; limited transportation options
West End & North End	Relatively affordable; close proximity to major sights; convenient transportation to other neighborhoods; great dining and shopping in North End	Few options in North End; desolate atmosphere in West End
Beacon Hill & Boston Common	Neighborhood charm; close proximity to major sights; great dining and shopping	Expensive
Downtown & Waterfront	Close proximity to major sights and waterfront; convenient transportation to other neighborhoods; hustle-and-bustle city atmosphere	Expensive; hustle-and-bustle city atmosphere (noisy, no neighborhood charm)
South End & Chinatown	Neighborhood charm; close proximity to major sights; convenient transportation to other neighborhoods; great dining, shopping and nightlife; hustle-and-bustle city atmosphere	Some areas can be dangerous for solo travelers and late-night revelers who are not cautious; hustle-and-bustle city atmosphere (noisy)
Back Bay	Neighborhood charm; close proximity to major sights; convenient transportation to other neighborhoods; great dining, shopping and nightlife	None
Kenmore Square & Fenway	Close proximity to major sights; convenient transportation to other neighborhoods; great dining and nightlife	None
Seaport District & South Boston	Close proximity to airport and waterfront; great harbor and skyline views	Removed from city center; can feel desolate at night; limited transportation options
Cambridge	Neighborhood charm; close proximity to some sights; convenient transportation to other neighborhoods; great dining, shopping and nightlife	Removed from city center
Streetcar Suburbs	Relatively affordable; neighborhood charm; close proximity to some sights; convenient transportation to other neighborhoods; great dining, shopping and nightlife	Removed from city center

⊨ Charlestown

TOP CHOICE ⟩ GREEN TURTLE   B&B $$$

Map p245 (☑617-337-0202; www.greenturtlebb.
com; Pier 8, 13th St, Charlestown; r $260; P❋@;
⛴F4 from Long Wharf) It's not just a B&B, but
a floating B&B. If you want to be lulled to
sleep by the sound of waves lapping and
wake up to the cry of seagulls, maybe you
should be sleeping on a houseboat. The two
contemporary guest rooms are surprisingly
spacious, complete with kitchenettes. Hot
coffee and fresh pastries are served in your
room.

Your seafaring hosts Karen and Jon
do their utmost to ensure an unrivaled
experience.

CONSTITUTION INN   HOTEL $$

Map p245 (☑617-241-8400, 617-495-9622; www.
constitutioninn.org; 150 Third Ave; d $179-189;
P❋@❋❋; ⛴F4 from Long Wharf) Housed in
a granite building in the historic Charlestown Navy Yard, this excellent, affordable
hotel accommodates active and retired
military personnel. But you don't have to
have a crew cut to stay here. The rooms are
clean, crisp, modern and freshly painted,
and decorated with plain cherry furniture;
some have kitchenettes. Guests gain free
access to the Olympic-class fitness center.

⊨ West End & North End

The North End's close-knit Italian community is not known for welcoming visitors –
for dinner, yes, but not to spend the night.
Save for one solitary B&B, all of the accommodation options are in the West End.

TOP CHOICE ⟩ LIBERTY HOTEL   HOTEL $$$

Map p246 (☑617-224-4000; www.libertyhotel.
com; 225 Charles St; r from $375; P❋@; Ⓜ
Charles/MGH) It is with intended irony that
the notorious Charles Street Jail has been
converted into the luxurious Liberty Hotel.
Today, the spectacular lobby soars under
a 90ft ceiling. Guest rooms boast floor-to-
ceiling windows with amazing views of the
Charles River and Beacon Hill, not to men-
tion luxurious linens and high-tech ameni-
ties such as LCD televisions and iPod dock-
ing stations.

LA CAPPELLA SUITES   B&B $$

Mapp248(☑617-523-9020;www.lacappellasuites.
com; 290 North St; ste $150-210; ❋@❋; ⓂHay-
market) 'La Cappella' refers to the small
chapel of La Societá di San Calogero di
Sciacca that previously occupied this red-
brick building. Now it is a private home
with three spacious guest suites on the upper floors, topped off by a shared roof deck.
Look for Italian marble flooring, panoramic
views of the skyline and the harbor, and access to a kitchen and common areas.

A small self-service breakfast is included
in the price.

∅ **ONYX HOTEL**   BOUTIQUE HOTEL $$

Map p246 (☑617-557-9955; www.onyxhotel.com;
155 Portland St; d $229-289; P❋@; ⓂNorth
Station) Done up in jewel tones and contem-
porary furniture, the Onyx exudes warmth
and style – two elements that do not always
go hand in hand. Attractive features of
the hotel (a member of the Kimpton Hotel
Group) include morning car service, passes
to a local gym and an evening wine recep-
tion. 'Pet-friendly' goes to a whole new level
with gourmet doggy biscuits and a dog-
sitting service.

FRIEND STREET HOSTEL   HOSTEL $

Map p246 (☑617-934-2413; www.friendstreethos
tel.com; 234 Friend St; dm $43-50) We believe
them when they say it's the friendliest hos-
tel in Boston. But there are other reasons to
love this affable hostelry, such as the spic-
and-span kitchen and the comfy common
area with the huge flatscreen TV. Sleeping
six to 10 people each, dorm rooms have
painted brick walls, wide-plank wood floors
and sturdy pine bunk beds.

Also: breakfast, bikes and lots of free ac-
tivities. What's not to love? Street noise.

BULFINCH HOTEL   BOUTIQUE HOTEL $$

Map p246 (☑617-624-0202; www.bulfinchhotel.
com; 107 Merrimac St; d $199-249; P❋@; Ⓜ
North Station) Exemplifying the up-and-
coming character of this once-downtrodden
district, this namesake hotel occupies a fully
restored 19th-century flatiron building on
the western edge of the Bulfinch Triangle.
The place oozes understated sophistication.
Inside, warm, creamy coffee colors complement the modern walnut furniture in the
guest rooms, all of which are fully equipped
with flatscreen TVs and other amenities.

FIVE-STAR JAILHOUSE

'Be captivated,' invites the Liberty Hotel. It's a rather blatant use of irony considering the building used to be the notorious Charles Street Jail.

Many people were skeptical about this project. At best it's gimmicky, some said. Many feared it would be downright tasteless, mocking the prisoners who spent years enduring inhumane conditions in the old Suffolk County prison.

But now even the critics agree that the end result is pretty classy. Most importantly, the Liberty Hotel has turned this graceful, granite building into a productive and – frankly – spectacular space, retaining much of the original architectural detailing. The catwalks still circle the five-story lobby, its original rose windows flooding the place with light. The hotel has also preserved the history of this building, with a gallery of historic photos in the lobby and plenty of whimsical nods to its former incarnation.

The hotel does not gloss over the building's rocky history. When the jail was first built in 1851, the architect collaborated with prison reformer Louis Dwight. Together they designed the facility, experimenting with principles of humanitarian incarceration that were *en vogue* at the time. The building is considered an archetype of the Boston Granite Style (with granite straight from Quincy, Mass). Over the years, the jail housed many famous residents, including the anarchists Sacco and Vanzetti, black liberationist Malcolm X and Boston's own James Michael Curley. (Indeed, this is where the would-be mayor lived when he was elected to the Board of Aldermen in 1904.)

Despite its auspicious start, the Charles Street Jail suffered from a lack of funding and therefore a lack of maintenance. By the middle of the 20th century, the building was overcrowded, conditions were miserable and there was a constant threat of revolt. On one occasion, two men found bugs in their soup and incited an uprising that caused $250,000 in damage. Guests can learn all this and more from the documentary video in the hotel gallery.

Finally, a group of inmates brought a lawsuit against the county. Judge Arthur Garrity actually spent a night in the prison – on murderers' row – before making his decision. In 1974, he ruled that the inhumane conditions were unacceptable and the prison should be closed immediately.

His ruling was finally carried out 16 years later. This is Boston, after all. And any job worth doing is worth doing over budget and past deadline.

By comparison, turning the low-down prison into a high-class hotel took only five years. Of the many tasks, one was inviting a group of monks to burn some incense, say some prayers and cleanse the property of any negative karma that might be lurking in the corners. No way were they starting a $150 million endeavor with bad feng shui.

Who would have thought that the notorious Charles Street Jail would get a second life as a five-star luxury hotel? These days it houses much more willing residents, no doubt. (Oh, they are willing... willing to pay $300-plus per night!)

🛏 Beacon Hill & Boston Common

BEACON HILL HOTEL & BISTRO
BOUTIQUE HOTEL **$$$**

Map p250 (📞617-723-7575; www.beaconhillhotel.com; 25 Charles St; r $305-365, ste $365-425; P✳︎🛜; MCharles/MGH) This upmarket European-style inn blends into its namesake neighborhood without flash or fanfare. Carved out of former residential buildings typical of Beacon Hill, the hotel has 12 small but stylish rooms, individually decorated with black-and-white photographs, louvered shutters and a designer's soothing palette of paint choices. Added perks include the exclusive roof deck and complimentary breakfast at the urbane, on-site bistro.

XV BEACON
BOUTIQUE HOTEL **$$$**

Map p250 (📞617-670-1500; www.xvbeacon.com; 15 Beacon St; r from $295; P✳︎🛜; MPark St) Housed in a turn-of-the-20th-century beaux-arts building, XV Beacon sets the standard for Boston's boutique hotels. Guestroom decor is soothing, taking advantage of color schemes rich with taupe, espresso and cream. You'll find custom-made gas fireplaces and built-in mahogany entertainment units; heated towel racks and rainforest shower heads in the bathrooms; and romantic canopy beds dressed in Frette linens.

CHARLES STREET INN   GUESTHOUSE $$$
Map p250 (617-314-8900, 617-772-8900; www.charlesstreetinn.com; 94 Charles St; r $250-375; P※@; MCharles/MGH) Built in 1860 as a showcase home, this Second Empire Victorian inn is now a model for how to meld the best of the 19th and 21st centuries. Ornate plaster cornices, ceiling medallions and window styles grace the nine rooms and common areas, where you're never vying for staff attention. Rooms are fitted with Victorian fabrics, handmade Turkish rugs, whirlpool tubs and working fireplaces.

For added romance, a complimentary continental breakfast is served in your room.

JOHN JEFFRIES HOUSE   HOTEL $$
Map p250 (617-367-1866; www.johnjeffrieshouse.com; 14 David Mugar Way; r $124-159, ste $174-194; P※奈♿; MCharles/MGH) Reproduction furnishings, original molding, hardwood floors and mahogany accents warmly recall the era when Dr John Jeffries founded what is now the world-renowned Massachusetts Eye & Ear Infirmary. Many patients reside here when they come to town for treatment, as do travelers.

While the parlor is a lovely spot to enjoy your complimentary breakfast, you can also whip up your own meal in your in-room kitchenette (available in most rooms).

🛏 Downtown & Waterfront

🎐 NINE ZERO   BOUTIQUE HOTEL $$$
Map p252 (617-772-5810; www.ninezero.com; 90 Tremont St; r from $259; P※奈; MPark St) This chic boutique hotel appeals to a broad audience, courting business travelers with a complimentary shoe-shine service and ergonomic workspace; techies with on-demand video games and iPod docking stations; and animal lovers with Kimpton's signature pet service. All of the above enjoy the marvelous views of the State House and the Granary from the upper floors.

HARBORSIDE INN   BOUTIQUE HOTEL $$
Map p252 (617-723-7500; www.harborsideinnboston.com; 185 State St; r from $199; P※@奈; MAquarium) Ensconced in a respectfully

renovated 19th-century warehouse, this waterfront hostelry strikes just the right balance between historic digs and modern conveniences. Apparently, the architects who did the renovation cared about preserving historic details, as guest rooms have original exposed brick and granite walls and hardwood floors. They're offset perfectly by Oriental area carpets, sleigh beds and reproduction Federal-era furnishings. Add $20 for a city view.

AMES HOTEL   BOUTIQUE HOTEL $$$
Map p252 (617-979-8100; www.ameshotel.com; 1 Court St; r from $320; P※奈; MState) It's easy to miss this understated hotel, tucked behind the granite facade of the historic Ames Building (Boston's first skyscraper). Starting in the lobby and extending to the guest rooms, the style is elegant but eclectic, artfully blending modern minimalism and old-fashioned ornamental details. The upper floors yield wonderful views over the city.

BOSTON HARBOR HOTEL   HOTEL $$$
Map p252 (617-493-7000; www.bhh.com; 70 Rowes Wharf; r $245-295; P※奈⊠; MAquarium) Everybody adores the attentive service at this waterside hotel, especially the above-and-beyond turn-down treats. And how is it – with 230 rooms – that the staff seems to know each and every guest? The rooms are plush even if the decor is a bit staid, and you can't beat the glorious harbor views.

In summertime, the hotel hosts live music, old movies and other entertainment on its outdoor plaza.

🎐 MILLENNIUM BOSTONIAN HOTEL   HOTEL $$
Map p252 (617-523-3600; www.millenniumhotels.com; 26 North St; d $239-259; P※奈; MHaymarket) The Bostonian proudly touts its roots as part of the Blackstone Block, the city's oldest block. From the moment you enter the cool, contemporary lobby, to the time you step out onto your balcony overlooking the bustle of Haymarket, you'll appreciate this hotel's singular position. All-new rooms feature high-def TVs, Frette linens, gas fireplaces and other luxuries.

🎐 INTERCONTINENTAL HOTEL   HOTEL $$$
Map p252 (617-747-1000; www.intercontinentalboston.com; 510 Atlantic Ave; r $240-260; P※奈⊠; MSouth Station) The fancy marble bathrooms alone are worth the price of

staying in this first-class hotel. The bathtub is enormous, perfect for soaking, with sliding windows yielding a view of the flatscreen TV in the bedroom, not to mention the separate shower, fragrant soaps and plush, luxurious towels.

The rooms are sumptuous and sophisticated, while the location – perched on the edge of the Seaport District – is ideal.

OMNI PARKER HOUSE HISTORIC HOTEL $$$

Map p252 (☑617-227-8600; www.omnihotels.com; 60 School St; r $289-389; ᴘ✳✸⚿; ᴍPark St) History and Parker House go hand in hand like JFK and Jackie O (who got engaged here). To wit: Malcolm X was a busboy here; Ho Chi Minh was a pastry chef; and Boston cream pie, the official state dessert, was created here. The lovely guest rooms are decorated in rich red and gold tones and equipped with all the high-tech gadgetry.

🛏 South End & Chinatown

All of the accommodation options are located in the South End and the Theater District (although isn't it nice to have Chinatown nearby when you get the munchies at 2am?).

TOP CHOICE ENCORE B&B $$

Map p256 (☑617-247-3425; www.encorebandb.com; 116 W Newton St; r $140-240; ᴘ✳✸; ᴍBack Bay) If you love the theater, or if you love innovative contemporary design, or if you just love creature comforts and warm hospitality, you will love Encore. Co-owned by an architect and a set designer, this 19th-century South End town house sets a stage for both of their passions.

Exposed brick walls are adorned with exotic masks, interesting art and theatrical posters; bold colors and contemporary furniture pieces furnish the spacious guest rooms. All three rooms have a sitting area or private deck that offers a sweet skyline view. Continental breakfast.

CHANDLER INN HOTEL $$

Map p256 (☑800-842-3450, 617-482-3450; www.chandlerinn.com; 26 Chandler St; r $115-185; ✳✸⚿; ᴍBack Bay) The Chandler Inn is looking fine, after a complete overhaul. Small but sleek rooms have benefited from a designer's touch, giving them a sophisticated, urban glow. Modern travelers will appreciate the plasma TVs and iPod docks,

all of which comes at surprisingly affordable prices. As a bonus, congenial staff provide super service. On site is the South End drinking institution, Fritz.

CLARENDON SQUARE INN B&B $$

Map p256 (☑617-536-2229; www.clarendonsquare.com; 198 W Brookline St; r from $195; ᴘ✳✸; ᴍPrudential) Located on a quiet residential street in the South End, this completely renovated brownstone is a designer's dream. Guest-room details might include Italian marble wainscoting, French limestone floors, a silver-leaf barrel-vaulted ceiling or a hand-forged iron and porcelain washbasin. Common areas are decadent (case in point: roof-deck hot tub); continental breakfast is served in the paneled dining room and butler's pantry.

40 BERKELEY HOSTEL $

Map p256 (☑617-375-2524; www.40berkeley.com; 40 Berkeley St; d/tr/q from $60/100/124; ✸⚿; ᴍBack Bay) Straddling the South End and Back Bay, this safe, friendly Y rents over 200 small rooms (some overlooking the garden) to guests on a nightly and long-term basis. Bathrooms are shared, as are other useful facilities such as the telephone, library, TV room and laundry. All rates include a generous and delicious breakfast. Weekly rates also available.

NEW HI BOSTON HOSTEL $

Map p258 (☑617-536-9455; www.hinewengland.org; 19 Stuart St; dm $31-48, d $80-130; ✳@✸⚿; ᴍChinatown or Boylston) HI Boston has a brand-new facility! The historic Dill Building has been completely revamped to allow for expanded capacity and community space, handicap access and, most impressively, state-of-the-art green amenities and energy efficiency. What stays the same? The reliably comfortable accommodations and excellent line-up of cultural activities that HI-Boston has offered for the past three decades.

82 CHANDLER B&B $$

Map p256 (☑617-482-0408; www.82chandler.com; 82 Chandler St; r $135-175; ✳; ᴍBack Bay) This beautiful brick Victorian town house contains four guest rooms for a few lucky travelers, who get to enjoy original fireplaces, carved mantelpieces and wrought-iron filigree. The place could use a bit of updating, but overall it's charming. Your hosts, Dominic and Jose, are rather hands-off, but they do serve breakfast in the sunlit penthouse.

MILNER HOTEL   HOTEL **$$**

Map p258 (☑617-426-6220, 617-453-1731; www.milner-hotels.com; 78 Charles St S; s/d from $149/169; P🛜; MBoylston) Mr Milner said it himself back in 1918: 'A bed and a bath for a buck and a half.' Prices have gone up since then, but the Milner Hotel still offers excellent value for this central location. Itinerant actors and international travelers frequent this affordable Theater District hostelry, which offers postage-stamp rooms with passable decor. The price includes a continental breakfast.

🛏 Back Bay

TOP CHOICE INN @ ST BOTOLPH   BOUTIQUE HOTEL **$$**

Map p260 (☑617-236-8099; www.innatstbotolph.com; 99 St Botolph St; ste $189-239; P❄🛜; MPrudential) Whimsical but wonderful, this delightful brownstone boutique emphasizes affordable luxury. Spacious, light-filled rooms feature bold patterns and contemporary decor, fully equipped kitchens, and all the high-tech bells and whistles. Foreshadowing a coming trend, the hotel keeps prices down by offering 'edited service,' with virtual check-in, keyless entry and 'touch-up' housekeeping, minimizing the need for costly staff. Complimentary continental breakfast.

NEWBURY GUEST HOUSE   GUESTHOUSE **$$**

Map p260 (☑617-437-7668, 617-437-7666; www.newburyguesthouse.com; 261 Newbury St; r $219-249; P❄🛜; MHynes or Copley) Dating to 1882, these three interconnected brick and brownstone buildings offer a prime location in the heart of Newbury St. A recent renovation has preserved the charming features like ceiling medallions and in-room fireplaces, but now the rooms feature clean lines, luxurious linens and modern amenities. Each morning, a complimentary continental breakfast is laid out next to the marble fireplace in the salon.

COLLEGE CLUB   GUESTHOUSE **$$$**

Map p260 (☑617-536-9510; www.thecollegeclubofboston.com; 44 Commonwealth Ave; s without bathroom from $129, d with bathroom $249-289; ❄🛜; MArlington) Originally a private club for female college graduates, the College Club has 11 spacious rooms with high ceilings, now open to both sexes. Period details – typical of the area's Victorian brownstones – include claw-tooth tubs, orna-

mental fireplaces and bay windows. Local designers have lent their skills to decorate the various rooms, with delightful results. Prices include a continental breakfast.

COLONNADE   HOTEL **$$**

Map p260 (☑617-424-7000; www.colonnadehotel.com; 120 Huntington Ave; r $179-249; P❄🛜 🏊♿; MPrudential) There are many reasons to stay at the Colonnade, such as its handsome guest rooms, which are well equipped with both high-tech gadgetry and simple pleasures (like a rubber duck in your bathtub). There's the VIPets program, complete with fluffy beds and walking services. And of course there's the excellent dining and the fabulous location.

But the real reason to stay at the Colonnade is the rooftop pool, or RTP, as it's known. A glamorous place to see and be seen in your bikini, it's also optimal for al fresco dining, sunbathing and yes, even swimming. Open to nonguests weekdays only.

BACK BAY HOTEL   HOTEL **$$**

Map p260 (☑617-266-7200; www.jurysdoyle.com; 350 Stuart St; r $209-309; P❄🛜♿; MBack Bay) Perched on the border of Back Bay and the South End, this stunner is housed in the former Boston Police Headquarters. The Irish brand (Doyles) brings a modern Euro flair to this historic edifice, with funky floor lights, intriguing artwork and a flowing waterfall. Rooms are luxurious, draped in rich ivory and copper tones, and well stocked with amenities.

LENOX HOTEL   HISTORIC HOTEL **$$$**

Map p260 (☑617-536-5300, 617-225-7676; www.lenoxhotel.com; 61 Exeter St; r $265-305; P❄🛜; MCopley) For three generations, the Saunders family has run this gem in Back Bay. And while the atmosphere is a tad old-world, you don't have to forgo modern conveniences to live with that ethos. Guest rooms are comfortably elegant (with chandeliers and crown molding), without being stuffy. If your pockets are deep enough, it's worth splurging for a junior suite, as they boast the best views.

The Lenox is a pioneer in green hospitality, implementing hundreds of initiatives to reduce its negative environmental impact.

CHARLESMARK HOTEL   BOUTIQUE HOTEL **$$**

Map p260 (☑617-247-1212; www.thecharlesmark.com; 655 Boylston St; r $209-269; P❄🛜;

MCopley) The Charlesmark's small but sleek rooms are at the crossroads of European style and functionality. The design is classic modernism; and the effect is upscale, urbane and surprisingly affordable. This hip hotel is backed by a small group of warmly efficient staff that see to every detail. The downstairs lounge spills out onto the sidewalk where the people-watching is tops. Complimentary continental breakfast.

COPLEY SQUARE HOTEL
HOTEL $$$

Map p260 (☎617-225-7062, 617-536-9000; www.copleysquarehotel.com; 47 Huntington Ave; r $269-319; P❋☎☏; MCopley or Back Bay) The Copley Square Hotel was always a nice place to stay, but after a multimillion-dollar reinvention, now it's downright sumptuous, with gorgeous contemporary rooms decorated in muted tones of taupe and gray, with subtle lines and soft fabrics. Flat-screen TVs and iPod docks are de rigueur. The morning coffee bar and afternoon Wine Down are lovely perks.

COMMONWEALTH COURT GUEST HOUSE
GUESTHOUSE $

Map p260 (☎888-424-1230, 617-424-1230; www.commonwealthcourt.com; 284 Commonwealth Ave; r per night $99-140, per week $500-800; ❋; MHynes) These 20 rooms with kitchenettes are not super spiffy, but the price is right for this great location. The Euro-style guesthouse is located in a turn-of-the-century brownstone in the heart of Back Bay. Once a private residence, it retains a homey feel and lots of lavish architectural details.

The service is pleasant but not overly attentive (maid service occurs only twice a week and the office closes in the evenings).

463 BEACON STREET GUEST HOUSE
GUESTHOUSE $

Map p260 (☎617-536-1302; www.463beacon.com; 463 Beacon St; d without/with bathroom from $89/139; P❋☎☏; MHynes) What's more 'Boston' than a handsome, historic brownstone in Back Bay? This guesthouse lets you live the blue-blood fantasy – and save your cash for the boutiques and bars on Newbury St. This c 1880 building retains plenty of highfalutin' architectural frolics, like a spiral staircase, wrought-iron filigrees and impossibly high ceilings. Alas, there is no elevator.

Rooms vary in size and decor, but they all have the basics (except daily maid service, which is not offered). Bathrooms are cramped, but hopefully you won't be spending too much time in there.

HOTEL 140
HOTEL $$

Map p260 (☎617-585-5440; www.hotel140.com; 140 Clarendon St; r $169-199, ste $199-219; @; MCopley or Back Bay) Once the headquarters of the YWCA, this classic brick building is now one of Boston's hidden hotel bargains. The standard rooms are quite basic, with dorm-style furniture and linoleum floors. Pricier rooms have a hint of contemporary style, with large windows and lots of sunlight. The price includes a continental breakfast. This is a popular spot among theater people, thanks to weekly and monthly rates.

COPLEY INN
GUESTHOUSE $$

Map p260 (☎617-232-0306, 617-236-0300; www.copleyinn.com; 19 Garrison St; r $175; MPrudential) This sweet old brownstone is tucked into the residential streets behind Copley Place: it's about as close as you can get to Newbury St while preserving the sense that you're nesting in a slightly quieter neighborhood. Equipped with kitchens, rooms in this four-story walk-up are relatively roomy, if a bit plain.

MIDTOWN HOTEL
MOTEL $$

Map p260 (☎617-262-1000, 617-343-1177; www.midtownhotel.com; 220 Huntington Ave; r $199-299; P❋☎☏☐; MSymphony) This low-rise motel looks like it belongs beside a highway instead of in the shadow of the Prudential Center, but its spacious rooms fill up with families, businesspeople and tour groups because the price is right and the location is unbeatable. The service is friendly and efficient; rooms are plain but clean.

Perks for families: kids under 18 stay for free, and they'll enjoy splashing around in the private outdoor swimming pool.

COPLEY HOUSE
APARTMENTS $$

Map p260 (☎617-236-8300, 617-331-1318; www.copleyhouse.com; 239 W Newton St; studio $145-175; ❋; MPrudential) Copley House occupies four different buildings, straddling Back Bay and the South End. The simple, somewhat run-down apartment-style rooms each have a kitchenette. A judicious use of antique wood and big windows beaming with light make this Queen Anne–style inn a place of respite, while the location makes it a handy base of operations for exploring Boston. Weekly rates are available.

Kenmore Square & Fenway

TOP CHOICE GRYPHON HOUSE B&B $$
Map p264 (617-375-9003; www.innboston.com; 9 Bay State Rd; r $215-265; P❄☂; MKenmore) A premier example of Richardson Romanesque, this beautiful five-story brownstone is a paradigm of artistry and luxury overlooking the picturesque Charles River. Eight spacious suites have different styles, including Victorian, Gothic and Arts and Crafts, but they all have 19th-century period details. And they all have home-away-from-home perks such as entertainment centers, wet bars and gas fireplaces.

Inquire about discounts for Red Sox fans (seriously!). Prices include a continental breakfast.

HOTEL COMMONWEALTH HOTEL $$$
Map p264 (617-933-5000, 617-784-4000; www.hotelcommonwealth.com; 500 Commonwealth Ave; r $229-329; P❄☂; MKenmore) Set amid Commonwealth Ave's brownstones and just steps away from Fenway Park, this independent luxury hotel enjoys prime real estate. Spacious Commonwealth rooms are more like suites, with king-size beds and two LCD TVs. Fenway rooms are slightly smaller, but they do offer a view into the ballpark. All guests can enjoy the amazing services and amenities, which range from turn-down service to iPods and PlayStations.

OASIS GUEST HOUSE GUESTHOUSE $$
Map p264 (617-267-2262, 617-230-0105; www.oasisgh.com; 22 Edgerly Rd; r without bathroom $99-129, with bathroom $159-204; P❄☂; MHynes or Symphony) True to its name, this homey guesthouse is a peaceful, pleasant oasis in the midst of Boston's chaotic city streets. Thirty-odd guest rooms occupy four attractive, brick, bow-front town houses on this tree-lined lane. The modest, light-filled rooms are tastefully and traditionally decorated, most with queen beds, floral quilts and nondescript prints.

The common living room does not exactly encourage lingering, but outdoor decks and kitchen facilities are nice touches. Complimentary continental breakfast.

ELIOT HOTEL BOUTIQUE HOTEL $$$
Map p264 (617-267-1607, 617-443-5468; www.eliothotel.com; 370 Commonwealth Ave; r $245-285, ste $285-345; P❄☂; MHynes) Akin to a small London hotel, the Eliot offers posh quarters, furnished in English chintz and Queen Anne mahogany; bathroom walls are dressed with Italian marble. Other upscale amenities include plush terry robes and down duvets, complimentary shoe-shine service and turn-down service. The acclaimed restaurant Clio is on the 1st floor.

HOTEL BUCKMINSTER HOTEL $$
Map p264 (617-727-2825, 617-236-7050; www.bostonhotelbuckminster.com; 645 Beacon St; r from $129, ste from $289; P❄☂; MKenmore) Designed by the architect of the Boston Public Library, the Buckminster is a convergence of Old Boston charm and affordable elegance. It offers nearly 100 rooms of varying shapes and sizes: economy rooms are small and stuffy, with slightly worn furniture (but still a great bargain); by contrast, the European-style suites are quite roomy, with all the tools and toys of comfort and convenience.

Each floor has its own laundry and kitchen facilities.

FENWAY SUMMER HOSTEL HOSTEL $
Map p264 (617-536-1027, 617-267-8599; www.bostonhostel.org; 575 Commonwealth Ave; dm $39-48, r $99-122; ☼Jun-Aug; ❄@; MKenmore) This former Howard Johnson hotel turned HI youth hostel doubles as a Boston University dorm, so it's open for travelers only in summer. Rooms have three beds each: rent the bed or rent the room. Each room has its own bathroom, which allows plenty of privacy in hostel-hopping terms.

Seaport District & South Boston

With the opening of the convention center, this district has become a hotbed of hotel development. It's a bit removed from the action unless you are actually attending an event at the convention center, but it's nirvana for seafood eaters and art connoisseurs. Bonus: it's also an easy trip from the airport.

SEAPORT BOSTON HOTEL HOTEL $$
Map p255 (617-385-4000; www.seaportboston.com; 1 Seaport Lane; r $219-309; P❄☂❄; MSouth Station, SL1 or SL2) With glorious views of the Boston Harbor, this business hotel is up-to-snuff when it comes to high-tech amenities (like automatic

motion-sensitive lights so you never have to enter a dark room, and privacy/service lights instead of the old-fashioned 'Do not disturb' signs). Soothing tones, plush linens and robes, and a unique no-tipping policy guarantee a relaxing retreat.

Now the Seaport is reaching out to families, offering Nintendo, baby gear and treats for your pet.

🛌 Cambridge

TOP CHOICE KENDALL HOTEL
BOUTIQUE HOTEL $$

Map p268 (☏617-566-1300; www.kendallhotel. com; 350 Main St; r from $169; P❄️🛜; MKendall/MIT) Once the Engine 7 Firehouse, this city landmark is now a cool and classy all-American hotel. The 65 guest rooms retain a firefighter riff, without a whiff of 'cutesy.' There's no scrimping at the breakfast table, either, with a full buffet included.

The on-site Black Sheep restaurant, filled with memorabilia from the good old days of fightin' fires, features organic, locally grown produce pleasing to omnivores and vegetarians alike.

TOP CHOICE HARDING HOUSE
INN $$

Map p268 (☏617-876-2888, 617-489-2888; www. harding-house.com; 288 Harvard St; r without bathroom $115-165, with bathroom $175-265; P❄️@🛜; MCentral) This treasure brilliantly blends refinement and comfort, artistry and efficiency. Old wooden floors toss back a warm glow and sport throw rugs. Antique furnishings complete the inviting atmosphere. The complimentary Thursday-night wine-and-cheese hour is a chance to meet fellow inn-mates, or sip and nosh in thoughtful solitude, gazing at the garden. Other perks: all-day munchies, a thoughtfully designed continental breakfast and complimentary museum passes.

HOTEL VERITAS
BOUTIQUE HOTEL $$$

Map p266 (☏617-520-5000; www.thehotelveritas. com; 1 Remington St; r from $279; P❄️🛜; MHarvard) Mosts guests agree that the super-chic design and top-notch service more than make up for the small size of the rooms at this Harvard Sq newcomer. Rich fabrics, shimmering textures and local artwork adorn the rooms. Dressed to the nines in Brooks Brothers uniforms, the Veritas team does whatever it takes to ensure a satisfying and truly special experience.

The on-site Simple Truth Lounge is a lovely spot for a drink, and guests have access to the gym at Karma Yoga across the street.

CHARLES HOTEL
HOTEL $$$

Map p266 (☏617-864-1200; www.charleshotel. com; 1 Bennett St; r from $269; P❄️🛜📶; MHarvard) 'Simple, Stylish, Smart.' Harvard Sq's most illustrious hotel lives up to its motto. Overlooking the Charles River, this institution has hosted the university's most esteemed guests, ranging from Bob Barker to the Dalai Lama. Design at the Charles – including rooms and restaurants – is surprisingly sleek, but the facilities do not lack the luxuries and amenities one would expect from a highly rated hotel.

IRVING HOUSE
GUESTHOUSE $$

Map p266 (☏617-547-4600; www.irvinghouse. com; 24 Irving St; s without bathroom $135-160, d without bathroom $160-190, r with bathroom $165-255; P❄️@🛜; MHarvard) Call it a big inn or a homey hotel, this property welcomes the world-weariest travelers. The 44 rooms range in size, but every bed is covered with a quilt and big windows let in plenty of light. There is a bistro-style atmosphere in the brick-lined basement, where you can browse the books on hand, plan your travels or munch on free continental breakfast.

Perks include museum passes and laundry facilities.

HOTEL MARLOWE
BOUTIQUE HOTEL $$

Map p268 (☏617-825-7140; www.hotelmarlowe. com; 25 Edwin Land Blvd; d $229-289, specials d $129; P❄️🛜📶; MLechmere or Science Park) The Kimpton Hotel Group's flagship property in the Boston area, just steps from the Charles River, embodies chic and unique as this organization always tries to do. Thoughtful perks include down comforters, Sony PlayStations and the *New York Times* delivered to your door – enough to please everyone, from the creatures of comfort to the free spirits to the intellectual snobs.

Hotel Marlowe is in East Cambridge, steps from the Museum of Science and the West End.

LE MÉRIDIEN CAMBRIDGE-MIT
HOTEL $$$

Map p268 (☏617-222-8733, 617-577-0200; www. starwoodhotels.com; 20 Sidney St; r $239-269; P❄️@🛜; MCentral) In the heart of the MIT campus, this contemporary hotel fuses art, design and science. Rooms and suites are awash with wood, chrome and ergonomically designed furniture. Guests may be world-famous geneticists or Nobel Prize–winning technologists, so this hip hotel doesn't skimp on providing them with all the high-tech and luxury amenities they expect.

ROYAL SONESTA — HOTEL $$$

Map p268 (☑617-806-4200; www.sonesta.com; 40 Edwin Land Blvd; r $199-399; P❄️🛜🐕; Ⓜ Science Park) Besides the luxurious rooms and up-to-date amenities, come to the Royal Sonesta to admire the incredible contemporary art collection, on display throughout the public spaces, including the awesome Art-Bar. This is a great spot for kids, with free ice cream, bikes and boat rides on the Charles.

🏄 INN AT HARVARD — INN $$

Map p266 (☑617-491-2222; www.hotelsinharvardsquare.com; 1201 Massachusetts Ave; d from $229; P❄️🛜; ⓂHarvard) The inn's collegiate atmosphere is appropriate for its setting, just outside the gates of Harvard Yard. The traditional guest rooms are a little outdated, but they do feature original artwork, flatscreen TVs and ergonomic chairs. On-site services are limited – this is not a full-service hotel after all – but all the resources of Harvard Sq are at your doorstep.

Breakfast is included in the price but afternoon tea is not. This place is scheduled for an overhaul in 2013.

HARVARD SQUARE HOTEL — HOTEL $$

Map p266 (☑617-864-5200; www.hotelsinharvardsquare.com; 110 Mt Auburn St; d $169-199; P❄️@🛜; ⓂHarvard) The square's namesake hotel offers a suitable (if unremarkable) place to sleep smack-dab in the middle of lively Harvard Sq. The downside: rooms are small and not particularly stylish; service is not particularly attentive; and you'll pay extra for amenities such as parking and internet access. The upside: location, location, location.

The hotel is scheduled for a long-overdue renovation in 2012, after which you can expect quality to improve and prices to increase.

A FRIENDLY INN — GUESTHOUSE $

Map p266 (☑617-547-7851; www.afinow.com/afi; 1673 Cambridge St; r $97-197; P❄️🛜; ⓂHarvard) While this Victorian-era inn gets mixed reviews, nobody disputes that it is indeed 'a friendly inn.' Service is accommodating and efficient, offering a clean and quiet respite for budget travelers. The old maxim holds true, however: you get what you pay for. Be prepared to sleep in cramped quarters and to forgo the fancy-pants amenities you may find at an upscale hotel.

A continental breakfast is included, but you are better off heading down the street to Darwin's Ltd for your morning meal.

🛏 Streetcar Suburbs

The streetcar suburbs are a sweet retreat if the city makes you feel claustrophobic. Grand elm trees shade the wide green lawns and gracious mansions, and a short ride on the T brings you into town.

TAYLOR HOUSE — B&B $$

Map p271 (☑617-983-9334; www.taylorhouse.com; 50 Burroughs St, Jamaica Inn; s $145-159, d $165-189, ste $199-219; P❄️🛜🐕; ⓂGreen St) Sitting pretty pond-side in Jamaica Plain, this gracious Italianate Victorian mansion has undergone a loving restoration – apparent from the ornamental details throughout the house and the gorgeous gardens outside. The spacious guest rooms have dark polished-wood floors, sleigh beds, bold contemporary art and plenty of sunshine. The suites are in the carriage house behind.

Dave is your designer, decorator and amazing host. PS: Must love dogs (two friendly golden retrievers live here too).

BERTRAM INN — B&B $$

Map p270 (☑617-295-3822, 617-566-2234; www.bertraminn.com; 92 Sewall Ave, Brookline; r $149-189; P❄️🛜; ⓂSt Paul) Brookline's tree-lined streets shelter this dreamy, Arts and Crafts–style inn, located only a quick jaunt from downtown Boston. A quiet elegance is accented with beautifully carved oak panels, leaded windows and, if you play your cards right, a working fireplace in your room. Amenities and services match those of high-end hotels.

The same owners run the **Samuel Sewall Inn** (☑617-713-0123, 888-713-2566; www.samuelsewallinn.com; 143 St Paul Ave, Brookline; r $149-189) across the street, an exquisitely restored Victorian with even more rooms. Both places boast tree-shaded patios, a full gourmet breakfast and a location that's just a heartbeat from the Hub of the Universe.

LONGWOOD INN — GUESTHOUSE $

Map p270 (☑617-566-8615; www.longwood-inn.com; 123 Longwood Ave, Brookline; s/d from

$119/129; P✷☎; MCoolidge Corner) This big old Victorian mansion is in an odd location midway between Coolidge Corner and Longwood. Affordable rates (including cheaper weekly rates) attract many long-term guests, especially folks working in the nearby medical district. Simple rooms have an old-fashioned charm, with floral bedspreads and antique furniture. The cheapest rooms have detached private bathrooms; add $15 for en suite.

Common areas include a modern kitchen and a comfy cozy library with leather furniture and beamed ceilings.

ANTHONY'S TOWN HOUSE GUESTHOUSE $

Map p270 (☏617-566-3972; www.anthonystown house.com; 1085 Beacon St, Brookline; r without bathroom $99-129; ✷☎; MHawes St) Halfway between Coolidge Corner and Kenmore Sq, this family-operated guesthouse puts the rolled 'r' in rococo. With more frills and flourishes than should be allowed in one place at one time, the Victorian-era brownstone is downright girly. The 10 rooms are spacious and comfortable and filled with antiques and lacy linens. Affable owners and cheap rates attract plenty of repeat visitors. Cash only!

BEECH TREE INN B&B $

Map p270 (☏617-227-1620; www.thebeechtree inn.com; 83 Longwood Ave, Brookline; s $99-129, d $129-159; ✷@; MLongwood) This turn-of-the-20th-century Victorian home now contains 10 guest rooms, each individually decorated with period furnishings and wallpaper, ornamental fireplaces with hand-painted screens, floral quilts and lacy curtains. Common areas include a cozy parlor and a pleasant patio. It's a romantic return to yesteryear, located on a quiet residential street not far from Coolidge Corner and the Back Bay Fens. Breakfast is included; parking costs $7.

Understand Boston

Boston Today

Recalling its revolutionary roots, Boston continues to claim its place among the country's forward-thinking and barrier-breaking cities. This is most evident in the political sphere – controversial issues like same-sex marriage and universal healthcare are already old news here. Physically, the city's changing landscape showcases some of the country's most cutting-edge architecture and innovative urban planning projects. Culturally, Boston has shed its staid and stodgy reputation, becoming a focal point for contemporary art.

Best on Film

The Verdict (1982) Paul Newman as a Boston lawyer.
Good Will Hunting (1997) Put Southie on the Hollywood map.
Next Stop Wonderland (1997) A heartwarming independent film with a bossa nova soundtrack.
The Departed (2006) A suspense-filled mob movie that won Best Picture.
The Social Network (2009) The fictionalized drama of the founding of Facebook.

Best in Print

The Scarlet Letter (Nathaniel Hawthorne; 1850) Hypocrisy and malice in Puritan New England.
The Friends of Eddie Coyle (George Higgins, 1972) A crime novel that provides a crash course in the Boston dialect.
Infinite Jest (David Foster Wallace; 1996) A 1000-page tome that is at once philosophical and satirical.
Interpreter of the Maladies (Jhumpa Lahiri; 1999) A Pulitzer Prize–winner that addresses the challenges of migration and multiculturalism.
Mystic River (Dennis Lehane; 2001) The dark story of three childhood friends who are thrown together in adulthood.

Greening the City

Bostonians have had the great fortune to witness the literal greening of their city. The Central Artery roadway, now underground and out of sight, has been replaced by the Rose Kennedy Greenway.

Like all good Boston public works projects, the Greenway is not without controversy. Many of the grand facilities that were promised – Boston Museum, YMCA, Garden under Glass, etc – do not exist, as investors have been forced to cancel their plans. The Greenway Conservancy has also come under fire for a lack of transparency in its finances.

Nonetheless, most Bostonians are pleased with the verdant thread that has successfully sutured its neighborhoods. And as more plans and plants come to fruition, the urban oasis keeps getting better. If all goes well, the future Rose Kennedy Greenway will be home to a local farmers' market, a custom-designed carousel and a newly conceived history museum.

The More Things Change...

Thanks to revitalization efforts, most of Boston is looking fantastic. Neighborhoods like the North End, West End and Waterfront have been rediscovered and reconnected to the rest of the city. Gentrification has transformed the South End and the Seaport District.

Unfortunately, other areas were left in the lurch by the recent recession. Downtown Crossing suffered from the closing of the iconic department store Filene's. Developers planned to preserve the historic facade and build a skyscraper behind it; the resulting building would be the centerpiece of the neighborhood's revitalization. But construction came to a standstill some time in 2008, leaving the Filene's facade teetering on the edge of an abyss – literally.

West of center, Allston was targeted for a complete overhaul at the expense of its wealthy neighbor across the river, Harvard. The university bought up all the land, tore down the buildings, then promptly ran out of money. Now the Allston Initiative is more like the Allston Interruption.

As the global economy emerges from the gutter, the city of Boston is anxious to move these projects forward. Investors are now at least talking about how to achieve this – which is a step in the right direction.

Local Pols Going National

Boston continues to play an influential role in national politics. Ironically – in this bastion of liberalism – it is Republicans who are making the headlines.

After the death of Senator Ted Kennedy in 2009, Massachusetts shocked the nation by replacing the beloved 'Liberal Lion' with the good-looking, truck-driving, barn-coat–wearing Scott Brown. He was the first Republican elected to the US Senate from Massachusetts since 1972.

Senator Brown has already made history, but it remains to be seen if his truck has legs. He is up for re-election in 2012, facing off in a competitive contest with Democratic candidate Elizabeth Warren. The nation waits and watches to see which party will fill the hotly contested senate seat.

Boston has also provided candidates for three recent presidential campaigns: Democrat John Kerry in 2004, and Republican Mitt Romney in 2008 and 2012 – with the outcome of that last bid still pending.

All Art Was Once Contemporary

When the Institute of Contemporary Art moved in 2006 from a cramped, converted police station to dramatic new quarters on the South Boston waterfront, it foreshadowed a phenom.

Less than a decade later, three more of Boston's most prominent and prestigious artistic institutions have upgraded their contemporary offerings in significant ways. In 2011, the Museum of Fine Arts opened the new Linde Family Wing for Contemporary Art, an expansion that tripled the size of exhibition space and increased the permanent collection of contemporary pieces. In 2012, the Isabella Stewart Gardner Museum unveiled its eye-catching new wing, featuring state-of-the-art facilities to support a dynamic artist-in-residency program. And in 2013, Harvard Art Museums will complete a renovation and expansion that is intended to transform the museum into a 'laboratory for the fine arts.'

Meanwhile, artists in Fort Point and SoWa regularly open their studios for public access. Tens of thousands of visitors are flooding the new museums. Boston is busting out of its conservative reputation and establishing itself, for the first time in over a century, on the cutting edge of contemporary art and culture.

if Boston were 100 people

47 would be Non-Hispanic Whites
22 would be Black or African American
18 would be Hispanic or Latino
9 would be Asian
2 would be two or more races
2 would be other

BOSTON TODAY

Educational attainment
(% of population)

High school not completed | High school degree | Bachelor's degree

Some college or associate's degree | Graduate or professional degree

population per sq mile

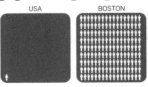

USA | BOSTON

↟ ≈ 87 people

History

In 1614 English explorer Captain John Smith, at the behest of the future King Charles I, set sail to assess the New World's commercial opportunities. Braving the frigid North Atlantic, the plucky explorer reached the rocky coast of present-day Maine and made his way southward to Cape Cod, making contact with the native population, mapping out the coastline and dubbing the region 'New England.' Smith noted a tricapped hilly peninsula, connected to the mainland by a narrow neck across a shallow back bay and with an excellent harbor fed by three rivers. The region was known to the natives as Shawmut.

THE SHAWMUT PENINSULA

Prior to the 17th century, there were as many as 100,000 native inhabitants of New England, mostly of the Algonquin nation, organized into small regional tribes that variously cooperated and quarreled with one another.

Before England's religious outcasts (the Puritans) showed up, local natives were already acquainted with Portuguese fishermen, French fur traders, Dutch merchants and Jesuit missionaries. The Europeans were welcomed as a source of valued goods, but they were also feared. In the Great Sadness of 1616–17, a smallpox epidemic devastated the native population, reducing it by three-quarters.

English colonial coastal encampments quickly spread, as seemingly unoccupied lands were claimed for king and commodity. According to John Winthrop, the first governor of the colony, 'God hath hereby cleared our title to this place.'

In 1675 Chief Metacomet, son of the famed Massasoit who befriended the starving Pilgrims, organized a desperate last stand against the ever-encroaching English. Known as King Philip to the settlers, he terrorized the frontier for more than a year before he was finally ambushed and killed. The chief's body was drawn and quartered and his heathen head perched on a pole, while his son was sold into slavery. In less than a hundred years, disease, war and forced migration had reduced the indigenous population by 90%.

TIMELINE	1614	1629	1630
	English explorer Captain John Smith surveys the coast of Maine and Massachusetts. Upon his return to England, he recounts the journey in his *Description of New England*.	The shareholders of the Massachusetts Bay Colony sign the Cambridge Agreement, which allows the emigrating Puritans to govern the colony and to answer only to the king.	Puritan settlers led by Governor John Winthrop flee the Church of England for the theocratic Massachusetts Bay Colony on the Shawmut Peninsula and on the north shore of the Charles River.

MISSION FROM GOD

Seventeenth-century England was torn by religious strife. The Puritans, austere Calvinists, wanted to purify the Anglican Church of all vestiges of pomp, pope and privilege. James I, annoyed by these nonconformists, threatened to 'harry them out of the country.'

As the fortunes of the faithful diminished, New England held out hope of renewal. The first trickle of Protestant immigrants came in 1620, when the Pilgrims established a small colony in Plymouth. Ten years later, the flagship *Arbella* led a flotilla of a thousand Puritans on the treacherous transatlantic crossing. In June 1630, their leader, country squire John Winthrop, gazed out on the Shawmut Peninsula and declared, 'we shall be as a City upon a Hill, with the eyes of all people upon us.'

They landed first near Salem and settled further south at present-day Charlestown. Across the river, the Shawmut Peninsula was at this time occupied by the Reverend William Blackstone, who had survived an earlier failed settlement. He invited Winthrop and his scurvy-ridden company to move closer to fresh water. They named their new home Boston, after the town in Lincolnshire where many of the Pilgrims had lived.

PIETY, POWER & PROFITS

The new settlement was governed by a spiritual elite – a Puritan theocracy. As such, the Church dominated early colonial life.

Divine Law was above all, and the state was put in service to the Church. The General Court, a select assembly of Church members, became the principal mechanism for lawmaking, while the governor was endowed with extensive powers to enforce the laws. Local affairs were settled at regular meetings, open to the freemen of each town. (Women were allowed to attend if they did not talk.) The tradition of town meetings became a cornerstone of American democracy.

Meanwhile, Boston became a boomtown. The first inhabitants were concentrated near the waterfront, behind the town dock. The back side of the hill served as 'common' lands. Newcomers fanned out along the rivers, looking for farmland and founding new settlements. Fortunes were made in the maritime trades – fishing, shipbuilding and commerce with the Old World. Well into the 18th century, Boston was the richest city in the American colonies.

But population and prosperity put pressure on Puritan principles. Modesty gave way to display. Red-brick mansions appeared on Beacon

1635	1636	1638	1675–76
The first public school, now the Boston Latin School, is founded in the Massachusetts Bay Colony, demonstrating the importance of literacy and education in the Puritan ethos.	Church leaders found a college to train ministers for their role in the theocracy. Three years later, the college is named for its first benefactor, the young minister John Harvard.	Anne Hutchinson is banished from the colony for contesting the ministers and encouraging dissent. She and her followers establish an outpost near present-day Portsmouth, Rhode Island.	Colonists engage in battle with the Wampanoag and other native tribes over the settlers' expansion and evangelism. Known as King Philip's War, the conflict devastates the indigenous population.

Hill, tables were set with fine china and silk linens, and women's shoulders were fashionably exposed.

The Church lost its monopoly on governing when the royal charter was revised to make property-holding the basis for political rights. Life in Colonial Boston increasingly felt tension between community and individual, piety and profit.

FROM EMPIRE TO INDEPENDENCE

The demands of empire kept England at war. Colonists were drawn into the fighting in the French–Indian War. Despite their victory, all the colonists got was a tax bill from the king. Covetous of New England's maritime wealth, the Crown pronounced a series of Navigation Acts, restricting colonial trade. Boston merchants conducted business as usual, except now it was on the sly.

The issue of taxation brought the clash between king and colony to a head. In the 1760s, Parliament passed the Stamp Act, the Townsend Acts and the Tea Act – all of which placed greater financial burdens on the colonists. With each new tax and toll, colonial resentment intensified, as exhibited by vocal protests and violent mobs. The acts of defiance were defended by respectable lawyer John Adams, who cited the Magna Carta's principle of 'no taxation without representation.'

To each act of rebellion, the British throne responded with increasingly severe measures, eventually dispatching Redcoat regiments known as 'regulars' to restore order and suspending all local political power.

Anne Hutchinson was a religious free-thinker who was banished from the Massachusetts Bay Colony. Hutchinson insisted on freedom of religion as a founding principle in the charter of Rhode Island, which would later influence the US Constitution.

Under siege on the street, unrepentant Bostonians went underground. The Sons of Liberty, a clandestine network of patriots, stirred up public resistance to British policy and harassed the king's loyalists. They were led by some well-known townsmen, including esteemed surgeon Dr Joseph Warren, upper-class merchant John Hancock, skilled silversmith Paul Revere and bankrupt brewer Sam Adams. Branded as treasonous rebels by the king, the Sons of Liberty became more radical and popular as the imperial grip tightened.

The resented Redcoat presence did not extinguish but rather inflamed local passions. In March 1770 a motley street gang provoked British regulars with slurs and snowballs until the troops fired into the crowd, killing five and wounding six. John Adams successfully defended the British troops, who were found to be acting in self-defense. The Sons of Liberty, however, scored a propaganda coup with their depictions of the Boston Massacre, as the incident came to be called.

1689	1700–50	1754–63	1760
The Glorious Revolution overthrows the Stuart kings. The royal governor, whose interference in local government and affiliation with the Church of England has angered the colonists, is run out of town.	Immigration to Massachusetts is spurred by the promise of land and by lucrative opportunities in fishing, shipbuilding and trade. By the middle of the century, Boston's population reaches 15,000.	The British fight over North American territory in the French–Indian War. The war debt causes the Crown to increase colonial taxes. Also, a royal proclamation restricts further western expansion.	A devastating fire starts in a local tavern and spreads throughout the city, destroying ten merchant ships in the harbor and more than 300 buildings. The city unsuccessfully seeks aid from the Crown.

SHOT HEARD ROUND THE WORLD

Until now, all but the most pugnacious of patriots would have been satisfied with colonial economic autonomy and political representation. But the king's coercive tactics aroused indignity and acrimony. Both sides were spoiling for a fight.

British General Gage was sent over with 4000 troops and a fleet of warships. Local townsfolk and yeoman farmers organized themselves into Minutemen groups, citizen militias that could mobilize in a minute. They drilled on town commons and stockpiled weapons in secret stores.

In April 1775 Gage saw the chance to break colonial resistance. Acting on a tip from a local informant, Gage dispatched 700 troops on the road west to arrest fugitives Sam Adams and John Hancock and to seize a hidden stash of gunpowder. Bostonians had their own informants, including Gage's wife, who tipped off Joseph Warren on the troop movement.

Word was then passed to the Old North Church sexton to hang two signal lanterns in the steeple. Paul Revere quietly slipped across the river into Charlestown, where he mounted Brown Beauty and galloped into the night to alert the Minutemen.

At daybreak, the confrontation finally occurred. 'Here once the embattled farmer stood,' Ralph Waldo Emerson later wrote, 'and fired the shot heard round the world.' Imperial troops skirmished with Minutemen on the Old North Bridge in Concord and the Lexington Green. By midmorning, more militia had arrived and chased the bloodied Redcoats back to Boston in ignominious defeat. The inevitable had arrived: the War for Independence.

> When royal revenue agents were sent from London to take control of the Boston customs house, they targeted one of the city's richest merchants, John Hancock, impounding his ship, *Liberty*, which was laden with undeclared cargo.

TEMPEST IN A TEAPOT

In May 1773 the British Parliament passed the Tea Act, granting a trade monopoly to the politically influential but financially troubled East India Company. In December three tea-bearing vessels arrived in Boston Harbor, but colonial merchants refused the shipments. When they tried to depart, Governor Hutchinson demanded their cargo be unloaded.

At a meeting in the Old South Church, the Sons of Liberty decided to take matters into their own hands. Disguised as Mohawk Indians, they descended on the waterfront, boarded the ships and dumped 90,000 pounds of taxable tea into the harbor.

The king's retribution was swift. Legislation was rushed through Parliament to punish Boston, 'the center of rebellious commotion in America, the ring leader in every riot.' The port was blockaded and the city placed under military rule. The Sons of Liberty spread the news of this latest outrage down the seaboard. The cause of Boston was becoming the cause of all the colonies – American Independence versus British Tyranny.

1767–68	1770	1773	1775
The British Parliament passes the Townsend Acts, a series of laws designed to enforce Crown's right to tax the colonies. Boston merchants scoff and British troops are sent to enforce the acts.	Provoked by a local gang throwing snowballs, British troops fire into a crowd, killing five people. The soldiers are later acquitted, but the incident becomes known as the Boston Massacre.	The British Parliament levies a tax on tea, which incites an angry mob to protest by raiding a merchant ship and dumping crates of tea into Boston Harbor.	British troops heed reports that colonists are stockpiling arms. Warned by Paul Revere and William Dawes, the Minutemen confront the troops in Lexington and Concord, initiating the War for Independence.

INDEPENDENCE

Boston figured prominently in the early phase of the American Revolution. In June 1775 Bostonians inflicted a hurtful blow on British morale at the Battle of Bunker Hill. The British took the hill after three tries, but their losses were greater than expected. Fighting on the front line, Dr Warren – who had achieved the rank of general – was killed by a musket shot to the head in the final British charge. A few weeks later, George Washington assumed command of the ragged Continental Army on the Cambridge Common.

Britain's military occupation of the city continued until March 1776, when Washington mounted captured British cannons on Dorchester Heights and trained them on the British fleet in Boston Harbor. Rather than see the king's expensive warships sent to the bottom, the British evacuated the city, trashing and looting as they went; Boston was liberated.

ATHENS OF AMERICA

In the early 19th century, Boston emerged as a center of enlightenment in the young republic. The city's second mayor, Josiah Quincy, led an effort to remake the city's underclass into a group of industrious and responsible citizens. He expanded public education and made the streets safer and cleaner. The 'Great Mayor' revitalized the decaying waterfront with a refurbished Faneuil Hall and the new Greek Revival marketplace, which bears his name.

Influenced by the idealistic legacy of Puritanism and revolution, Boston gave rise to the first uniquely American intellectual movement. Led by Unitarian minister Ralph Waldo Emerson, the transcendentalists shocked and challenged the Christian establishment with their belief in the inherent goodness of human nature and an emphasis on individual self-reliance to achieve spiritual fulfillment. Transcendental influences are exemplified in the romantic literature of Nathaniel Hawthorne and the civil disobedience of Henry David Thoreau. Besides philosophy, the city also became a vibrant cultural center for poetry, painting, architecture, science and scholarship, earning Boston a reputation as the 'Athens of America.'

On July 18, 1776, Bostonians first heard the Declaration of Independence read from the balcony of the Old State House, and there was much rejoicing.

FROM SAIL TO STEAM

Boston thrived during the Age of Sail. In the 17th century the infamous 'triangular trade' route was developed, involving sugar, rum and slaves. Merchants who chose not to traffic in human cargo could still make large profits by illicitly undercutting European trade monopolies

1776	1780	1813	1831
The Continental Army takes Dorchester Heights, giving them a clear shot at the Royal Navy's fleet. The British evacuate Boston on May 17; the colonies declare independence from the Crown.	Massachusetts ratifies its constitution (written mostly by John Adams), which will serve as the model for the US Constitution with its Declaration of Rights and Frame of Government.	Merchant Francis Cabot Lowell establishes the Boston Manufacturing Company for the production of cotton textiles, launching the Industrial Revolution in New England.	Abolitionist agitator William Lloyd Garrison, cofounder of the American Anti-Slavery Society, publishes the first issue of radical newspaper The Liberator from his office on Beacon Hill.

in the West Indies. In his East Boston shipyard, Donald McKay perfected the design of the clipper ship. The advent of the steam engine in the second half of the 19th century marked the decline of Boston seafaring prominence.

Early on, Boston's industry was related to overseas trading: shipbuilding, fishing and rum. Besides this, the city had small-scale artisan shops. During the war, the disruption of commerce caused acute shortages of manufactured goods. In response, some merchants shifted their investments into industry, with revolutionary results.

By the middle of the 19th century, steam power and metal machines transformed the city. Boston became the railroad hub of New England. Leather works and shoe-making factories appeared on the edge of the city. Even Paul Revere abandoned his silversmith shop and set up a rolling copper mill and foundry.

Industrial wealth transformed the landscape. The tops of hills were cropped and used for landfill to expand its size. Back Bay became a French-style neighborhood of elegant boulevards, and the South End, an English-style quarter of intimate courtyards.

What Made the Athens of America?

Museum of Fine Arts (Fenway)

Boston Symphony Orchestra (Fenway)

Trinity Church (Back Bay)

Boston Public Library (Back Bay)

BOSTON MELTING POT

For nearly two centuries, the city was ruled by a select group of leading families, collectively known as the Boston Brahmins. A reference to the exclusive ruling class in India, the self-deprecating term was coined by Oliver Wendell Holmes Sr, but was readily adopted by the caste-conscious. Their elite status was claimed through lineage to the colonial founders or through wealth from the merchant heyday. They dominated city politics and business, mimicked the style and manners of the European aristocracy, and created exclusive clubs for themselves and cultural institutions for the city.

The rapid rise of industry led to social change. The industrial workforce was initially drawn from the region's young farm women, who lived in dormitories under paternalistic supervision. The 'mill girls' were replaced by cheaper immigrant Irish labor in the 1820s. Although their numbers were still modest, the effect of immigration on local attitudes was great. The world of English-descended Whig Protestants was thrown into turmoil.

Disparaged by 'proper' Bostonians, the Irish were considered an inferior race of moral delinquents, whose spoken brogue was not endearing, but rather suggested a shoe in one's mouth. They undercut workers in the job market. Worse yet, the Irish brought the dreaded religion of pomp and popery that the Puritans so detested.

1840s

The potato famine spurs Irish immigration to Boston. The influx sparks conflict over religious and cultural differences. By the middle of the century, the Irish population reaches 35,000.

1850s

The Fugitive Slave Law requires citizens to return runaway slaves to their owners. Enforcement of this law leads to the arrests of Boston abolitionists in 1850 and 1854.

Quote from Frederick Douglass outside the African Meeting House

A potato famine back home spurred an upsurge in Irish immigration. Between 1846 and 1856 more than 1000 new immigrants stepped off the boat every month. It was a human flood tide that the city was not prepared to absorb. Anti-immigrant and anti-Catholic sentiments were shrill. The Know Nothing Party sprang up as a political expression of this rabid nativist reaction.

Subsequent groups of Italian, Portuguese and East European Jewish immigrants suffered similar indignities. By the end of the 19th century, the urban landscape resembled a mosaic of clannish ethnic enclaves.

ALL POLITICS IS LOCAL

With social change, Brahmin dominance of Boston politics slipped away. By the end of the 19th century, ethnic-based political machines wrested control of local government from the old elite.

While the Democratic Party was initially associated with rural and radical interests, it became the political instrument of the working poor. Irish immigrant neighborhoods provided ready-made voting blocs, which empowered a new type of political boss. These flamboyant populists took an activist approach to government and traded in patronage and graft.

No other Boston boss outshone James Michael Curley. He was conniving, corrupt and beloved. The Rascal King had a seemingly endless supply of holiday turkeys and city jobs for constituents, who between 1914 and 1949 elected him mayor four times and a governor and congressman once.

After more than 125 years, Massachusetts once again took center stage in national politics with John F Kennedy's election to the presidency in 1960. The youthful JFK was the pride of Boston's Irish Catholics for being the one who finally made it. Kennedy's brief Camelot inspired a new generation of Americans into public service and founded a political family dynasty that rivaled the Adams.

In 1952, Thomas 'Tip' O'Neill inherited Kennedy's recently vacated congressional seat. O'Neill climbed to the top of the legislative ladder, becoming Speaker of the House in 1977, all the while sticking to the adage that 'All Politics is Local.'

In the 1830s, rumors of licentiousness led a Protestant mob to torch the Catholic Ursuline Convent in present-day Somerville. In another incident, an Irish funeral procession met a volunteer fire company along Boston's Broad Street, and a melee ensued, leaving a row of Irish flats burned to the ground.

REFORM & RACISM

The legacy of race relations in Boston is marred by contradictions. Abolitionists and segregationists, reformers and racists have all left their mark. Massachusetts was the first colony to recognize slavery as a legal institution in 1641, and the first to abolish slavery in 1783.

1857–1900	1863	1870–76
Boston is transformed when the marshland along the Charles River's south shore is filled with landfill from the city's three hills. New neighborhoods are created: Back Bay, Kenmore and Fenway.	Local boy Robert Gould Shaw is placed in command of the 54th Massachusetts Volunteer Infantry, one of the first all-black regiments in the Union Army.	With a generous donation from the private collection of the Boston Athenaeum, the Museum of Fine Arts is established in a Gothic Revival building on Copley Sq.

Museum of Fine Arts

Boston emerged as a nucleus of the abolition movement. Newspaper publisher William Lloyd Garrison, Unitarian minister Theodore Parker and aristocratic lawyer Wendell Phillips launched the American Anti-Slavery Society to agitate public sentiment. The city provided safe houses for runaway slaves who took the Underground Railroad to freedom in Canada.

After the Civil War, many blacks rose to prominent positions in Boston society, including John S Rock, who became the first African American to practice in the US Supreme Court; John J Smith, who was elected to the Massachusetts House of Representatives; Lewis Hayden, who was elected to the Massachusetts General Court; and William DuBois, who was the first African American to receive a PhD from Harvard.

In the early 20th century manufacturing jobs attracted southern blacks as part of the Great Migration. For newcomers, the north promised refuge from racism and poverty. More than 20,000 strong, Boston's expanding black community relocated to Roxbury and the South End, where a thriving jazz and dance scene enlivened city nights. At one point, Boston was home to both Martin Luther King, a Boston University divinity student, and Malcolm X, a pool hall–hustling teenager.

Boston did not have Jim Crow laws per se, but it did have its own informal patterns of racial segregation, with African Americans as an underclass. As the city's economy declined, racial antagonism increased. In the 1970s, a judge determined that separate was not equal in the public school system. His court order to desegregate the schools through forced busing violated the sanctity of the city's ethnic neighborhoods and exposed underlying racial tensions. The school year was marked by a series of violent incidents involving students and parents, most infamously in South Boston. The experiment in racial integration was eventually abandoned, and the healing was slow.

Black History

....

African Meeting House (Beacon Hill)

....

Robert Gould Shaw Memorial (Boston Common)

....

Black Heritage Trail (Beacon Hill)

....

Copp's Hill Burying Ground (North End)

HISTORY MAKING BOSTON MODERN

MAKING BOSTON MODERN

In the mid-20th century, the city underwent a remarkable physical transformation. Two of the city's oldest neighborhoods were targeted: Scollay Sq, which was once an area bustling with theaters and music halls, but had since become a rundown red-light district; and the West End, where poor immigrants eked out an existence amid a grubby labyrinth of row houses and alleyways. Urban renewal came in the form of the grim bulldozer, which sent both neighborhoods into oblivion.

Next came the cement mixers that filled the modernist moldings of a new Government Center for Boston's sizable civil-servant sector. The centerpiece was an inverted pyramid, the monumental and cavernous

1918	1927	1960	1960s
Babe Ruth leads the Boston Red Sox to their fifth World Series victory in 15 years. He is subsequently traded to the New York Yankees, which fans will remember for the rest of the century.	Two Italian anarchists, Nicola Sacco and Bartolomeo Vanzetti, are executed on trumped-up murder charges, revealing the persistence of class and ethnic animosities.	After six years in the House of Representatives and eight years in the Senate, Boston native John F Kennedy is elected president, ushering in the era of Camelot.	In a fit of urban renewal, the city razes Scollay Sq. Over 1000 buildings are destroyed and 20,000 residents are displaced to make way for the new Government Center.

City Hall, which has since become prime evidence in the architectural case against 1960s modernism.

The city's skyline reached upwards with luxury condominiums and office buildings. The old customs tower on the waterfront, long the tallest building in town, was overtaken by the proud Prudential Tower and Henry Cobb's elegant John Hancock Tower. Boston was on the rebound.

PAST FORWARD

Since colonial times, Boston has been a champion of political equality, civil rights and social reform; and the tradition continues in the 21st century. In 2004, Boston became a battle site for gay and lesbian rights, when the country's first legally recognized gay marriage took place in Cambridge. In reaction to the queer nuptials, busloads of protesters descended on Boston, but they failed to sway the locals or overturn the ruling. By 2008, the state had recognized over 10,000 same-sex marriages.

The politics of Boston, as well as the People's Republic of Cambridge, have long been left-leaning. In 2007, Massachusetts elected Harvard grad Deval Patrick, the state's first African American governor and the country's second.

Boston would not be Boston without a major redevelopment project. The recently completed Big Dig was an unmatched marvel of civil engineering, urban planning and pork-barrel politics: the project employed the most advanced techniques of urban engineering and environmental science, in order to reroute the Central Artery underground through the center of the city. The project fell far behind schedule and went way over budget. When it finally opened in 2004, the walls leaked and a falling ceiling panel killed a motorist. The investigations and litigations over mismanagement, misappropriation and malfeasance are likely to last longer than the construction time. But now, finally, Bostonians are enjoying a quick drive to the airport and a peaceful stroll along the Rose Kennedy Greenway.

In the new millennium, nothing has inspired Bostonians' passion and pride more than their local sports teams. After more than eight decades of heartbreaking near-misses, the Boston Red Sox finally won baseball's World Series in 2004 and then again in 2007. The Red Sox shared the sports spotlight with local gridiron gladiators, the New England Patriots, who won an amazing three Super Bowls in four years from 2002 to 2005. In 2008, the Boston Celtics piled on, winning a historic 17th basketball title. And in 2011, the Boston Bruins brought home the Stanley Cup, completing the city's 'Grand Slam of American Sports.' Now that's something to cheer about.

In 1976, the city organized a triumphant bicentennial celebration, capped with spectacular fireworks and a spirited concert by the Charles River. Half a million people attended the patriotic party, including Queen Elizabeth II, who showed no hard feelings over past misunderstandings in her salute from the balcony of the Old State House.

1974	1974–76	1991–2006	2004
The city of Boston institutes a mandatory busing program in an attempt to desegregate schools. This sparks violence between black and white students and parents in Charlestown and South Boston.	Designed by Henry Cobb, the John Hancock Tower, Boston's tallest building, is built on Copley Sq. A flaw in the design is revealed when glass windowpanes crash to the ground on windy days.	The Central Artery/ Tunnel Project keeps Boston under construction for 15 years and $15 billion. Behind schedule and over budget, the project nonetheless transforms the surface of the city.	Massachusetts becomes the first state in the union to legalize same-sex marriage. The city of Cambridge becomes the first municipality to issue marriage licenses to gay and lesbian couples.

Arts & Architecture

The Puritans were a spiritual people, uninterested in such small-minded pursuits as art or music. It was not until the 19th century that Boston developed as an artistic center, earning its nickname the Athens of America. Boston can thank the Puritans, however, for founding Harvard College, and thus establishing the Boston area as a center for learning. Attracted by the intellectual atmosphere, other institutions followed suit; not only traditional universities but also art schools, music colleges, conservatories and more. To this day, the university culture enhances the breadth and depth of the city's cultural offerings.

LITERATURE

By the 19th century, the city's universities had become a magnet for writers, poets and philosophers, as well as publishers and bookstores. The local literati were expounding on social issues such as slavery, women's rights and religious reawakening. Boston, Cambridge and Concord were fertile breeding grounds for ideas, nurturing the seeds of America's literary and philosophical flowering. Ralph Waldo Emerson, Henry David Thoreau, Nathaniel Hawthorne, Louisa May Alcott and Henry Wadsworth Longfellow were born of this era. This was the Golden Age of American literature, and Boston was its nucleus.

In the 20th century, Boston continued to foster authors, poets and playwrights, but the Golden Age was over. This city was no longer the center of progressive thought and social activism that had so inspired American literature. Moral crusaders and city officials promoted stringent censorship of books, films and plays that they deemed offensive or obscene. Many writers were 'banned in Boston' – a trend that contributed to the city's image as a provincial outpost instead of a cultural capital.

Boston never regained its status as the hub of the literary solar system, but its rich legacy and ever-influential universities ensure that the city continues to contribute to American literature. Many of Boston's most prominent writers are transplants from other cities or countries, drawn to its academic and creative institutions. John Updike, Ha Jin, Jhumpa Lahiri and David Foster Wallace all came to the Boston area to study or teach at local universities.

Boston's 19th-century luminaries congregated one Saturday a month at the old Parker House. Presided over by Oliver Wendell Holmes, the Saturday Club was known for its jovial atmosphere and stimulating discourse, attracting such renowned visitors as Charles Dickens. The prestigious literary magazine *Atlantic Monthly* was born out of these meetings.

PAINTING & VISUAL ARTS

Boston began supporting a world-class artistic movement in the late 19th century, when new construction and cultural institutions required adornment. Boston's most celebrated artist is John Singer Sargent, whose murals decorate the staircases at the Museum of Fine Arts and the Boston Public Library, both of which were built during this time. Prolific sculptors Daniel Chester French and Augustus St Gaudens also left their marks in parks and public spaces all over town. During this period, Winslow Homer became famous for his paintings of the New England coast, while Childe Hassam used local cityscapes as subjects for his impressionist works.

Critics claim that Boston lost pace with the artistic world in the second half of the 20th century. But the visual arts are returning to the forefront of contemporary cultural life in the new millennium. The 2006 opening of the new ICA has shone the spotlight onto Boston's long-overshadowed

FINE ARTS

contemporary art scene. Almost in response, the Museum of Fine Arts, the Isabella Steward Gardner Museum and the Harvard Art Museums have upgraded their facilities for contemporary art with new and expanded exhibit spaces and programming. Artists are transforming the South End and the Seaport District into vibrant art districts that feed off the growing and changing art institutions.

ARCHITECTURE

After the American Revolution, Boston set to work repairing and rebuilding the city, now the capital of the Commonwealth of Massachusetts. Charles Bulfinch took responsibility for much of it, creating Faneuil Hall and the Massachusetts State House as well as private homes for Boston's most distinguished citizens.

As the city expanded, so too did the opportunities for creative art and architecture, especially with the new construction in Back Bay. Frederick Law Olmsted designed the Charles River Esplanade and the Emerald Necklace, two magnificent green spaces that snake around the city. Copley Sq represents the pinnacle of 19th-century architecture with Henry Hobson Richardson's Romanesque Trinity Church, and the Renaissance Revival Boston Public Library, designed by McKim, Mead and White.

The 20th century witnessed plenty of noteworthy additions. IM Pei is responsible for the much-hated City Hall Plaza and the much-beloved John F Kennedy Library. His partner James Cobb designed the stunning John Hancock Tower. Reflecting Trinity Church in its facade, this prominent modern tower takes its design cues from Boston's past, a recurring trope in the city.

The century closed with a remarkable project in urban planning – not building, but un-building – as parts of the Central Artery were rerouted underground and replaced by a network of green parks and plazas, the Rose Kennedy Greenway. And where the Central Artery is not hidden, it is on display, as it soars over the Charles River on the new Zakim Bunker Hill Bridge, one of the widest cable-stayed bridges in the world.

Several new buildings on the MIT campus – mainly Frank Gehry's Stata Center – have made industrial East Cambridge the city's most daring neighborhood for design of late. Meanwhile, the dramatic new space for the Institute of Contemporary Art has kicked off a spate of construction along the South Boston waterfront.

Boston artist John Singleton Copley is considered the first great American portrait painter, but he completed many of his best-known works after relocating to London (though you can see a huge collection of his works at the Museum of Fine Arts).

MUSIC

Contemporary Music

Boston has a tradition of grooving to great music. Classic rockers remember Aerosmith, the Cars and the J Geils Band. (Peter Wolf, lead singer of the J Geils Band, is frequently sighted at celebrity events around Boston.)

The pinnacle of the Boston music scene, however, is reserved for the punk rockers of the 1990s. Bostonians still pine for the Mighty Mighty Bosstones and the Pixies, the most influential of many B-town bands from this era. Nowadays, no one makes more real, honest hardcore punk than the wildly popular Dropkick Murphys, a bunch of blue-collar Irish boys from Quincy.

Boston is also home to a thriving folk tradition, thanks to the venerable nonprofit Club Passim, while the Berklee College of Music sustains a lively jazz and blues scene.

Classical Music

Possibly Boston's most venerated cultural institution, the Boston Symphony Orchestra was founded in 1881 and is rated among the world's best orchestras, thanks to the leadership of several talented conductors. It was under Serge Koussevitsky's reign that the BSO gained its world-renowned reputation, due to its radio broadcasts and its noteworthy world premieres. Seiji Ozawa, the BSO's longest-tenured maestro (1973–2002), was beloved in Boston for his passionate style. Ozawa's successor, James Levine, was known for challenging Boston audiences with a less traditional repertoire, but he resigned in 2011 due to health issues.

The Boston Pops was founded as an effort to offer audiences lighter fare, such as popular classics, marches and show tunes. Arthur Fiedler, who took the helm of the Pops in 1930, was responsible for realizing its goal of attracting more diverse audiences, thanks to free concerts on the Charles River Esplanade. The Pops' current conductor is the young, charismatic Keith Lockhart, who has reached out to audiences in new ways – namely by bringing in pop and rock singers to perform with the orchestra.

THEATER

Boston's strong Puritan roots have always exercised a stranglehold over its desire to become a world-class city, and this clash is most apparent in the city's stunted theater tradition. Only in recent years has the city developed as a destination for interesting alternative or cutting-edge theatrical productions. Nowadays, there are several excellent professional drama theater companies – namely the Huntington Theatre Company and the American Repertory Theater – which perform outside the Theater District. The Boston Center for the Arts in the South End hosts a slew of smaller companies that stage engaging and unconventional shows.

DANCE

Boston's preeminent dance company is the Boston Ballet, founded by E Virginia Williams in 1965. The current director is Mikko Nissenen, veteran of the Finnish National Ballet and the Kirov Ballet in St Petersburg, Russia. The season usually includes timeless pieces by choreographers such as Rudolph Nureyev and George Balanchine, as well as more daring work by choreographers-in-residence. And it always includes the classic performance of *The Nutcracker* at Christmas. The Boston Ballet performs at the Opera House.

The Carpenter Center on the Harvard campus is the only Le Corbusier building in the country, and across town, MIT boasts buildings by Eero Saarinen and Alvar Aalto – emblematic of how these academic institutions have enabled design prowess.

Colleges & Universities

No single element has influenced the city so profoundly as its educational institutions. Aside from the big ones mentioned here, dozens of smaller schools are located in Fenway. The residential areas west of the center (Brighton and Allston) have been dubbed the 'student ghetto.' Academic suburban sprawl means there are also excellent schools in Medford, Waltham and Wellesley, north and west of Boston.

THE BIG BOYS

Harvard University

A slew of superlatives accompany the name of this venerable institution in Cambridge. It is America's oldest university, founded in 1636. It still has the largest endowment, measuring $32 billion in 2011, despite losing almost a third of it playing the market in previous years. It is often ranked first in the list of national universities, according to *US News & World Report.* Harvard actually comprises 10 independent schools dedicated to the study of medicine, dentistry, law, business, divinity, design, education, public health and public policy, in addition to the traditional Faculty of Arts & Sciences.

Harvard Yard is the heart and soul of the university campus, with buildings dating back to its founding. But the university continues to expand in all directions. Most recently, Harvard acquired extensive land across the river in Allston, with intentions of converting this working-class residential area into a satellite campus with parkland and community services.

MIT computer scientist Joseph Carl Robnett Licklider first conceived of a 'galactic network' in the early 1960s, which would later spawn the internet.

Massachusetts Institute of Technology

At the opposite end of Mass Ave, the Massachusetts Institute of Technology (MIT) offers an interesting contrast (and complement) to Harvard. Excelling in sciences and engineering – pretty serious stuff, by most standards – MIT nonetheless does not take itself too seriously. The campus is dotted with whimsical sculptures and offbeat art, not to mention some of Boston's most daring and dumbfounding contemporary architecture. MIT students are notorious practical jokers, and their pranks usually leave the bemused public wondering 'How did they do that?'

Despite the atmosphere of fun and funniness, these smarty-pants are hard at work. The school has claimed some 77 Nobel Laureates and 52 recipients of the National Medal of Science since its founding in 1861. Some recent accomplishments include: artifically duplicating the process of photosynthesis to store solar energy; developing computer programs to decipher ancient languages; and creating an acrobatic robotic bird.

The MIT campus stretches out for about a mile along the Charles River. The university has a few museums, but it's really the art, architecture and atmosphere of innovation that make the place unique.

THE BEST OF BOSTON

Boston University

Boston University (BU) is a massive urban campus sprawling west of Kenmore Sq. BU enrolls about 30,000 undergraduate and graduate students in all fields of study. The special collections of BU's Mugar Memorial Library

A WALK ACROSS THE HARVARD BRIDGE

The Harvard Bridge – from Back Bay in Boston to MIT in Cambridge – is the longest bridge across the Charles River. It is not too long to walk, but it is long enough to do some wondering while you walk. You might wonder, for example, why the bridge that leads into the heart of MIT is named the Harvard Bridge.

According to legend, the state offered to name the bridge after Cambridge's second university. But the brainiac engineers at MIT analyzed the plans for construction and found the bridge was structurally unsound. Not wanting the MIT moniker associated with a faulty feat of engineering, it was suggested that the bridge better be named for the neighboring university up the river. That the bridge was subsequently rebuilt validated the superior brainpower of MIT.

That is only a legend, however (one invented by an MIT student, no doubt). The fact is that the Harvard Bridge was first constructed in 1891, and MIT moved to its current location only in 1916. The bridge was rebuilt in the 1980s to modernize and expand it, but the original name has stuck, at least officially. Most Bostonians actually refer to this bridge as the 'Mass Ave bridge' because, frankly, it makes more sense.

When walking across the bridge it is likely you will notice the graffiti reading: '50 smoots... 69 smoots... 100 smoots... Halfway to Hell...' At his point you might well wonder 'What is a smoot?'

A smoot is an obscure unit of measurement that was used to measure the distance of the Harvard Bridge, first in 1958 and every year since. One smoot is approximately 5ft 7in, the height of Oliver R Smoot, who was a pledge of the MIT fraternity Lambda Chi Alpha in '58. He was the shortest pledge that year. And yes, his physical person was actually used for all the measurements.

And now that you have reached the other side of the river, surely you are wondering exactly how long this bridge is. We can't say about the Harvard students, but certainly every MIT student knows that the Harvard Bridge is 364.4 smoots plus one ear.

include an outstanding 20th-century archive. Public exhibits showcase the holdings, which include the papers of Isaac Asimov, Bette Davis, Martin Luther King, Jr and more. The BU Terriers excel at ice hockey, with frequent appearances in the national college championships, the Frozen Four, as well as victories in the local Beanpot Tournament.

Boston College

Not to be confused with BU, Boston College (BC) could not be more different. BC is situated between Brighton in Boston and Chestnut Hill in the tony suburb of Newton; the attractive campus is recognizable by its neo-Gothic towers. It is home to the nation's largest Jesuit community. Its Catholic influence makes it more socially conservative and more social-service oriented than other universities. Visitors to the campus will find a good art museum and excellent Irish and Catholic ephemera collections in the library. Aside from the vibrant undergraduate population, it has a strong education program and an excellent law school. Its basketball and football teams – the BC Eagles – are usually high in national rankings.

Northeastern University

Located in the midst of student central, aka Fenway, Northeastern is a private regional university with programs emphasizing health, security and sustainability. Northeastern University (NU) boasts one of the country's largest work-study cooperative programs, whereby most students complete two or three semesters of full-time employment in addition to their eight semesters of studies. This integration of classroom learning with real-world experience is the university's strongest feature.

Since 1952, one of Boston's biggest annual sporting events is the Beanpot, a local hockey tournament – between Harvard, BU, BC and Northeastern – which takes place on the first two Mondays (men) and Tuesdays (women) in February.

ART & MUSIC SCHOOLS

Massachusetts College of Art and Design

The country's first and only four-year independent public art college was founded along with MIT and the Museum of Fine Arts in the late 19th century, when local leaders wanted to influence the state's development by promoting fine arts and technology. It seems safe to say that their long-term goal was successfully met. Nowadays, Massachusetts College of Art and Design (MassArt) offers a highly ranked art program, with specializations in industrial design, fashion design, illustration and animation, as well as the more traditional fine arts.

Berklee College of Music

Housed in and around Back Bay in Boston, Berklee is an internationally renowned school for contemporary music, especially jazz. The school was founded in 1945 by Laurence Berk (the Lee came from his son's first name). Created as an alternative to the classical agenda and stuffy attitude of traditional music schools, Berk taught courses in composition and arrangement for popular music. He wasn't big on musical theory, and emphasized learning by playing. This system was a big success and the school flourished. Among Berklee's Grammy-laden alumni are: jazz musicians Gary Burton, Al Di Meola, Keith Jarrett and Diana Krall; pop/rock artists Quincy Jones, Donald Fagen and John Mayer; and filmmaker Howard Shore.

Emerson College

Founded in 1880, Emerson is a liberal arts college that specializes in communications and the performing arts. Located in the Boston theater district, the college operates the Cutler Majestic Theatre and the Paramount Center, and its students run Boston's coolest radio station, WERS. Emerson celebs include Norman Lear, Jay Leno and Henry Winkler (better known as the Fonz).

COMEDY

Boston is a funny place, and we mean funny ha-ha. Many of Boston's famous jokesters are graduates of Emerson College, which offers scholarships and workshops specifically devoted to comedy.

Boston Bikes

For three years straight, *Bicycling* magazine put Boston on its list of 'Worst Bicycling Cities.' Old, narrow streets, weird traffic patterns and endless traffic jams – not to mention notorious scofflaw drivers – do not make for a pleasant or safe bike ride. Mayor Thomas Menino took note. In 2007, he created a new position in his city administration, Bike Czar, and hired Olympic cyclist Nicole Freedman to oversee the city's efforts to turn Boston into a world-class cycling city. Five years later, Boston is on the magazine's list of top bike-friendly cities. (It's number 25, but at least it's the right list.)

MAKING CYCLING SAFER

Bike lanes, bike lanes, bike lanes. Since implementing its cycling promotion program, Boston Bikes, the city has painted more than 50 miles of bike lanes on major and minor thoroughfares around town. And it's only getting started. The goal is a city-wide bike network that will allow cyclists to travel from one end of Boston to the other on dedicated bike lanes and paths. Most recently, Boston Bikes has replaced the parking lanes on

NICOLE FREEDMAN, DIRECTOR, BOSTON BIKES

Nicole Freedman was an Olympic and professional bike racer; since 2007 she has been Boston's Bike Czar.

Greatest Accomplishment
The launch of the New Balance Hubway program, making Boston one of only a few cities in the US to offer a bike-share program. This is a great way for tourists to get around town.

Plans for the Future
We will be introducing some more progressive facilities, like protected bike lanes and bike tracks, which are more comfortable for novice riders. We are expanding the Hubway to Cambridge, Somerville and Brookline.

Politics of Cycling
The mayor is the driving force making things happen and he is committed to transforming Boston into one of the best cycling cities in the world in a reasonable time. Already, in the last four years, we went from the worst-ranked city to one of the top-ranked cities.

Best Riding Route for Visitors
For riding downtown, there are now bike lanes along the Greenway on Commercial St and Atlantic Ave around the North End. It's also nice to ride around the Boston Common and Public Garden and into Back Bay.

The Charles River bike path and the Emerald Necklace are great rides away from the busiest part of town.

Tips for New Riders
➡ Start on an off-road path, such as the Charles River bike path.
➡ When riding in the street, avoid the 'door zone' by riding at least 3ft away from parked cars. It's OK to claim your lane.
➡ Follow local traffic laws. Ultimately, it's the same rules as for driving. Or, if you're not comfortable acting like a car, for example making a left-hand turn, you can stop and cross at the light like a pedestrian.

Massachusetts Ave with bike lanes. Cyclists are ecstatic; local car-owners who need somewhere to park, not so much.

MAKING CYCLING MORE ACCESSIBLE

Not everyone can afford a bike. Mayor Menino wanted to increase bike ridership across the board, not just among the affluent. Boston Bikes aims to promote biking as an easy, affordable transportation option for anybody.

The solution was to implement a city-wide bike-share program, the New Balance Hubway. Rolled out in 2011, it's an impressive network of 60 bicycle stations all around town. Each station is stocked with bikes that are available for short-term rental. For a few bucks, anyone can borrow a bike for an hour or a day.

In its first four months of operation, the Hubway recorded 140,000 station-to-station trips, which exceeded all expectations. The bike-share program signed up 3650 long-term members, but the majority of users were tourists or others with short-term passes.

As part of its efforts to make cycling accessible to everyone, the City of Boston has donated more than 1000 bicycles to low-income residents, has trained 7700 youth in bike skills and safety, and has offered free bike repairs at some 80 farmers markets around town.

MAKING BOSTON NICER

What's the biggest challenge facing this bike-crazed administration? Possibly, it's the car drivers. The animosity between cars and bikes in Boston would be comical if it were not so dangerous. Cyclists are vulnerable – and defensive – with no patience for cars they perceive as inattentive or unwilling to share the road. Drivers are resentful that bikes run red lights and sap precious lane space (never mind that the shortage of lane space is due to an excess of cars, not an excess of bikes).

But the car drivers do have a good point: cyclists should also follow the rules. Boston Bikes is making an effort to raise awareness all around by encouraging cyclists to learn and follow traffic laws, and encouraging drivers to notice bikes and give them space. (Bike lanes go a long way in that regard.)

Best Bike Adventures

Charles River Bike Path (Back Bay)

Minuteman Bikeway (Cambridge)

Urban AdvenTours (Transportation)

MAKING BOSTON LEANER & GREENER

A journalist asked Bike Czar Nicole Freedman what's so important about cycling. Her answer was succinct but compelling: sustainability and health. 'Every time someone drives they are contributing to climate change and obesity; go by bike and you tackle both of these issues head on.'

Freedom Trail

The best introduction to revolutionary Boston is the Freedom Trail. The red-brick path winds its way past 16 sites that earned this town its status as the cradle of liberty. The 2.5-mile trail follows the course of the conflict, from the Old State House to the Old North Church, from the Boston Common to Bunker Hill. But even though it's called the Freedom Trail, it covers much more than just revolutionary history. Here you'll find some of Boston's oldest landmarks, as well as the sites where Boston prospered in the post-revolutionary period.

❶ BOSTON COMMON

The Freedom Trail kicks off at the Boston Common (p68), America's oldest public park and the centerpiece of the city. The 50-acre green is criss-crossed with walking paths and dotted with monuments. Don't miss the powerful monument to the victims of the Boston Massacre, erected in 1888.

❷ MASSACHUSETTS STATE HOUSE

Overlooking the Boston Common from the northeast corner, the Massachusetts State House (p71) occupies a proud spot atop the city's last remaining hill – land that was previously part of John Hancock's cow pasture. Other Sons of Liberty literally had their hands in building the new capitol: Samuel Adams and Paul Revere laid the cornerstones on July 4, 1795.

❸ PARK STREET CHURCH

Just south of the State House, the soaring spire of Park Street Church (p72) has been an unmistakable landmark since 1809. The church earned the moniker 'Brimstone Corner' for its usage as a gunpowder storage place during the War of 1812 and for its fiery preaching.

❹ GRANARY BURYING GROUND

Walk north on Tremont St, where you will pass the Egyptian Revival gates of the Granary Burying Ground (p72). Steeped in history, the serene cemetery is the final resting place of many of the Sons of Liberty, as well as the victims of the Boston Massacre and other historical figures.

STEPS TO FREEDOM

1635
The Puritans establish the first public school in the home of the schoolmaster. Now the Boston Latin School, it still operates in Fenway.

1688
Amid much wrangling with the local leadership, King's Chapel is founded as an Anglican congregation in Puritan Boston.

March 5, 1770
The Boston Massacre is the first violent conflict leading up to the War for Independence.

December 16, 1773
Angry protesters have a Tea Party, storming out of the Old South Meeting House, raiding a merchant ship docked nearby and dumping crates of tea overboard.

April 18, 1775
The sexton hangs two lanterns in the Old North Church to signal the Redcoats' route to Concord. Paul Revere rides from his home on North Sq to warn the patriots of the Redcoats' approach.

June 17, 1775
The Battle of Bunker Hill inflicts significant damage to British troops both physically and psychologically.

July 18, 1776
The Declaration of Independence is read for the first time in Boston, from the balcony of the Old State House.

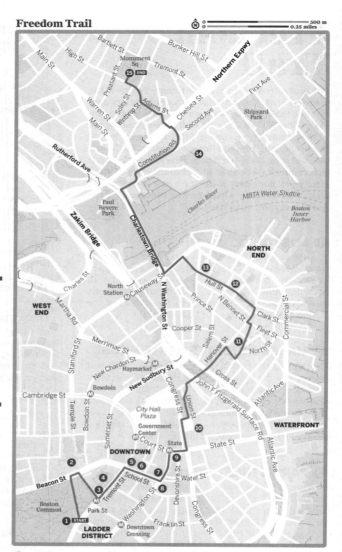

Freedom Trail

The Boston Common is site of the Great Elm, which was not only a rallying place for the Sons of Liberty, but also a popular spot for hanging religious heretics during Puritan times. Ironic.

❺ KING'S CHAPEL & BURYING GROUND

Continue north to School St, where the Georgian King's Chapel (p86) overlooks its adjacent burying ground. It is perhaps an odd choice for inclusion on the Freedom Trail, since it was founded as an Anglican Church in 1688. It does contain a large bell crafted by Paul Revere, and the prestigious Governor's pew, once occupied by George Washington.

❻ SITE OF THE FIRST PUBLIC SCHOOL

Turn east on School St, and take note of the bronze statue of Benjamin Franklin outside Old City Hall (p86). A plaque commemorates this spot as the site of the first public school. Enter the courtyard to discover some of the school's distinguished alumni and some quirky artwork.

❼ OLD CORNER BOOKSTORE

Continue down School St to Washington St, where the little brick building is known as the Old Corner Bookstore (p86), a literary and intellectual hotspot for 75 years. Strangely, now it is an option for lunch if you're in the mood for Mexican fast food.

❽ OLD SOUTH MEETING HOUSE

Kitty-corner across Washington St, the Old South Meeting House (p87) saw the beginnings of one of the American Revolution's most vociferous protest, the Boston Tea Party. Come off the street and listen to a re-enactment of what went down that day.

❾ OLD STATE HOUSE

Before the revolution, the seat of the Massachusetts government was the Old State House (p84), a red-brick colonial building that is now surrounded by modern buildings and busy streets. Dodge the traffic to inspect the cobblestone circle that marks the site of the Boston Massacre, the revolution's first violent conflict in 1770; gaze up at the balcony, where the Declaration of Independence was first read to Bostonians.

❿ FANEUIL HALL

Nearly every visitor to Boston stops at Quincy Market to grab a beer or shop for souvenirs, but most bypass historic Faneuil Hall (p85), the original market and public meeting place that was built in 1740. Pause to admire the bronze statue of Samuel Adams, who sits astride his horse in Dock Square. Then ascend to the 2nd-floor hall, where Adams was one of many orators to speak out against the British rule.

⓫ PAUL REVERE HOUSE

From Faneuil Hall, cross the Rose Kennedy Greenway and head into the heart of the North End. Turn east on Richmond St and you will find yourself in charming North Sq, once home to Paul Revere. The weathered clapboard house – the Paul Revere House (p56) – is the oldest example in Boston, as most other wooden construction was destroyed by the fires that ravaged the city. This is likely where Paul Revere commenced his famous midnight ride.

1797
The 44-gun USS *Constitution* is launched from a Boston shipyard, just in time for victorious battles in the new nation's first naval wars.

1798
Symbolic of the new state, the new Massachusetts State House becomes the seat of government for the Commonwealth.

FREEDOM TRAIL SITE OF THE FIRST PUBLIC SCHOOL

Pay your respects to Paul Revere at the Granary Burying Ground; but the politically-savvy silversmith was not the only patriot who rode to Lexington and Concord. He was joined by young William Dawes, buried in King's Chapel Burying Ground, and Samuel Prescott, buried in Concord.

BATTLE OF BUNKER HILL

⑫ OLD NORTH CHURCH

Back on Hanover St, walk two blocks north to Paul Revere Mall. Besides a dramatic statue of the patriot himself, this park also provides a lovely vantage point to view your next destination, the Old North Church (p55). In addition to playing a crucial revolutionary role, the 1723 church is also Boston's oldest house of worship. Take a breather in the delightful gardens behind the church.

⑬ COPP'S HILL BURYING GROUND

From the church, head west on Hull St to Copp's Hill Burying Ground (p57). This quiet corner contains some of the city's oldest gravestones and offers grand views across the river to Charlestown. See if you can find the headstone of Daniel Malcolm, which is littered with bullet holes from British troops who apparently took offense at his epitaph. Incidentally, little is known about Malcolm's actual role in protests or revolution; historical records only show that he was arrested for failing to pay duty on 60 casks of wine.

⑭ USS CONSTITUTION

Continue west on Hull St to its end. Turn left on Commercial St and walk across the Charlestown Bridge. Turning right on Constitution Rd brings you to the Charlestown Navy Yard, home of the world's oldest commissioned warship, the USS *Constitution* (p46). Board the ship for a tour of the upper decks, where you will learn about its exploits in America's earliest naval battles.

⑮ BUNKER HILL MONUMENT

Walk through the winding cobblestone streets up to the 220ft granite obelisk that is the Bunker Hill Monument (p48). Check out the dioramas in the museum to better understand what transpired on that fateful day in June 1775, when the Battle of Bunker Hill took place. Then climb 295 steps to the top of the monument to enjoy the panorama of the city, the harbor and the North Shore.

Turns out the so-called Battle of Bunker Hill actually took place on Breed's Hill, which is where the monument stands today.

Survival Guide

Transportation

GETTING TO BOSTON

Most travelers arrive in Boston by airplane, with many national and international flights in and out of Logan International Airport. Two smaller regional airports – Manchester Airport in New Hampshire and TF Green Airport near Providence, Rhode Island – offer alternatives that are also accessible to Boston and are sometimes less expensive.

Most trains operated by **Amtrak** (☑800-872-7245; www.amtrak.com; South Station) go in and out of South Station. Boston is the northern terminus of the Northeast Corridor, which sends frequent trains to New York (4½ hours), Philadelphia (six hours) and Washington DC (eight hours). The Lakeshore Express goes daily to Buffalo (12 hours) and Chicago (23 hours), while the Downeaster goes from North Station to Portland, Maine (2½ hours, five daily).

Buses are most useful for regional destinations, although **Greyhound** (☑617-526-1800, 800-231-2222; www.greyhound.com) operates services around the country. In recent years there has been a spate of new companies (p221) offering super-cheap (and sometimes efficient) services to New York City (four to five hours).

Flights, tours and rail tickets can be booked online at www.lonelyplanet.com.

Logan International Airport

On MA 1A in East Boston, **Logan International Airport** (☑800-235-6426; www.massport.com/logan) has five separate terminals that are connected by the frequent shuttle bus 11.

Downtown Boston is just a few miles from Logan International Airport and is accessible by subway (the T), water shuttle and taxi.

Silver Line Bus

The silver line is the MBTA's 'bus rapid transit service.' It travels between Logan International Airport and South Station, with stops in the Seaport District. Silver line buses pick up at the airport terminals and connect directly to the subway station, so you don't have to buy another ticket for the T.

This is the most convenient way to get into the city if you are staying in the Seaport District or Chinatown, or anywhere along the red line (Downtown, Beacon Hill, Cambridge). Prices and hours are the same as the T.

Subway

The T, or the **MBTA subway** (☑617-222-3200, 800-392-6100; www.mbta.com; per ride $1.70-2; ☺5:30am-12:30am), is a fast and cheap way to reach the city from the airport. From any terminal, take a free, well-marked shuttle bus (22 or 33) to the blue-line T station called Airport and you'll be downtown within 30 minutes.

Boat

Several water shuttles operate between Logan and the Boston waterfront. In both cases, fares to the North End and Charlestown are twice as much as fares to downtown. Take the free water transportation shuttle bus No 66 from the airport terminal to the ferry dock.

City Water Taxi (www.citywatertaxi.com; Long Wharf; one-way/round-trip $10/17; ☺7am-10pm Mon-Sat, to 8pm Sun) Use the checkerboard call box at Logan dock to summon the water taxi.

Rowes Wharf Water Transport (☑617-406-8584; www.roweswharfwatertransport.com; Rowes Wharf; one way/round trip $10/17; ☺7am-10pm Mon-Sat, to 8pm Sun Apr-Nov, 7am-7pm daily Dec-Mar) Offers a zero-emissions service.

Car

If you're driving from the airport into Boston or to points north of the city, the Sumner Tunnel ($3.50 toll) will lead you to Storrow Dr or over the Zakim Bridge to I-93 North. To points south of Boston, use the Ted Williams Tunnel ($3.50) to I-93 South. To or from points west, the Mass Pike connects directly with the Ted Williams Tunnel. When you're heading to the airport from downtown Boston, take the Callahan Tunnel. All three tunnels are off I-93 and free when heading inbound.

Manchester Airport

A quiet alternative to Logan, **Manchester Airport** (☑603-624-6556; www.flymanchester. com) is just 55 miles north of Boston in New Hampshire.

Flight Line Inc (☑800-245-2525; www.flightlineinc.com; 1/2/3/4 people $39/49/59/59; ⊙9am-11pm) This shuttle runs every 30 minutes from Manchester Airport to Boston Logan. Reservations recommended.

TF Green Airport

Just outside the city of Providence (Rhode Island), **TF Green Airport** (www.pvd airport.com) is also serviced by major carriers. Southwest Airlines, in particular, offers very competitively priced tickets.

The airport is one hour south of Boston. The **MBTA commuter rail** (☑800-392-6100, 617-222-3200; www. mbta.com) travels between TF Green Airport and South Station ($8.25, 90 minutes, 10 daily), with stops at Ruggles and Back Bay stations along the way.

South Station

South Station is a stop on the red line of the T. It is also the junction where the silver line buses connect to the subway system.

GETTING AROUND BOSTON

For a city of its stature, Boston is geographically small and logistically manageable. The sights and activities of

FROM NEW YORK TO BOSTON BY BUS

The infamous 'Chinatown Buses' originated in the late 1990s as a cheap way for Chinese workers to travel to and from jobs. They offered super cheap-tickets between Boston and New York, traveling from Chinatown to Chinatown. Young, savvy travelers caught wind of the bargain transportation, and the phenomenon began to spread. It was crowded and confusing and probably not that safe, but it sure was cheap.

In recent years, more and more companies are running buses on this route. With competition come improved service and safety records. They don't always start and end in Chinatown. Many offer free wireless service on board. But the prices remain blissfully low.

➡ **Boston Deluxe** (www.bostondeluxe.com; 177 Huntington Ave, Christian Science Plaza; one-way $15; ⓂPrudential) Not technically a Chinatown bus, since it departs from Back Bay, but still cheap. Travels by way of Hartford, Connecticut.

➡ **Fung Wah Bus Company** (www.fungwahbus.com; South Station; one-way $15; ⓂSouth Station) The original Chinatown bus.

➡ **Lucky Star Bus** (www.luckystarbus.com; South Station; one-way $1-20; ☎; ⓂSouth Station) Reserve way in advance for the cheapest tickets (really $1).

➡ **Megabus** (www.megabus.com; South Station; one way $1-24; ☎; ⓂSouth Station) The one-dollar tickets are very limited, but with minimal foresight you can get your fare for $10 or less.

➡ **Worldwide Bus** (www.worldwidebus.com; Alewife Brook Pkwy, Cambridge; one-way $25; ☎; ⓂAlewife) Departs from Alewife station in Cambridge.

principal interest to travelers are contained within an area that's only about 1 mile wide by 3 miles long.

This makes Boston a wonderful walking or cycling city. Otherwise, most of the main attractions are accessible by subway (or the 'T'). Some outlying sites require a bus ride. And a few – namely the Boston Harbor Islands – require a boat ride or two.

Incidentally, Boston is a waterside city, and riding in boats is part of the fun. Water shuttles are a convenient transportation option for a few harborside destinations, including the airport.

Bicycle

In recent years, Boston has made vast improvements in its infrastructure for cyclists, including painting miles of bicycle lanes, upgrading bike facilities on and around public transportation and implementing a cutting-edge bike-share program.

Many students, commuters and messenger services get around by bike. Boston drivers are used to sharing the roads with their two-wheeled friends (and they are used to arriving *after* their two-wheeled friends, who are less impeded by traffic snarls). Cyclists should always obey traffic rules and ride defensively.

The Hubway

Boston's brand new bike-share program (sponsored by New Balance, as you will be repeatedly reminded) is the **Hubway** (www.thehubway.com; 1/3-day membership $5/12, 30-min free, 60/90/120-min $2/6/14; ⊙24hr). There are now 60 Hubway stations around town, stocked with 600 bikes that are available for short-term loan. Purchase a temporary membership at any bicycle kiosk, then pay by the half-hour for the use of the bikes (free under 30 minutes). Return the bike to any station in the vicinity of your destination. Check the website for a map of Hubway stations.

The Hubway pricing is designed so a bike ride can substitute for a cab ride (eg to make a one-way trip or run an errand), not for leisurely riding or long trips, which would be expensive. Lower usage rates are available to committed riders who sign up for a one-year membership.

Bikes on the MBTA

You can bring bikes on the T, the bus and the commuter rail for no additional fare. Bikes are not allowed on green-line trains or silver-line buses, nor are they allowed on any trains during rush hour (7am to 10am and 4pm to 7pm, Monday to Friday). Bikes are not permitted inside buses, but most MBTA buses have bicycle racks on the outside.

Bicycle Rental

Urban AdvenTours (www.urbanadventours.com; 103 Atlantic Ave; per day $35; ⊙9am-6pm Mon-Sat; ⓂAquarium) Bikes available for rental include road bikes and mountain bikes in addition to the standard hybrids. For an extra fee these guys will bring your bike to your doorstep in a BioBus powered by vegetable oil.

Cambridge Bicycle (www.cambridgebicycle.com; 259 Massachusetts Ave; per day/week $30/$150; ⊙10am-7pm Mon-Sat, noon-6pm Sun; ⓂCentral) Convenient for cycling along the Charles River. Rentals are three-speed commuter bikes – nothing fancy but solid for city riding.

Bicycle Exchange (www.cambridgebicycleexchange.com; 2067 Massachusetts Ave; per day/week $25/100; ⊙9am-6pm Tue-Sat, noon-5pm Sun; ⓂPorter) This bike shop is located just north of Porter Sq, convenient to the Minuteman Bikeway.

Bus

The **MBTA** (☑617-222-5215; www.mbta.com) operates bus routes within the city. These can be difficult to figure out for the short-term visitor, but schedules are posted on its website and at some bus stops along the routes. The standard bus fare is $1.50, or $1.25 with a Charlie Card. If you're transferring from the T on a Charlie Card the bus fare is free.

The silver line, a so-called 'rapid' bus, starts at Downtown Crossing and runs along Washington St in the South End to Roxbury's Dudley Sq. Another route goes from South Station to the Seaport District, then under the harbor to Logan International Airport. This waterfront route costs $2 ($1.70 with a Charlie Card), instead of the normal bus fare.

The silver line is different from the regular MBTA buses because it drives in a designated lane (supposedly reducing travel time). More importantly, the silver line starts/terminates inside the South Station or Downtown Crossing subway terminal, so you can transfer to/from the T without purchasing an additional ticket.

Boat

While boats will likely not be your primary means of transportation, they are useful for a few destinations, primarily the Boston Harbor Islands and Charlestown. Ferries to Provincetown and Salem provide a pleasant transportation alternative for day trips out of the city. There is also a water-shuttle service (p220) to the airport.

Subway (The T)

The **MBTA** (☑800-392-6100, 617-222-3200; www.mbta.com) operates the USA's oldest subway, built in 1897 and known locally as the 'T.' There are four lines – red, blue, green and orange – that radiate from the principal downtown stations: Downtown Crossing, Government Center, Park St and State. When traveling away from any of these stations, you are heading 'outbound.' Although the MBTA might like you to believe otherwise, the silver line is a bus line with a dedicated traffic lane – not a subway line.

Tourist passes with unlimited travel (on subway, bus or water shuttle) are available for periods of one week ($15) and one day ($9). Kids under 11 ride for free. Passes may be purchased at the Boston Welcome Center on Tremont St and at the following T stations: Park St, Government Center, Back Bay, Alewife, Copley, Quincy Adams, Harvard, North Station, South Station, Hynes and Airport. For longer stays, you can buy a monthly pass allowing unlimited use of the subway and local bus ($59). Otherwise, buy a paper fare card ($2 per ride) or a Charlie Card ($1.70 per ride) at all stations.

The T operates from approximately 5:30am to 12:30am. The last red-line trains pass through Park St at about 12:30am (depending on the direction), but all T stations and lines are different: check the posting at the station.

Taxi

Cabs are plentiful but expensive. Rates are determined by the meter, which calculates miles. Expect to pay about $12 to $18 between most tourist points within the city limits, without much traffic. If you have any trouble hailing a cab, head to any nearby hotel, where they congregate. Recommended taxi companies:

Chill Out First Class Cab (☑617-212-3763)

Cabbie's Cab (☑617-547-2222; www.cabbiescab.com)

PlanetTran (☑617-756-8876; www.planettran.com) An environmentally friendly service using hybrid vehicles

Green & Yellow Cab (☑617-628-0600; www.green andyellowcab.com)

Train

The **MBTA commuter rail** (☑800-392-6100, 617-222-3200; www.mbta.com) services destinations in the metropolitan Boston area. Trains heading west and north of the city, including to Concord and Salem, leave from bustling North Station on Causeway St. Trains heading south, including to Plymouth, leave from South Station.

TOURS

Bicycle Tours

Urban AdvenTours (Map p248; ☑office 617-233-7595; www.urbanadventours.com; 103 Atlantic Ave; tours $50; ♿; Ⓜ Aquarium) Founded by avid cyclists who believe the best views of Boston are from a bicycle. The City View Ride

CHARLIE ON THE MTA

Did he ever return?
No, he never returned
And his fate is still unlearned
He may ride forever
'Neath the streets of Boston
He's the man who never returned.

Immortalized by the Kingston Trio, Charlie's sad story was that he could not get off the Boston T because he did not have the exit fare.

Now Charlie has been immortalized – yet again – by the MBTA's fare system: the Charlie Card. The plastic cards are available from the attendant at any T station. Once you have a card, you can add money at the automated fare machines; at the turnstile you will be charged $1.70 per ride.

The system is designed to favor commuters and cardholders. If you do not request a Charlie Card, you can purchase a paper fare card from the machine, but the turnstile will charge you $2 per ride. Similarly, Charlie Card–holders pay $1.25 to ride the bus, while cash-holders pay $1.50.

provides a great overview of how to get around by bike, but there are other specialty tours such as Bikes at Night and Bike & Brew Tour.

Boat Tours

Boston Green Cruises (Map p252; www.bostongreen cruises.com; 60 Rowes Wharf; adult/child from $28/24; ♿; Ⓜ Aquarium or South Station) See the sights and hear the sounds of the city from Boston's first super quiet, zero-emissions electric boat. Spend an hour floating in the Boston Harbor or cruising on the River Charles (or upgrade to a 90-minute combo trip for adult/child $39/35).

Boston Duck Tours (Map p260; www.bostonducktours. com; adult/child/senior $33/22/27; ♿; Ⓜ Prudential or Science Park) These ridiculously popular tours use WWII amphibious vehicles that cruise the downtown streets before splashing into the Charles River. Tours depart from the

Museum of Science or from behind the Prudential Center. Reserve in advance.

Boston Harbor Cruises (Map p252; www.boston harborcruises.com; 1 Long Wharf; Ⓜ Aquarium) Boston Harbor Cruises offers a slew of options for those who want to get out on the water, from a Historic Sightseeing Tour around the Inner Harbor (adult/child/senior $23/19/21) to an all-day Lighthouse Tour that goes out to Boston Light (adult/child/senior $67/57/62). River rats might prefer the Charles River & Locks Tour (adult/child/senior $23/19/21), a 90-minute loop around the whole of the Shawmut Peninsula.

Trolley Tours

Overheard on a Duck Tour: 'Trolleys can go in the water too...once.' That said, trolley tours offer great flexibility because you can hop off at sites along the route and hop on the next trolley that comes along. All trolleys offer discounts for online purchase.

Upper Deck Trolley Tours (Map p252; www.bostonsupertrolleytours.com; adult/child/senior $36/17/32; ⊕; Ⓜ Aquarium) Super-tall trolleys give passengers a view over the traffic. This is the only trolley tour that goes to Cambridge. The ticket – which is good for two days – also includes admission to a few museums.

Old Town Trolley Tours (Map p252; www.historictours.com; Long Wharf; adult/child/senior $42/16/39; ⊕; Ⓜ Aquarium) The price includes free admission to the Old State House and a free Boston Harbor cruise.

Ghosts & Gravestones (Map p252; www.ghostsandgravestones.com; Long Wharf; adult/child $38/24; ⊕; Ⓜ Aquarium) A hair-raising tour telling tales of Boston's darker side, hosted by a cursed gravedigger.

Walking Tours

The granddaddy of walking tours in Boston is the **Freedom Trail**, a 2½-mile trail that traverses the city from the Boston Common to Charlestown. Most of the companies listed here lead tours of the Freedom Trail, as does the **National Park Service** (Map p252; www.nps.gov/bost; Faneuil Hall; ⊙10am & 2pm Apr-Nov; ⊕; Ⓜ State). Tours that focus on a particular neighborhood are covered in their respective neighborhood chapters.

Boston by Foot (www.bostonbyfoot.com; tours $8-15; ⊕) This fantastic nonprofit offers 90-minute walking tours, with specialty theme tours like Literary Landmarks, Boston Underfoot (with highlights from the Big Dig and the T) and Boston for Little Feet – a kid-friendly version of the Freedom Trail.

Photo Walks (www.photowalks.com; adult/youth $30/15; ⊕) A walking tour combined with a photography lesson. Different routes cover

Boston's most photogenic neighborhoods.

Freedom Trail Foundation (www.thefreedomtrail.org) This educational nonprofit group leads excellent tours of the Freedom Trail, broken up into bite-size portions (eg Boston Common to Faneuil Hall, North End, etc). Frequent departures from Faneuil Hall and Boston Common make this a convenient option. Tour guides are in period costume too.

On Location Tours (www.screentours.com; tours $22) More than 30 films were shot along Boston's Movie Mile, which you will see along this 90-minute walking tour. For even more movie madness, the company offers a three-hour bus tour that visits 40-plus sites.

Boston Chocolate Tours (www.bostonchocolatetours.com; tours $48) If you believe 'the best things in life are chocolate,' then pick a neighborhood and let the experts show you where to sate your craving.

Directory
A–Z

Business Hours

→ **Banks** 8:30am to 4pm Monday to Friday; sometimes to 6pm on Friday and/or 9am to noon on Saturday

→ **Bars & Clubs** Open to midnight daily, and often stay open to 1am or 2am on Friday and Saturday nights

→ **Businesses** 9am to 5pm Monday to Friday

→ **Restaurants** 11am or 11:30am to 9pm or 10pm; restaurants serving breakfast open from 7am; some places close from 2:30pm to 5:30pm

→ **Shops** From 10am or 11am until 6pm or 7pm, Monday to Saturday; sometimes noon to 5pm Sunday. Major shopping areas and malls keep extended hours.

Customs Regulations

For up-to-date information, see www.customs.gov.

→ **Alcohol & Tobacco** Each visitor is allowed to bring 1L of liquor and 200 cigarettes duty-free into the US, but you must be at least 21 and 18 years of age, respectively.

→ **Gift Items** In addition, each traveler is permitted to bring up to $100 worth of gift merchandise into the US without incurring any duty.

Discount Cards

Thanks to its student-heavy population, Boston is one of the few US cities that usually offers students discounted admission, so bring your student ID and always inquire.

Other programs that offer discounted admission to area museums and attractions:

→ **Go Select Boston Pass** (www.smartdestinations.com; prices variable) Pick a package or design your own, choosing two or more sites from the 31 included options. You have 30 days to use your pass, which usually results in a savings of around 20%.

→ **Boston City Pass** (www.citypass.com; adult/child $46/29) Includes admission to five popular spots: Museum of Fine Arts, Museum of Science, New England Aquarium and Skywalk Observatory and either the John F Kennedy Library & Museum or the Harvard Museum of Natural History. You have nine days for a busy week, but if you use them all, you'll save $40.

→ **Go Boston Card** (www.smartdestinations.com; adult/child 1 day $48/32, 3 days $88/72, 7 days $148/112) This card allows unlimited admission to over 60 Boston-area attractions, including most museums, tours and historic sites, and up to 20% restaurant and retail discounts. The card is good for one to seven days, depending on what you pay. In reality, you have to have a pretty ambitious itinerary to make this worthwhile.

PRACTICALITIES

→ **Radio** Boston is blessed with two public radio stations – WGBH (89.7FM) and WBUR (90.9FM) – broadcasting news, classical music and radio shows. For sports talk radio all the time, tune into 850AM.

→ **Weights & Measures** US customary units are based on imperial units, measuring distance by mile, weight by pound and volume by pint, quart or gallon.

→ **Smoking** No smoking in Boston hotels, restaurants or bars. Cambridge hotels may reserve a few rooms for smokers, but it is banned in Boston.

→ **Currency** The US dollar ($) is divided into 100 cents. Coins come in denominations of 1¢ (penny), 5¢ (nickel), 10¢ (dime), 25¢ (quarter) and the rare 50¢ piece (half-dollar). Banknotes come in $1, $2, $5, $10, $20, $50 and $100 denominations.

Electricity

120v/60hz

120v/60hz

Emergencies

→ **Ambulance/police/fire** (☎911)

Gay & Lesbian Travelers

Out and active gay communities are visible all around Boston, especially in the South End and Jamaica Plain, and in the nearby town of Provincetown. Stop by **Calamus Bookstore** (Map p258; www.calamusbooks.com; 92 South St; ⊗9am-7pm Mon-Sat, noon-6pm Sun; ⓂSouth Station), which is an excellent source of information about community events and organizations.

There is no shortage of entertainment options catering to GLBT travelers. From drag shows to dyke nights, this sexually diverse community has something for everybody.

The biggest event of the year for the Boston gay and lesbian community is June's **Boston Pride**, a week of parades, parties, festivals and flag-raisings.

Other excellent sources of information for the gay and lesbian community:

→ **Bay Windows** (www.baywindows.com)

→ **EDGE Boston** (www.edgeboston.com)

Internet Access

Most hotels and hostels offer internet access in one way or another. Usually that means wireless access (indicated by the 🛜 icon in the listings), though some hotels also have an on-site business center or internet corner which provides computers (indicated by the @ icon).

Aside from hotels, wireless access is common at cafes, on buses and even in public spaces like shopping malls and airports. Many cafes charge a fee, though they may offer the first hour free of charge. Again, look for the 🛜 icon in the listings.

→ **Boston Public Library** (www.bpl.org; 700 Boylston St; access free; ⊗9am-9pm Mon-Thu, 9am-5pm Fri & Sat, 1-5pm Sun Oct-May only; @🛜; ⓂCopley) Internet access free for 15-minute intervals. Or get a visitor courtesy card at the circulation desk and sign up for one hour of free terminal time. Arrive first thing in the morning to avoid long waits.

→ **Cambridge Public Library** (www.cambridgema.gov/cpl; 449 Broadway; ⊗9am-9pm Mon-Thu, 9am-5pm Fri and Sat; @🛜; ⓂHarvard) The sparkling new glass library has dozens of zippy computers that are free to the public. It's a busy place so you may have to wait your turn.

→ **Wired Puppy** (www.wiredpuppy.com; 250 Newbury St; ⊗6:30am-8pm; @🛜; ⓂHynes) This cafe offers free wireless access and free computer use in case you don't have your own. This is also a comfortable, cozy place to just come and drink coffee.

→ **Tech Superpowers Digilounge** (http://techsuperpowers.com/digilounge; 252 Newbury St; $3 per 15min; ⊗9am-7pm Mon-Fri, 11am-4pm Sat; @🛜; ⓂHynes) Internet cafe that rents out Macs fully loaded with Skype and other useful stuff.

Money

ATMs

Automatic teller machines (ATMs) are great for quick cash influxes and can negate the need for traveler's checks entirely, but watch out for ATM surcharges. Most banks in Boston charge at least $1.50 per withdrawal.

The Cirrus and Plus systems both have extensive ATM networks that will give cash advances on major credit cards and allow cash withdrawals with affiliated ATM cards. Look for ATMs outside banks and in large grocery stores, shopping centers and gas stations.

Changing Money

If you are carrying foreign currency, it can be exchanged for US dollars at Logan International Airport.

Bank outlets around the city are not so reliable about offering currency exchange, but this service is provided at any full-service branch of the **Bank of America** (www.bankofamerica.com).

Credit Cards

Major credit cards are accepted at hotels, restaurants, gas stations, shops and car-rental agencies. In fact, you'll find it hard to perform certain transactions, such as renting cars or purchasing concert tickets, without one. Some small B&Bs and family-owned shops and restaurants may not accept credit cards (noted in reviews where relevant). Visa and MasterCard are the most widely accepted.

Tipping

Many members of the service industry depend on tips to earn a living. Servers and bartenders, in particular, get paid less than minimum wage in the US, so tips constitute their wages. Use the following guidelines for tipping your service providers:

➡ **Baggage carriers** $1 to $2 per bag

➡ **Bar & restaurant staff** 20% for good service; 15% for adequate service; any less than 15% indicates dissatisfaction with the service.

➡ **Housekeeping** $3 to $5 for one or two nights, more for longer stays

➡ **Taxi drivers** 10% to 15%

Traveler's Checks

Traveler's checks provide protection from theft and loss. Most companies now offer a convenient Traveler's Check Card, a prepaid card that is not linked to a bank account. For refunds on lost or stolen traveler's checks or cards, call **American Express** (📞800-221-7282; www.americanexpress.com) or **Thomas Cook** (📞800-713-3424). Keeping a record of check numbers and those you have used is vital for replacing lost checks, so keep your records separate from the checks themselves. Traveler's checks are as good as cash in the US, but only if they are in US dollars.

Newspapers & Magazines

➡ **Boston Globe** (www.boston.com) The *Globe,* One of two major daily newspapers, publishes an extensive Calendar section every Thursday and the daily Sidekick, both of which include entertainment options.

➡ **Boston Herald** (www.bostonherald.com) The more right-wing daily, competing with the Globe; has its own Scene section published every Friday.

➡ **Boston Magazine** (www.bostonmagazine.com) The city's monthly glossy magazine.

➡ **Boston Phoenix** (www.bostonphoenix.com) The free, 'alternative' paper that focuses on arts and entertainment; published weekly.

➡ **Improper Bostonian** (www.improper.com) A sassy biweekly distributed free from sidewalk dispenser boxes.

➡ **Stuff@Night** (www.stuffatnight.com) A free, offbeat bi-weekly publication focusing on entertainment events.

Public Holidays

New Year's Day January 1

Martin Luther King Jr's Birthday Third Monday in January

Presidents' Day Third Monday in February

Evacuation Day March 17

Patriot's Day Third Monday in April

Memorial Day Last Monday in May

Independence Day July 4

Labor Day First Monday in September

Columbus Day Second Monday in October

Veterans Day November 11

Thanksgiving Day Fourth Thursday in November

Christmas Day December 25

Safe Travel

As with most big US cities, there are run-down sections of Boston in which crime is a problem. These are primarily in Roxbury, Mattapan and Dorchester (where tourist attractions are limited). Parts of the South End border Roxbury, as does Jamaica Plain.

➡ In the South End, avoid areas southeast of Harrison Ave and southwest of Massachusetts Ave after dark.

➡ In Jamaica Plain, stay on the west side of Hyde Park Ave, Washington St and Columbus Ave at night.

➡ Avoid parks such as Franklin Park and the Back Bay Fens after dark. The same goes for streets and subway stations that are otherwise empty of people.

Taxes & Refunds

The state of Massachusetts charges a 5% sales tax on all items that are not considered necessities. Foodies and fashionistas will be happy to hear that food (purchased from a store, not a restaurant) and clothing (up to $175) are indeed considered necessities!

In addition to the 5% sales tax, hotel rooms are subject to a 12.45% tax in Boston and Cambridge (which includes a city and state hotel tax, as well as a convention center tax). B&Bs with three rooms or fewer are exempt from this tax.

Telephone

Phone Codes

➡ **Area codes** Boston ✍617; Suburban Boston ✍781; North Shore ✍978; South Shore ✍508

➡ **Country code** ✍1 for USA

➡ **International dialing code** ✍011

All US phone numbers consist of a three-digit area code followed by a seven-digit local number. Even if you are calling locally, you must dial all 10 digits. If you are calling long distance, dial ✍1 + area code + seven-digit number.

Cell Phones

The US uses a variety of cell-phone systems, most of which are incompatible with the GSM 900/1800 standard used throughout Europe and Asia. The main cell-phone companies that have extensive coverage in Boston and around New England are **Cingular** (www.cingular.com), **Sprint** (www.sprint.com) and **Verizon** (www.verizon.com), which have outlets around Boston (see their websites for details).

Time

Boston is on Eastern Standard Time, five hours behind Greenwich Mean Time. When it's noon in Boston, it's:

➡ 9am in San Francisco

➡ 5pm in London

➡ 9pm in Moscow

➡ 2am in Tokyo

➡ 4am in Melbourne

This region observes daylight saving time from the second Sunday in March until the first Sunday in November.

Tourist Information

Boston Common Information Kiosk (GBCVB Visitors Center; www.bostonusa.com; Boston Common; ⊙8:30am-5pm; ⓜPark St) Starting point for the Freedom Trail and many other walking tours.

➡ **Boston Harbor Islands Pavilion** (www.boston harborislands.org; Rose Kennedy Greenway; ⊙9am-5pm May-Oct; ⓜAquarium) Ideally located on the Rose Kennedy Greenway, this information center will tell you everything you need to know to plan your visit to the Boston Harbor Islands.

➡ **Cambridge Visitor Information Kiosk** (www.cambridge-usa.org; Harvard Sq; ⊙9am-5pm Mon-Sat & 1-5pm Sun; ⓜHarvard) Detailed information on current Cambridge happenings and self-guided walking tours.

➡ **Massachusetts Office of Travel & Tourism** (www.massvacation.com) Information about events and activities throughout the state, including an excellent guide to green tourism and resources especially for gay and lesbian travelers.

➡ **National Park Service Visitors Center** (NPS Faneuil Hall; www.nps.gov/bost; Faneuil Hall; ⊙9am-6pm; ⓜState) The brand-new NPS Visitors Center has loads of information about the Freedom Trail sights. This is also the starting point for the free NPS Freedom Trail Tour. There is an additional NPS Visitors Center at the Charlestown Navy Yard.

Travelers with Disabilities

Boston attempts to cater to residents and visitors with disabilities by providing cut curbs, accessible restrooms

and ramps on public buildings; but old streets, sidewalks and buildings mean that facilities are not always up to snuff.

➡ **Sights** Most major museums are accessible to wheelchairs, while the Isabella Stewart Gardner Museum, the Museum of Fine Arts and the Museum of Science offer special programs and tours for travelers with disabilities.

➡ **Activities** Many tours use vehicles that are wheelchair accessible, including Boston Duck Tours and New England Aquarium Whale Watch. Walking tours like the Freedom Trail and the student tour of Harvard Yard are also accessible, though the historic buildings may not be.

➡ **Transportation** MBTA buses and commuter trains are accessible, although not all subway trains and stations are. See **MBTA Accessibility** (www.mbta.com/accessibility) for more information. Ferries to the Boston Harbor Islands, Provincetown and Salem are all accessible.

Visas

Since the establishment of the Department of Homeland Security following the events of September 11, 2001, immigration now falls under the purview of the **US Citizenship and Immigration Service** (www.uscis.gov).

Getting into the United States can be a bureaucratic nightmare, depending on your country of origin, and the rules are rapidly changing. For up-to-date visa and immigration information, check with the **US State Department** (www.unitedstatesvisas.gov).

Visa Waiver Program

The US has Visa Waiver Program in which citizens of certain countries may enter the US for stays of 90 days or less without first obtaining a

US visa. This list is subject to continual re-examination and bureaucratic rejigging. As of January 2012 these countries include: Andorra, Australia, Austria, Belgium, Brunei, Czech Republic, Denmark, Estonia, Finland, France, Germany, Greece, Hungary, Iceland, Ireland, Italy, Japan, Latvia, Liechtenstein, Lithuania, Luxembourg, Malta, Monaco, the Netherlands, New Zealand, Norway, Portugal, San Marino, Singapore, Slovakia, Slovenia, South Korea, Spain, Sweden, Switzerland and the UK.

Under this program you must have the following:

➡ A round-trip ticket (or onward ticket to any foreign destination) that is nonrefundable in the US

➡ A machine-readable passport

➡ A passport that will be valid for at least six months longer than your intended stay; in any case, you will not be able to extend your stay beyond 90 days

Electronic System for Travel Authorization

Since January 2009 the US has an Electronic System for Travel Authorization (ESTA), a system that has been implemented to mitigate security risks concerning travelers to the US by air or sea (this does not apply to those entering by land, such

as Canada). This pre-authorization system **applies to citizens of all countries that fall under the Visa Waiver Program**. This process requires that you register specific information online, prior to entering the US.

Information required includes details like your name, current address and passport information including the number and expiration date and details about any communicable diseases you may carry (including HIV). It is recommended to fill out the online form as early as possible, and at least 72 hours prior to departure.

You will receive one of three responses:

➡ **Authorization Approved** This usually comes within minutes; most applicants can expect to receive this response

➡ **Authorization Pending** In which case you can check back online to check the status within roughly 72 hours

➡ **Travel Not Authorized** This means your application is not approved and you will need to apply for a visa

Once approved, registration is valid for two years, but note that if you renew your passport or change your name, you will need to re-register. It costs $4

to apply, and a further $10 when an application is approved. The entire process is stored electronically and linked to your passport, but it is recommended that you bring a printout of the ESTA approval just to be safe.

Visa Applications

The validity period for a US visitor visa depends on your home country. The actual length of time you'll be allowed to stay in the US is determined by the Bureau of Citizenship and Immigration Services at the port of entry. Applicants may be required to submit any or all of the following:

➡ A recent photo (50.8mm x 50.8mm)

➡ Documents of financial stability and/or guarantees from a US resident (particularly for travelers from developing countries)

➡ Applicants may be required to 'demonstrate binding obligations' that ensure their return home; anyone planning to travel through other countries before arriving in the US is generally better off applying for a US visa while still in their home country rather than while on the road

➡ Your passport should be valid for at least six months longer than your intended stay

Behind the Scenes

SEND US YOUR FEEDBACK

We love to hear from travelers – your comments keep us on our toes and help make our books better. Our well-traveled team reads every word on what you loved or loathed about this book. Although we cannot reply individually to postal submissions, we always guarantee that your feedback goes straight to the appropriate authors, in time for the next edition. Each person who sends us information is thanked in the next edition – the most useful submissions are rewarded with a selection of digital PDF chapters.

Visit **lonelyplanet.com/contact** to submit your updates and suggestions or to ask for help. Our award-winning website also features inspirational travel stories, news and discussions.

Note: We may edit, reproduce and incorporate your comments in Lonely Planet products such as guidebooks, websites and digital products, so let us know if you don't want your comments reproduced or your name acknowledged. For a copy of our privacy policy visit lonelyplanet.com/privacy.

OUR READERS

Many thanks to the travelers who used the last edition and wrote to us with helpful hints, useful advice and interesting anecdotes:

Bill Lawford, Thomas Seymour.

AUTHOR THANKS
Mara Vorhees

I am grateful to Barbara Lynch and Nicole Freedman, for sharing their insights with our readers, and all my Bostonian friends and family, for divulging their best favorite spots.

Special thanks to Shay and Van, who made me an instant expert on kids' Boston. Speaking of which, I couldn't have written this book without Elsida, who came to our rescue in the nick of time. As always, Jerry deserves the most credit for turning me into a true Bostonian and keeping the good juju in the pink house.

ACKNOWLEDGMENTS

Cover photograph: The Boston skyline over the Charles River; Stuart Pearce/Alamy. Many of the images in this guide are available for licensing from Lonely Planet Images: www.lonelyplanetimages.com.

THIS BOOK

This 5th edition of *Boston* was researched and written by Mara Vorhees, who also wrote the previous edition. This guidebook was commissioned in Lonely Planet's Oakland office, and produced by the following:

Commissioning Editors Jennye Garibaldi, Catherine Craddock

Coordinating Editors Briohny Hooper, Mardi O'Connor

Coordinating Cartographer Mark Griffiths

Coordinating Layout Designer Jacqui Saunders

Managing Editors Barbara Delissen, Anna Metcalfe, Martine Power, Angela Tinson

Managing Cartographer Alison Lyall

Managing Layout Designer Jane Hart

Assisting Editors Carolyn Bain, Elin Berglund, Samantha Forge, Kate James, Bella Li, Sonya Mithen, Simon Williamson

Assisting Cartographer James Leversha

Assisting Layout Designer Kerrianne Southway

Cover Research Naomi Parker

Internal Image Research Nicholas Colicchia

Thanks to Imogen Bannister, Lucy Birchley, Daniel Corbett, Laura Crawford, Janine Eberle, Ryan Evans, Liz Heynes, Gabrielle Innes, Laura Jane, David Kemp, Ali Lemer, Ross Macaw, Erin McManus, Tad O'Biegly, Darren O'Connell, Trent Paton, Piers Pickard, Averil Robertson, Lachlan Ross, Michael Ruff, Dianne Schallmeiner, Julie Sheridan, Amanda Sierp, Laura Stansfeld, John Taufa, Gerard Walker, Clifton Wilkinson

See also separate subindexes for:

✗ **EATING P238**

● **DRINKING & NIGHTLIFE P239**

☆ **ENTERTAINMENT P239**

🛍 **SHOPPING P240**

🏃 **SPORTS & ACTIVITIES P241**

🛏 **SLEEPING P241**

Index

✕ EATING

🛍 SHOPPING

🏃 SPORTS & ACTIVITIES

🛏 SLEEPING

Sights 000
Map Pages **000**
Photo Pages **000**

Boston Maps

Map Legend

Sights
- 🏖 Beach
- 🔱 Buddhist
- 🏰 Castle
- ✝ Christian
- 🕉 Hindu
- ☪ Islamic
- ✡ Jewish
- ❶ Monument
- 🏛 Museum/Gallery
- Ruin
- Winery/Vineyard
- Zoo
- Other Sight

Eating
- Eating

Drinking & Nightlife
- Drinking & Nightlife
- Cafe

Entertainment
- Entertainment

Shopping
- Shopping

Sleeping
- Sleeping
- Camping

Sports & Activities
- Diving/Snorkelling
- Canoeing/Kayaking
- Skiing
- Surfing
- Swimming/Pool
- Walking
- Windsurfing
- Other Sports & Activities

Information
- Post Office
- Tourist Information

Transport
- Airport
- Border Crossing
- Bus
- Cable Car/ Funicular
- Cycling
- Ferry
- Metro
- Monorail
- Parking
- S-Bahn
- Taxi
- Train/Railway
- Tram
- Tube Station
- U-Bahn
- Other Transport

Routes
- Tollway
- Freeway
- Primary
- Secondary
- Tertiary
- Lane
- Unsealed Road
- Plaza/Mall
- Steps
- Tunnel
- Pedestrian Overpass
- Walking Tour
- Walking Tour Detour
- Path

Boundaries
- International
- State/Province
- Disputed
- Regional/Suburb
- Marine Park
- Cliff
- Wall

Geographic
- Hut/Shelter
- Lighthouse
- Lookout
- Mountain/Volcano
- Oasis
- Park
- Pass
- Picnic Area
- Waterfall

Hydrography
- River/Creek
- Intermittent River
- Swamp/Mangrove
- Reef
- Canal
- Water
- Dry/Salt/ Intermittent Lake
- Glacier

Areas
- Beach/Desert
- Cemetery (Christian)
- Cemetery (Other)
- Park/Forest
- Sportsground
- Sight (Building)
- Top Sight (Building)

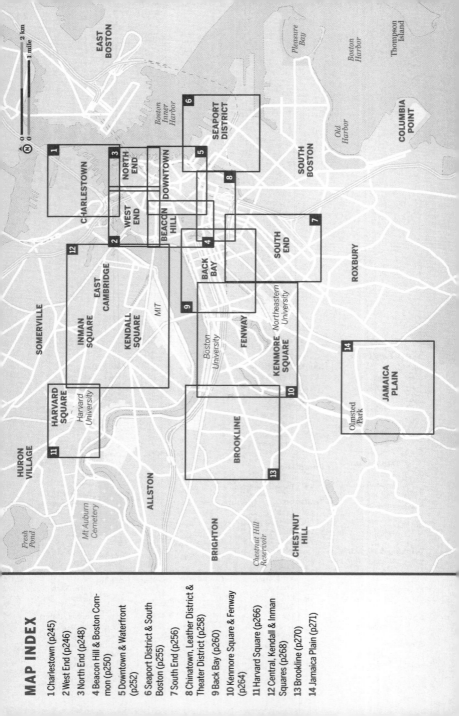

MAP INDEX

EAST BOSTON

Pleasure Bay

Boston Harbor

Thompson Island

COLUMBIA POINT

Old Harbor

SEAPORT DISTRICT

SOUTH BOSTON

Boston Inner Harbor

CHARLESTOWN

NORTH END

DOWNTOWN

WEST END

BEACON HILL

BACK BAY

SOUTH END

ROXBURY

EAST CAMBRIDGE

SOMERVILLE

INMAN SQUARE

KENDALL SQUARE

MIT

Boston University

FENWAY

Northeastern University

KENMORE SQUARE

HARVARD SQUARE

Harvard University

HURON VILLAGE

Fresh Pond

Mt Auburn Cemetery

ALLSTON

BRIGHTON

Chestnut Hill Reservoir

CHESTNUT HILL

BROOKLINE

Olmsted Park

JAMAICA PLAIN

N

0   2 km
0   1 mile

CHARLESTOWN

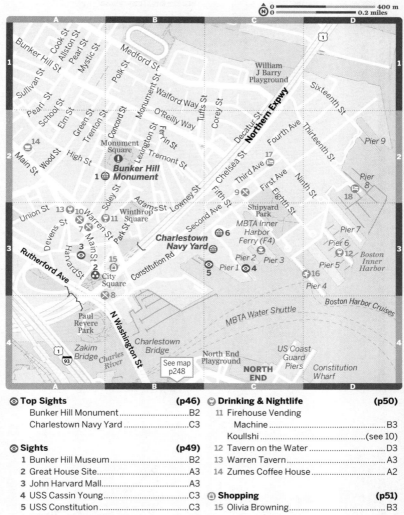

WEST END

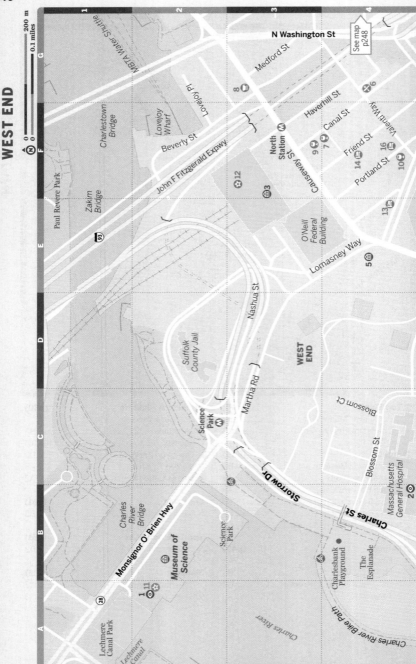

N Washington St

See map p248

Medford St

MBTA Water Shuttle

Lovejoy Pl

Charlestown Bridge

Lovejoy Wharf

Beverly St

John F Fitzgerald Expwy

Paul Revere Park

Zakim Bridge

93

Haverhill St

North Station

Canal St

Valenti Way

Causeway St

Friend St

Portland St

O'Neill Federal Building

Lomasney Way

Nashua St

Suffolk County Jail

WEST END

Martha Rd

Science Park

Blossom Ct

Blossom St

Storrow Dr

Charles St

Massachusetts General Hospital

Science Park

Museum of Science

Charles River Bridge

Monsignor O' Brien Hwy

Science Park

Charleshbank Playground

The Esplanade

Charles River Bike Path

Lechmere Canal Park

Lechmere Canal

28

Charles River

0   200 m
0   0.1 miles

WEST END

Top Sights (p54)
Museum of Science.....................B2

Sights (p56)
1 Charles Hayden Planetarium.......A2
2 Ether Dome...............................B4
3 New England Sports Museum.......F3
4 Otis House.................................D6
5 West End Museum.......................E4

Eating (p57)
6 Cafe Rustico................................G4
Clink....................................(see 15)
Scampo................................(see 15)

Drinking & Nightlife (p60)
Alibi...................................(see 15)
7 Boston Beer
   Works......................................F4

8 Equal Exchange Cafe...................G3
9 Fours...F3
10 West End Johnnies....................F4

Sports & Activities
TD Banknorth Garden.............(see 12)

Entertainment (p61)
11 Mugar Omni Theater..................A2
12 TD Banknorth
    Garden....................................F4

Sleeping (p185)
13 Bulfinch Hotel...........................E4
14 Friend Street Hostel..................F4
15 Liberty Hotel.............................B5
16 Onyx Hotel................................F3

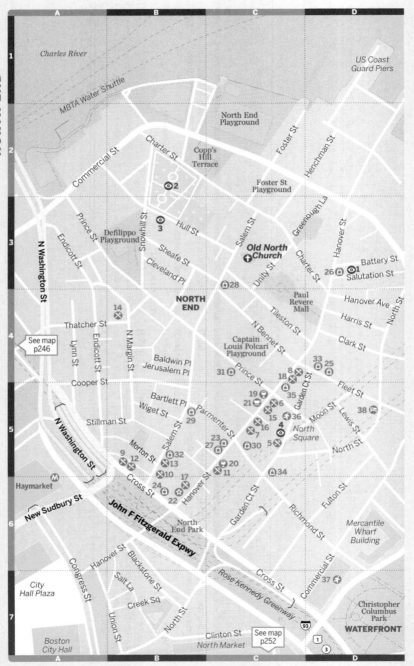

A   B   C   D

Charles River

US Coast
Guard Piers

MBTA Water Shuttle

North End
Playground

Commercial St

Charter St

Copp's
Hill
Terrace

Foster St

Henchman St

Foster St
Playground

Greenough La

⊙2

Prince St

Snowhill St

Hull St

Salem St

Old North
Church

Charter St

Hanover St

Battery St

26⊙1

Endicott St

Defilippo
Playground

Sheafe St

Unity St

26⊙ Salutation St

N Washington St

See map
p246

Thatcher St

Cleveland Pl

NORTH
END

🔒28

Paul
Revere
Mall

Hanover Ave

Harris St

North St

14🗶

N Margin St

Tileston St

N Bennet St

Clark St

33🔒 25🔒

Fleet St

Lynn St

Endicott St

Cooper St

Baldwin Pl
Jerusalem Pl

Captain
Louis Polcari
Playground

31🔒

Prince St

18🗶

8🗶

Garden Ct St

Moon St

Lewis St

38🖵

N Washington St

Bartlett Pl

Wiget St

Parmenter St

29🔒

19🍴
21🍴

15🗶 36
35

North
Square

16🗶

Stillman St

Salem St

23🗶
27🔒

4⊙

5🔒

North St

9🗶
12🗶

Morton St

32🔒
13🗶

17🌸

20🍴

30🗶

34🔒

Haymarket Ⓜ

10🗶

11

Richmond St

Fulton St

New Sudbury St

24🗶
22🌸

Hanover St

Cross St

North
End Park

Garden Ct St

Mercantile
Wharf
Building

John F Fitzgerald Expwy

Congress St

Hanover St

Blackstone St

Salt La

Creek Sq

North St

Cross St

Rose Kennedy Greenway

Commercial St

37 ✈

Christopher
Columbus
Park

WATERFRONT

City
Hall Plaza

Boston
City Hall

Union St

Clinton St
North Market

See map
p252

93

1
3

NORTH END

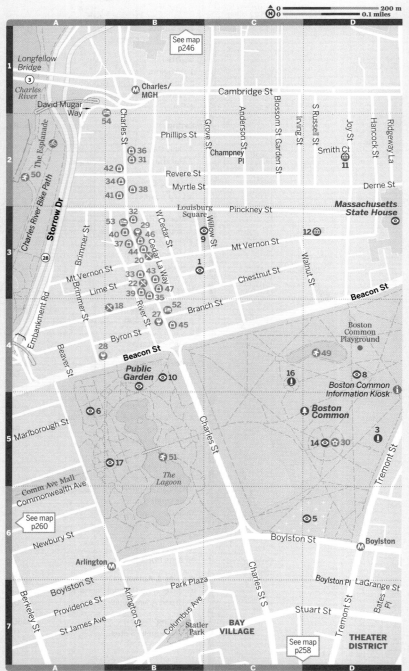

BEACON HILL & BOSTON COMMON

0 ___ 200 m
0 ___ 0.1 miles

Longfellow Bridge
Charles River
David Mugar Way
The Esplanade
Charles River Bike Path
Storrow Dr

Charles/MGH

Cambridge St

Charles St
Phillips St
Grove St
Anderson St
Blossom St
Garden St
Irving St
S Russell St
Joy St
Hancock St
Ridgeway La

Champney Pl
Smith Ct

Revere St
Myrtle St
Derne St

Louisburg Square
Pinckney St
Willow St
Massachusetts State House

W Cedar St
Cedar La Way
Mt Vernon St
Walnut St

Brimmer St
Mt Vernon St
Lime St
Chestnut St

Brimmer St
River St
Branch St
Beacon St

Byron St
Beacon St

Beaver St
Public Garden

Boston Common Playground

Marlborough St

Boston Common Information Kiosk

Boston Common

Comm Ave Mall
Commonwealth Ave
The Lagoon

Newbury St

Boylston St

Boylston

Arlington
Boylston St
Providence St
Arlington St
Park Plaza
Charles St S
Boylston Pl
LaGrange St
Tremont St
Bates Pl

Berkeley St
St James Ave
Columbus Ave
Statler Park
BAY VILLAGE
Stuart St
THEATER DISTRICT

See map p246
See map p260
See map p258

54
36
31
42
34
38
41
32
53
29
40
46
37
44
20
33
43
22
47
39
35
18
52
27
45
28
10
6
17
51
49
16
8
5
14
30
3
1
9
11
12
50

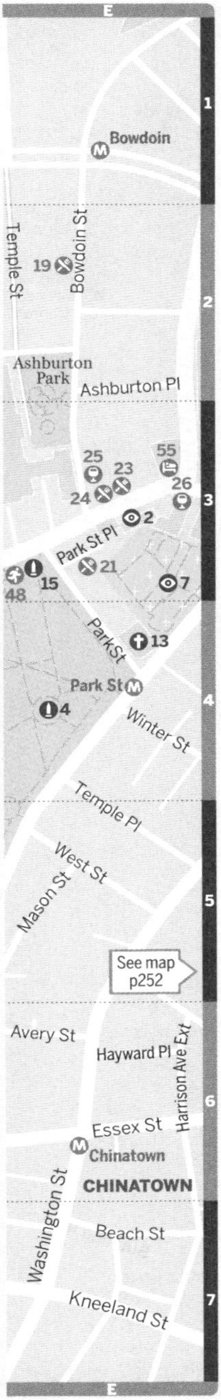

Bowdoin Ⓜ

Temple St
Bowdoin St

19 ✕ Bowdoin St

Ashburton
Park   Ashburton Pl

25   55
23
24 ✕   26

Park St Pl   ◎2

15   ✕21
48

Park St

◎7

Park St Ⓜ

4   Winter St

Temple Pl

West St

Mason St

See map
p252

Avery St

Hayward Pl   Harrison Ave Ext

Essex St
Ⓜ Chinatown
CHINATOWN

Washington St

Beach St

Kneeland St

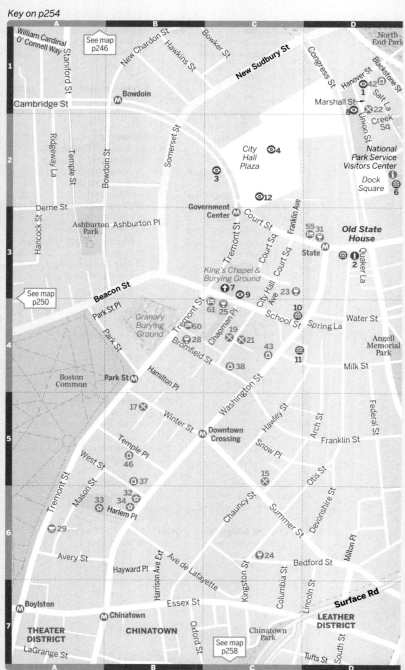

DOWNTOWN & WATERFRONT

William Cardinal O' Connell Way

Staniford St

New Chardon St

Hawkins St

Bowker St

New Sudbury St

Congress St

North End Park

Hanover St

42

Blackstone St

Salt La

1

Marshall St

8

22

Creek Sq

Union St

Cambridge St

M Bowdoin

Ridgeway La

Temple St

Bowdoin St

Somerset St

City Hall Plaza

4

3

National Park Service Visitors Center

Derne St

Hancock St

Ashburton Park

Ashburton Pl

Government Center

12

Court St

Franklin Ave

Dock Square

6

55 31

Old State House

Tremont St

Court Sq

Court Sq

State M

2

Quaker La

See map p250

Beacon St

Park St Pl

Granary Burying Ground

King's Chapel & Burying Ground

7

9

City Hall Ave

23

10

School St

Spring La

Water St

Angell Memorial Park

Park St

61

25 Pl

Chapman Pl

19

43

11

Milk St

60

28

21

Bromfield St

38

Boston Common

Park St M

Hamilton Pl

Washington St

Hawley St

Arch St

Federal St

17

Winter St

Downtown Crossing

Snow Pl

Franklin St

West St

Temple Pl

46

Chauncy St

Summer St

15

Otis St

Devonshire St

Tremont St

Mason St

37

32

33

34

Harlem Pl

29

Avery St

Hayward Pl

Ave de Lafayette

Harrison Ave Ext

Kingston St

Columbia St

24

Bedford St

Milton Pl

Lincoln St

Surface Rd

M Boylston

THEATER DISTRICT

LaGrange St

M Chinatown

CHINATOWN

Essex St

Oxford St

Chinatown Park

See map p258

LEATHER DISTRICT

Tufts St

South St

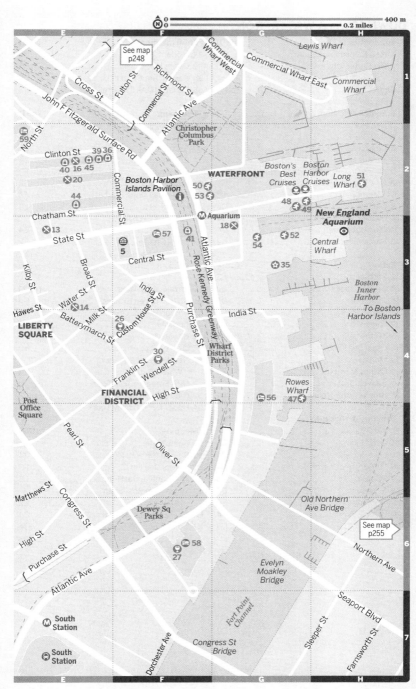

0 400 m
N
0 0.2 miles

See map
p248

Lewis Wharf

Commercial Wharf West

Commercial Wharf East

Commercial Wharf

Cross St

Fulton St

Richmond St

Commercial St

Atlantic Ave

John F Fitzgerald Surface Rd

Christopher Columbus Park

North St 59

Clinton St 39 36

40 16 45

20

44

Chatham St

Commercial St

Boston Harbor Islands Pavilion

WATERFRONT

Boston's Best Cruises

Boston Harbor Cruises

Long 51
Wharf

50
53

48
49

13

State St

Aquarium

18

New England Aquarium

Kilby St

Broad St

Water St

Central St

57

5

41

Atlantic Ave-Rose Kennedy Greenway

54

52

Central Wharf

35

Boston Inner Harbor

Hawes St

14

Milk St

Batterymarch St

India St

Custom House St

26

India St

To Boston Harbor Islands

LIBERTY SQUARE

Purchase St

Franklin St

30

Wendell St

Wharf District Parks

FINANCIAL DISTRICT

High St

Rowes Wharf

56
47

Post Office Square

Pearl St

Oliver St

Matthews St

Congress St

Old Northern Ave Bridge

See map
p255

High St

Purchase St

Atlantic Ave

Dewey Sq Parks

27 58

Evelyn Moakley Bridge

Northern Ave

Seaport Blvd

South Station

South Station

Dorchester Ave

Fort Point Channel

Congress St Bridge

Sleeper St

Farnsworth St

DOWNTOWN & WATERFRONT *Map on p252*

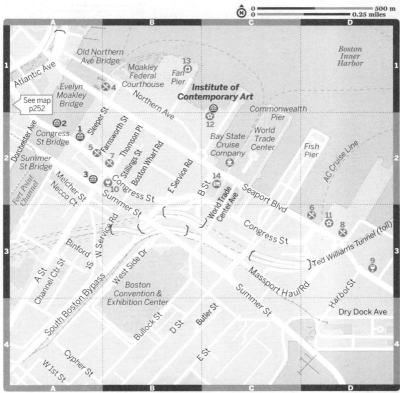

◎ **Top Sights** **(p136)**
Institute of Contemporary Art C1

◎ **Sights** **(p137)**
1 Boston Children's Museum A2
2 Boston Tea Party Ships & Museum A2
3 Fort Point Arts Community A2

⊗ **Eating** **(p138)**
4 Barking Crab B1
Channel Café .... (see 3)
5 Flour A2
6 Legal Harborside D3
Sam's .... (see 13)
7 Sportello B2
8 Yankee Lobster Fish Co D3

◎ **Drinking & Nightlife** **(p140)**
Drink .... (see 7)
9 Harpoon Brewery D3
10 Lucky's Lounge B2

✪ **Entertainment** **(p140)**
11 Bank of America Pavilion D3
12 Institute of Contemporary Art C2

🛍 **Shopping** **(p141)**
13 Louis Boston B1
Made in Fort Point .... (see 5)

🛏 **Sleeping** **(p191)**
14 Seaport Boston Hotel C2

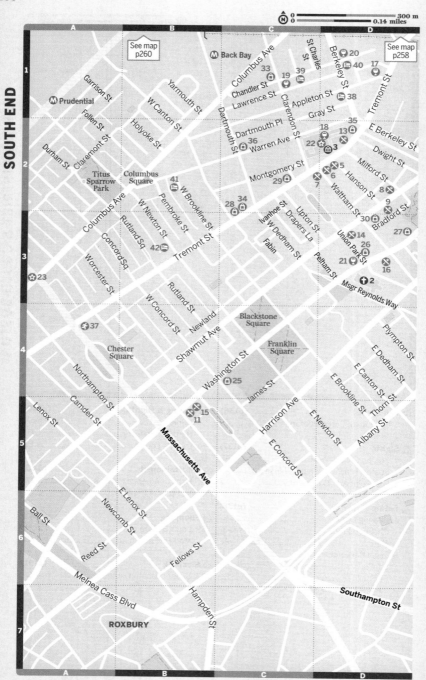

SOUTH END

See map p260

See map p258

M Back Bay

M Prudential

Garrison St

Yarmouth St

W Canton St

Holyoke St

Follen St

Claremont St

Durham St

Columbus Ave

Columbus Square

Titus Sparrow Park

Columbus Ave

Rutland Sq

W Newton St

Pembroke St

W Brookline St

Concord Sq

Worcester St

23

37

Chester Square

Northampton St

W Concord St

Rutland St

Newland St

Shawmut Ave

Lenox St

Camden St

E Lenox St

Newcomb St

Ball St

Reed St

Melnea Cass Blvd

ROXBURY

Hampden St

Columbus Ave

St Charles St

Chandler St

Lawrence St

Dartmouth St

Dartmouth Pl

Warren Ave

Montgomery St

Clarendon St

Appleton St

Gray St

Berkeley St

Tremont St

E Berkeley St

Dwight St

Milford St

Hanson St

Waltham St

Bradford St

Union Park St

Pelham St

W Dedham St

Drapers La

Upton St

Ivanhoe St

Fabin

Tremont St

Msgr Reynolds Way

Blackstone Square

Franklin Square

Washington St

James St

Harrison Ave

E Newton St

E Concord St

Massachusetts Ave

Fellows St

Southampton St

E Dedham St

E Canton St

E Brookline St

Thorn

Albany St

Plympton St

33
19
39
20
40
17
38
18
13
35
22
3
5
6
29
7
8
9
30
27
14
26
21
16
2
41
28
34
42
25
15
11

SOUTH END

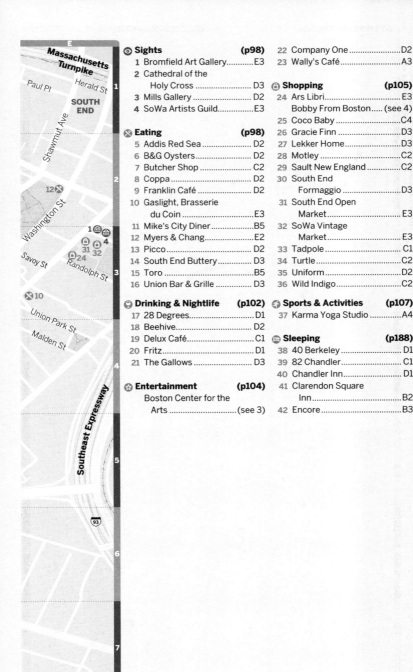

CHINATOWN, LEATHER DISTRICT & THEATER DISTRICT

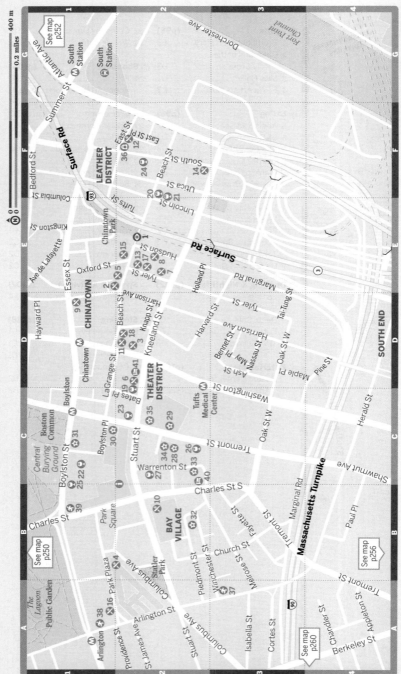

See map p252

See map p250

See map p256

See map p260

400 m
0.2 miles

South Station

Fort Point Channel

Dorchester Ave

Summer St

Atlantic Ave

Surface Rd

Bedford St

Columbia St

Kingston St

LEATHER DISTRICT

East St

East St Pl

Beach St

South St

Utica St

Lincoln St

Tufts St

Chinatown Park

Ave de Lafayette

Essex St

Oxford St

Hayward Pl

Hudson St

Tyler St

Surface Rd

Holland Pl

Marginal Rd

CHINATOWN

Beach St

Harrison Ave

Knapp St

Kneeland St

Harvard St

Tyler St

Tai-Tung St

SOUTH END

Chinatown

LaGrange St

Bates Pl

THEATER DISTRICT

Ash St

Bennet St

May St

Nassau St

Oak St W

Maple Pl

Pine St

Washington St

Herald St

Boylston

Boylston St

Stuart St

Tufts Medical Center

Oak St W

Tremont St

Boston Common

Central Burying Ground

Warren ton St

Charles St S

Marginal Rd

Shawmut Ave

Massachusetts Turnpike

BAY VILLAGE

Park Square

Piedmont St

Fayette St

Tremont St

Charles St

Park Plaza

Stuart St

Church St

Winchester St

Melrose St

The Lagoon

Public Garden

Columbus Ave

Providence St

St James Ave

Arlington St

Isabella St

Cortes St

Paul Pl

Chandler St

Appleton St

Berkeley St

Tremont St

CHINATOWN, LEATHER DISTRICT & THEATER DISTRICT

◎ **Sights** (p98)
1 Chinatown Gate..E2

🞖 **Eating** (p100)
2 Café de Lulu...E1
3 Empire Garden...D2
4 Finale Desserterie..B2
5 Gourmet Dumpling House................................E2
6 Jacob Wirth..D2
7 Jade Garden...E2
8 Jumbo Seafood...E2
9 Kaze Shabu Shabu...D1
10 Market by Jean-Georges.................................B2
11 My Thai Vegan Café.......................................D2
12 O Ya...F2
13 Peach Farm...E2
14 South Street Diner..F2
15 Taiwan Cafe..E2
16 Via Matta..A1

17 Winsor Dim Sum Cafe.....................................E2
18 Xinh Xinh..D2

🍸 **Drinking & Nightlife** (p103)
19 Bijou...C2
20 Corner Pub..F2
21 District..F2
22 Estate..C1
23 Intermission Tavern...C2
24 Les Zygomates..F2
25 Troquet..B1
26 Underbar...C2
27 Venu & Rumor...C2

🎭 **Entertainment** (p104)
28 Boston Lyric Opera..C2
29 Citi Performing Arts
   Center..C2
30 Cutler Majestic Theatre...................................A1

31 Dick's Beantown Comedy Vault.......................C1
32 Jacques Cabaret..B2
   Opera Boston...(see 30)
33 Shear Madness..C2
34 Shubert Theatre...C2
35 Wilbur Theatre...C2

🛍 **Shopping** (p106)
36 Calamus Bookstore..F2

❀ **Sports & Activities** (p107)
37 Boston Center for Adult
   Education...A3
38 Exhale Spa..A1
39 Grub Street...B1

🛏 **Sleeping** (p188)
40 Milner Hotel..C2
41 New HI Boston...D2

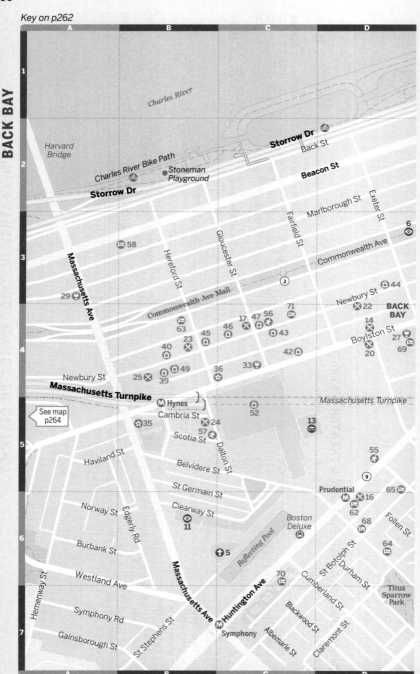

Key on p262

BACK BAY

Charles River

Harvard Bridge

Charles River Bike Path

Stoneman Playground

Storrow Dr

Storrow Dr

Back St

Beacon St

58

Marlborough St

Fairfield St

Exeter St

6

29

Commonwealth Ave

Hereford St

Gloucester St

Commonwealth Ave Mall

2

Newbury St

44

BACK BAY

63

17 47 56
46   71
45   43
23
40   42
25   39 49 36 33

22

14
Boylston St
20   27
69

Hynes

Cambria St

52

Massachusetts Turnpike

13

35

24
57
Scotia St

Dalton St

Belvidere St

55

9

St Germain St

Prudential

16
62

65

Clearway St

11

Boston Deluxe

68

64

5

Reflecting Pool

70

Massachusetts Ave

Huntington Ave

Cumberland St

St Botolph St

Durham St

Follen St

Titus Sparrow Park

Haviland St

Norway St

Edgerly Rd

Burbank St

Westland Ave

Hemenway St

Symphony Rd

Gainsborough St

St Stephens St

Symphony

Blackwood St

Albemarle St

Claremont St

Massachusetts Ave

See map p264

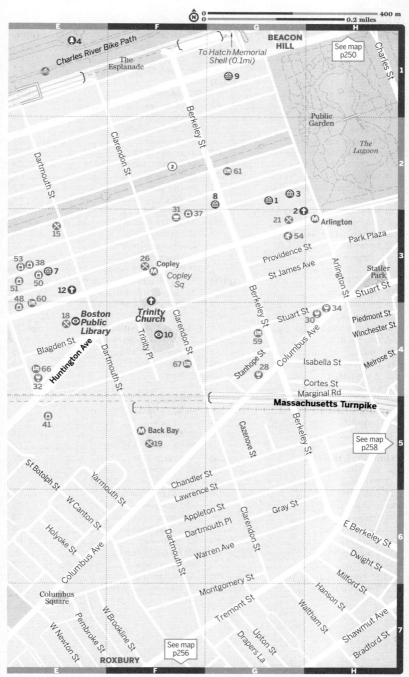

0 400 m
0 0.2 miles

BEACON HILL

To Hatch Memorial Shell (0.1mi)

Charles River Bike Path

The Esplanade

See map p250

Charles St

Public Garden

The Lagoon

Berkeley St

Clarendon St

Dartmouth St

4
6

9

2
61
8
31 37
1 3
2
21
Arlington
54

Park Plaza

Providence St
St James Ave

Statler Park
Stuart St

15

53 38
7
51 50
48 60
12
18
Boston Public Library
26
Copley
Copley Sq

Trinity Church
10

Blagden St
Huntington Ave
66
32

Trinity Pl
Clarendon St

Berkeley St

Stuart St
30 34
Piedmont St
Winchester St

59
67
28

Columbus Ave

Isabella St
Cortes St
Marginal Rd

Massachusetts Turnpike

41

Back Bay
19

Dartmouth St

Cazenove St

Berkeley St

See map p258

St Botolph St
Yarmouth St
W Canton St
Holyoke St
Columbus Ave

Chandler St
Lawrence St
Appleton St
Dartmouth Pl
Warren Ave

Dartmouth St

Clarendon St

Gray St

E Berkeley St
Dwight St
Milford St

Columbus Square
W Brookline St
W Newton St
Pembroke St

Montgomery St
Tremont St
Upton St
Drapers La

Hanson St
Waltham St
Shawmut Ave
Bradford St

See map p256

ROXBURY

BACK BAY

KENMORE SQUARE & FENWAY *Map on p264*

KENMORE SQUARE & FENWAY

Key on p263

KENMORE SQUARE & FENWAY

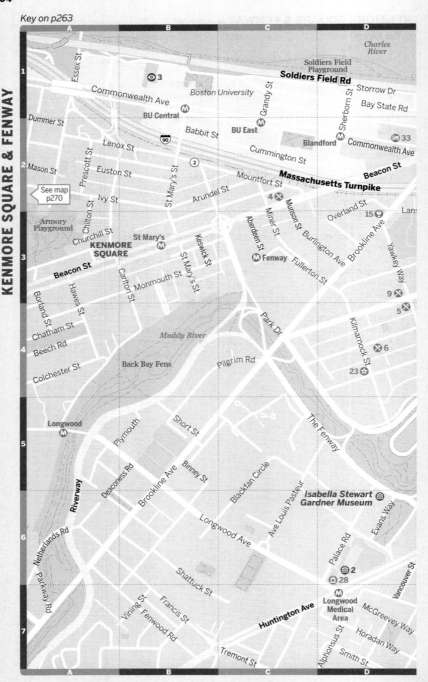

See map p270

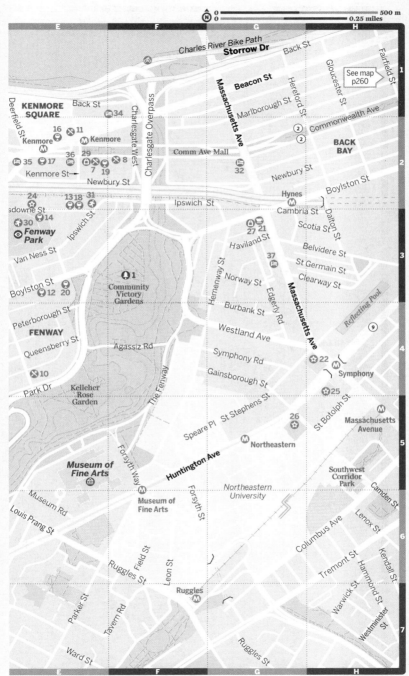

KENMORE SQUARE & FENWAY

0 500 m
0 0.25 miles

Charles River Bike Path
Storrow Dr
Back St
Fairfield St
See map p260
Beacon St
Gloucester St
Hereford St
Back St
Marlborough St
Commonwealth Ave
BACK BAY
Deerfield St
KENMORE SQUARE
Back St
34
Charlesgate Overpass
Massachusetts Ave
Comm Ave Mall
Newbury St
Boylston St
16 11
Kenmore Kenmore
Charlesgate West
32
Hynes
Dalton St
35 17 36 29 8
7 19
Kenmore St
Newbury St
Cambria St
Ipswich St
Scotia St
Belvidere St
24 13 18 31
sdowne St 14
30
Fenway Park
Ipswich St
Haviland St
27 21
37
St Germain St
Clearway St
Reflecting Pool
Van Ness St
Hemenway St
Norway St
Edgerly Rd
9
Boylston St
12 20
Community Victory Gardens
Burbank St
Westland Ave
Massachusetts Ave
Peterborough St
FENWAY
Queensberry St
Agassiz Rd
Symphony Rd
22
Symphony
10
The Fenway
Gainsborough St
25
Park Dr
Kelleher Rose Garden
Speare Pl St Stephens St
26
St Botolph St
Massachusetts Avenue
Museum of Fine Arts
Forsyth Way
Northeastern
Southwest Corridor Park
Camden St
Museum Rd
Louis Prang St
Forsyth St
Forsyth St
Northeastern University
Columbus Ave
Lenox St
Tremont St
Hammond St
Kendall St
Ruggles St
Field St
Leon St
Ruggles
Warwick St
Parker St
Tavern Rd
Ward St
Ruggles St
Westminster St

HARVARD SQUARE

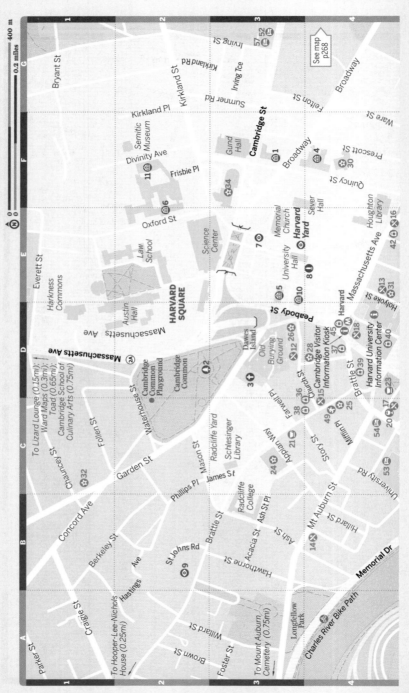

See map p268

N

0.2 miles
400 m

HARVARD SQUARE

CENTRAL, KENDALL & INMAN SQUARES

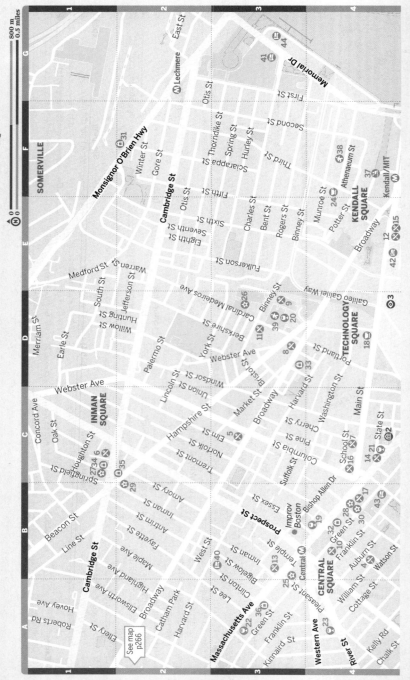

800 m
0.5 miles

SOMERVILLE

Monsignor O'Brien Hwy

East St

Lechmere

Memorial Dr

Otis St

First St

Second St

Thorndike St

Spring St

Hurley St

Third St

Sciarappa St

Winter St

Gore St

Cambridge St

Fifth St

Otis St

Charles St

Bent St

Rogers St

Binney St

Munroe St

Athenaeum St

Potter St

Broadway

Kendall / MIT

KENDALL SQUARE

Sixth St

Seventh St

Eighth St

Fulkerson St

Cardinal Medeiros Ave

Binney St

Galileo Galilei Way

TECHNOLOGY SQUARE

Portland St

Main St

Medford St

Warren St

South St

Jefferson St

Hunting St

Willow St

Palermo St

Berkshire St

York St

Webster Ave

Bristol St

Harvard St

Washington St

Merriam St

Earle St

Concord Ave

Oak St

Houghton St

Webster Ave

INMAN SQUARE

Lincoln St

Union St

Market St

Broadway

Pine St

Cherry St

State St

School St

Columbia St

Springfield St

Tremont St

Hampshire St

Norfolk St

Elm St

Windsor St

Suffolk St

Amory St

Essex St

Improv Boston

Prospect St

Bishop Allen Dr

Green St

Franklin St

Auburn St

CENTRAL SQUARE

Central

Pleasant St

Temple St

Inman St

Bigelow St

Magazine St

Lee St

Clinton St

West St

Maple Ave

Highland Ave

Ellsworth Ave

Broadway

Catham Park

Harvard St

Green St

Franklin St

Kinnaird St

Massachusetts Ave

Cambridge St

Beacon St

Line St

Fayette St

Antrim St

Roberts Rd

Ellery St

Hovey Ave

Western Ave

River St

William St

Cottage St

Watson St

Kelly Rd

Chalk St

See map p266

CENTRAL, KENDALL & INMAN SQUARES

Longfellow Bridge

Charles River

BROOKLINE

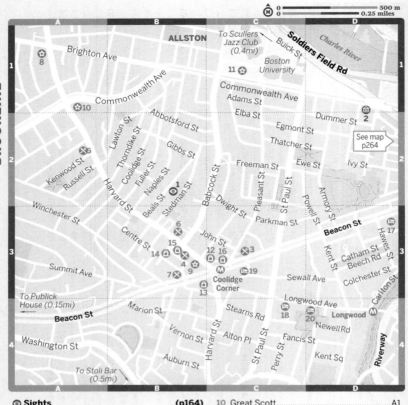

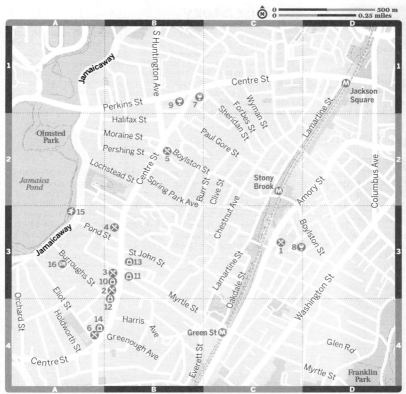

JAMAICA PLAIN

Our Story

A beat-up old car, a few dollars in the pocket and a sense of adventure. In 1972 that's all Tony and Maureen Wheeler needed for the trip of a lifetime – across Europe and Asia overland to Australia. It took several months, and at the end – broke but inspired – they sat at their kitchen table writing and stapling together their first travel guide, *Across Asia on the Cheap*. Within a week they'd sold 1500 copies. Lonely Planet was born.

Today, Lonely Planet has offices in Melbourne, London and Oakland, with more than 600 staff and writers. We share Tony's belief that 'a great guidebook should do three things: inform, educate and amuse.'

Our Writer

Mara Vorhees

Born and raised in St Clair Shores, Michigan, Mara traveled the world (if not the universe) before finally settling in the Hub. She spent several years pushing papers and tapping keys at Harvard University, but has since embraced the life of a full-time travel writer, traveling to destinations as diverse as Russia and Belize. She now lives in a pink house in Somerville, Massachusetts with her husband, two kiddies and two kitties. She is often spotted sipping Sam Seasonal in Union Square and pedaling her road bike along the River Charles. The pen-wielding traveler is the author of Lonely Planet's guide to New England, among others. Follow her adventures online at www.maravorhees.com.

Read more about Mara at:
lonelyplanet.com/members/mvorhees

Published by Lonely Planet Publications Pty Ltd
ABN 36 005 607 983
5th edition – Aug 2012
ISBN 978 1 74179 718 3
© Lonely Planet 2012   Photographs © as indicated 2012
10 9 8 7 6 5 4 3 2 1
Printed in China